THE LEGACY OF
GREECE

OXFORD UNIVERSITY
PRESS
LONDON: AMEN HOUSE, E.C. 4
EDINBURGH GLASGOW LEIPZIG
COPENHAGEN NEW YORK TORONTO
MELBOURNE CAPETOWN BOMBAY
CALCUTTA MADRAS SHANGHAI
HUMPHREY MILFORD
PUBLISHER TO THE
UNIVERSITY

Impression of 1928
First edition, 1921

The Legacy of GREECE

Essays by GILBERT MURRAY, W. R. INGE, J. BURNET, Sir T. L. HEATH, D'ARCY W. THOMPSON, CHARLES SINGER, R. W. LIVINGSTONE, A. TOYNBEE, A. E. ZIMMERN, PERCY GARDNER, Sir REGINALD BLOMFIELD

Edited by

R. W. LIVINGSTONE

OXFORD
AT THE CLARENDON PRESS

PRINTED IN ENGLAND AT THE
UNIVERSITY PRESS, OXFORD
BY JOHN JOHNSON
PRINTER TO THE UNIVERSITY

PREFACE

In spite of many differences, no age has had closer affinities with Ancient Greece than our own; none has based its deeper life so largely on ideals which the Greeks brought into the world. History does not repeat itself. Yet, if the twentieth century searched through the past for its nearest spiritual kin, it is in the fifth and following centuries before Christ that they would be found. Again and again, as we study Greek thought and literature, behind the veil woven by time and distance, the face that meets us is our own, younger, with fewer lines and wrinkles on its features and with more definite and deliberate purpose in its eyes. For these reasons we are to-day in a position, as no other age has been, to understand Ancient Greece, to learn the lessons it teaches, and, in studying the ideals and fortunes of men with whom we have so much in common, to gain a fuller power of understanding and estimating our own. This book—the first of its kind in English—aims at giving some idea of what the world owes to Greece in various realms of the spirit and the intellect, and of what it can still learn from her.

THE EDITOR.

October 1921.

CONTENTS

PAGE

THE VALUE OF GREECE TO THE FUTURE OF THE WORLD. By GILBERT MURRAY, F.B.A., Regius Professor of Greek in the University of Oxford   1

RELIGION. By W. R. INGE, D.D., Dean of St. Paul's .   25

PHILOSOPHY. By J. BURNET, F.B.A., Professor of Greek in the University of St. Andrews   57

MATHEMATICS AND ASTRONOMY. By Sir T. L. HEATH, K.C.B., K.C.V.O., F.R.S.   .   .   97

NATURAL SCIENCE. By D'ARCY W. THOMPSON, F.R.S., Professor of Natural History in the University of St. Andrews   137

BIOLOGY. By CHARLES SINGER, Lecturer in the History of Medicine in University College, London   163

MEDICINE. By CHARLES SINGER   .   .   .   201

LITERATURE. By R. W. LIVINGSTONE, Fellow of Corpus Christi College, Oxford .   .   .   249

HISTORY. By ARNOLD TOYNBEE, Koraés Professor of Byzantine and Modern Greek Language, Literature, and History in the University of London   .   289

CONTENTS

PAGE

POLITICAL THOUGHT. By A. E. Zimmern,
   late Wilson Professor of International Politics,
   University College of Wales, Aberystwyth . . 321

THE LAMPS OF GREEK ART. By Percy Gardner,
   F.B.A., Merton Professor of Classical Archaeology
   in the University of Oxford 353

ARCHITECTURE. By Sir Reginald Blomfield,
   F.S.A., R.A. 397

LIST OF ILLUSTRATIONS

NATURAL SCIENCE

FIGURE   PAGE

1. Lioness and young, from an Ionian vase of the sixth century B. C. .   165
2. A, Jaw bones of lion ; B, head of lioness from Caere vase .   .   165
3. Paintings of fish on plates : Italo-Greek work of the fourth century B. C.   166
4. Head and talons of the Sea-eagle, *Haliaëtus albicilla* : A, from an Ionic vase of the sixth century B. C. ; B, drawn from the object   167
5. Minoan gold cup, sixteenth century B. C. .   .   .   *facing* 170
6. Horse's head, from Parthenon. 440 B. C.   .   .   ,, 170
7. Aristotle. From Herculaneum ; probably work of fourth century B. C.   .   .   .   .   ,, 176
8. Theophrastus. From Villa Albani ; copy (second century A. D. ?) of earlier work   .   .   .   .   .   .   ,, 182
9, 10. Fifth-century drawings from Juliana Anicia MS., copied from originals of the first century B. C. (?) : 9, Σόγκος τρυφερός = *Crepis paludosa*, Moen. ; 10, Γεράνιον = *Geranium pyrenaicum*, L. .   .   .   .   .   .   ,, 186
11. Illustrating Galen's physiological teaching   .   .   .   189

MEDICINE

1. Hippocrates. British Museum, second or third century B. C. *facing* 212
2. Asclepius. British Museum, fourth century B. C.   .   .   ,, 212
3, 4. From MS. of Apollonius of Kitium, of ninth century (copied from a pre-Christian original) : 3, reducing dislocated shoulder ; 4, reducing dislocated jaw .   .   .   ,, 224
5. A Greek clinic of about 400 B. C. : from a vase-painting .   226
6. A kylix, from the Berlin Museum, of about 490 B. C. .   .   227
7. Athenian funerary monument. British Museum, second century A. D. .   .   .   .   *facing* 234
8. Votive tablet, representing cupping and bleeding instruments, from Temple of Asclepius at Athens .   .   .   ,, 240

ART

FIGURE   PAGE

1. Vase representing sunrise   .   .   .   .   .   *facing* 358
2. Caryatid of Erechtheum ⎫
3. Caryatid, by Rodin   ⎬   .   .   .   .   ,,   359
4. Charioteer of Delphi   ⎫
5. Artemis of Gabii   ⎬   .   .   .   .   ,,   362
6. Knight and Lady, by Peter Vischer   .   .   .   ,,   363
7. Sarcophagus from Sidon   .   .   .   .   .   ,,   372
8. Demosthenes, by Polyeuctus . ⎫
9. Abraham Lincoln, by Barnard ⎬   .   .   .   .   ,,   374
10. Aged Shepherdess, Alexandrian ⎫
11. La Vieille Héaulmière, by Rodin ⎬ .   .   .   .   ,,   378
12. Athlete with strigil   . ⎫
13. Athlete, by Tait McKenzie ⎬   .   .   .   .   ,,   380

ARCHITECTURE

1. Lion Gate, Mycenae   .   .   .   .   .   .   *facing* 400
2. Temple of Neptune at Paestum   .   .   .   .   ,,   406
3. Doric Temple, Corinth .   .   .   .   .   .   ,,   410
4. Temple of Theseus, Athens   .   .   .   .   ,   ,,   416

THE VALUE OF GREECE TO THE FUTURE OF THE WORLD

IF the value of man's life on earth is to be measured in dollars and miles and horse-power, ancient Greece must count as a poverty-stricken and a minute territory; its engines and implements were nearer to the spear and bow of the savage than to our own telegraph and aeroplane. Even if we neglect merely material things and take as our standard the actual achievements of the race in conduct and in knowledge, the average clerk who goes to town daily, idly glancing at his morning newspaper, is probably a better behaved and infinitely better informed person than the average Athenian who sat spellbound at the tragedies of Aeschylus. It is only by the standard of the spirit, to which the thing achieved is little and the quality of mind that achieved it much, which cares less for the sum of knowledge attained than for the love of knowledge, less for much good policing than for one free act of heroism, that the great age of Greece can be judged as something extraordinary and unique in value.

By this standard, if it is a legitimate and reasonable one to apply, we shall be able to understand why classical Greek literature was the basis of education throughout all later antiquity; why its re-discovery, however fragmentary and however imperfectly understood, was able to intoxicate the keenest minds of Europe and constitute a kind of spiritual 'Re-birth', and how its further and further exploration may be still a task worth men's spending their lives upon and capable of giving mankind guidance as well as inspiration.

But is such a standard legitimate and reasonable? We shall gain nothing by unanalysed phrases. But I think surely it is merely the natural standard of any philosophical historian. Suppose it is argued that an average optician at the present day knows more optics than Roger Bacon, the inventor of spectacles ; suppose it is argued that therefore he is, as far as optics go, a greater man, and that Roger Bacon has nothing to teach us ; what is the answer? It is, I suppose, that Roger Bacon, receiving a certain amount of knowledge from his teachers, had that in him which turned it to unsuspected directions and made it immensely greater and more fruitful. The average optician has probably added a little to what he was taught, but not much, and has doubtless forgotten or confused a good deal. So that, if by studying Roger Bacon's life or his books we could get into touch with his mind and acquire some of that special moving and inspiring quality of his, it would help us far more than would the mere knowledge of the optician.

This truth is no doubt hard to see in the case of purely technical science ; in books of wider range, such as Darwin's for instance, it is easy for any reader to feel the presence of a really great mind, producing inspiration of a different sort from that of the most excellent up-to-date examination text-book. In philosophy, religion, poetry, and the highest kinds of art, the greatness of the author's mind seems as a rule to be all that matters ; one almost ignores the date at which he worked. This is because in technical sciences the element of mere fact, or mere knowledge, is so enormous, the elements of imagination, character, and the like so very small. Hence, books on science, in a progressive age, very quickly become ' out of date ', and each new edition usually supersedes the last. It is the rarest thing for a work of science to survive as a text-book more than ten years or so. Newton's *Principia* is almost an isolated instance among modern writings.

Yet there are some few such books. Up till about the year 1900 the elements of geometry were regularly taught, throughout Europe, in a text-book written by a Greek called Eucleides in the fourth or third century B.C.[1] That text-book lasted over two thousand years. Now, of course, people have discovered a number of faults in Euclid, but it has taken them all that time to do it.

Again, I knew an old gentleman who told me that, at a good English school in the early nineteenth century, he had been taught the principles of grammar out of a writer called Dionysius Thrax, or Denis of Thrace. Denis was a Greek of the first century B.C., who made or carried out the remarkable discovery that there was such a thing as a science of grammar, i. e. that men in their daily speech were unconsciously obeying an extraordinarily subtle and intricate body of laws, which were capable of being studied and reduced to order. Denis did not make the whole discovery himself; he was led to it by his master Aristarchus and others. And his book had been re-edited several times in the nineteen-hundred odd years before this old gentleman was taught it.

To take a third case: all through later antiquity and the middle ages the science of medicine was based on the writings of two ancient doctors, Hippocrates and Galen. Galen was a Greek who lived at Rome in the early Empire, Hippocrates a Greek who lived at the island of Cos in the fifth century B.C. A great part of the history of modern medicine is a story of emancipation from the dead hand of these great ancients. But one little treatise attributed to Hippocrates was in active use in the training of medical students in my own day in Scotland and is still in use in some American Universities. It was the

[1] Since this paper was first written *Euclid*, Book I, in the Greek, has been edited with a commentary by Sir Thomas Heath (Cambridge Press, 1920). It is full of interest and instruction.

Oath taken by medical students in the classic age of Greece when they solemnly faced the duties of their profession. The disciple swore to honour and obey his teacher and care for his children if ever they were in need ; always to help his patients to the best of his power ; never to use or profess to use magic or charms or any supernatural means ; never to supply poison or perform illegal operations ; never to abuse the special position of intimacy which a doctor naturally obtains in a sick house, but always on entering to remember that he goes as a friend and helper to every individual in it.

We have given up that oath now : I suppose we do not believe so much in the value of oaths. But the man who first drew up that oath did a great deed. He realized and defined the meaning of his high calling in words which doctors of unknown tongues and undiscovered countries accepted from him and felt to express their aims for well over two thousand years.

Now what do I want to illustrate by these three instances? The rapidity with which we are now at last throwing off the last vestiges of the yoke of Greece? No, not that. I want to point out that even in the realm of science, where progress is so swift and books so short-lived, the Greeks of the great age had such genius and vitality that their books lived in a way that no others have lived. Let us get away from the thought of Euclid as an inky and imperfect English school-book, to that ancient Eucleides who, with exceedingly few books but a large table of sand let into the floor, planned and discovered and put together and re-shaped the first laws of geometry, till at last he had written one of the great simple books of the world, a book which should stand a pillar and beacon to mankind long after all the political world that Eucleides knew had been swept away and the kings he served were conquered by the Romans, and the Romans in course of time conquered by the barbarians, and the barbarians themselves, with much labour and reluctance, partly by means of Eucleides' book, eventually educated; so that at last, in our own day, they can manage to learn their geometry without it. The time has come for Euclid to be superseded; let him go. He has surely held the torch for mankind long enough; and books of science are born to be superseded. What I want to suggest is that the same extraordinary vitality of mind which made Hippocrates and Euclid and even Denis of Thrace last their two thousand years, was also put by the Greeks of the great age into those activities which are, for the most part at any rate, not perishable or progressive but eternal.

This is a simple point, but it is so important that we must dwell on it for a moment. If we read an old treatise on medicine or mechanics, we may admire it and feel it a work of genius, but we also feel that it is obsolete : its work is over ; we have got beyond it. But when we read Homer or Aeschylus, if once we have the power to admire and understand their writing, we do not for the most part have any feeling of having got beyond them. We have done so no doubt in all kinds of minor things, in general knowledge, in details of technique, in civilization and the like ; but hardly any sensible person ever imagines that he has got beyond their essential quality, the quality that has made them great.

Doubtless there is in every art an element of mere knowledge or science, and that element is progressive. But there is another element, too, which does not depend on knowledge and which does not progress but has a kind of stationary and eternal value, like the beauty of the dawn, or the love of a mother for her child, or the joy of a young animal in being alive, or the courage of a martyr facing torment. We cannot for all our progress get beyond these things ; there they stand, like light upon the mountains. The only question is whether we can rise to them. And it is the same with all the greatest births of human imagination. As far as we can speculate, there is not the faintest probability of any poet ever setting to work on, let us say, the essential effect aimed at by Aeschylus in the Cassandra-scene of the *Agamemnon*, and doing it better than Aeschylus. The only thing which the human race has to do with that scene is to understand it and get out of it all the joy and emotion and wonder that it contains.

This eternal quality is perhaps clearest in poetry : in poetry the mixture of knowledge matters less. In art there is a constant development of tools and media and technical processes. The modern artist can feel that, though he cannot, perhaps, make as good a statue as Pheidias, he could here and there have taught Pheidias something : and at any rate he can try his art on subjects far more varied and more stimulating to his imagination. In philosophy the mixture is more subtle and more profound. Philosophy always depends in some sense upon science, yet the best philosophy seems generally to have in it some eternal quality of creative imagination. Plato wrote a dialogue about the constitution of the world, the *Timaeus*, which was highly influential in later Greece, but seems to us, with our vastly superior scientific knowledge, almost nonsensical. Yet when Plato writes about the theory of knowledge or the ultimate meaning of Justice or of Love, no good philosopher can afford to leave him aside : the chief question is whether we can rise to the height and subtlety of his thought.

And here another point emerges, equally simple and equally important if we are to understand our relation to the past. Suppose a man says : ' I quite understand that Plato or Aeschylus may have had fine ideas, but surely anything of value which they said must long before this have become common property. There is no need to go back to the Greeks for it. We do not go back and read Copernicus to learn that the earth goes round the sun.' What is the answer? It is that such a view ignores exactly this difference between the progressive and the eternal, between knowledge and imagination. If Harvey discovers that the blood is not stationary but circulates, if Copernicus discovers that the earth goes round the sun and not the sun round the earth, those discoveries can easily be communicated in the most abbreviated form. If a mechanic invents an improvement on the telephone, or a social reformer puts some good usage in the place of a bad one, in a few years we shall probably all be using the improvement without even knowing what it is or saying Thank you. We may be as stupid as we like, we have in a sense got the good of it.

But can one apply the same process to *Macbeth* or *Romeo and Juliet*? Can any one tell us in a few words what they come to? Or can a person get the good of them in any way except one—the way of vivid and loving study, following and feeling the author's meaning all through? To suppose, as I believe some people do, that you can get the value of a great poem by studying an abstract of it in an encyclopaedia or by reading cursorily an average translation of it, argues really a kind of mental deficiency, like deafness or colour-blindness. The things that we have called eternal, the things of the spirit and the imagination, always seem to lie more in a process than in a result, and can only be reached and enjoyed by somehow going through the process again. If the value of a particular walk lies in the scenery, you do not get that value by taking a short cut or using a fast motor-car.

In looking back, then, upon any vital and significant age of the past we shall find objects of two kinds. First, there will be things like the Venus of Milo or the Book of Job or Plato's *Republic*, which are interesting or precious in themselves, because of their own inherent qualities ; secondly, there will be things like the Roman code of the Twelve Tables or the invention of the printing-press or the record of certain great battles, which are interesting chiefly because they are causes of other and greater things or form knots in the great web of history—the first having artistic interest, the second only historical interest, though, of course, it is obvious that in any concrete case there is generally a mixture of both.

Now Ancient Greece is important in both ways. For the artist or poet it has in a quite extraordinary degree the quality of beauty. For instance, to take a contrast with Rome : if you dig about the Roman Wall in Cumberland you will find quantities of objects, altars, inscriptions, figurines, weapons, boots and shoes, which are full of historic interest but are not much more beautiful than the contents of a modern rubbish heap. And the same is true of most excavations all over the world. But if you dig at any classical or sub-classical site in the Greek world, however unimportant historically, practically every object you find will be beautiful. The wall itself will be beautiful ; the inscriptions will be beautifully cut ; the figurines, however cheap and simple, may have some intentional grotesques among them, but the rest will have a special truthfulness and grace ; the vases will be of good shapes and the patterns will be beautiful patterns. If you happen to dig in a burying-place and come across some epitaphs on the dead, they will practically all—even when the verses do not quite scan and the words are wrongly spelt—have about them this inexplicable touch of beauty.

I am anxious not to write nonsense about this. One could prove the point in detail by taking any collection of Greek epitaphs, and that is the only way in which it can be proved. The beauty is a fact, and if we try to analyse the sources of it we shall perhaps in part understand how it has come to pass.

In the first place, it is not a beauty of ornament; it is a beauty of structure, a beauty of rightness and simplicity. Compare an athlete in flannels playing tennis and a stout dignitary smothered in gold robes. Or compare a good modern yacht, swift, lithe, and plain, with a lumbering heavily gilded sixteenth-century galleon, or even with a Chinese state junk : the yacht is far the more beautiful though she has not a hundredth part of the ornament. It is she herself that is beautiful, because her lines and structure are right. The others are essentially clumsy and, therefore, ugly things, dabbed over with gold and paint. Now ancient Greek things for the most part have the beauty of the yacht. The Greeks used paint a good deal, but apart from that a Greek temple is almost as plain as a shed : people accustomed to arabesques and stained glass and gargoyles can very often see nothing in it. A Greek statue has as a rule no ornament at all : a young man racing or praying, an old man thinking, there it stands expressed in a stately and simple convention, true or false, the anatomy and the surfaces right or wrong, aiming at no beauty except the truest. It would probably seem quite dull to the maker of a mediaeval wooden figure of a king which I remember seeing in a town in the east of Europe : a crown blazing with many-coloured glass, a long crimson robe covered with ornaments and beneath them an idiot face, no bones, no muscles, no attitude. That is not what a Greek meant by beauty. The same quality holds to a great extent of Greek poetry. Not, of course, that the artistic convention was the same, or at all similar, for treating stone and for treating language. Greek poetry is statuesque in the sense that it depends greatly on its organic structure ; it is not in the least so in the sense of being cold or colourless or stiff. But Greek poetry on the whole has a bareness and severity which disappoints a modern reader, accustomed as he is to lavish ornament and exaggeration at every turn. It has the same simplicity and straightforwardness as Greek sculpture. The poet has something to say and he says it as well and truly as he can in the suitable style, and if you are not interested you are not. With some exceptions which explain themselves he does not play a thousand pretty tricks and antics on the way, so that you may forget the dullness of what he says in amusement at the draperies in which he wraps it.

But here comes an apparent difficulty. Greek poetry, we say, is very direct, very simple, very free from irrelevant ornament. And yet when we translate it into English and look at our translation, our main feeling, I think, is that somehow the glory has gone : a thing that was high and lordly has become poor and mean. Any decent Greek scholar when he opens one of his ancient poets feels at once the presence of something lofty and rare—something like the atmosphere of *Paradise Lost*. But the language of *Paradise Lost* is elaborately twisted and embellished into loftiness and rarity ; the language of the Greek poem is simple and direct. What does this mean?

I can only suppose that the normal language of Greek poetry is in itself in some sense sublime. Most critics accept this as an obvious fact, yet, if true, it is a very strange fact and worth thinking about. It depends partly on mere euphony : *Khaireis horôn fôs* is probably more beautiful in sound than ' You rejoice to see the light ', but euphony cannot be everything. The sound of a great deal of Greek poetry, either as we pronounce it, or as the ancients pronounced it, is to modern ears almost ugly. It depends partly, perhaps, on the actual structure of the Greek language : philologists tell us that, viewed as a specimen, it is in structure and growth and in power of expressing things, the most perfect language they know. And certainly one often finds that a thought can be expressed with ease and grace in Greek which becomes clumsy and involved in Latin,

English, French or German. But neither of these causes goes, I think, to the root of the matter.

What is it that gives words their character and makes a style high or low? Obviously, their associations ; the company they habitually keep in the minds of those who use them. A word which belongs to the language of bars and billiard saloons will become permeated by the normal standard of mind prevalent in such places ; a word which suggests Milton or Carlyle will have the flavour of those men's minds about it. I therefore cannot resist the conclusion that, if the language of Greek poetry has, to those who know it intimately, this special quality of keen austere beauty, it is because the minds of the poets who used that language were habitually toned to a higher level both of intensity and of nobility than ours. It is a finer language because it expresses the minds of finer men. By ' finer men ' I do not necessarily mean men who behaved better, either by our standards or by their own ; I mean men to whom the fine things of the world, sunrise and sea and stars and the love of man for man, and strife and the facing of evil for the sake of good, and even common things like meat and drink, and evil things like hate and terror, had, as it were, a keener edge than they have for us and roused a swifter and a nobler reaction.

Let us resume this argument before going further. We start from the indisputable fact that the Greeks of about the fifth century b. c. did for some reason or other produce various works of art, buildings and statues and books, especially books, which instead of decently dying or falling out of fashion in the lifetime of the men who made them, lasted on and can still cause high thoughts and intense emotions. In trying to explain this strange fact we notice that the Greeks had a great and pervading instinct for beauty, and for beauty of a particular kind. It is a beauty which never lies in irrelevant ornament, but always in the very essence and structure of the object made. In literature we found that the special beauty which we call Greek depends partly on the directness, truthfulness, and simplicity with which the Greeks say what they want to say, and partly on a special keenness and nobility in the language, which seems to be the natural expression of keen and noble minds. Can we in any way put all these things together so as to explain them—or at any rate to hold them together more clearly?

An extremely old and often misleading metaphor will help us. People have said : 'The world was young then.' Of course, strictly speaking, it was not. In the total age of the world or of man the two thousand odd years between us and Pericles do not count for much. Nor can we imagine that a man of sixty felt any more juvenile in the fifth century B.C. than he does now. It was just the other way, because at that time there were no spectacles or false teeth. Yet in a sense the world *was* young then, at any rate our western world, the world of progress and humanity. For the beginnings of nearly all the great things that progressive minds now care for were then being laid in Greece.

Youth, perhaps, is not exactly the right word. There are certain plants—some kinds of aloe, for instance—which continue for an indefinite number of years in a slow routine of ordinary life close to the ground, and then suddenly, when they have stored enough vital force, grow ten feet high and burst into flower, after which, no doubt, they die or show signs of exhaustion. Apart from the dying, it seems as if something like that happened from time to time to the human race, or to such parts of it as really bear flowers at all. For most races and nations during the most of their life are not progressive but simply stagnant, sometimes just managing to preserve their standard customs, sometimes slipping back to the slough. That is why history has nothing to say about them. The history of the world consists mostly in the memory of those ages, quite few in number, in which some part of the world has risen above itself and burst into flower or fruit.

We ourselves happen to live in the midst or possibly in the close of one such period. More change has probably taken place in daily life, in ideas, and in the general aspect of the earth during the last century than during any four other centuries since the Christian era : and this fact has tended to make us look on rapid progress as a normal condition of the human race, which it never has been. And another such period of bloom, a bloom comparatively short in time and narrow in area, but amazingly swift and intense, occurred in the lower parts of the Balkan peninsula from about the sixth to the fourth centuries before Christ.

Now it is this kind of bloom which fills the world with hope and therefore makes it young. Take a man who has just made a discovery or an invention, a man happily in love, a man who is starting some great and successful social movement, a man who is writing a book or painting a picture which he knows to be good ; take men who have been fighting in some great cause which before they fought seemed to be hopeless and now is triumphant ; think of England when the Armada was just defeated, France at the first dawn of the Revolution, America after Yorktown : such men and nations will be above themselves. Their powers will be stronger and keener ; there will be exhilaration in the air, a sense of walking in new paths, of dawning hopes and untried possibilities, a confidence that all things can be won if only we try hard enough. In that sense the world will be young. In that sense I think it was young in the time of Themistocles and Aeschylus. And it is that youth which is half the secret of the Greek spirit.

And here I may meet an objection that has perhaps been

lurking in the minds of many readers. ' All this,' they may say, ' professes to be a simple analysis of known facts, but in reality is sheer idealization. These Greeks whom you call so " noble " have been long since exposed. Anthropology has turned its searchlights upon them. It is not only their ploughs, their weapons, their musical instruments, and their painted idols that resemble those of the savages ; it is everything else about them. Many of them were sunk in the most degrading superstitions : many practised unnatural vices : in times of great fear some were apt to think that the best " medicine " was a human sacrifice. After that, it is hardly worth men-tioning that their social structure was largely based on slavery ; that they lived in petty little towns, like so many wasps' nests, each at war with its next-door neighbour, and half of them at war with themselves ! '

If our anti-Greek went further he would probably cease to speak the truth. We will stop him while we can still agree with him. These charges are on the whole true, and, if we are to understand what Greece means, we must realize and digest them. We must keep hold of two facts : first, that the Greeks of the fifth century produced some of the noblest poetry and art, the finest political thinking, the most vital philosophy, known to the world ; second, that the people who heard and saw, nay perhaps, even the people who produced these wonders, were separated by a thin and precarious interval from the savage. Scratch a civilized Russian, they say, and you find a wild Tartar. Scratch an ancient Greek, and you hit, no doubt, on a very primitive and formidable being, somewhere between a Viking and a Polynesian.

That is just the magic and the wonder of it. The spiritual effort implied is so tremendous. We have read stories of savage chiefs converted by Christian or Buddhist missionaries, who within a year or so have turned from drunken corroborees and bloody witch-smellings to a life that is not only godly but even philanthropic and statesmanlike. We have seen the Japanese lately go through some centuries of normal growth in the space of a generation. But in all such examples men have only been following the teaching of a superior civilization, and after all, they have not ended by producing works of extraordinary and original genius. It seems quite clear that the Greeks owed exceedingly little to foreign influence. Even in their decay they were a race, as Professor Bury observes, accustomed ' to take little and to give much '. They built up their civilization for themselves. We must listen with due attention to the critics who have pointed out all the remnants of savagery and superstition that they find in Greece : the slave-driver, the fetish-worshipper and the medicine-man, the trampler on women, the bloodthirsty hater of all outside his own town and party. But it is not those people that constitute Greece ; those people can be found all over the historical world, commoner than blackberries. It is not anything fixed and stationary that constitutes Greece : what constitutes Greece is the movement which leads from all these to the Stoic or fifth-century ' sophist ' who condemns and denies slavery, who has abolished all cruel superstitions and preaches some religion based on philosophy and humanity, who claims for women the same spiritual rights as for man, who looks on all human creatures as his brethren, and the world as ' one great City of gods and men '. It is that movement which you will not find elsewhere, any more than the statues of Pheidias or the dialogues of Plato or the poems of Aeschylus and Euripides.

From all this two or three results follow. For one thing, being built up so swiftly, by such keen effort, and from so low a starting-point, Greek civilization was, amid all its glory, curiously unstable and full of flaws. Such flaws made it, of course, much worse for those who lived in it, but they hardly make it less interesting or instructive to those who study it. Rather the contrary. Again, the near neighbourhood of the savage gives to the Greek mind certain qualities which we of the safer and solider civilizations would give a great deal to possess. It springs swift and straight. It is never jaded. Its wonder and interest about the world are fresh. And lastly there is one curious and very important quality which, unless I am mistaken, belongs to Greek civilization more than to any other. To an extraordinary degree it starts clean from nature, with almost no entanglements of elaborate creeds and customs and traditions.

I am not, of course, forgetting the prehistoric Minoan civilization, nor yet the peculiar forms—mostly simple enough—into which the traditional Greek religion fell. It is possible that I may be a little misled by my own habit of living much among Greek things and so forgetting through long familiarity how odd some of them once seemed. But when all allowances are made, I think that this clean start from nature is, on the whole, a true claim. If a thoughtful European or American wants to study Chinese or Indian things, he has not only to learn certain data of history and mythology, he has to work his mind into a particular attitude; to put on, as it were, spectacles of a particular sort. If he wants to study mediaeval things, if he takes even so universal a poet as Dante, it is something the same. Curious views about the Pope and the emperor, a crabbed scholastic philosophy, a strange and to the modern mind rather horrible theology, floating upon the flames of Hell : all these have somehow to be taken into his imagination before he can understand his Dante. With Greek things this is very much less so. The historical and imaginative background of the various great poets and philosophers is, no doubt, highly important. A great part of the work of modern scholarship is now devoted to getting it clearer. But on the whole, putting aside for the moment the possible inadequacies of translation, Greek philosophy speaks straight to any human being who is willing to think simply, Greek art and poetry to any one who can use his imagination and enjoy beauty. He has not to put on the fetters or the blinkers of any new system in order to understand them ; he has only to get rid of his own—a much more profitable and less troublesome task.

This particular conclusion will scarcely, I think, be disputed, but the point presents difficulties and must be dwelt upon.

In the first place, it does not mean that Greek art is what we call ' naturalist ' or ' realist '. It is markedly the reverse. Art to the Greek is always a form of *Sophia*, or Wisdom, a *Techne* with rules that have to be learnt. Its air of utter simplicity is deceptive. The pillar that looks merely straight is really a thing of subtle curves. The funeral bas-relief that seems to represent in the simplest possible manner a woman saying good-bye to her child is arranged, plane behind plane, with the most delicate skill and sometimes with deliberate falsification of perspective. There is always some convention, some idealization, some touch of the light that never was on sea or land. Yet all the time, I think, Greek art remains in a remarkable degree close to nature. The artist's eye is always on the object, and, though he represents it in his own style, that style is always normal and temperate, free from affectation, free from exaggeration or morbidity and, in the earlier periods, free from conventionality. It is art without doubt ; but it is natural and normal art, such as grew spontaneously when mankind first tried in freedom to express beauty. For example, the language of Greek poetry is markedly different from that of prose, and there are even clear differences of language between different styles of poetry. And further, the poetry is very seldom about the present. It is about the past, and that an ideal past. What we have to notice there is that this kind of rule, which has been usual in all great ages of poetry, is apparently not an artificial or arbitrary thing but a tendency that grew up naturally with the first great expressions of poetical feeling.

Furthermore, this closeness to nature, this absence of a unifying or hide-bound system of thought, acting together with other causes, has led to the extraordinary variety and many-sidedness which is one of the most puzzling charms of Ancient Greece as contrasted, say, with Israel or Assyria or early Rome. Geographically it is a small country with a highly indented coast-line and an interior cut into a great number of almost isolated valleys. Politically it was a confused unity made up of numerous independent states, one walled city of a few thousand inhabitants being quite enough to form a state. And the citizens of these states were, each of them, rather excessively capable of forming opinions of their own and fighting for them. Hence came in practice much isolation and faction and general weakness, to the detriment of the Greeks themselves ; but the same cause led in thought and literature to immense variety and vitality, to the great gain of us who study the Greeks afterwards. There is hardly any type of thought or style of writing which cannot be paralleled in ancient Greece, only they will there be seen, as it were, in their earlier and simpler forms. Traces of all the things that seem most un-Greek can be found somewhere in Greek literature : voluptuousness, asceticism, the worship of knowledge, the contempt for knowledge, atheism, pietism, the religion of serving the world and the religion of turning away from the world : all these and almost all other points of view one can think of are represented somewhere in the records of that one small people. And there is hardly any single generalization in this chapter which the author himself could not controvert by examples to the contrary. You feel in general a great absence of all fetters : the human mind free, rather inexperienced, intensely interested in life and full of hope, trying in every direction for that excellence which the Greeks called *aretê*, and guided by some peculiar instinct toward Temperance and Beauty.

The variety is there and must not be forgotten ; yet amid the variety there are certain general or central characteristics, mostly due to this same quality of freshness and closeness to nature.

If you look at a Greek statue or bas-relief, or if you read an average piece of Aristotle, you will very likely at first feel bored. Why? Because it is all so normal and truthful ; so singularly free from exaggeration, paradox, violent emphasis ; so destitute of those fascinating by-forms of insanity which appeal to some similar faint element of insanity in ourselves. ' We are sick ', we may exclaim, ' of the sight of these hand-some, perfectly healthy men with grave faces and normal bones and muscles ! We are sick of being told that Virtue is a mean between two extremes and tends to make men happy ! We shall not be interested unless some one tells us that Virtue is the utter abnegation of self, or, it may be, the extreme and ruthless assertion of self ; or again, that Virtue is all an infamous mistake ! And for statues, give us a haggard man with starved body and cavernous eyes, cursing God—or give us something rolling in fat and colour. . . .'

What is at the back of this sort of feeling? which I admit often takes more reasonable forms than these I have suggested. It is the same psychological cause that brings about the changes of fashion in art or dress : which loves ' stunts ' and makes the fortunes of yellow newspapers. It is boredom or *ennui*. We have had too much of A ; we are sick of it, we know how it is done and despise it ; give us some B, or better still some Z. And after a strong dose of Z we shall crave for the beginning of the alphabet again. But now think of a person who is not bored at all ; who is, on the contrary, immensely interested in the world, keen to choose good things and reject bad ones ; full of the desire for knowledge and the excitement of discovery. The joy to him is to see things as they are and to judge them normally. He is not bored by the sight of normal, healthy muscles in a healthy, well-shaped body; he is delighted. If you distort the muscles for emotional effect, he would say with disappointment : ' But that is ugly ! ' or ' But a man's muscles do *not* go like that ! ' He will have noted that tears are salt and rather warm ; but if you say like a modern poet that your heroine's tears are ' more hot than fire, more salt than the salt sea', he will probably think your statement ἀπίθανον ' unpersuasive ', and therefore ψυχρόν ' chilling '.

It is perhaps especially in the religious and moral sphere that we are accustomed to the habitual use of ecstatic language : expressions that are only true of exalted moments are used by us as the commonplaces of ordinary life. ' It is a thousand times worse to see another suffer than to suffer oneself.' ' True love only desires the happiness of the beloved object.' This kind of ' high falutin'' has become part of our regular mental habit, just as dead metaphors by the bushel are a part of our daily language. Consequently we are a little chilled and disappointed by a language in which people hardly ever use a metaphor except when they vividly realize it, and never utter heroic sentiments except when they are wrought up to the pitch of feeling them true. Does this mean that the Greek always remains, so to speak, at a normal temperature, that he never has intense or blinding emotions? Not in the least. It shows a lack of faith in the value of life to imagine such a conclusion. It implies that you can only reach great emotion by pretence, or by habitually exaggerating small emotions, whereas probably the exact reverse is the case. When the great thing comes, then the Greek will have the great word and the great thought ready. It is the habitual exaggerator who will perhaps be bankrupt. And after all—the great things are sure to come !

The power of seeing things straight and knowing what is beautiful or noble, quite undisturbed by momentary boredoms or changes of taste, is a very rare gift and never perhaps possessed in full by any one. But there is a profound rule of art, bidding a man in the midst of all his study of various styles or his pursuit of his own peculiar imaginations, from time to time *se retremper dans la nature*—' to steep himself again in nature '. And in something the same way it seems as if the world ought from time to time to steep itself again in Hellenism : that is, it ought, amid all the varying affectations and extravagances and changes of convention in art and letters, to have some careful regard for those which arose when man first awoke to the meaning of truth and beauty and saw the world freely as a new thing.

Is this exaggeration? I think not. But no full defence of it can be attempted here. In this essay we have been concerned almost entirely with the artistic interest of Greece. It would be equally possible to dwell on the historical interest. Then we should find that, for that branch of mankind which is responsible for western civilization, the seeds of almost all that we count best in human progress were sown in Greece. The conception of beauty as a joy in itself and as a guide in life was first and most vividly expressed in Greece, and the very laws by which things are beautiful or ugly were to a great extent discovered there and laid down. The conception of Freedom and Justice, freedom in body, in speech and in mind, justice between the strong and the weak, the rich and the poor, penetrates the whole of Greek political thought, and was, amid obvious flaws, actually realized to a remarkable degree in the best Greek communities. The conception of Truth as an end to pursue for its own sake, a thing to discover and puzzle out by experiment and imagination and especially by Reason, a conception essentially allied with that of Freedom and opposed both to anarchy and to blind obedience, has perhaps never in the world been more clearly grasped than by the early Greek writers on science and philosophy. One stands amazed sometimes at the perfect freedom of their thought. Another conception came rather later, when the small City States with exclusive rights of citizenship had been merged in a larger whole : the conception of the universal fellowship between man and man. Greece realized soon after the Persian war that she had a mission to the world, that Hellenism stood for the higher life of man as against barbarism, for Aretê, or Excellence, as against the mere effortless average. First came the crude patriotism which regarded every Greek as superior to every barbarian ; then came reflection, showing that not all Greeks were true bearers of the light, nor all barbarians its enemies ; that Hellenism was a thing of the spirit and not dependent on the race to which a man belonged or the place where he was born : then came the new word and conception ἀνθρωπότης, *humanitas*, which to the Stoics made the world as one brotherhood. No people known to history clearly formulated these ideals before the Greeks, and those who have spoken the words afterwards seem for the most part to be merely echoing the thoughts of old Greek men.

These ideas, the pursuit of Truth, Freedom, Beauty, Excellence are not everything. They have been a leaven of unrest in the world ; they have held up a light which was not always comforting to the eyes to see. There is another ideal which is generally stronger and may, for all we know, in the end stamp them out as evil things. There is Submission instead of Freedom, the deadening or brutalizing of the senses instead of Beauty, the acceptance of tradition instead of the pursuit of Truth, the belief in hallucination or passion instead of Reason and Temperate Thought, the obscuring of distinctions between good and bad and the acceptance of all human beings and all states of mind as equal in value. If something of this kind should prove in the end to be right for man, then Greece will have played the part of the great wrecker in human history. She will have held up false lights which have lured our ship to dangerous places. But at any rate, through calm and storm, she does hold her lights; she lit them first of the nations and held them during her short reign the clearest; and whether we believe in an individual life founded on Freedom, Reason, Beauty, Excellence and the pursuit of Truth, and an international life aiming at the fellowship between man and man, or whether we think these ideals the great snares of human politics, there is good cause for some of us in each generation at the cost of some time and trouble to study such important forces where they first appear consciously in the minds of our spiritual ancestors. In the thought and art of ancient Greece, more than any other, we shall find these forces, and also to some extent their great opposites, fresh, clean and comparatively uncomplicated, with every vast issue wrought out on a small material scale and every problem stated in its lowest terms.

GILBERT MURRAY.

RELIGION

THOSE who write about the Greeks must beware of a heresy which is very rife just now—the theory of *racialism*. Political ethnology, which is no genuine science, excused the ambition of the Germans to themselves, and helped them to wage war; it has suggested to the Allies a method of waging peace. The false and mischievous doctrine of superior and inferior races is used to justify oppression in Europe, and murder by torture in America. It will not help us to understand the Greeks. The Greeks were a nation of splendid mongrels, made up of the same elements, differently mixed, as ourselves. Their famous beauty, which had almost disappeared when Cicero visited Athens, was mainly the result of a healthy outdoor life and physical training, combined with a very becoming costume. They were probably not handsomer than Oxford rowing crews or Eton boys. Their flowering time of genius was due to the same causes which produced similar results in the Italian Renaissance. The city-state is a forcing-house of brilliant achievement, though it quickly uses up its human material. We cannot even regard the Greeks as a homogeneous mixed race. The Spartiates were almost pure Nordics; the Athenians almost pure Mediterraneans. The early colonists, from whom sprang so many of the greatest names in the Hellenic roll of honour, are not likely to have kept their blood pure. Nor was there ever a Greek culture shared by all the Greeks. The Spartan system, that of a small fighting tribe encamped in a subject country, recalls that of Chaka's Zulus; Arcadia was bucolic, Aetolia barbarous, Boeotia stolid, Macedonia half outside the pale. The consciousness of race among the Greeks counted practically for about as much as the consciousness of being white men, or Christians, does in modern civilization.

Greece for our purposes means not a race, but a culture, a language and literature, and still more an attitude towards life, which for us begins with Homer, and persists, with many changes but no breaks, till the closing of the Athenian lecture-rooms by Justinian. The changes no doubt were great, when politically Greece was living Greece no more, and when the bearers of the tradition were no longer the lineal descendants of those who established it. But the tradition, enshrined in literature, in monuments, and in social customs, survived. The civilization of the Roman Empire was not Italian but Greek. After the sixth century, Hellenism—the language, the literature, and the attitude towards life—was practically lost to the West for nearly a thousand years. It was recovered at the Renaissance, and from that time to this has been a potent element in western civilization. The Dark Ages, and the early Middle Ages, are the period during which the West was cut off from Hellenism. Yet even then the severance was not complete. For these were the ages of the Catholic theocracy ; and if we had to choose one man as the founder of Catholicism as a theocratic system, we should have to name neither Augustine nor St. Paul, still less Jesus Christ, but Plato, who in the *Laws* sketches out with wonderful prescience the conditions for such a polity, and the form which it would be compelled to take. Even in speculative thought we know that Augustine owed much to the Platonists, the Schoolmen to Aristotle, the mystics to the pupil of Proclus whom they called Dionysius. Only Greek science, and the scientific spirit, were almost completely lost, and a beginning *de novo* had to be made when the West shook off its fetters.

Hellenism then is not the mind of a particular ethnic type, nor of a particular period. It was not destroyed, though it was emasculated, by the loss of political freedom; it was neither killed nor died a natural death. Its philosophy was continuous from Thales to Proclus, and again from Ficino and Pico to Lotze and Bradley, after a long sleep which was not death. Its religion passes into Christian theology and cultus without any real break. The early Church spoke in Greek and thought in Greek. In the days of Greek freedom to be a Greek had meant to be a citizen of a Greek canton; after Alexander it meant to have Greek culture. None of the great Stoics were natives of Greece proper; Zeno himself was a Semite. Of the later Greek writers, Marcus Aurelius was a Romanized Spaniard, Plotinus possibly a Copt, Porphyry and Lucian Syrians, Philo, St. Paul, and probably the Fourth Evangelist were Jews. These men all belong to the history of Greek culture. And if these were Greeks how shall we deny the name to Raphael and Michael Angelo, to Spenser and Sidney, to Keats and Shelley? When Blake wrote—

> The sun's light when he unfolds it,
> Depends on the organ that beholds it,

he was summing up, not only the philosophy of the Lake Poets but the fundamental dogma of the maturest Greek thought. Would not Plato have rejoiced in Michael Angelo's confession of faith, which Wordsworth has translated for us?

> Heaven-born, the soul a heavenward course must hold;
> Beyond the visible world she soars to seek
> (For what delights the sense is false and weak)
> Ideal Form, the universal mould.
> The wise man, I affirm, can find no rest
> In that which perishes; nor will he lend
> His heart to aught that doth on time depend.

Has the highest aspect of Greek religion ever been better expressed than by Wordsworth himself, to whom, as to Blake, it came by inspiration and not from books?

While yet a child, and long before his time
Had he perceived the presence and the power
Of greatness ; and deep feelings had impressed
So vividly great objects that *they lay*
Upon his mind like substances, whose presence
Perplexed the bodily sense.

The spirit of man does not live only on tradition ; it can draw direct from the fountain-head. We are dealing with a permanent type of human culture, which is rightly named after the Greeks, since it attained its chief glory in the literature and art of the Hellenic cities, but which cannot be separated from western civilization as an alien importation. Without what we call our debt to Greece we should have neither our religion nor our philosophy nor our science nor our literature nor our education nor our politics. We should be mere barbarians. We need not speculate how much we might ultimately have discovered for ourselves. Our civilization is a tree which has its roots in Greece, or, to borrow a more appropriate metaphor from Clement of Alexandria, it is a river which has received affluents from every side ; but its head waters are Greek. The continuity of Greek thought and practice in religion and religious philosophy is especially important, and it is necessary to emphasize it because the accident of our educational curriculum leaves in the minds of most students a broad chasm between the Stoics and the Christians, ignores the later Greek philosophy of religion altogether, and traces Christian dogma back to Palestine, with which it has very little connexion.

Our sense of continuity is dulled in another way. There is a tendency to isolate certain aspects of Hellenic life and thought as characteristic, and to stamp others, which are equally found among the ancient Greeks, as untypical and exceptional. In the sphere of religion, with which we are concerned in this essay, we are bidden to regard Plato and Euripides as rebels against the national tradition, and not as normal products of their age and country. I do not feel at liberty to pick and choose in this fashion. A national character may be best exemplified in its rebels, a religion in its heretics. If Nietzsche was right in calling Plato a Christian before Christ, I do not therefore regard him as an unhellenic Greek. Rather, I trace back to him, and so to Greece, the religion and the political philosophy of the Christian Church, and the Christian type of mysticism. If Euripides anticipated to an extraordinary degree the devout agnosticism, the vague pantheism, the humanitarian sentiment of the nineteenth (rather than of the twentieth) century, I do not consider that he was a freak in fifth-century Athens, but that Greece showed us the way even in paths where we have not been used to look to her for guidance. I am equally reluctant to assume, without evidence, that the later Platonism, whether we call it religion or philosophy, is unhellenic. It is quite unnecessary to look for Asiatic influences in a school which clung close to the Attic tradition. It is more to the purpose to show how a religious philosophy of mystical revelation and introspection grew naturally out of the older nature-philosophies, just as in our own day metaphysics and science have both been driven back upon the theory of knowledge and psychology. It should not be necessary to remind Hellenists that ' Know thyself ' passed for the supreme word of wisdom in the classical period, or that Heracleitus revealed his method in the words ' I searched myself '.

We shall come presently to certain parts of our modern heritage which are not Greek either by origin or by affinity. These will not be found in Euripides or Plato any more than in Herodotus or Sophocles. But some developments of religion which our Hellenists particularly dislike, and are therefore anxious to disclaim as alien to Greek thought and practice, such as asceticism, sacramental magic, religious persecution, and timid reliance on authority, are maladies of the Greek spirit, and came into the Church from Hellenistic and not from Jewish sources. It was Cleanthes who wished to treat Aristarchus as the Church treated Galileo, for anticipating Galileo's discovery. It was Plutarch, or rather his revered father, who said, ' You seem to me to be handling a very great and dangerous subject, or rather to be raising questions which ought not to be raised at all, when you question the opinion we hold about the gods, and ask reasons and proofs for everything. The ancient and ancestral faith is enough ; and if on one point its fixed and traditional character be disturbed, it will be undermined and no one will trust it '. It is true that Celsus accused the Christians of saying, ' Do not inquire ; only believe.' But this was not the attitude of Clement and Origen, still less of that most courageous pioneer St. Paul ; it was rather the attitude of the average devout pagan. At this time the defence of popular superstition was no longer a matter of mere policy but of heartfelt need. Marcus Aurelius was a great immolator of white cows. The Christians were disliked, not as superstitious, but as impious. Alexander of Abunoteichos expelled ' Christians and Epicureans ' by name from his *séances*. Lucian is the Voltaire of a credulous age. As for sacerdotal magic, Ovid explicitly ascribed the *ex opere operato* doctrine to the Greeks.

> Graecia principium moris fuit ; illa nocentes
>   impia lustratos ponere facta putat,
> a nimium faciles, qui tristia crimina caedis
>   fluminea tolli posse putatis aqua.

The Christian Church was the last great creative achievement of the classical culture. It is neither Asiatic nor mediaeval in its essential character. It is not Asiatic ; Christianity is the least Oriental of all the great religions. The Semites either shook it off and reverted to a Judaism purged of its Hellenic elements, or enrolled themselves with fervour under the banner of Islam, which Westcott called ' a petrified Judaism '.

Christian missions have had no success in any Asiatic country. Nor is there anything specifically mediaeval about Catholicism. It preserved the idea of Roman imperialism, after the secular empire of the West had disappeared, and even kept the tradition of the secular empire alive. It modelled all its machinery on the Roman Empire, and consecrated the Roman claim to universal dominion, with the Roman law of *maiestas* against all who disputed its authority. Even its favourite penalty of the ' avenging flames ' is borrowed from the later Roman codes. It maintained the official language of antiquity, and the imperial title of the autocrat who reigned on the Seven Hills. Nor were the early Christians so anxious as is often supposed to disclaim this continuity. At first, it is true, their apologetic was directed to proving their continuity with Judaism ; but Judaism ceased to count for much after the destruction of the Holy City in A. D. 70, and the second-century apologists appeal for toleration on the ground that the best Greek philosophers taught very much the same as what Christians believe. ' We teach the same as the Greeks ', says Justin Martyr, ' though we alone are hated for what we teach.' ' Some among us ', says Tertullian, ' who are versed in ancient literature, have written books to prove that we have embraced no tenets for which we have not the support of common and public literature.' ' The teachings of Plato ', says Justin again, ' are not alien to those of Christ ; and the same is true of the Stoics.' ' Heracleitus and Socrates lived in accordance with the divine Logos ', and should be reckoned as Christians. Clement says that Plato wrote ' by inspiration of God '. Augustine, much later, finds that ' only a few words and phrases ' need be changed to bring Platonism into complete accord with Christianity. The ethics of contemporary paganism, as Harnack shows, with special reference to Porphyry, are almost identical with those of the Christians of his day. They differ in many points from the standards of 500 years earlier and from those of 1,500 years later, but the divergences are neither racial nor credal. Catholic Christianity is historically continuous with the old civilization, which indeed continued to live in this region after its other traditions and customs had been shattered. There are few other examples in history of so great a difference between appearance and reality. Outwardly, the continuity with Judaism seems to be unbroken, that with paganism to be broken. In reality, the opposite is the fact.

This most important truth has been obscured from many causes. The gap in history made by our educational tradition has been already mentioned. And our histories of the early Church are too often warped by an unfortunate bias. Christianity has been judged at its best, paganism at its worst. The rhetorical denunciations of writers like Seneca, Juvenal, and Tacitus are taken at their face value, and few have remembered the convention which obliged a satirist to be scathing, or the political prejudice of the Stoics against the monarchy, or the non-representative character of fashionable life in the capital. The modern Church historian, as Mr. Benn says, has gathered his experience in a college quadrangle or a cathedral close, and knows little enough about his own country, next to nothing about what morality was in the Middle Ages, and nothing at all about what it still is in many parts of Europe. In the most recent books, however, there is a real desire to hold the scales fairly, and Christianity has nothing to fear from an impartial judgement.

There is also an assumption, which we find even in such learned writers as Harnack and Hatch, that the Hellenic element in Christianity is an accretion which transformed the new religion from its original purity and half-paganized Europe again. They would like to prove that underneath Catholicism was a primitive Protestantism, which owed nothing to Greece. The truth is that the Church was half Greek from the first, though, as I shall say presently, the original Gospel was not. St. Paul was a Jew of the Dispersion, not of Palestine, and the Christianity to which he was converted was the Christianity of Stephen, not of James the Lord's brother. His later epistles are steeped in the phraseology of the Greek mysteries. The Epistle to the Hebrews and the Fourth Gospel are unintelligible without some knowledge of Philo, whose theology is more Greek than Jewish. In the conflict about the nature of the future life, it was the Greek eschatology which prevailed over the Jewish. St. Paul's famous declaration, ' We look not at the things which are seen, but at the things which are not seen ; for the things which are seen are temporal, but the things which are not seen are eternal ', is pure Platonism and quite alien to Jewish thought. Judaic Christianity was a local affair, and had a very short life.

Further, too much is made of the conflict between the official cults of paganism and Christian public worship. It is forgotten how completely, in Hellenistic times, religion and philosophy were fused. Without under-estimating the simple piety which, especially in country districts, still attached itself to the temples and their ritual, we may say confidently that the vital religion of the empire was associated with the mystery-religions and with the discipline of the ' philosophic life '. It is in this region that the continuity of Catholicism with Hellenism is mainly to be found. The philosophers at this time were preachers, confessors, chaplains, and missionaries. The clerical profession, in nearly all its activities, is directly descended from the Hellenistic philosophers.

This claim of continuity may seem paradoxical when we remember the savage persecutions of the Christians by the imperial government. Of these persecutions there were several causes. The empire, like all empires of the same type, rested partly on religious support. Augustus encouraged his court poets to advocate a revival of piety and sound morals. A government cannot inquire into religious conviction, but it can enforce conformity and outward respect for the forms of worship as ' by law established '. The Christians and Epicureans were held guilty of the same political offence—' atheism '. The State had no quarrel with the mystery-religions, which were a private matter, but open disrespect to the national deities was flat disloyalty. The pagans could not understand why the Church would make no terms with the fusion of religions (θεοκρασία) which seemed to them the natural result of the fusion of nationalities. Apuleius makes Isis say, when she reveals herself to Lucius, ' cuius numen unicum multiformi specie, ritu vario, nomine multiiugo totus veneratur orbis ' ; and she then recounts her various names. This more than tolerant hospitality of the spirit seemed to the mixed population of the empire the logical recognition of the actual political situation, and those who deliberately stood outside it were at least potentially enemies of society. This was the real quarrel between the Church and the empire. It is the old State religion which Augustine attacks, ridiculing the innumerable Roman godlings whose names he perhaps found in Varro. It is true that Plato, Euripides, and Xenophanes had attacked the official mythology with hardly less asperity ; but they did not escape censure, and the Christian alienation from the Olympians was far more fundamental.

The pagan revival under the empire was rather like Neo-Catholicism in France. It was patriotic, nationalistic, and conservative, rather than strictly religious. Celsus, in his lost book against the Christians, seems to have appealed to their patriotism, urging them to support their country and its government in dangerous times. As the Church grew in numbers and power, and the old traditions crumbled away, largely from the fall in the birth-rate among the upper and middle classes, the conservatives became more anxiously attached to their own culture, and saw in Christianity a ' shapeless darkness ' which threatened to extinguish ' all the beautiful things in the world '. We can partly sympathize with this alarm, though not with the foolish policy which it inspired. The early persecutions were like Russian ' pogroms ', instigated or connived at by the government as a safety valve for popular discontent. For at this time the common people hated the Christians, and half believed the monstrous stories about them. The attacks were not continuous, and were half-hearted, very unlike the systematic extermination of Jews and Protestants in Spain. At Alexandria Hadrian found a money-loving population worshipping Christ and Sarapis almost indifferently. A wrong impression is formed if we picture to ourselves two sections of society engaged in constant war. The first real war was the last, under Diocletian ; it was to decide whether paganism or Christianity was to be the state religion. However, there is no doubt that the persecutions helped to seal the fate of the old culture.

Harnack traces three stages in the Hellenization of Christianity. ' In the earliest Christian writings, apart from Paul, Luke, and John ', he cannot find any considerable traces of Greek influence. ' The real influx of Greek thought and life ' began about 130. The exception is so important as to make this statement of little or no value. After 130, he says, ' the philosophy of Greece went straight to the core of the new religion '. A century or so later, ' Greek mysteries and Greek civilization in the whole range of its development exercise their influence on the Church, but as yet not its mythology and polytheism ; these were still to come '. ' Another century had to elapse before Hellenism as a whole and in every phase of its development was established in the Church.' The process which he describes began, in fact, as soon as Christian preachers used the Greek language, and was never so complete as he says. The Logos-Christology, to which he justly attributes the greatest importance, is already present in St. Paul's epistles ;

the name only is wanting ; and the sharp contradiction which he finds between the Christian idea of a revelation made through a person at a certain date, and the Greek idea of an apprehension of timeless and changeless truth, always open to individuals after the appropriate discipline, was faced and in part overcome by the Greek Fathers. Harnack also regards Gnosticism as an embodiment of the genuinely Greek view of revelation, forgetting that orthodox Platonism was as hostile to Gnosticism as the Church itself. In rejecting Gnosticism, the Church in fact decided for genuine Hellenism against a corrupted and barbarized development of it. On the other hand, there is no period at which we can speak of a complete conquest of Christianity by Greek ideas. There was a large part of the old tradition which perished with its defenders, who, obeying the melancholy law which directs human survival, died out to make way for immigrants and for the formerly submerged classes, the people with few wants, who were indifferent to a culture which they had never been allowed to share.

One more cause of misunderstanding may be illustrated from the writings of Matthew Arnold. He divides the human race into Hebraizers and Hellenizers, and classifies the modern English and Americans as Hebraizers. The fundamental maxim of Hebrew ethics, according to him, is ' Walk by the light you have ' ; of Greek ethics, ' Take heed that the light which is in thee is not darkness '. The Hebraizer is conscientious but unenlightened ; the Hellenizer is clear-headed but unscrupulous. Professor Santayana has lately noted the same difference between the type of character developed by the Latin nations and by the Anglo-Saxons. The Mediterranean civilization, older and more sophisticated, is careful to get its values right ; the northern man is bent on doing something big, no matter what, and follows Clough's advice :

Go ! say not in thine heart, And what then, were it accom-
    plished,
  Were the wild impulse allayed, what is the use and the good ?

But Santayana does not make the mistake of regarding the
Reformation as a return to Palestinian Christianity. This was,
indeed, the opinion of the Reformers themselves ; but all
religious innovation seeks to base itself on some old tradition.
Christianity at first sought for its credentials in Judaism,
though the Jews saw very quickly that it ' destroyed the Law '.
The belief of the Reformers was plausible ; for they rejected
just those parts of Catholicism which had nothing to do with
Palestine, but were taken over from the old Hellenic or Hellenistic culture. But the residuum was less Jewish than
Teutonic. On one side, indeed, the Reformation was a return
to Hellenism from Romanism. Early Christian philosophy
was mainly Platonic ; early Christian ethics (as exemplified
especially in writers like Ambrose) were mainly Stoical. There
had been a considerable fusion of Plato and the Stoa among
the Neoplatonists, so that it was easy for the two to flourish
together. Augustine banished Stoical ethics from the Church,
and they were revived only at the Reformation. Calvinism is
simply baptized Stoicism ; it is logically pantheistic, since it
acknowledges only one effective will in the universe. The
creed of nineteenth-century science is very similar. Puritanism
was not at all like Judaism, in spite of its fondness for the Old
Testament ; it was very like Stoicism. The Reformation was
a revolt against Latin theocracy and the hereditary paganism
of the Mediterranean peoples ; it was not really a return to
pre-Hellenic Christianity. It sheltered the humanism of
Erasmus and the late-flowering English Renaissance, and
Christian Platonism has nowhere had a more flourishing record
than in Protestant Britain.

  At the present time a more drastic revolt is in progress
among the *plebs urbana,* which does in truth threaten with

destruction ' what we owe to Greece '. The industrial revolution has generated a new type of barbarism, with no roots
in the past. For the second time in the history of Western
Europe, continuity is in danger of being lost. A generation
is growing up, not uneducated, but educated in a system
which has little connexion with European culture in its
historical development. The Classics are not taught ; the Bible
is not taught ; history is not taught to any effect. What is
even more serious, there are no social traditions. The modern
townsman is *déraciné* : he has forgotten the habits and sentiments of the village from which his forefathers came. An
unnatural and unhealthy mode of life, cut off from the sweet
and humanizing influences of nature, has produced an unnatural and unhealthy mentality, to which we shall find no
parallels in the past. Its chief characteristic is profound
secularity or materialism. The typical town artisan has no
religion and no superstitions ; he has no ideals beyond the
visible and tangible world of the senses. This of course opens an
impassable gulf between him and Greek religion, and a still
wider gulf between him and Christianity. The attempts
which are occasionally made, especially in this country, to
dress up the Labour movement as a return to the Palestinian
Gospel, are little short of grotesque. The contrast is well
summed up by Belfort Bax, in a passage quoted by Professor
Gardner. ' According to Christianity, regeneration must
come from within. The ethics and religion of modern socialism
on the contrary look for regeneration from without, from
material conditions and a higher social life.' Here the gauntlet
is thrown down to Christ and Plato alike.

Quite logically the new spirit is in revolt against what it
calls intellectualism, which means the application of the dry
light of reason to the problems of human life. It wishes to
substitute for reason what some of its philosophers call instinct,
but which should rather be called sentiment and emotion.

There is no reconciliation between this view of life and Hellenism. For science is the eldest and dearest child of the Greek spirit. One of the great battles of the future will be between science and its enemies. The misologists have numbers on their side; but 'Nature', whom all the Greeks honoured and trusted, will be justified in her children.

The new spirit is especially bitter against the Stoical ethics, which as we have seen were taken over, with the Platonic metaphysics, by Christianity. Stoicism teaches men to venerate and obey natural law; to accept with proud equanimity the misfortunes of life; to be beneficent, but to inhibit the emotion of pity; to be self-reliant and self-contained; to practise self-denial for the sake of self-conquest; and to regard this life as a stern school of moral discipline. All this is simply detestable to the new spirit, which is sentimental, undisciplined, and hedonistic. It remembers the hardness of Puritanism, and has no admiration for its virtues.

It is often said that the modern man has entirely lost the Greek love of beauty. This is, I think, untrue, and unjust to our present civilization, unlovely as it undoubtedly is in many ways. It is curious that modern critics of the Greeks have not called attention to the *aesthetic* obtuseness which showed itself in the defective reaction of the ancients against cruelty. It was not that they excluded beautiful actions from the sphere of aesthetics; they never thought of separating the beautiful from the good in this way. But they were not disgusted at the torture of slaves, the exposure of new-born children, or the massacre of the population of a revolted city. The same callousness appears in the Italian cities at the Renaissance; Ezzelino was a contemporary of the great architects and painters. I cannot avoid the conclusion that it is connected in some obscure way with the artistic creativeness of these two closely similar epochs. The extreme sensibility to physical suffering which characterizes modern civilization arose together with industrialism, and is most marked in the most highly industrialized countries. It has synchronized with the complete eclipse of spontaneous and unconscious artistic production, which we deplore in our time. Evelyn, in the seventeenth century, was still able to visit a prison in Paris to gratify his curiosity by seeing a prisoner tortured, and though he did not stay to the end of the exhibition he shows that his stomach was not easily turned. It is certain that our repugnance to such sights is aesthetic rather than moral, and probable that it is strongest in the lower social strata. Several years ago I went to the first night of a rather foolish play about ancient Rome, in which an early Christian is brought in to be very mildly tortured on the stage. At the first crack of the whip my neighbours sprang from their seats, crying, ' Shame ! Stop that ! ' ; and the scene had to be removed in subsequent performances. The operatives in a certain factory stopped the engines for an hour because they heard a cat mewing among the machinery. Having with difficulty rescued the animal from being crushed they strangled it. The explanation of this extreme susceptibleness must be left to psychologists ; but I am convinced that we have here a case of transferred aesthetic sensibility. We can walk unmoved down the streets of Plaistow, but we cannot bear to see a horse beaten. The Athenians set up no Albert Memorials, but they tortured slave-girls in their law-courts and sent their prisoners to work in the horrible galleries of the Laureion silver-mines.

This emergence of a new spirit, which seems to be almost independent of all traditions, makes it difficult to estimate our present indebtedness to Greece in matters of religion. It would be difficult even if the industrial revolution had not taken place. The northern Europeans have hardly yet attained to self-expression. Their religion is a mixture of Greek, Latin, and Hebrew elements which refuse to be harmonized, and

which in this country sometimes clash with the ideal of
a gentleman, that lay religion of the English-speaking peoples,
which has no longer any connexion with heraldry or property
in land. The English gentleman is not a Greek any more than
he is a Jew. His code makes Odysseus an amusing rascal;
Achilles a violent and sulky savage; and Aristotle's μεγαλό-
ψυχος (as has been said) is rather like a nobleman in a novel
by Disraeli, but not like any other sort of gentleman. The
Englishman is by nature religious; but Christianity in its
developed form is a Mediterranean religion; in all external
features it might have been very different if it had been first
planted north of the Alps. There is, therefore, a chronic
confusion in Protestantism which makes its conflicts with the
Latin Church like the battles of undisciplined barbarians
against well-drilled troops.

Nevertheless, though it is so difficult to separate out the
various threads which make up the tangled skein of our modern
religion, it may be worth while to make the attempt to distinguish, first, those parts of current Christianity which are not
Greek, in the wide sense which I have chosen for the word,
and then those which, in the same sense, are Greek by origin
or affinity.

Among those elements which are not Greek, the first place
must be given to the original Gospel, of which I have said
nothing yet. Our records of the Galilean ministry, contained
in the three synoptic Gospels, were not compiled till long after
the events which they describe, and must not be used uncriti-
cally. But in my opinion, at any rate, the substance of the
teaching of Christ comes out very clearly in these books. No
Hellenic influence can be traced in it; there is not even any
sign of the Hellenized Judaism which for us is represented by
his contemporary Philo. But neither is it possible to call the
Gospel Jewish, except with many qualifications. Christ came
before his countrymen as a prophet; he deliberately placed

himself in the line of the prophetic tradition. Like other
prophets of his nation, he did not altogether eschew the
framework of apocalyptic which was at that time the natural
mould for prophecy. But he preached neither the popular
nationalism, nor the popular ecclesiasticism, nor the popular
ethics. His countrymen rejected him as soon as they understood him. The Gospel was, as St. Paul said, a new creation. It is most significant that it at once introduced a new
ethical terminology. The Greek words which we translate
love (or charity), joy, peace, hope, humility, are no part
of the stock-in-trade of Greek moralists before Christ. Men
do not coin new words for old ideas. Taken as a whole the
Gospel is profoundly original ; and a Christian can find strong
evidence for his belief that in Christ a revelation was made to
humanity at large, in which the religion of the Spirit, in its
purest and most universal form, was for the first time presented
to mankind. This revelation has to a considerable extent
passed into the common consciousness of the civilized world ;
but its implications in matters of conduct, individual, social,
and international, are still imperfectly understood and have
never been acted upon, except feebly and sporadically. It is
a reproach to us that the teaching of Christ must be regarded
as only one of many elements which make up what we call
Christianity. The Quakers, as a body, seem to me to come
nearest to what a genuinely Christian society would be.

Secondly, the Greeks escaped the evils of priestly government. The Oriental type of theocracy, with which they were
familiar in the Egypt of the Pharaohs, was alien to their
civilization. Their sacrifices were for the most part of the
genial type, a communion-meal with the god. But even in
Greece we must remember the gloomy chthonian rites, and
the degradations of Orphism mentioned by Plato in the
Republic. 'They persuade not only individuals but whole
cities that expiations and atonements for sin may be made

by sacrifices and amusements which fill a vacant hour, and are equally at the service of the living and of the dead ; the latter sort they call mysteries, and they redeem us from the pains of hell, but if we neglect them no one knows what awaits us.' This exploitation of sacramentalism was common enough in Greece ; but the characteristic Caesaro-Papism of Byzantium and modern imperialism was wholly foreign to Hellenism. It was introduced by Constantine as part of the Orientalizing of the empire begun by Diocletian. As Seeley says, 'Constantine purchased an indefeasible title by a charter. He gave certain liberties and received in return passive obedience. He gained a sanction for the Oriental theory of government ; in return he accepted the law of the Church. He became irresponsible to his subjects on condition of becoming responsible to Christ.'

The Greeks never had a book-religion, in the sense in which Judaism became, and Islam always was, a book-religion. But they were in some danger of treating Homer and Hesiod as inspired scriptures. To us it is plain that a long religious history lies behind Homer, and that the treatment of the gods in Epic poetry proves that they had almost ceased to be the objects of religious feeling. Some of them are even comic characters, like the devil in Scottish folklore. To turn these poems into sacred literature was to court the ridicule of the Christians. But Homer was never supposed to contain ' the faith once delivered to the saints ' ; no religion of authority could be built upon him, and Greek speculation remained far more unfettered than the thought of Christendom has been until our own day.

Those who have observed the actual state of Christianity in Mediterranean countries cannot lay much stress on the difference between Christian monotheism and pagan polytheism. The early Church fought against the tendency to interpose objects of worship between God and man ; but Mariolatry came in through a loophole, and the worship of the masses in Roman Catholic countries is far more pagan than the service-books. In the imagination of many simple Catholics, Jesus, Mary, and Joseph are the chief potentates in their Olympus.

The doctrine of the creation of the world in time, which was denied by most pagan thinkers and affirmed by most Christian divines, belongs to philosophy rather than to religion. The disbelief in the pre-existence of the soul, a doctrine which for Greek thought stands or falls with the belief in survival after death, is more important, and may be partly attributable to Jewish influence. But pre-existence does not seem to have been believed by the majority of Greeks, and in fact almost disappears from Greek thought between Plato and the Neo-platonists. It is possible that the Pythagorean and Platonic doctrine may still have a future.

There are some who will insist that these differences are insignificant by the side of the fact that Christianity was the idealistic side of a revolt of the proletariat against the whole social order of the time. This notion, which made Christ 'le bon sans-culotte', has again become popular lately; some have even compared the early Christians with Bolsheviks. It is a fair question to ask at what period this was even approximately true. Christ and his apostles belonged to the prosperous peasantry of Galilee, a well-educated and comfortable middle class. The domestic slaves of wealthy Romans, who embraced the new faith in large numbers, were legally defenceless, but by no means miserable or degraded. After the second century the comparison of the Christians to modern revolutionists becomes too absurd for discussion. There is a good deal of rhetorical declamation about riches and poverty in the Christian Fathers; but unfortunately the Church seems to have done very little to protest against the crying economic injustices of the fourth and fifth centuries. From first to last there was nothing of the 'Spartacus' movement about the

Catholic Church. As soon as the persecutions ceased, the bishops took their place naturally among the nobility.

When we turn to the obligations of modern religion to Greece, it is difficult to know where to begin.

The conception of philosophy as an *ars vivendi* is characteristically Greek. Nothing can be further from the truth than to call the Greeks 'intellectualists' in the disparaging sense in which the word is now often used. The object of philosophy was to teach a man to live well, and with that object to think rightly about God, the world, and himself. This close union between metaphysics, morals, and religion has remained as a permanent possession of the modern world. Every philosopher is now expected to show the bearing of his system on morality and religion, and the criticism is often justified that however bold the speculations of the thinker, he is careful, when he comes to conduct, to be conventional enough. The Hellenistic combination of Platonic metaphysics with Stoic ethics is still the dominant type of Christian religious philosophy. It is curious to observe how competing tendencies in these systems—the praise of isolated detachment and of active social sympathy—have continued to struggle against each other within the Christian Church.

The place of asceticism in religion is so important, and so much has been written rather unintelligently about the contrast between Hellenism and Christianity in this matter, that I propose to deal with it, briefly indeed, but with a little more detail than a strict attention to proportion would justify. It has often been assumed that a nation of athletes, who made heroes of Heracles and Theseus, Achilles and Hector, could have had nothing but contempt for the ascetic ideal. But in truth asceticism has a continuous history within Hellenism. Even Homer knows of the priests of chilly Dodona, the Selli, whose bare feet are unwashed, and who sleep on the ground. This is probably not, as Wilamowitz-Moellendorff thinks, a description of savage life, but of an ascetic school of prophets. For the fastdays which introduced the Thesmophoria were observed by the Athenian matrons in the same way; they went unshod and sat on the bare earth; and we may compare the Nudipedalia, ordered by the Romans in time of dearth and mentioned by Petronius and Tertullian. Prophets and prophetesses fasted at Miletus, Colophon, and other places. National fasts were ordered in times of calamity or danger, and Tarentum kept a yearly fast of thankfulness for deliverance from a siege. The flagellation of boys at Sparta hardly comes into account, being probably a substitute for human sacrifice; but the continuance of the cruel rite till nearly the end of antiquity causes surprise. The worship of Dionysus Zagreus in Thrace was accompanied by ascetic practices before Pythagoras. Vegetarianism, which has always played an important part in the ascetic life, was obligatory on all Pythagoreans; but in this school there was another motive besides the desire to mortify the flesh. Those who believe in the transmigration of souls into the bodies of animals must regard flesh-eating as little better than cannibalism. The Pythagorean and the Orphic rules of life were well known throughout antiquity, and were probably obeyed by large numbers. The rule of continence was far less strict than in the Catholic ' religious ' life; but Empedocles, according to Hippolytus, advised abstinence from marriage and procreation, and the tendency to regard celibacy as part of the ' philosophic life ' increased steadily. The Cynic Antisthenes is quoted by Clement of Alexandria as having expressed a wish to ' shoot Aphrodite, who has ruined so many virtuous women '. But the asceticism of the early Cynics and of some Stoics was based not on self-devotion and spirituality but on the desire for independence, and often took repulsive forms. Of some among them it may be said that they did not object to sensual pleasure, they only objected to having to pay for it. Desire for self-sufficiency is always part of asceticism, but in the Christian saints it has been a small part. The Greeks who practised it were from first to last too anxious to be invulnerable; this was the main attraction of the philosophic life from the time of Antisthenes, and it remained the main attraction to the end. But Cynicism and Stoicism (which tend to run together) became gentler, more humane, and more spiritual under the Roman empire. Seneca, Epictetus, and Marcus Aurelius often seem to be half Christian. Direct influence of Christian ethics at this early period is perhaps unlikely; it is enough to suppose that the spirit of the age affected in a similar way all creeds and denominations. Self-mortification tended to assume more and more violent forms, till it culminated in the strange aberrations of Egyptian eremitism. It is impossible to regard these as either Greek or Christian; they indicate a pathological state of society, which can be partly but not entirely accounted for by the conditions of the time. After a few centuries a far more wholesome type of monachism supplanted the hermits; the anchorites of the Middle Ages retained the solitary life, but were very unlike the crazy savages of the Thebaid. In modern times, those who have been most under the Greek spirit have generally lived with austere simplicity, but without any of the violent self-discipline which is said to be still practised by some devout Catholics. The assiduous practice of self-mastery and the most sparing indulgence in the pleasures of sense are the 'philosophic life' which the Greek spirit recommends as the highest. The best Greeks would blame the life of an English clergyman, professor, or philosopher as too self-indulgent; we often forget how frugally and hardily the Greeks lived at all times. But here we have to consider the differences of climate, and the apparent necessity of a rather generous diet for the Nordic race.

The influence of the Greek mysteries upon Christianity is a keenly debated question, in which passion and prejudice play

too large a part. The information necessary for forming
a judgement has been much enlarged by recent discoveries
in Egypt and elsewhere, and, as usually happens, the importance
of the new facts has been sometimes exaggerated. Protestant
theology has on the whole minimized the influence of the
mysteries, and has post-dated it, from an unwillingness to allow
that there was already a strong Catholic element in the Christianity of the first century. Orthodox Catholicism has ignored
it from different but equally obvious motives. Modernist
Catholicism has in my opinion antedated the irruption of crude
sacramentalism into the Church, and has greatly overstated
its importance in the religion of the first-century Christians.
This school practically denies anything more than a half-
accidental continuity between the preaching of the historical
Christ, whom they strangely suppose to have been a mere
apocalyptist, one of the many Messiahs or Mahdis who arose
at this period in Palestine, and the Catholic Church, which
according to them belonged to the same type of religion as
the worship of Isis and Mithra. Another bone of contention
is the value of the mystery-religions of Greece. The very
able German scholars who have written on the subject, such
as Reitzenstein and still more Rohde, seem to me much too
unsympathetic in their treatment of the mystery-cults. Lastly,
some competent critics have lately urged that this side of
Christianity owed more to Judaism—Hellenized Judaism,
of course—than has been hitherto supposed.

Plato in the *Phaedo* says that ' those who established our
mysteries declare that all who come to Hades uninitiated will
lie in the mud ; while he who has been purified and initiated
will dwell with the gods '. For, as they say in the mysteries,
' Many are the thyrsus-bearers, but few are the inspired '.
This sacramentalism was not unchallenged, as we have already
seen from Plato himself. Diogenes is said to have asked whether
the robber Pataecion was better off in the other world than the

hero Epaminondas, because the former had been initiated, and the latter had not. But Orphism, though liable to degradation, purified and elevated the old Bacchic rites. As Miss Harrison says, the Bacchanals hoped to attain unity with God by intoxication, the Orphics by abstinence. The way to salvation was now through ' holiness ' (ὁσιότης). To the initiated the assurance was given, ' Happy and blessed one ! Thou shalt be a god instead of a mortal.' To be a god meant for a Greek simply to be immortal ; the Orphic saint was delivered from the painful cycle of recurring births and deaths. And Orphic purity was mainly, though not entirely, the result of moral discipline. Cumont says that the mystery-cults brought with them two new things—mysterious means of purification by which they proposed to cleanse away the defilements of the soul, and the assurance that an immortality of bliss would be the reward of piety. The truth, says Mr. H. A. Kennedy, was presented to them in the guise of divine revelations, esoteric doctrines to be carefully concealed from the gaze of the profane, doctrines which placed in their hands a powerful apparatus for gaining deliverance from the assaults of malicious demonic influences, and above all for overcoming the relentless tyranny of fate. This demonology was believed everywhere under the Roman empire, the period of which Mr. Kennedy is thinking in this sentence, and it has unfortunately left more traces in St. Paul's epistles than we like to allow. The formation of brotherhoods for mystic worship was also an important step in the development of Greek religion. These brotherhoods were cosmopolitan, and seem to have flourished especially at great seaports. They were thoroughly popular, drawing most of their support from the lower classes, and within them national and social distinctions were ignored. Their ultimate aim cannot be summed up better than in Mr. Kennedy's words—' to raise the soul above the transiency of perishable matter through actual union with the Divine '. It has been usual to distinguish between the dignified and officially recognized mysteries, like those of Eleusis, and the independent voluntary associations, some of which became important. But there was probably no essential difference between them. In neither case was there much definite teaching; the aim, as Aristotle says, was to produce a certain emotional state (οὐ μαθεῖν τι δεῖν ἀλλὰ παθεῖν). A passion-play was enacted amid the most impressive surroundings, and we need not doubt that the moral effect was beneficial and sometimes profound. When the Egyptian mysteries of Isis and Osiris were fused with the Hellenic, a type of worship was evolved which was startlingly like Christianity. A famous Egyptian text contains the promise: ' As truly as Osiris lives, shall he [the worshipper] live; as truly as Osiris is not dead, shall he not die.' The thanksgiving to Isis at the end of the *Metamorphoses* of Apuleius is very beautiful in itself, though it is an odd termination of a licentious novel. The Hermetic literature also contains doctrine of a markedly Johannine type, as notably in a prayer to Isis: ' Glorify me, as I have glorified the name of thy son Horus.' I agree with those critics (Cumont, Zielinski, and others) who attach the ' higher ' Hermetic teaching to genuinely Hellenic sources. But it is not necessary to ascribe all the higher teaching to Greece and the lower to Egypt.

Much of St. Paul's theology belongs to the same circle of ideas as these mysteries. Especially important is the psychology which divides human nature into spirit, soul, and body, spirit being the divine element into which those who are saved are transformed by the ' knowledge of God '. This knowledge is a supernatural gift, which (in the *Poimandres*) confers ' deification '. St. Paul usually prefers ' Pneuma ' as the name of this highest part of human nature; in the Hermetic literature it is not easy to distinguish between Pneuma and Nous, which holds exactly the same place in Neoplatonism. The notion of salvation as consisting in the knowledge of God is not infrequent in St. Paul ; compare, for example, 1 Cor. xiii. 12 and a still more important passage, Phil. ii. 8–10. This knowledge was partly communicated by visions and revelations, to which St. Paul attributed some importance ; but on the whole he is consistent in treating knowledge as the crown and consummation of faith. The pneumatic transformation of the personality is the centre of St. Paul's eschatology. 'Though our outward man perish, our inward man is renewed day by day.' The 'spiritual body' is the vehicle of the transformed personality ; for 'flesh and blood cannot inherit the kingdom of God'. The expression 'to be born again' is common in the mystery literature.

It would be easy to find many other parallels in St. Paul's epistles, in the Johannine books which are the best commentary upon them, and in the theology of the Greek Fathers, which prove the close connexion of early Christianity with the mystery-religions of the empire. Twenty years ago it might have been worth while to draw out these resemblances in greater detail, even in so summary a survey as this. But at present the tendency is, if not to over-estimate the debt of the Christian religion to Hellenistic thought and worship, at any rate to ignore the great difference between the higher elements in the mystery-religions, which the new faith could gladly and readily assimilate, and the lower type, the theosophy, magic, and theurgy, which was not in the line of Hellenic development, and is not to be found in the New Testament. Wendland, always a judicious critic, has said very truly that St. Paul stands to the mystery-religions as Plato to Orphism ; they are not the centre of his religious life, but they gave him effective forms of expression for his religious experience. Or, as Weinel says, ' St. Paul's doctrine of the Spirit and of Christ is not an imitation of mystery-doctrine, but inmost personal experience metaphysically interpreted after the manner of his time.' Writers like Loisy, who say that for St. Paul Jesus was 'a Saviour God, after the manner of Osiris, Attis, or Mithra ', and who proceed to draw out obvious parallels between the sufferings, death, and resurrection of these mythological personages and the gospels of the Christian Church, surely forget that St. Paul was a Jew, and that there are some transformations of which the religious mind is incapable. He never speaks of Christ as a ' Saviour God '. Even more perverse are the arguments which are used to prove that the centre of St. Paul's religion was a gross and materialistic sacramental magic. The apostle, whose antipathy to ritual in every shape is stamped upon all his writings, who thanks God that he baptized very few of the Corinthians, who declares that ' Christ sent him not to baptize but to preach the Gospel ', is accused of regarding baptism as ' an *opus operatum* which secures a man's admission into the kingdom apart from the character of his future conduct '. And yet in the Epistle to the Romans, as Weinel says, ' baptism only once enters his mind, and the Lord's Supper not even once '. Baptism for him is no *opus operatum*, but a ceremony of social significance, a symbol conditioning a deeper experience of divine grace, already embraced by faith. These same critics proceed to illustrate St. Paul's doctrine of the Lord's Supper by references to the religion of the Aztecs and other barbarians. But it is hardly worth while to argue with those who suppose that a man with St. Paul's upbringing and culture could have dallied with the notion of ' eating a god '. The ' table of the Lord ' is the table at which the Lord is the spiritual host, not the table on which his flesh is placed. Does any one suppose that ' the table of demons ' which is contrasted with the ' table of the Lord ' is the table at which demons are eaten ? Demons had no bodies, as we learn from the οὐκ εἰμι δαιμόνιον ἀσώματον of a well-known passage in a New Testament manuscript.

Crude sacramentalism certainly came in later. Its parentage

may be traced, if we will, to those mystery-mongers whom Plato mentions with disapproval. If Hellenism is the name of a way of thinking, this form of religion is not healthy Hellenism; that it was held by many Hellenes cannot be denied.

The biblical doctrine of the Fall of Man, which the Hebrews would never have evolved for themselves, remained an otiose dogma in Jewish religion. It was revivified in Christianity under Greek influence. Man, as Empedocles and others had taught, was 'an exile and vagabond from God'; his body was his tomb; he is clothed in 'an alien garment of flesh'. He is in a fallen state and needs redemption. Hellenism had become a religion of redemption; the empire was quite ready to accept this part of Christian doctrine. The sin of Adam became the first scene in the great drama of humanity, which led up to the Atonement. At the same time the whole process was never mere history; its deepest meaning was enacted in the life-story of each individual. Greek thought gave this turn to dogmas which for a Jew would have been a flat historical recital. In modern times the earlier scenes in the story, at any rate, are looked upon as little more than the dramatization of the normal experience of a human soul. But Greek thought, while it remained true to type, never took sin so tragically as Christianity has done. The struggle against evil has become sterner than it ever was for the Greeks. It must, however, be remembered that the large majority of professing Christians do not trouble themselves much about their sins, and that the best of the Greeks were thoroughly in earnest in seeking to amend their lives.

Redemption was brought to earth by a Redeemer who was both God and Man. This again was in accordance with Greek ideas. The Mediator between God and Man must be fully divine, since an intermediate Being would be in touch with neither side. The victory of Athanasius was in no sense a defeat for Hellenism. The only difficulty for a Greek thinker was that an Incarnate God ought to be impassible. This was a puzzle only for philosophers ; popular religion saw no difficulty in a *Christus patiens*. The doctrine of the Logos brought Christianity into direct affinity with both Platonism and Stoicism, and the Second Person of the Trinity was invested with the same attributes as the Nous of the Neoplatonists. But the attempts to equate the Trinity with the three divine hypostases of Plotinus was no more successful than the later attempt of Hegel to set the Trinity in the framework of his philosophy.

The subject of eschatology is so vast that it is hopeless to deal with it, even in the most summary fashion, in one paragraph. It is usually said that the resurrection of the body is a Jewish doctrine, the immortality of the soul a Greek doctrine. But the Jews were very slow to bring the idea of a future life into their living faith ; to this day it does not seem to be of much importance in Judaism. Some form of Millenarianism—a reign of the saints on earth—would seem to be the natural form for Jewish hopes to take. This belief, which was the earliest mould into which the treasure of the new revelation was poured, has never quite disappeared from the Church, and in times of excitement and upheaval it tends to reassert itself. The maturest Greek philosophy regards eternity as the divine mode of existence, while mortals are born, live, and die in time. Man is a microcosm, in touch with every rung of the ladder of existence ; and he is potentially a ' participator ' in the divine mode of existence, which he can make his own by living, so far as may be, in detachment from the vain shadows and perishable goods of earth. That this conception of immortality has had a great influence upon Christian thought and practice needs no demonstration. It is and always has been the religion of the mystic. But the Orphic tradition, with its pictures of purgatory and of eternal bliss and torment, has on the whole dominated the other two in popular Christian belief. It has been stripped of its accessories—the belief in reincarnation and the transmigration of souls, doctrines which maintain a somewhat uneasy existence within the scheme of the Neoplatonists. The picture of future retribution is even more terrifying without them. Both the philosophical and the popular beliefs about the other world are far more Greek than Jewish; but the attempt to hold these very discrepant beliefs together has reduced Christian eschatology to extreme confusion, and many Christians have given up the attempt to formulate any theories about what are called the four last things. On such a mysterious subject, definiteness is neither to be expected nor desired. The original Gospel does not encourage the natural curiosity of man to know his future fate; and the three types of eschatology which we have described have all their value as representing different aspects of religious faith and hope. We must after all confess the truth of St. Paul's words, that 'eye hath not seen, nor ear heard, neither hath it entered into the heart of man to conceive, the things that God hath prepared for them that love him'. The same apostle reminds us that 'now we see through a mirror, in riddles, and know only in part'; the face to face vision, and the knowledge which unites the knower and the known, may be ours when we have finished our course. In these words, which recall Plato's famous myth of the Cave, St. Paul is fundamentally at one with the Platonists; and it may well be that it is by this path that our contemporaries may recover that belief in eternal life which is at present burning very dimly among us.

In conclusion, what has the religion of the Greeks to teach us that we are most in danger of forgetting? In a word, it is the faith that Truth is our friend, and that the knowledge of Truth is not beyond our reach. Faith in honest seeking (ζήτησις) is at the heart of the Greek view of life. 'Those who would rightly judge of truth', says Aristotle, 'must be arbitrators, not litigants'. 'Happy is he who has learnt the value of research' (ἱστορία), says Euripides in a fragment. Curiosity, as the Greeks knew and the Middle Ages knew not, is a virtue, not a vice. Nature, for Plato, is God's vicegerent and revealer, the Soul of the universe. Human nature is the same nature as the divine; no one has proclaimed this more strongly. Nature is for us; chaos and 'necessity' are the enemy. The divorce between religion and humanism began, it must be admitted, under Plato's successors, who unhappily were indifferent to natural science, and did not even follow the best light that was to be had in physical knowledge. In the Dark Ages, when the link with Greece was broken, the separation became absolute. The luxuriant mythology of the early Greeks was not unscientific. In the absence of knowledge gaps were filled up by the imagination, and the 'method of trial and error'. The dramatic fancy which creates myths is the raw material of both poetry and science. Of course religious myths may come to be a bar to progress in science; they do so when, in a rationalizing age, the question comes to be one of fact or fiction. It is a mistake to suppose that the faith of a 'post-rational' age, to use a phrase of Santayana, can be the same as that of an unscientific age, even when it uses the same formulas. The Greek spirit itself is now calling us away from some of the vestments of Greek tradition. The choice before us is between a 'post-rational' traditionalism, fundamentally sceptical, pragmatistic, and intellectually dishonest, and a trust in reason which rests really on faith in the divine Logos, the self-revealing soul of the universe. It is the belief of the present writer that the unflinching eye and the open mind will bring us again to the feet of Christ, to whom Greece, with her long tradition of free and fearless inquiry, became a speedy and willing captive, bringing her manifold treasures to Him, in the well-grounded confidence that He was not come to destroy but to fulfil.

W. R. INGE.

PHILOSOPHY

IF we consider the philosophical tendencies of the day, we shall probably observe first of all that the artificial wall of partition between philosophy and science—and especially mathematical science—is beginning to wear very thin. On the other hand, we cannot fail to notice a reaction against what is called intellectualism. This reaction takes many forms, the most characteristic perhaps of which is a renewed interest in Mysticism. It leads also to a strong insistence on the practical aspect of philosophic thought, and to a view of its bearing on what had been regarded as primarily theoretical issues, which is known by the rather unfortunate name of Pragmatism. Now it is just on these points that we have most to learn from the Greeks, and Greek philosophy is therefore of special importance for us at the present time. At its best, it was never divorced from science, while it found a way of reconciling itself both with the interests of the practical life and with mysticism without in any way abating the claims of the intellect. It is solely from these points of view that it is proposed to regard Greek philosophy here. It would be futile to attempt a summary of the whole subject in the space available, and such a summary would have no value. Many things will therefore be passed over in silence which are important in themselves and would have to be fully treated in a complete account. All that can be done now is to indicate the points at which Greek philosophy seems to touch our actual problems. It will be seen that here, as elsewhere, ' all history is contemporary history ', and that the present can only be understood in the light of the past.

The word ' philosophy ' is Greek and so is the thing it denotes. Unless we are to use the term in so wide a sense as to empty it of all special meaning, there is no evidence that philosophy has ever come into existence anywhere except under Greek influences. In particular, mystical speculation based on religious experience is not itself philosophy, though it has often influenced philosophy profoundly, and for this reason the pantheism of the *Upanishads* cannot be called philosophical. It is true that there is an Indian philosophy, and indeed the Hindus are the only ancient people besides the Greeks who ever had one, but Indian science was demonstrably borrowed from Greece after the conquest of Alexander, and there is every reason to believe that those Indian systems which can be regarded as genuinely philosophical are a good deal more recent still. On the other hand, the earliest authenticated instance of a Greek thinker coming under Indian influence is that of Pyrrho (326 B.C.), and what he brought back from the East was rather the ideal of quietism than any definite philosophical doctrine. The barrier of language was sufficient to prevent any intercourse on important subjects, for neither the Greeks nor the Indians cared to learn any language but their own. Of course philosophy may culminate in theology, and the best Greek philosophy certainly does so, but it begins with science and not with religion.

By philosophy the Greeks meant a serious endeavour to understand the world and man, having for its chief aim the discovery of the right way of life and the conversion of people to it. It would not, however, be true to say that the word had always borne this special sense. At any rate the corresponding verb (φιλοσοφεῖν) had at first a far wider range. For instance, Herodotus (i. 30) makes Croesus say that Solon had travelled far and wide ' as a philosopher ' (φιλοσοφέων), and it is clear from the context that this refers to that love of travel for the sake of the ' wonders ' to be seen in strange lands which was so characteristic of the Ionian Greeks in the fifth century B.C. That is made quite plain by the phrase ' for the sake of sightseeing ' (θεωρίης εἵνεκεν) with which the word is coupled. Again, when Thucydides (ii. 40) makes Pericles say of his fellow citizens ' we follow philosophy without loss of manliness ' (φιλοσοφοῦμεν ἄνευ μαλακίας), it is certainly not of philosophy in the special sense he is thinking. He is only contrasting the culture of Athens with the somewhat effeminate civilization of the Ionians in Asia Minor. Even in the next century, Isocrates tried to revert to this wider sense of the word, and he regularly uses it of the art of political journalism which he imparted to his pupils.

Tradition ascribes the first use of the term ' philosophy ' in the more restricted sense indicated above to Pythagoras of Samos, an Ionian who founded a society for its cultivation in southern Italy in the latter half of the sixth century B.C. It is notoriously difficult to make any positive statements about Pythagoras, seeing that he wrote nothing ; but it is safer on general grounds to ascribe the leading ideas of the system to the master rather than to his followers. Moreover, this particular tradition is confirmed by the fact, for which there is sufficient evidence, that the name ' philosophers ' originally designated the Pythagoreans in a special way. For instance, we know that Zeno of Elea (c. 450 B.C.) wrote a book ' Against the Philosophers ', and in his mouth that can only mean 'Against the Pythagoreans '. Now the Pythagorean use of the term depends on a certain way of regarding man, which there is good reason for ascribing to Pythagoras himself. It has become more or less of a commonplace now, but we must try to seize it in its original freshness if we wish to understand the associations the word ' philosophy ' came to have for the Greeks. To state it briefly, it is the view that man is something intermediate between God and ' the other animals ' (τἆλλα ζῷα). As compared with God, he is ' mere man ', liable to error and

death (both of which are spoken of as specially *human*, ἀνθρώπινα);
as compared with ' the other animals ', he is kindly and capable
of civilization. The Latin word *humanus* took over this double
meaning, which is somewhat arbitrarily marked in English
by the spellings *human* and *humane*. Now it is clear that, for
a being subject to error and death, wisdom (σοφία) in the full
sense is impossible ; that is for God alone. On the other hand,
man cannot be content, like ' the other animals ' to remain
in ignorance. If he cannot be wise, he can at least be ' a lover
of wisdom ', and it follows that his chief end will be ' assimilation to God so far as possible ' (ὁμοίωσις τῷ θεῷ κατὰ τὸ δυνατόν),
as Plato put it in the *Theaetetus*. The mathematical studies of
the Pythagoreans soon brought them face to face with the
idea of a constant approximation which never reaches its
goal. There is, then, sufficient ground for accepting the
tradition which makes Pythagoras the author of this special
sense of the word ' philosophy ' and for connecting it with
the division of living creatures into God, men and ' the other
animals '. If the later Pythagoreans went a step further and
classified rational animals into gods, men and ' such as Pythagoras ', that was due to the enthusiasm of discipleship,
and is really a further indication of the genuinely Pythagorean
character of this whole range of ideas. We may take it,
then, that the word ' philosophy ' had acquired its special
sense in southern Italy before the beginning of the fifth
century B.C.

It is even more certain that this sense was well known at
Athens, at least in certain circles, not long after the middle of the
fifth century. To all appearance, this was the work of Socrates
(470–399 B.C.). Whatever view may be taken of the philosophy
of Socrates or of its relation to that expounded in Plato's earlier
dialogues (a point which need not be discussed here), it is at
least not open to question that he was personally intimate
with the leading Pythagoreans who had taken refuge at Thebes

and at Phlius in the Peloponnesus when their society came to
be regarded as a danger to the state at Croton and elsewhere
in southern Italy. That happened about the middle of the
fifth century, and Socrates must have made the acquaintance
of these men not long after. At that time it would be quite
natural for them to visit Athens; but, after the beginning
of the Peloponnesian War (431 B. C.), all intercourse with
them must have ceased. They were resident in enemy states,
and Socrates was fighting for his country. With the exception
of the brief interval of the Peace of Nicias (421 B.C.), he can have
seen nothing of them for years. Nevertheless it is clear that they
did not forget him; for we must accept Plato's statement
in the *Phaedo* that many of the most distinguished philosophers
of the time came to Athens to be with Socrates when he was
put to death, and that those of them who could not come
were eager to hear a full account of what happened. It is
highly significant that, even before this, two young disciples
of the Pythagorean Philolaus, Simmias and Cebes, had come
from Thebes and attached themselves to Socrates. For that
we have the evidence of Xenophon as well as of Plato, and
Xenophon's statement is of real value here; for it was just
during these few years that he himself associated with Socrates,
though he saw him for the last time a year or two before his
trial and death. Whatever other inferences may be drawn
from these facts, they are sufficient to prove that Socrates
had become acquainted with some of the leading philosophers
of the Greek world before he was forty, and to make it highly
probable that it was he who introduced the word 'philosophy'
in its Pythagorean sense to the Athenians.

So much for the word; we have next to ask how there came
to be such a thing as philosophy at all. It has been mentioned
that Pythagoras was an Ionian, and we should naturally expect
to find that he brought at least the beginnings of what he
called philosophy from eastern Hellas. Now it has been

pointed out that Greek philosophy was based on science, and science originated at Miletus on the mainland of Asia Minor nearly opposite the island of Samos, which was the original home of Pythagoras. The early Milesians were, in fact, men of science rather than philosophers in the strict sense. The two things were not differentiated yet, however, and the traditional account of the matter, according to which Greek philosophy begins with Thales (*c.* 585 B.C.), is after all quite justified. The rudimentary mathematical science of which, as explained elsewhere in this volume, he was the originator in fact led him and his successors to ask certain questions about the ultimate nature of reality, and these questions were the beginning of philosophy on its theoretical side. It is true that the Milesians were unable to give any but the crudest answers to these questions, and very likely they did not realise their full importance. These early inquirers only wanted to know what the world was made of and how it worked, but the complete break with mythology and traditional views which they effected cleared the way for everything that followed. It was no small thing that they were able to discard the old doctrine of what were afterwards known as the 'elements'—Fire, Air, Earth, and Water—and to regard all these as states of a single substance, which presented different appearances according as it was more or less rarefied or condensed. Moreover, Anaximander at least (*c.* 546 B.C.), the successor of Thales, shook himself free of the idea that the earth required support of some kind to keep in its place. He held that it swung free in space and that it remained where it was because there was no reason for it to fall in one direction rather than another. In general these early cosmologists saw that weight was not an inherent quality of bodies and that it could not be used to explain anything. On the contrary, weight was itself the thing to be explained. Anaximander also noted the importance of rotary or vortex motion in the cosmical scheme, and he inferred that there might be an indefinite number of rotating systems in addition to that with which we are immediately acquainted. He also made some very important observations of a biological character, and he announced that man must be descended from an animal of a different species. The young of most animals, he said, can find their food at once, while that of the human species requires a prolonged period of nursing. If, then, man had been originally such as he is now, he could never have survived. All this, no doubt, is rudimentary science rather than philosophy, but it was the beginning of philosophy in this sense, that it completely transformed the traditional view of the world, and made the raising of more ultimate problems inevitable.

This transformation was effected in complete independence of religion. What we may call secularism was, in fact, characteristic of all eastern Ionian science to the end. We must not be misled by the fact that Anaximander called his innumerable worlds ' gods ' and that his successor Anaximenes spoke of Air as a ' god '. These were never the gods of any city and were never worshipped by any one, and they did not therefore answer at all to what the ordinary Greek meant by a god. The use of the term by the Milesians means rather that the place once occupied by the gods of religion was now being taken by the great fundamental phenomena of nature, and the later Greeks were quite right, from their own point of view, in calling that atheism. Aristophanes characterizes this way of speaking very accurately indeed in the *Clouds* when he makes Strepsiades sum up the teaching he has received in the words ' Vortex has driven out Zeus and reigns in his stead ', and when he makes Socrates swear by ' Chaos, Respiration and Air '. So too the Milesians spoke of the primary substance as ' ageless and deathless ', which is a Homeric phrase used to mark the difference between gods and men, but this only means that the emotion formerly attached to the divine was now being transferred to the natural.

The Milesians, then, had formed the conception of an eternal matter out of which all things are produced and into which all things return, and the conception of Matter belongs to philosophy rather than to science. But besides this they had laid the foundations of geometry, and that led in other hands to the formulation of the correlative conception of Limit or Form. It is needless to enumerate here the Milesian and Pythagorean contributions to plane geometry ; it will be sufficient to remind the reader that they covered most of the ground of *Euclid*, Books I, II, IV, and VI, and probably also of Book III. In addition, Pythagoras founded Arithmetic, that is, the scientific theory of numbers (ἀριθμητική), as opposed to the practical art of calculation (λογιστική). We also know that he discovered the sphericity of the earth, and the numerical ratios of the intervals between the concordant notes of the octave. It is obvious that he was a scientific genius of the first order, and it is also clear that his methods included those of observation and experiment. The discovery of the earth's spherical shape was due to observation of eclipses, and that of the intervals of the octave can only have been based on experiments with a stretched string, though the actual experiments attributed by tradition to Pythagoras are absurd. It was no doubt this last discovery that led him to formulate his doctrine in the striking saying ' Things are numbers ', thus definitely giving the priority to the element of form or limit instead of to the indeterminate matter of his predecessors.

Pythagoras further differed from his predecessors in one respect which proved of vital moment. So far was he from ignoring religion, that he founded a society in southern Italy which was primarily a religious community. It is quite possible that he was influenced by the growth of the Orphic societies which had begun to spread everywhere in the course of the sixth century, but his religion differed from the Orphic in many ways. In particular, Apollo and not Dionysus was the chief god of the Pythagoreans, and all our evidence points to the conclusion that Pythagoras brought his religion, as he had brought his science, from eastern Hellas, though rather from the islands of the Aegean than from mainland Ionia. He was much influenced, we can still see, by certain traditions of the temple of Delos, which had become the religious centre of the Ionic world. There had, of course, been plenty of religious speculation among the Greeks before Pythagoras, and it was of a type not unlike that we find in India, though there are insuperable difficulties in the way of assuming any Aegean influence on India or any Indian influence on the Aegean at this date. It may be that the beginnings of such ideas go back to the time when the Greeks and the Hindus were living together, though it is still more likely that both the Greeks and the Indians were affected by a movement originating in the north, which brought to both of them a new view of the soul. The Delian legend of the Hyperboreans may be thought to point in this direction. However that may be, the main purpose of the religious observances practised by the Orphics and Pythagoreans alike was to secure by means of ' purifications ' (καθαρμοί) the ransom (λύσις) of the soul, which was regarded as a fallen god, from the punishment of imprisonment in successive bodies. There is no reason to suppose that Pythagoras displayed any particular originality in this part of his teaching. It all depends on the doctrine of transmigration or rebirth (παλιγγενεσία), which is often incorrectly designated by the late and inaccurate term ' metempsychosis '. There is no doubt that Pythagoras taught this, and also the rule of abstinence from animal flesh which is its natural corollary, but such ideas had been well known in many parts of Greece before his time. The real difficulty is to see the connexion between all this and his scientific work. Here we are of course confined to inferences from what we are told by later writers ;

but, if the doctrine which Plato makes Socrates expound in the early part of the *Phaedo* is Pythagorean, as it is generally supposed to be, we may say that what Pythagoras did was to teach that, while the ordinary methods of purification were well enough in their way, the best and truest purification for the soul was just scientific study. It is only in some such way as this that we can explain the religious note which is characteristic of all the best Greek science. It involves the doctrine that the Theoretic Life is the highest way of life for man, a belief still held by Plato and Aristotle, and to which we shall have to return. We may note at once, however, that it is not an 'intellectualist' ideal. There is no question of idle contemplation; it is a strenuous way of life, the aim of which is the soul's salvation, and it gives rise to an eager desire to convert other men. Just for that reason, the Pythagorean philosopher will take part in practical life when the opportunity offers, and he will even rule the state if called upon to do so. The Pythagorean society was a proselytizing body from the first, and it tried to bring in all it could reach, without distinction of nationality, social position, or sex (for women played a great part in it from the first). It was precisely its zeal for the reform of human life, and its attempt to set up a Rule of the Saints in the cities of southern Italy that led to its unpopularity. If the Pythagoreans had contented themselves with idle speculation, they would not have been massacred or forced to take refuge in flight, a fate which overtook them before the middle of the fifth century.

It soon proved, however, that the Pythagorean doctrine in its entirety was too high a one for its adherents, and a rift between Pythagorean religion and Pythagorean science was inevitable. Those who were capable of appreciating the scientific side of the movement would tend more and more to neglect the religious rule which it prescribed, and we find accordingly that before the end of the fifth century the leading

Pythagoreans, the men whose names we know, are first of all men of science, and more and more inclined to drop what they doubtless regarded as the superstitious side of the doctrine. In the end they were absorbed in the new philosophical schools which arose at Athens. The mass of the faithful, on the other hand, took no interest in arithmetic, geometry, music, and astronomy, and with them to follow Pythagoras meant to go barefoot and to abstain from animal flesh and beans. These continued the tradition even after scientific Pythagoreanism had become extinct as such, and they were a favourite subject of ridicule with the comic poets of the fourth century B.C.

It is easy for us to see now that all this indicates a real weakness in Pythagoreanism. Science and religion are not to be brought into union by a simple process of juxtaposition. We do not know how far Pythagoras himself was conscious of the ambiguity of his position; it would not be surprising if he came to feel it towards the end of his life, and we know for certain that he lived long enough to witness the beginnings of the revolt against his society in Croton and elsewhere. It is for this reason that he removed to Metapontum where he died, and where Cicero was able to visit his tomb long afterwards. We shall see later what the weak point in his system was, and we shall have to consider how the discord he had left unresolved was ultimately overcome. For the present, it is more important to note that he was the real founder both of science and of philosophy as we understand them now. It is specially true of science that it is the first steps which are the most difficult, and Pythagoras left a sufficient achievement in mathematics behind him for others to elaborate. The Greeks took less than three centuries to complete the edifice, and that was chiefly due to Pythagoras, who had laid the foundations truly and well.

We have now seen how the two great conceptions of Matter

and Form were reached ; the next problem Greek philosophy had to face was that of Motion. At first the fact of movement had simply been taken for granted. The Ionian tendency was to see motion everywhere ; it was rest that had to be explained, or rather the appearance of it. However, when the new conception of an eternal matter began to be taken seriously, difficulties made themselves felt at once. If reality was regarded as continuous, it appeared that there was no room for anything else, not even for empty space, which could only be identified with the unreal, and it was easy to show that the unreal could not exist. But, if there is no empty space, it seems impossible that there should be any motion, and the world of which we suppose ourselves to be aware must be an illusion. Such, briefly stated, was the position taken up by another Ionian of southern Italy, Parmenides of Elea (*c.* 475 B.C.), who had begun as a Pythagorean, but had been led to apply the rigorous method of reasoning introduced into geometry with such success by the Pythagoreans to the old question of the nature of the world which had occupied the Milesians. The remarkable thing about the earliest geometers is, in fact, that they did not formulate the conception of Space, which seems to us at the present day fundamental. They were able to avoid it because they possessed the conception of Matter, and regarded Air as the normal state of the material substratum. The confusion of air with empty space is, of course, a natural one, though it may be considered surprising that it should not have been detected by the founders of geometrical science. Such failures to draw all the consequences from a new discovery are common enough, however, in the history of scientific thought.

Parmenides cleared up this ambiguity, not by affirming the existence of empty space, but by denying the possibility of such a thing, even before it had been asserted by any one. He saw that the Pythagoreans really implied it, though they were quite unconscious of the fact. He is interesting to us as the first philosopher who thought of expounding his system in verse. It was not a very happy thought, as the arguments in which he deals do not readily lend themselves to this mode of expression, and we may be thankful that none of his successors except Empedocles followed his example. It has the very great inconvenience of making it necessary to use different words for the same thing to suit the exigencies of metre. And if there ever was an argument that demanded precise statement, it was that of Parmenides. As it is, his poem has the faults we should look for in a metrical version of Euclid. On the other hand, Parmenides is the first philosopher of whom we have sufficient remains to enable us to follow a continuous argument; for we have nothing of Pythagoras at all, and only detached fragments of the rest. We can see that he was ready to follow the argument wherever it might lead. He took the conception of matter which had been elaborated by his predecessors and he showed that, if it is to be taken seriously, it must lead to the conclusion that reality is continuous, finite, and spherical, with nothing outside it and no empty space within it. For such a reality motion is impossible, and the world of the senses is therefore an illusion. Of course that was not a result in which it was possible for men to acquiesce for long, and historically speaking, the Eleatic doctrine must be regarded as a *reductio ad absurdum* of earlier speculation. There is no reason to believe, however, that Parmenides himself meant it to be understood in this way. He believed firmly that he had found the truth.

Several attempts were made to escape the conclusions of Parmenides, and they all start by abandoning the assumption of the homogeneity and continuity of matter which had been implicit in the earlier systems, though it was first brought to the light of day by Parmenides. Here again the influence of contemporary science on philosophic thought is clearly marked. Empedocles of Agrigentum (*c.* 460 B. C.), the only citizen of a Dorian state who finds a place in the early history of science and philosophy, was the founder of the Sicilian school of medicine, and it was probably his pre-occupation with that science that led him to revive the old doctrine of Fire, Air, Earth, and Water, which the Milesians had cast aside, but which lent itself readily to the physio-logical theories of the day. He did not use the word after-wards translated 'elements' ($\sigma\tau o\iota\chi\epsilon\hat{\iota}a$) for these. It means literally 'letters of the alphabet', and appears to have been first employed in this connexion by the Pythagoreans at a later date, when they found it necessary to take account of the new theory. Empedocles spoke of the 'four roots' of things, and by this he meant to imply that these four forms of matter were equally original and altogether disparate. That furnished at least a partial answer to the arguments of Parmenides, which depended on the assumption that matter was homo-geneous. He also found it necessary to assume two sources of motion or forces, as we might call them, though Empedocles thought of them as substances, one of which tended to separate the 'four roots' and the other to combine them. These he called Love and Strife, and he supposed the life of the world to take the form of alternate cycles, in which one or the other prevailed in turn. In all this he was plainly influenced by his physiological studies. He thinks of the world as an animal organism subject to what are now called anabolism and cata-bolism. The details of the theory make this quite clear. A similar doctrine was taught by Anaxagoras (*c.* 460 B. C.), who came from Clazomenae in Asia Minor to Athens after the Persian Wars, and was one of the teachers of Pericles. His doctrine of ' seeds ', in which the traditional 'opposites'—wet and dry, cold and hot—were combined in different proportions, is rather more subtle than that of Empedocles, and it is possible to see in it a curious anticipation of certain features in modern chemistry. Anaxagoras too felt it necessary to assume a force or source of motion, but he thought that one would suffice to account for the rotation (περιχώρησις) to which he attributed the formation of the world. He called that force Mind (νοῦς), but his own description of it shows that he regarded it as corporeal, though he thought it was something more tenuous and unmixed than other bodies. There is little doubt that he selected the term in order to mark the identity of the source of motion in the world with that in the animal organism. That again is in accordance with the scientific interests of the time. In his astronomical theories, however, Anaxagoras showed himself a true eastern Ionian, and lagged far behind the Pythagoreans. For him, as for the Ionians of the Aegean down to and including Democritus, the earth was flat, and the eddy or vortex which gave rise to the world was still rotation in a plane. A more satisfying answer to Parmenides was the doctrine of Atomism, which frankly accepted the existence of space, and asserted that it was just as real as body. The first hint of such a solution was given by Melissus (*c.* 444 B. C.), who was a Samian but a member of the Eleatic school. He said, ' If things are a many, then each of them must be such as I have shown the One to be.' That was meant as a *reductio ad absurdum* ; but, when Leucippus of Miletus (*c.* 440 B. C.), who had also studied in the school of Elea, ventured to assert the existence of the Void, there was no longer any reason for shirking the conclusion which Melissus had stated only to show its impossibility. The atoms are, in fact, just the continuous indivisible One of Parmenides multiplied *ad infinitum* in an infinite empty space. On that side at least, the theory of body was now complete, and the question asked by Thales was answered, and it is of great interest to observe that this was brought about by the renewal of intercourse between the Ionians of Italy and those of the Aegean, a renewal which was made possible by the establishment of the Athenian Empire. Nothing makes us feel the historical connexion more vividly than the re-emergence of the names of Miletus and Samos after all these years. There were, however, certain more fundamental problems which Atomism could not solve, and which were first attacked at Athens itself. So far, it will be noted, Athens has played no part at all in our story, and in fact no more than two Athenians ever became philosophers of the first rank. It is true that they were called Socrates and Plato, so the exception is a considerable one. It was the foundation of the Athenian Empire that made Athens the natural meeting-place of the most diverse philosophical and scientific views. It was here that the east and west of Hellas came together, and that the two streams of tradition became one, with the result that a new tradition was started which, though often interrupted for a time, continues to the present day.

If we wish to understand the development of Greek philosophy, it is of the first importance that we should realize the intellectual ferment which existed at Athens in the great days of the Periclean age. It has been mentioned already that Anaxagoras of Clazomenae had settled there, and it was not long before his example was followed by others. In particular, Zeno of Elea (*c.* 450 B.C.), the favourite disciple of Parmenides, had a considerable following at Athens. He made it his business to champion the doctrine of his master by showing that those who refused to accept it were obliged to give their assent to views which were at least as repugnant to common sense, and in this way he incidentally did much for mathematics and philosophy by raising the difficulties of infinite divisibility and continuity in an acute form. All that is something quite apart from the influence of the ' sophists ' at a rather later date, though they too came both from the east and from the west, and though they had been influenced by the more strictly philosophical schools of these regions. It was into this Athens that Socrates was born (470 B. C.) about ten years after the battle of Salamis, and he was naturally exposed to all these conflicting influences, of which Plato has given us a vivid description in the *Phaedo*, from his earliest youth. He cannot, in fact, be understood at all unless this historical background is kept constantly in view. There can be no reasonable doubt that at a very early age he attached himself to Archelaus, an Athenian who had succeeded Anaxagoras, when that philosopher had to leave Athens for Lampsacus. Ion of Chios, a contemporary witness, said that Socrates had visited Asia Minor with Archelaus, and that appears to refer to the siege of Samos, when Socrates was under thirty. There is no reason whatever to doubt the statement, which Plato makes more than once, that he had met Parmenides and Zeno at a still earlier date. At any rate, the influence of Zeno on the dialectic of Socrates is unmistakable. We may also take it that he was familiar with all sorts of Orphic and Pythagorean sectaries. Aeschines of Sphettos wrote a dialogue entitled *Telauges*, in which he represented Socrates as rallying the extreme asceticism of the strict followers of Pythagoras. So far, however, as we can form a picture of him for ourselves, he was not the sort of man to become the disciple of any one. He was a genuine Athenian in respect of what is called his ' irony ', which implies a certain humorous reserve which kept him from all extravagances, however interested he might be in the extravagances of others. Nevertheless, while still quite a young man, he had somehow acquired a reputation for ' wisdom ', though he himself disclaimed anything of the sort. He had also, it appears, gathered round him a circle of ' associates ' (ἑταῖροι). The only direct evidence we have for these early days is the *Clouds* of Aristophanes (423 B.C.), which is of course a comedy and must not be taken too literally. On the other hand, a comic poet who knew his business (and surely Aristophanes did) could hardly present a well-known man to the Athenian public in a manner which had no relation to fact at all. It is fortunate that there is a passage in Xenophon's *Memorabilia* (i. 6) which seems to supply us with the very background we need to make the *Clouds* intelligible. It represents Socrates in an entirely different light from that in which he appears in the rest of the work, and it can hardly be Xenophon's own invention. It seems to refer to a time when Plato and Xenophon were babies, if not to a time before they were born, and it is probable that it comes from some literary source which we can no longer trace. We are told, then, that Antiphon the sophist was trying to detach his companions (συνουσιασταί) from Socrates, and a conversation followed in which he charged him with teaching his followers to be miserable rather than happy, and added that he was right not to charge a fee for his teaching, since in fact it was of no value. It will be seen that this implies a regular relation between Socrates and his followers which was sufficiently well known to arouse professional jealousy. Socrates does not attempt to deny the fact. He says that what he and his companions do is to spend their time together in studying the wisdom of the men of old which they have left behind them in books, and that, if they come upon anything which they think is good, they extract it for their own use, and count it great gain if, in doing this, they become friends to one another. It is obvious that this suggests something quite different from the current view of Socrates as a talker at street corners, something much more like a regular school, and that, so far as it goes, it explains the burlesque of Aristophanes.

The Socrates of whom we know most is, however, quite differently engaged. He has devoted his life to a mission to his fellow men, and especially to his fellow citizens. If we may so far trust Plato's *Apology*, the occasion of that was the answer received from the Delphic oracle by Chaerephon, whom we know from Aristophanes as one of the leading disciples of

Socrates in the earlier part of his life. Chaerephon asked the god of Delphi whether there was any one wiser than Socrates, and this of course implies that Socrates had a reputation for ' wisdom ' before his mission began. The oracle declared that there was no one wiser, and Plato makes Socrates say in the *Apology* that this was the real beginning of that mission. He set out at first to prove that the oracle was wrong, and for that purpose he tried to discover some one wiser than himself, a search in which he was disappointed, since he could only find people who thought they were wise, and no one who really was so. He therefore concluded that what the oracle really meant was that Socrates was wiser than other people in one respect only. Neither he nor any one else was really ' wise ', but Socrates was wiser than the rest because he knew he was not wise and they thought they were. It ought to be clear that this is mostly ' irony ', and it is not to be supposed that Socrates attached undue importance to the oracle, which he speaks of quite lightly, but he could hardly have told the story at all unless it was generally known that his mission did in fact date roughly from that period of his life. Historically it would probably be truer to say that the outbreak of the Peloponnesian War, in which Socrates served with great distinction as a hoplite, marked the decisive turning-point. It was in the camp at Potidaea that he once stood in a trance for twenty-four hours (431 B.C.), and that seems to point to some great psychological change, which may very well have been occasioned or accelerated by his experiences in the war. At any rate we now find him entirely devoted to the con-version of his fellow citizens, and we must try to understand what the message he had for them was.

In the *Apology* Socrates declares that his mission was divinely imposed upon him, so that he dare not neglect it, even if it should lead to his death, as in fact it did. The tone here is quite different from the half-humorous style in which he deals with the Delphic oracle, and even the 'divine sign'. That only warned him not to do things, mostly quite trivial things, which he was about to do, and never told him to do anything ; this, on the contrary, was a positive command, laid upon him by God, and there can be no doubt that Plato means us to understand this to have been the innermost conviction of Socrates. It is hard to believe that Plato could have misrepresented his master's attitude on such a point. He was present at the trial, and the *Apology* must have been written not very long afterwards, when the memory of it was still fresh in people's minds. Now Plato tells us quite clearly that what Socrates tried to get the Athenians to understand was the duty of ' caring for their souls '($\psi v \chi \hat{\eta}s \ \dot{\epsilon}\pi\iota\mu\dot{\epsilon}\lambda\epsilon\iota a$). That is confirmed from other sources, and indeed it is generally admitted. The phrase has, however, become so familiar that it does not at once strike us as anything very new or important. To an Athenian of the fifth century B.C., on the other hand, it must have seemed very strange indeed. The word translated ' soul ' ($\psi v \chi \acute{\eta}$) occurs often enough, no doubt, in the literature of the period, but it is never used of anything for which we could be called upon to ' care ' in the sense evidently intended by Socrates. Its normal use is to denote the breath of life, the ' ghost ' a man ' gives up ' at the moment of death. It can therefore be rendered by ' life ' in all cases where there is a question of risking or losing life or of clinging to it when we ought to be prepared to sacrifice it, but it is not used for the seat of conscious life at all. It is sometimes employed to signify the seat of the dream-consciousness or of what is now called the subconscious or subliminal self, but never of the ordinary waking consciousness which is the seat of knowledge and ignorance, goodness and badness.[1] On the other hand, that use of the word is quite common in the fourth century,

---

[1] See my paper on 'The Socratic Doctrine of the Soul '. *Proceedings of the British Academy*, 1915-16, pp. 235 sqq.

and it may be inferred that this change was due to Socrates. More than once Aristophanes ridicules him for holding some strange view of the ' soul ', and these jests were made at a time when Plato was only a child. We cannot, of course, expect to get any very definite idea from them as to the real teaching of Socrates on this subject, but it is not impossible to see what it was, if we take into account the views of the soul which had been held by the philosophical schools of eastern and western Ionia.

The Ionians of Asia Minor had certainly identified the soul with that in us which is conscious, and which is the seat of goodness and badness, wisdom and folly ; but they did not regard it as what we call the self or treat it as an individual. Anaximenes and his school held that the soul was what they called Air, but that was just because they regarded Air as the primary substance of which all things are made. The soul was something, in fact, that comes to us from outside ($\theta\acute{\nu}\rho\alpha\theta\epsilon\nu$) by means of respiration. As Diogenes of Apollonia expresses it, it is ' a small portion of the god ', that is, of the primary substance, enclosed in a human body for a time, and returning at death to the larger mass of the same substance outside. The formula ' Earth to earth and air to air ' was accepted as an adequate description of what takes place at death. The western Ionians, and especially the Pythagoreans, held a very different view. For them, the soul was something divine. It was, in fact, a fallen god, imprisoned in the body as a punishment for antenatal sin, and it deserved our care in this sense, that it was our chief business in life to purify it so as to secure its release from the necessity of reincarnation in another body. But, during this present life, they held that this divine element slumbers, except in prophetic dreams. As Pindar puts it, ' It sleeps when the limbs are active.' Neither of these views was familiar to the ordinary Athenian, but Socrates of course knew both well, and felt satisfied with neither. When he spoke of the soul he did not mean any mysterious fallen god which was the temporary tenant of the body, but the conscious self which it lies with us to try to make wise and good. On the other hand, his insistence on our duty to ' care for ' it is quite inconsistent with the view that it is merely something extrinsic, as all the eastern Ionians down to Anaxagoras had taught. It is, on the contrary, our very self, the thing in us which is of more importance to us than anything else whatever. It was to this doctrine of the soul and our duty to it that Socrates felt he must convert mankind and especially his fellow-citizens. It was a strange and novel doctrine then ; and, if it has become a commonplace since, that only shows that he was successful, if not in persuading his fellowmen to act on this knowledge, at least in making them aware of it. It was in this way that Socrates healed the rift between science and religion which had proved fatal to the Pythagorean society, and it may be suggested that the significance of his teaching is not exhausted yet. As has been indicated above it is to be found clearly stated in Plato's *Apology of Socrates*, and it furnishes the only clue to a right understanding of the great series of Platonic dialogues down to and including the *Republic* in which Socrates is represented as the chief speaker. Whether Plato added much or little of his own to the doctrine of his master in these dialogues is an interesting historical problem, but it need not concern the ordinary reader, at least in the first instance. We know from the allusions of Aristophanes that Socrates himself taught a new doctrine of the soul when Plato was a child, and no sympathetic reader can fail to see that the passage of the *Apology* to which we have referred is intended to be a faithful account of that doctrine. All the rest is simply its legitimate development, and it is not of very great importance for us to determine whether that development is due to Socrates or to Plato. The inspiration which has been derived from these writings by many generations will not be lessened by any decision we may come to on this point, so long as we keep clearly in mind that the new doctrine of soul is their principal theme, and that this must be understood in the light of the doctrines which had prepared the way for it. What Socrates did was really this. He deepened the meaning of the Eastern Ionian doctrine by informing it with some of the feeling and emotion which had characterized the Pythagorean teaching on the subject, while on the other hand he rationalized the Pythagorean theory by identifying the soul with our conscious personality.

Now if this is a correct account of what Socrates taught, he must be regarded as inaugurating an entirely new period in the history of philosophy. That is implied in the common term 'Presocratics' generally applied to his predecessors, though the ordinary textbooks are by no means clear as to the grounds for assigning this pre-eminent position to Socrates. We can also see how natural it was for him to lay such emphasis on the conversion of souls as he certainly did. That purpose continued to dominate Greek philosophy to the very end. No doubt successive schools varied in their conception of what conversion meant, but that is the link which binds them all together. In fact, it gave rise to a new literary form, the 'hortatory discourse' (προτρεπτικὸς λόγος), which was more and more cultivated as time went on, and was at last taken over by the fathers of the Christian church along with much else of a more fundamental character.

It has been noted already that Socrates had followers among all the leading philosophical schools of the time, and the possibility is not to be excluded that we may still learn more of him from the discovery of new sources. For the present, the recovery of some new and fairly extensive fragments of the *Alcibiades* of Aeschines of Sphettos is the chief addition to our sources of information. We know that Aeschines was a disciple of Socrates, and the tradition of antiquity was that his dialogues gave the most faithful picture of the man as he really was. If so, that was probably because Aeschines had no philosophy of his own. For us the chief importance of the new fragments is that, if we read them along with those already known (and it is unfortunate that the old and the new have not yet been printed together), they strongly confirm the impression we get from Plato of the manner of Socrates and his method of argument, and that helps to reassure us as to the essentially historical character of the Platonic Socrates. The fragments of Aeschines also corroborate Plato by showing that the conversion of Alcibiades (whose life he had saved when a young man) was one of the things that lay nearest his heart.

But the real successor of Socrates was, of course, Plato himself (427–347 B.C.). It is not possible to give even an outline of Plato's philosophy here. Indeed the time has hardly come for that yet, though much admirable work is now being done, especially by a French professor, M. Robin, which promises more certain conclusions than have yet been possible. All that can be attempted here is to indicate the attitude of Plato to some of the problems we have been discussing. His very great contributions to the theory of knowledge will be passed over, as they are beginning to be well understood, and the *Theaetetus* in particular, with its sequel the *Sophist*, is more and more coming to occupy its rightful place as the best introduction to philosophy in general. It is necessary, however, just to notice in passing a fundamental question of method which the Platonic dialogues themselves suggest. It is this. While Socrates is present in every one of them except the *Laws*, he takes practically no part in some of them, and the dialogues in which this is the case are known on other grounds to belong to the later years of Plato's life. There must be some reason for this, and it is obviously prudent to treat these later dialogues in the first instance as our primary evidence for Plato's own views. Indeed, it is only after his philosophy has been reconstructed from these sources and from the sometimes obscure references to it in Aristotle, that it will be safe to attempt an answer to the question of how much there may be in the dialogues of his early life which is properly to be assigned to Plato himself rather than to Socrates. That is a historical question of great interest ; but, as has been said, the solution of it, if that should ever prove possible, would not greatly affect the impression that Athenian philosophy leaves upon us as a whole.

Now, if we consider Plato's later, and presumably therefore most independent writings, we find, just as we should expect from a disciple of Socrates, that the doctrine of soul holds the first place, but that it has certain features of its own which there is no sufficient ground for attributing to Socrates. We are too apt to think of Plato as mainly occupied with what is called the ' theory of Ideas ', a theory which is discussed once or twice in his earlier dialogues, and which is there ascribed to Socrates, but which plays no part at all in his mature works. There the chief place is undoubtedly taken by the doctrine of the soul, and we can see that it is of the first importance for Plato. Soul is regarded as the source of all motion in the world, because it is the only thing in the world that moves without being itself moved by anything else. It is this and this alone that enables Plato to account for the existence of the world and of mankind, and to avoid the theory of ' two worlds ' into which, as he points out in the *Sophist*, ' the friends of the Ideas ', whoever they may have been, were only too apt to fall. In Plato this view of the soul culminates in theology of a kind which he nowhere attributes to Socrates. He represents him, indeed, as a man of a deeply religious nature, but we do not gather that he had felt the need of a formal doctrine of God. Plato, on the other hand, has left us the first systematic defence of Theism we know of, and it is based entirely on his doctrine of soul as the self-moved mover. But the highest soul, or God, is not only the ultimate source of motion, but also supremely good. Now, since there are many things in the world which are not good, and since it would be blasphemy to attribute these to God, there must be other souls in the world which are relatively at least independent. God is not, directly at least, the cause of all things, but it is not easy to discover the relation in which these other souls are thought of as standing to God. In the *Timaeus*, the matter is put in this way. The soul of the world, and all other souls human and divine, are the work of the Creator, who is identified with God, and they are not inherently indestructible, since anything that has been made can be unmade. They are, however, practically indestructible, since God made all things because He was good and wished them also to be as good as possible. His goodness, therefore, will not suffer Him to destroy what He has once made. That of course is mythically expressed, and Plato is not committed to it as a statement of his own belief, since it is only the account which *Timaeus* puts into the mouth of the Creator. We can see, however, what was the problem with which he was occupied, and it is not perhaps illegitimate to infer that he approached the question which still baffles speculation from the point of view that God's omnipotence, as we should call it, is limited by his goodness. This is a much more important limitation than that imposed by the existence of matter, to which Timaeus also refers. In that, he is simply following the tradition of the Pythagorean society to which he belonged, as is shown by his identification of matter with space, or rather with 'room'. So far as can be seen at present, we are not entitled to ascribe this view to Plato without more ado, but that is a point on which the last word has not yet been said.

The description of the creation given by Timaeus is of course to be regarded as mythical in its details, but it has features from which we may learn a good deal as to the direction taken by Plato's thoughts about the world. In particular, while the important part played by geometry is quite intelligible in the mouth of a Pythagorean, he makes use of certain theories which we know to belong to the most recent mathematics of the day, in particular the complete doctrine of the five regular solids, which was due to Theaetetus, who was one of the earliest members of the Academy, and whom Plato represents as having made the acquaintance of Socrates just before the master's death. Theaetetus died young, but we know enough of him to feel sure that he was one of the few great original mathematicians who have appeared in history. In the *Timaeus* the theory of the regular solids is used to get rid once more of the doctrine of four ultimate ' elements '. These, Timaeus says, are so far from being elements or letters of the alphabet, that they are not even syllables. The way in which the so-called elements are built up out of molecules corresponding in their configuration to the regular solids, and the explanations of their transmutation into one another based on the geometrical construction of these figures, is apt to strike the average reader as fantastic, but one of the most distinguished living mathematicians and physicists has stated that he is struck most of all by their resemblance to the scientific theories of the twentieth century. It will be well, therefore, to avoid hasty judgements on this point. It is at any rate easy to understand how the study of mathematics came to hold the preponderating place it did in the Platonic Academy.

In accordance with the plan of this paper, something must now be said of Plato's attitude to the practical life, a point on which it is very easy to make mistakes. No one has insisted more strongly than he has on the primacy of the Theoretic Life. The philosopher is the man who is in love with the spectacle of all time and all existence and that is what delivers him from petty ambitions and low desires. He has made the toilsome ascent out of the Cave in which the mass of men dwell, and in which they only behold the shadows of reality. But, even in this enthusiastic description of the philosophic life, an equal stress is laid on the duty of philosophers to descend into the

Cave in turn and to rescue as many of their former fellow-prisoners as may be, even against their will, by turning them to the light and dragging them up into the world of truth and reality. It is quite easy to understand, in view of this, that Plato devoted some of the best years of his life to practical affairs and that he relinquished the studies of the Academy for a time in order to direct the education of Dionysius II. The thing appeared well worth doing; for Greek civilization in Sicily, and consequently, as we can now see, the civilization of western Europe, was seriously threatened by the Carthaginians. They had been held at bay by Dionysius I, but after his death everything depended on his successor. Now the education of Dionysius II had been completely neglected, but he had good natural abilities, and his uncle Dion, who was Plato's friend, was ready to answer for his good intentions. Plato could not turn a deaf ear to such a call. Unfortunately Dionysius was vain and obstinate, and he soon became impatient of the serious studies which Plato rightly regarded as necessary to prepare him for his task. The result was a growing estrangement between Plato and his pupil, which made it impossible to hope for a successful issue to the plans of Dion. It is unnecessary to tell the whole story here, but it is right to say that there was nothing at all impracticable in what Plato undertook, and that he was certainly justified in holding that the education of Dionysius must be completed before it would be safe to entrust him with the championship of the cause of Hellenism in the west.

His failure to make anything of Dionysius did not lead Plato to abandon his efforts to heal the wounds of Hellenism. One of the studies most ardently pursued in the Academy was Jurisprudence, of which he is the real founder. It was not uncommon for Greek states to apply to the Academy for legislators to codify existing law or to frame a new code for colonies which had just been founded. That is the real explanation of the remarkable work entitled the *Laws*, which must have occupied Plato for many years, and which was probably begun while he was still directing the studies of Dionysius. It appears to have been left unfinished ; for, while some parts of it are highly elaborated, there are others which make upon us the impression of being a first draft. Even so, it is a great work if we regard it from the proper point of view. It is, in the first place, a codification of Greek, and especially Athenian law, of course with those reforms and improvements which suggest themselves when the subject is systematically treated, and it formed the basis of Hellenistic, and through that of Roman law, to which the world owes so much. There is no more useful corrective of the popular notion of Plato as an unpractical visionary than the careful study of the dullest and most technical parts of the *Laws* in the light of the *Institutes*.

No attempt has been made here to describe the system of Plato as a whole, and indeed the time has not yet come when such an attempt can profitably be made. We have no direct knowledge of his teaching in the Academy ; for we only possess the works which he wrote with a wider public in view. In the case of Aristotle (384–322 B.C.), a similar reservation must be made, though for just the opposite reason. We have only fragments of his published works and what we possess is mainly the groundwork of his lectures in the Lyceum. It will be seen that there is still very much to be done here too. From the nature of the case, notes for lectures take a great deal for granted that would be more fully explained when the lectures were delivered, and some of the most important points are hardly developed at all. Nevertheless there are certain things which come out clearly enough, and it so happens that they are points of great importance from which we can learn something with regard to the philosophical problems of the present day.

In the first place, it is desirable to point out that Aristotle was not an Athenian, but an Ionian from the northern Aegean, and that he was strongly influenced by eastern Ionian science, especially by the system of Democritus (which Plato does not appear to have known) and by the medical theories of the time. That is why he is so unsympathetic to the western schools of philosophy, and especially to the Pythagoreans and the Eleatics. Empedocles alone, who was a biologist like himself, and the founder of a medical school, finds favour in his eyes. He is not, therefore, at home in mathematical matters and his system of Physics can only be regarded as retrograde when we compare it with that of the Academy. He did indeed accept the doctrine of the earth's sphericity, but with that exception his cosmological views must be called reactionary. Where he is really great is in biology, a field of research which was not entirely neglected by the Academy, but which had been treated as secondary in comparison with mathematics and astronomy. The contrast between Plato and Aristotle in this respect seems to repeat on a higher plane that between Pythagoras and Empedocles, and this suggests something like a law of philosophical development which may perhaps throw light on the present situation. It seems as if this alternation of the mathematical and the biological interest was fundamental in the development of scientific thought and that the philosophy of different periods takes its colour from it. The philosophy of the nineteenth century was dominated in the main by biological conceptions, while it seems as if that of the twentieth was to be chiefly mathematical in its outlook on the world. We must not, of course, make too much of such formulas, but it is instructive to study such alternations in the philosophy of the Greeks, where everything is simpler and more easily apprehended.

On the other hand, Aristotle had been a member of the Academy for twenty years, and that could not fail to leave its mark upon him. This no doubt explains the fact, which has often been noted, that there are two opposite and inconsistent strains in all Aristotle's thinking. On the one hand, he is determined to avoid everything 'transcendental', and his dislike of Pythagorean and Platonist mathematics is mainly due to that. On the other hand, despite his captious and sometimes unfair criticisms of Plato, he evidently admired him greatly and had been much influenced by him. It may be suggested that the tone of his criticisms is partly due to his annoyance at finding that he could not shake off his Platonism, do what he would. This is borne out by the fact that, when he has come to the furthest point to which his own system will take him, he is apt to take refuge in metaphors of a mythical or 'transcendental' character, for which we are not prepared in any way and of which no explanation is vouchsafed us. That is particularly the case when he is dealing with the soul and the first mover. On the whole his account of the soul is simply a development of eastern Ionian theories, and we feel that we are far removed indeed from the Platonist conception of the soul's priority to everything else. But, when he has told us that the highest and most developed form of soul is Mind, we are suddenly surprised by the statement that Mind in this sense is merely passive, while there is another form of it which is separable from matter, and that alone is immortal and everlasting. This has given rise to endless controversy which does not concern us here, but it seems best to interpret it as an involuntary outburst of the Platonism Aristotle could not wholly renounce. Very similar is the passage where he tries to explain how the first mover, though itself unmoved, communicates motion to the world. 'It moves it like a thing beloved,' he tells us, and leaves us to make what we can of that. And yet we cannot help feeling that, in passages like this, we come far nearer to the beliefs Aristotle really cared about than we do anywhere else. At heart he is a Platonist in spite of himself.

Aristotle's attitude to the practical life is also dependent on

Plato's. In the Tenth Book of the *Ethics* he puts the claims of the Contemplative Life even higher than Plato ever did, so that the practical life appears to be only ancillary to it. He does not feel in the same degree as Plato the call for the philosopher to descend once more into the Cave for the sake of the prisoners there, and altogether he seems far more indifferent to the practical interests of life. Nevertheless he followed Plato's lead in giving much of his time to the study of Politics and that too with the distinctly practical aim of training legislators. He has often been criticized for his failure to see that the days of the city-state were numbered, and for the way in which he ignores the rise of an imperial monarchy in the person of his own pupil Alexander the Great. That, however, is not quite fair. Aristotle had a healthy dislike of princes and courts, and the city-state still appealed to him as the normal form of political organization. He could not believe that it would ever be superseded, and he wished to contribute to its better administration. He had, in fact, a much more conservative outlook than Plato, who was inclined to think with Isocrates, that the revival of monarchy was the only thing that could preserve Hellenism as things were then. We must remember that Aristotle was not himself a citizen of any free state, and that he could hardly be expected to have the same political instincts as Plato, who belonged by birth to the governing classes of Athens and had inherited the liberal traditions of the Periclean Age. This comes out best of all perhaps, in the attitude of the two philosophers to the question of slavery. In the *Laws*, which deals with existing conditions, Plato of course recognizes the *de facto* existence of slavery, though he is very sensible of its dangers and makes many legislative proposals with a view to their mitigation. In the *Republic*, on the other hand, where there is no need to trouble about existing conditions, he makes Socrates picture for us a community in which there are apparently no slaves at all. Aristotle is also anxious to mitigate the worst abuses of slavery, but he justifies the institution as a permanent one by the consideration that barbarians are ' slaves by nature ' and that it is for their own interest to be ' living tools '. This insistence upon the fundamental distinction between Greeks and barbarians must have seemed an anachronism to many of Aristotle's contemporaries and it had been expressly denounced by Plato as unscientific.

The immediate effect of Aristotle's rejection of Platonist mathematics was one he certainly neither foresaw nor intended. It was to make a breach between philosophy and science. Mathematical science, whether Aristotle realized it or not, was still in the vigour of its first youth, and mathematicians were stirred by the achievements of the last generation to attempt the solution of still higher problems. If the Lyceum turned away from them, they were quite prepared to carry on the Academic tradition by themselves, and they succeeded for a time beyond all expectation. The third century B. c. was, in fact, the Golden Age of Greek mathematics, and it has been suggested that this was due to the emancipation of mathematics from philosophy. If that were true, it would be very important for us to know it ; but it can, I think, be shown that it is not true. The great mathematicians of the third century were certainly carrying on the tradition of their predecessors who had been philosophers as well as mathematicians, and it is not to be wondered at that they were able to do so for a time. But the really striking fact is surely that Greek mathematics became sterile in a comparatively short time, and that no further advance was made till the days of Descartes and Leibniz, with whom philosophy and mathematics once more went hand in hand.

Nor was the effect of this divorce on philosophy itself less disastrous. Theophrastus continued Aristotle's work on Aristotle's lines, and founded the science of Botany as his predecessor had founded that of Zoology, but the Peripatetic School practically died out with him and had very little influence till the study of Aristotle was revived long afterwards by the Neoplatonists.

For the present, the divorce of science and philosophy was complete. The Stoics and the Epicureans had both, indeed, a scientific system, but their philosophy was in no sense based upon it. The attitude of Epicurus to science is particularly well marked. He took no interest in it whatever as such, but he used it as an instrument to free men from the religious fear to which he attributed human unhappiness. For that purpose, the science of the Academy, which had led up to a theology, was obviously unsuitable, and, like a true eastern Ionian as he was, Epicurus harked back to the atomic theory of Democritus, adding to it, however, certain things which really made nonsense of it, such, for instance, as the theory of absolute weight and lightness, which Aristotle had unfortunately taught. The Stoics too were corporealists, and found such science as they required in the system of Heraclitus, though they also adopted for polemical purposes much of Aristotle's Logic, taking pains, however, to alter his terminology. Both these schools, in fact, while remaining faithful to the idea of philosophy as conversion, forgot that it had always been based on science in its best days. It was this, no doubt, which chiefly commended Stoicism and Epicureanism to the Romans, who were never really interested in science. Both Stoicism and Epicureanism made a practical appeal, though of a different kind, and that served to gain credit for them at Rome.

The Academy which Plato had founded still continued to exist, though it was diverted from its original purpose not more than a generation after Plato's death. Mathematics, we have seen, had made itself independent, and the most pressing necessity of the time was certainly the criticism of the new dogmatism which the Stoics had introduced. That was really carrying on one side of Platonism and not the least important. It is true indeed that the Academy appears to us at this distance of time mainly as a school of scepticism, but we must remember that its scepticism was directed entirely to the sensible world, as to which the attitude of Plato himself was not fundamentally different. The real sceptics always refused to admit that the Academics were sceptics in the proper sense of the word, and it is possible that the tradition of Platonism proper was never wholly broken. At any rate, by the first century B.C., we begin to notice that Stoicism tends to become more and more Platonic. The study of Plato's *Timaeus* came into favour again, and the commentary which Posidonius (*c.* 100 B.C.) wrote upon it had great influence on the development of philosophy down to the end of the Middle Ages. It is this period of eclecticism which is reflected for us in the philosophical writings of Cicero. It had great importance for the history of civilization, but it is far removed from the spirit of genuine Greek philosophy. That was dead for the present, and it did not come to life again till the third century of our era, when Platonism was revived at Rome by Plotinus.

It is only quite recently that historians of Greek philosophy have begun to do justice to 'Neoplatonism'. That is partly due to the contemporary philosophical tendencies noted at the beginning of this paper, and partly to historical investigations into the philosophy of the Middle Ages, which is more and more seen to be dependent mainly on Neoplatonism down to and including the system of St. Thomas Aquinas. It was in fact the most decisive fact in the history of Western European civilization that Plotinus founded his school at Rome rather than at Athens or Alexandria; for that is how Western Europe became the real heir to the philosophy of Greece. Every one knows, of course, that Plotinus was a ' mystic ', but the term is apt to suggest quite wrong ideas about him. He is often spoken of still as a man who introduced oriental ideas into Greek philosophy, and he is popularly supposed to have been an Egyptian. That is most improbable ; and, if it were true, it would only make it the more remarkable that, though he certainly studied at Alexandria for eleven years, he never even mentions the religion of Isis, which was so fashionable at Rome in his day, and which had fascinated so genuine a Greek as Plutarch some generations before. There is no doubt that what Plotinus believed himself to be teaching was genuine Platonism, and that he had prepared himself for the task by a careful study of Aristotle and even of Stoicism, so far as that served his purpose. No doubt he was too great a man to make himself the mere mouthpiece of another's thought ; but, for all that, he was the legitimate successor of Plato, and it may be added that M. Robin, who has taken upon himself the arduous task of extracting Plato's real philosophy from the writings of Aristotle, has come to the conclusion that there is a great deal more ' Neoplatonism ' in Plato than is sometimes supposed.

Plotinus is a mystic, then, though not at all in the sense in which the term is often misused. He sets before his disciples a ' way of life ' which leads by stages to the highest life of all, but that is just what Pythagoras and Plato had done, and it is only the continuation of a tradition which goes back among the Greeks to the sixth century B.C., nearly a thousand years before the time of Plotinus. His aim, like that of his predecessors, is the conversion of souls to this way of life, and he differs from such thinkers as the Stoics and the Epicureans in holding that the ' way of life ' to which he calls them must be based once more on a systematic doctrine of God, the World and Man. The result was that the divorce which had existed for centuries between science and philosophy was once more annulled. We cannot say, indeed, that Plotinus himself made any special study of Mathematics, but there is no doubt at all that his followers did, and it is due to them, and especially to Proclus, that we know as much of Greek Mathematics as we do. Proclus was indeed the systematizer of the doctrine of Plotinus, though he differs from him on certain points, and his influence on later philosophy cannot be overestimated. It can be distinctly traced even in Descartes, whom it reached through a number of channels, the study of which has recently been undertaken by a French scholar, Professor Gilson, of the University of Strasbourg. When his researches are complete, the continuity of Greek and modern philosophy will be plainly seen, and the part played by Platonism in the making of the modern European mind will be made manifest. We shall then understand better than ever why Greek philosophy is a subject of perennial interest.

The history of Greek philosophy is, in fact, the history of our own spiritual past, and it is impossible to understand the present without taking it into account. In particular, the Platonist tradition underlies the whole of western civilization. It was at Rome, as has been pointed out, that Plotinus taught, and it was in certain Latin translations of the writings of his school that St. Augustine found the basis for a Christian philosophy he was seeking. It was Augustine's great authority in the Latin Church that made Platonism its official philosophy for centuries. It is a complete mistake to suppose that the thinking of the Middle Ages was dominated by the authority of Aristotle. It was not till the thirteenth century that Aristotle was known at all, and even then he was studied in the light of Platonism, just as he had been by Plotinus and his followers. It was only at the very close of the Middle Ages that he acquired the predominance which has made so strong an impression on the centuries that followed. It was from the Platonist tradition, too, that the science of the earlier Middle Ages came. A considerable portion of Plato's *Timaeus* had been translated into Latin in the fourth century by Chalcidius with a very elaborate commentary based on ancient sources, while the *Consolation of Philosophy*, written in prison by the Roman Platonist Boethius in A.D. 525, was easily the most popular book of the Middle Ages. It was translated into English by Alfred the Great and by Chaucer, and into many other European languages. It was on these foundations that the French Platonism of the twelfth century, and especially that of the School of Chartres, was built up, and the influence of that school in England was very great indeed. The names of Grosseteste and Roger Bacon may just be mentioned in this connexion, and it would not be hard to show that the special character of the contribution which English writers have been able to make to science and philosophy is in large measure attributable to this influence.

But the interest of Greek philosophy is not only historical ; it is full of instruction for the future too. Since the time of Locke, philosophy has been apt to limit itself to discussions about the nature of knowledge, and to leave questions about the nature of the world to specialists. The history of Greek philosophy shows the danger of this unnatural division of the province of thought, and the more we study it, the more we shall feel the need of a more comprehensive view. The ' philosophy of things human ', as the Greeks called it, is only one department among others, and the theory of knowledge is only one department of that. If studied in isolation from the whole, it must inevitably become one-sided. From Greek philosophy we can also learn that it is fatal to divorce speculation from the service of mankind. The notion that philosophy could be so isolated would have been wholly unintelligible to any of the great Greek thinkers, and most of all perhaps to the Platonists who are often charged with this very heresy. Above all, we can learn from Greek philosophy the paramount importance of what we call the personality and they called the soul. It was just because the Greeks realized this that the genuinely Hellenic idea of conversion played so great a part in their thinking and in their lives. That, above all, is the lesson they have to teach, and that is why the writings of their great philosophers have still the power to convert the souls of all that will receive their teaching with humility.

J. BURNET.

MATHEMATICS AND ASTRONOMY

It has been well said that, if we would study any subject properly, we must study it as something that is alive and growing and consider it with reference to its growth in the past. As most of the vital forces and movements in modern civilization had their origin in Greece, this means that, to study them properly, we must get back to Greece. So it is with the literature of modern countries, or their philosophy, or their art ; we cannot study them with the determination to get to the bottom and understand them without the way pointing eventually back to Greece.

When we think of the debt which mankind owes to the Greeks, we are apt to think too exclusively of the masterpieces in literature and art which they have left us. But the Greek genius was many-sided ; the Greek, with his insatiable love of knowledge, his determination to see things as they are and to see them whole, his burning desire to be able to give a rational explanation of everything in heaven and earth, was just as irresistibly driven to natural science, mathematics, and exact reasoning in general, or logic.

To quote from a brilliant review of a well-known work : ' To be a Greek was to seek to know, to know the primordial substance of matter, to know the meaning of number, to know the world as a rational whole. In no spirit of paradox one may say that Euclid is the most typical Greek : he would know to the bottom, and know as a rational system, the laws of the measurement of the earth. Plato, too, loved geometry and the wonders of numbers ; he was essentially Greek because he was essentially mathematical. . . . And if one thus finds the

Greek genius in Euclid and the *Posterior Analytics*, one will understand the motto written over the Academy, μηδεὶς ἀγεωμέτρητος εἰσίτω. To know what the Greek genius meant you must (if one may speak ἐν αἰνίγματι) begin with geometry.'

Mathematics, indeed, plays an important part in Greek philosophy : there are, for example, many passages in Plato and Aristotle for the interpretation of which some knowledge of the technique of Greek mathematics is the first essential. Hence it should be part of the equipment of every classical student that he should have read substantial portions of the works of the Greek mathematicians in the original, say, some of the early books of Euclid in full and the definitions (at least) of the other books, as well as selections from other writers. Von Wilamowitz-Moellendorff has included in his *Griechisches Lesebuch* extracts from Euclid, Archimedes and Heron of Alexandria ; and the example should be followed in this country.

Acquaintance with the original works of the Greek mathematicians is no less necessary for any mathematician worthy of the name. Mathematics is a Greek science. So far as pure geometry is concerned, the mathematician's technical equipment is almost wholly Greek. The Greeks laid down the principles, fixed the terminology and invented the methods *ab initio* ; moreover, they did this with such certainty that in the centuries which have since elapsed there has been no need to reconstruct, still less to reject as unsound, any essential part of their doctrine.

Consider first the terminology of mathematics. Almost all the standard terms are Greek or Latin translations from the Greek, and, although the mathematician may be taught their meaning without knowing Greek, he will certainly grasp their significance better if he knows them as they arise and as part of the living language of the men who invented them. Take the word *isosceles* ; a schoolboy can be shown what an isosceles triangle is, but, if he knows nothing of the derivation, he will wonder why such an apparently outlandish term should be necessary to express so simple an idea. But if the mere appearance of the word shows him that it means a thing *with equal legs*, being compounded of ἴσος, equal, and σκέλος, a leg, he will understand its appropriateness and will have no difficulty in remembering it. *Equilateral*, on the other hand, is borrowed from the Latin, but it is merely the Latin translation of the Greek ἰσόπλευρος, *equal-sided*. *Parallelogram* again can be explained to a Greekless person, but it will be far better understood by one who sees in it the two words παράλληλος and γραμμή and realizes that it is a short way of expressing that the figure in question is contained by parallel lines; and we shall best understand the word *parallel* itself if we see in it the statement of the fact that the two straight lines so described go *alongside one another*, παρ' ἀλλήλας, all the way. Similarly a mathematician should know that a *rhombus* is so called from its resemblance to a form of spinning-top (ῥόμβος from ῥέμβω, to spin) and that, just as a parallelogram is a figure formed by two pairs of parallel straight lines, so a *parallelepiped* is a solid figure bounded by three pairs of parallel planes (παράλληλος, parallel, and ἐπίπεδος, plane); incidentally, in the latter case, he will be saved from writing ' parallel*o*piped ', a monstrosity which has disfigured not a few textbooks of geometry. Another good example is the word *hypotenuse*; it comes from the verb ὑποτείνειν (c. ὑπό and acc. or simple acc.), to *stretch under*, or, in its Latin form, to *subtend*, which term is used quite generally for ' to be opposite to '; in our phraseology the word *hypotenuse* is restricted to that side of a right-angled triangle which is opposite to the right angle, being short for the expression used in Eucl. i. 47, ἡ τὴν ὀρθὴν γωνίαν ὑποτείνουσα πλευρά, ' the side subtending the right angle ', which accounts for the feminine participial form ὑποτείνουσα, *hypotenuse*. If mathematicians had had more Greek, perhaps the misspelt form 'hypot*h*enuse' would not have survived so long.

To take an example outside the Elements, how can a mathematician properly understand the term *latus rectum* used in conic sections unless he has seen it in Apollonius as the *erect side* (ὀρθία πλευρά) of a certain rectangle in the case of each of the three conics ? [1] The word *ordinate* can hardly convey anything to one who does not know that it is what Apollonius describes as ' the straight line drawn down (from a point on the curve) in the *prescribed* or *ordained* manner (τεταγμένως κατηγμένη) '. *Asymptote* again comes from ἀσύμπτωτος, *non-meeting*, *non-secant*, and had with the Greeks a more general signification as well as the narrower one which it has for us : it was sometimes used of parallel lines, which also ' do not meet '.

Again, if we take up a textbook of geometry written in accordance with the most modern Education Board circular or University syllabus, we shall find that the phraseology used (except where made more colloquial and less scientific) is almost all pure Greek. The Greek tongue was extraordinarily well adapted as a vehicle of scientific thought. One of the characteristics of Euclid's language which his commentator Proclus is most fond of emphasizing is its marvellous *exactness* (ἀκρίβεια). The language of the Greek geometers is also wonderfully concise, notwithstanding all appearances to the contrary. One of the complaints often made against Euclid is that he is ' diffuse '. Yet (apart from abbreviations in writing) it will be found that the exposition of corresponding

---

[1] In the case of the parabola, the base (as distinct from the ' erect side ') of the rectangle is what is called the *abscissa* (Gk. ἀποτεμνομένη, ' cut off ') of the ordinate, and the rectangle itself is equal to the square on the ordinate. In the case of the central conics, the base of the rectangle is ' the transverse side of the figure ' or the transverse diameter (the diameter of reference), and the rectangle is equal to the square on the diameter conjugate to the diameter of reference.

matters in modern elementary textbooks generally takes up, not less, but more space. And, to say nothing of the perfect finish of Archimedes's treatises, we shall find in Heron, Ptolemy and Pappus veritable models of concise statement. The purely geometrical proof by Heron of the formula for the area of a triangle, $\Delta = \sqrt{\{s(s-a)\ (s-b)\ (s-c)\}}$, and the geometrical propositions in Book I of Ptolemy's *Syntaxis* (including ' Ptolemy's Theorem ') are cases in point.

The principles of geometry and arithmetic (in the sense of the theory of numbers) are stated in the preliminary matter of Books I and VII of Euclid. But Euclid was not their discoverer ; they were gradually evolved from the time of Pythagoras onwards. Aristotle is clear about the nature of the principles and their classification. Every demonstrative science, he says, has to do with three things, the subject-matter, the things proved, and the things from which the proof starts (ἐξ ὧν). It is not everything that can be proved, otherwise the chain of proof would be endless ; you must begin somewhere, and you must start with things admitted but indemonstrable. These are, first, principles common to all sciences which are called *axioms* or *common opinions*, as that 'of two contradictories one must be true ', or ' if equals be subtracted from equals, the remainders are equal ' ; secondly, principles peculiar to the subject-matter of the particular science, say geometry. First among the latter principles are definitions ; there must be agreement as to what we mean by certain terms. But a definition asserts nothing about the existence or non-existence of the thing defined. The existence of the various things defined has to be *proved* except in the case of a few primary things in each science the existence of which is indemonstrable and must be *assumed* among the first principles of the science ; thus in geometry we must assume the existence of points and lines, and in arithmetic of the unit. Lastly, we must assume certain other things which are less obvious and cannot be proved but yet have to be accepted ; these are called *postulates*, because they make a demand on the faith of the learner. Euclid's Postulates are of this kind, especially that known as the parallel-postulate.

The methods of solution of problems were no doubt first applied in particular cases and then gradually systematized ; the technical terms for them were probably invented later, after the methods themselves had become established.

One method of solution was the *reduction* of one problem to another. This was called ἀπαγωγή, a term which seems to occur first in Aristotle. But instances of such reduction occurred long before. Hippocrates of Chios reduced the problem of duplicating the cube to that of finding two mean proportionals in continued proportion between two straight lines, that is, he showed that, if the latter problem could be solved, the former was thereby solved also ; and it is probable that there were still earlier cases in the Pythagorean geometry.

Next there is the method of mathematical *analysis*. This method is said to have been ' communicated ' or ' explained ' by Plato to Leodamas of Thasos ; but, like reduction (to which it is closely akin), analysis in the mathematical sense must have been in use much earlier. *Analysis* and its correlative *synthesis* are defined by Pappus : ' in analysis we assume that which is sought as if it were already done, and we inquire what it is from which this results, and again what is the antecedent cause of the latter, and so on, until by so retracing our steps we come upon something already known or belonging to the class of principles. But in synthesis, reversing the process, we take as already done that which was last arrived at in the analysis, and, by arranging in their natural order as consequences what were before antecedents and successively connecting them one with another, we arrive finally at the construction of that which was sought.'

The method of *reductio ad absurdum* is a variety of analysis.

Starting from a hypothesis, namely the contradictory of what we desire to prove, we use the same process of analysis, carrying it back until we arrive at something admittedly false or absurd. Aristotle describes this method in various ways as *reductio ad absurdum*, proof *per impossibile*, or proof leading to the impossible. But here again, though the term was new, the method was not. The paradoxes of Zeno are classical instances.

Lastly, the Greeks established the form of exposition which still governs geometrical work, simply because it is dictated by strict logic. It is seen in Euclid's propositions, with their separate formal divisions, to which specific names were afterwards assigned, (1) the *enunciation* (πρότασις), (2) the *setting-out* (ἔκθεσις), (3) the διορισμός, being a re-statement of what we are required to do or prove, not in general terms (as in the *enunciation*), but with reference to the particular data contained in the *setting-out*, (4) the *construction* (κατασκευή), (5) the *proof* (ἀπόδειξις), (6) the *conclusion* (συμπέρασμα). In the case of a problem it often happens that a solution is not possible unless the particular data are such as to satisfy certain conditions ; in this case there is yet another constituent part in the proposition, namely the statement of the conditions or limits of possibility, which was called by the same name διορισμός, definition or delimitation, as that applied to the third constituent part of a theorem.

We have so far endeavoured to indicate generally the finality and the abiding value of the work done by the creators of mathematical science. It remains to summarize, as briefly as possible, the history of Greek mathematics according to periods and subjects.

The Greeks of course took what they could in the shape of elementary facts in geometry and astronomy from the Egyptians and Babylonians. But some of the essential characteristics of the Greek genius assert themselves even in their borrowings from these or other sources. Here, as everywhere else, we see their directness and concentration; they always knew what they wanted, and they had an unerring instinct for taking only what was worth having and rejecting the rest. This is illustrated by the story of Pythagoras's travels. He consorted with priests and prophets and was initiated into the religious rites practised in different places, not out of religious enthusiasm 'as you might think' (says our informant), but in order that he might not overlook any fragment of knowledge worth acquiring that might lie hidden in the mysteries of divine worship.

This story also illustrates an important advantage which the Greeks had over the Egyptians and Babylonians. In those countries science, such as it was, was the monopoly of the priests; and, where this is the case, the first steps in science are apt to prove the last also, because the scientific results attained tend to become involved in religious prescriptions and routine observances, and so to end in a collection of lifeless formulae. Fortunately for the Greeks, they had no organized priesthood; untrammelled by prescription, traditional dogmas or superstition, they could give their reasoning faculties free play. Thus they were able to create science as a living thing susceptible of development without limit.

Greek geometry, as also Greek astronomy, begins with Thales (about 624–547 B. C.), who travelled in Egypt and is said to have brought geometry from thence. Such geometry as there was in Egypt arose out of practical needs. Revenue was raised by the taxation of landed property, and its assessment depended on the accurate fixing of the boundaries of the various holdings. When these were removed by the periodical flooding due to the rising of the Nile, it was necessary to replace them, or to determine the taxable area independently of them, by an art of land-surveying. We conclude from the Papyrus Rhind (say 1700 B. C.) and other documents that Egyptian geometry consisted mainly of practical rules for measuring, with more or less accuracy, (1) such areas as squares, triangles, trapezia, and circles, (2) the solid content of measures of corn, &c., of different shapes. The Egyptians also constructed pyramids of a certain slope by means of arithmetical calculations based on a certain ratio, *se-qet*, namely the ratio of half the side of the base to the height, which is in fact equivalent to the co-tangent of the angle of slope. The use of this ratio implies the notion of similarity of figures, especially triangles. The Egyptians knew, too, that a triangle with its sides in the ratio of the numbers 3, 4, 5 is right-angled, and used the fact as a means of drawing right angles. But there is no sign that they knew the general property of a right-angled triangle (= Eucl. I. 47), of which this is a particular case, or that they proved any general theorem in geometry.

No doubt Thales, when he was in Egypt, would see diagrams drawn to illustrate the rules for the measurement of circles and other plane figures, and these diagrams would suggest to him certain similarities and congruences which would set him thinking whether there were not some elementary general principles underlying the construction and relations of different figures and parts of figures. This would be in accord with the Greek instinct for generalization and their wish to be able to account for everything on rational principles.

The following theorems are attributed to Thales : (1) that a circle is bisected by any diameter (Eucl. I, Def. 17), (2) that the angles at the base of an isosceles triangle are equal (Eucl. I. 5), (3) that, if two straight lines cut one another, the vertically opposite angles are equal (Eucl. I. 15), (4) that, if two triangles have two angles and one side respectively equal, the triangles are equal in all respects (Eucl. I. 26). He is said (5) to have been the first to inscribe a right-angled triangle in a circle, which must mean that he was the first to discover that the angle in a semicircle is a right angle (cf. Eucl. III. 31).

Elementary as these things are, they represent a new departure of a momentous kind, being the first steps towards a *theory* of geometry. On this point we cannot do better than quote some remarks from Kant's preface to the second edition of his *Kritik der reinen Vernunft*.

' Mathematics has, from the earliest times to which the history of human reason goes back, (that is to say) with that wonderful people the Greeks, travelled the safe road of a *science*. But it must not be supposed that it was as easy for mathematics as it was for logic, where reason is concerned with itself alone, to find, or rather to build for itself, that royal road. I believe on the contrary that with mathematics it remained for long a case of groping about—the Egyptians in particular were still at that stage—and that this transformation must be ascribed to a *revolution* brought about by the happy inspiration of one man in trying an experiment, from which point onward the road that must be taken could no longer be missed, and the safe way of a science was struck and traced out for all time and to distances illimitable. . . . A light broke on the first man who demonstrated the property of the isosceles triangle (whether his name was Thales or what you will). . . .'

Thales also solved two problems of a practical kind : (1) he showed how to measure the distance of a ship at sea, and (2) he found the heights of pyramids by means of the shadows thrown on the ground by the pyramid and by a stick of known length at the same moment ; one account says that he chose the time when the lengths of the stick and of its shadow were equal, but in either case he argued by similarity of triangles.

In astronomy Thales predicted a solar eclipse which was probably that of the 28th May 585 B.C. Now the Babylonians, as the result of observations continued through centuries, had discovered the period of 223 lunations after which eclipses recur. It is most likely therefore that Thales had heard of this period, and that his prediction was based upon it. He is further said to have used the Little Bear for finding the pole, to have discovered the inequality of the four astronomical seasons, and to have written works *On the Equinox* and *On the Solstice*.

After Thales come the Pythagoreans. Of the Pythagoreans Aristotle says that they applied themselves to the study of mathematics and were the first to advance that science, going so far as to find in the principles of mathematics the principles of all existing things. Of Pythagoras himself we are told that he attached supreme importance to the study of arithmetic, advancing it and taking it out of the region of practical utility, and again that he transformed the study of geometry into a liberal education, examining the principles of the science from the beginning.

The very word μαθήματα, which originally meant ‘ subjects of instruction ’ generally, is said to have been first appropriated to mathematics by the Pythagoreans.

In saying that arithmetic began with Pythagoras we have to distinguish between the uses of that word then and now. Ἀριθμητική with the Greeks was distinguished from λογιστική, the science of calculation. It is the latter word which would cover arithmetic in our sense, or practical calculation ; the term ἀριθμητική was restricted to the science of numbers considered in themselves, or, as we should say, the Theory of Numbers. Another way of putting the distinction was to say that ἀριθμητική dealt with absolute numbers or numbers in the abstract, and λογιστική with numbered *things* or concrete numbers ; thus λογιστική included simple problems about numbers of apples, bowls, or objects generally, such as are found in the Greek Anthology and sometimes involve simple algebraical equations.

The Theory of Numbers then began with Pythagoras (about

572–497 B.C.). It included definitions of the unit and of number, and the classification and definitions of the various classes of numbers, odd, even, prime, composite, and sub-divisions of these such as odd-even, even-times-even, &c. Again there were figured numbers, namely, triangular numbers, squares, oblong numbers, polygonal numbers (pentagons, hexagons, &c.) corresponding respectively to plane figures, and pyramidal numbers, cubes, parallelepipeds, &c., corresponding to solid figures in geometry. The treatment was mostly geometrical, the numbers being represented by dots filling up geometrical figures of the various kinds. The laws of formation of the various figured numbers were established. In this investigation the *gnomon* played an important part. Originally meaning the upright needle of a sun-dial, the term was next used for a figure like a carpenter's square, and then was applied to a figure of that shape put round two sides of a square and making up a larger square. The arithmetical application of the term was similar. If we represent a unit by one dot and put round it three dots in such a way that the four form the corners of a square, *three* is the first gnomon. *Five* dots put at equal distances round two sides of the square containing four dots make up the next square (3^2), and *five* is the second gnomon. Generally, if we have n^2 dots so arranged as to fill up a square with n for its side, the gnomon to be put round it to make up the next square, $(n+1)^2$, has $2n+1$ dots. In the formation of squares, therefore, the successive gnomons are the series of odd numbers following 1 (the first square), namely 3, 5, 7, . . . In the formation of *oblong* numbers (numbers of the form $n(n+1)$), the first of which is 1 . 2, the successive gnomons are the terms after 2 in the series of *even* numbers 2, 4, 6 . . . Triangular numbers are formed by adding to 1 (the first triangle) the terms after 1 in the series of natural numbers 1, 2, 3 . . .; these are therefore the gnomons (by analogy) for triangles. The gnomons for pentagonal numbers

are the terms after 1 in the arithmetical progression 1, 4, 7, 10 . . .
(with 3, or 5 − 2, as the common difference) and so on ; the
common difference of the successive gnomons for an *a*-gonal
number is $a − 2$.

From the series of gnomons for squares we easily deduce
a formula for finding square numbers which are the sum of
two squares. For, the gnomon $2n + 1$ being the difference
between the successive squares n^2 and $(n + 1)^2$, we have only
to make $2n + 1$ a square. Suppose that $2n + 1 = m^2$; therefore
$n = \frac{1}{2}(m^2 − 1)$, and $\{\frac{1}{2}(m^2 − 1)\}^2 + m^2 = \{\frac{1}{2}(m^2 + 1)\}^2$, where *m* is
any odd number. This is the formula actually attributed to
Pythagoras.

Pythagoras is said to have discovered the theory of proportionals or proportion. This was a numerical theory and
therefore was applicable to commensurable magnitudes only ;
it was no doubt somewhat on the lines of Euclid, Book VII.
Connected with the theory of proportion was that of *means*,
and Pythagoras was acquainted with three of these, the
arithmetic, geometric, and sub-contrary (afterwards called
harmonic). In particular Pythagoras is said to have introduced
from Babylon into Greece the ' most perfect ' proportion,
namely :

$$a : \frac{a+b}{2} = \frac{2\,ab}{a+b} : b,$$

where the second and third terms are respectively the arithmetic and harmonic mean between *a* and *b*. A particular case
is $12 : 9 = 8 : 6$.

This bears upon what was probably Pythagoras's greatest
discovery, namely that the musical intervals correspond to
certain arithmetical ratios between lengths of string at the
same tension, the octave corresponding to the ratio $2 : 1$, the
fifth to $3 : 2$ and the fourth to $4 : 3$. These ratios being the
same as those of 12 to 6, 8, 9 respectively, we can understand

how the third term, 8, in the above proportion came to be called the ' harmonic ' mean between 12 and 6.

The Pythagorean arithmetic as a whole, with the developments made after the time of Pythagoras himself, is mainly known to us through Nicomachus's *Introductio arithmetica*, Iamblichus's commentary on the same, and Theon of Smyrna's work *Expositio rerum mathematicarum ad legendum Platonem utilium*. The things in these books most deserving of notice are the following.

First, there is the description of a ' perfect ' number (a number which is equal to the sum of all its parts, i.e. all its integral divisors including 1 but excluding the number itself), with a statement of the property that all such numbers end in 6 or 8. Four such numbers, namely 6, 28, 496, 8128, were known to Nicomachus. The law of formation for such numbers is first found in Eucl. IX. 36 proving that, if the sum (S_n) of n terms of the series 1, 2, 2^2, 2^3 ... is prime, then $S_n . 2^{n-1}$ is a perfect number.

Secondly, Theon of Smyrna gives the law of formation of the series of ' side- ' and ' diameter- ' numbers which satisfy the equations $2x^2 - y^2 = \pm 1$. The law depends on the proposition proved in Eucl. II. 10 to the effect that $(2x+y)^2 - 2(x+y)^2 = 2x^2 - y^2$, whence it follows that, if x, y satisfy either of the above equations, then $2x+y$, $x+y$ is a solution in higher numbers of the other equation. The successive solutions give values for y/x, namely $\frac{1}{1}$, $\frac{3}{2}$, $\frac{7}{5}$, $\frac{17}{12}$, $\frac{41}{29}$, ..., which are successive approximations to the value of $\sqrt{2}$ (the ratio of the diagonal of a square to its side). The occasion for this method of approximation to $\sqrt{2}$ (which can be carried as far as we please) was the discovery by the Pythagoreans of the incommensurable or irrational in this particular case.

Thirdly, Iamblichus mentions a discovery by Thymaridas, a Pythagorean not later than Plato's time, called the ἐπάνθημα (' bloom ') of Thymaridas, and amounting to the solution

of any number of simultaneous equations of the following
form:

$$x + x_1 + x_2 + \ldots + x_{n-1} = s,$$
$$x + x_1 = a_1,$$
$$x + x_2 = a_2,$$
$$\ldots \ldots$$
$$x + x_{n-1} = a_{n-1},$$

the solution being $x = \dfrac{(a_1 + a_2 + \ldots + a_{n-1}) - s}{n-2}$.

The rule is stated in general terms, but the above representation
of its effect shows that it is a piece of pure algebra.

The Pythagorean contributions to geometry were even more
remarkable. The most famous proposition attributed to
Pythagoras himself is of course the theorem of Eucl. I. 47
that the square on the hypotenuse of any right-angled triangle
is equal to the sum of the squares on the other two sides.
But Proclus also attributes to him, besides the theory of proportionals, the construction of the 'cosmic figures', the five
regular solids.

One of the said solids, the dodecahedron, has twelve regular
pentagons for faces, and the construction of a regular pentagon
involves the cutting of a straight line 'in extreme and mean
ratio' (Eucl. II. 11 and VI. 30), which is a particular case of
the method known as the *application of areas*. This method
was fully worked out by the Pythagoreans and proved one of
the most powerful in all Greek geometry. The most elementary case appears in Eucl. I. 44, 45, where it is shown how to
apply to a given straight line as base a parallelogram with one
angle equal to a given angle and equal in area to any given
rectilineal figure; this construction is the geometrical
equivalent of arithmetical *division*. The general case is that
in which the parallelogram, though applied to the straight
line, overlaps it or falls short of it in such a way that the part

of the parallelogram which extends beyond or falls short of the parallelogram of the same angle and breadth on the given straight line itself (exactly) as base is similar to any given parallelogram (Eucl. VI. 28, 29). This is the geometrical equivalent of the solution of the most general form of quadratic equation $ax \pm mx^2 = C$, so far as it has real roots ; the condition that the roots may be real was also worked out (= Eucl. VI. 27). It is in the form of ' application of areas ' that Apollonius obtains the fundamental property of each of the conic sections, and, as we shall see, it is from the terminology of application of areas that Apollonius took the three names *parabola, hyperbola,* and *ellipse* which he was the first to give to the three curves.

Another problem solved by the Pythagoreans was that of drawing a rectilineal figure which shall be equal in area to one given rectilineal figure and similar to another. Plutarch mentions a doubt whether it was this problem or the theorem of Eucl. I. 47 on the strength of which Pythagoras was said to have sacrificed an ox.

The main particular applications of the theorem of the square on the hypotenuse, e. g. those in Euclid, Book II, were also Pythagorean ; the construction of a square equal to a given rectangle (Eucl. II. 14) is one of them, and corresponds to the solution of the pure quadratic equation $x^2 = ab$.

The Pythagoreans knew the properties of parallels and proved the theorem that the sum of the three angles of any triangle is equal to two right angles.

As we have seen, the Pythagorean theory of proportion, being numerical, was inadequate in that it did not apply to incommensurable magnitudes ; but, with this qualification, we may say that the Pythagorean geometry covered the bulk of the subject-matter of Books I, II, IV and VI of Euclid's *Elements*. The case is less clear with regard to Book III of the *Elements* ; but, as the main propositions of that Book were known to Hippocrates of Chios in the second half of the fifth century B. C., we conclude that they, too, were part of the Pythagorean geometry.

Lastly, the Pythagoreans discovered the existence of the incommensurable or irrational in the particular case of the diagonal of a square in relation to its side. Aristotle mentions an ancient proof of the incommensurability of the diagonal with the side by a *reductio ad absurdum* showing that, if the diagonal were commensurable with the side, it would follow that one and the same number is both odd and even. This proof was doubtless Pythagorean.

A word should be added about the Pythagorean astronomy. Pythagoras was the first to hold that the earth (and no doubt each of the other heavenly bodies also) is spherical in shape, and he was aware that the sun, moon and planets have independent movements of their own in a sense opposite to that of the daily rotation ; but he seems to have kept the earth in the centre. His successors in the school (one Hicetas of Syracuse and Philolaus are alternatively credited with this innovation) actually abandoned the geocentric idea and made the earth, like the sun, the moon, and the other planets, revolve in a circle round the ' central fire ', in which resided the governing principle ordering and directing the movement of the universe.

The geometry of which we have so far spoken belongs to the Elements. But, before the body of the Elements was complete, the Greeks had advanced beyond the Elements. By the second half of the fifth century B. C. they had investigated three famous problems in higher geometry, (1) the squaring of the circle, (2) the trisection of any angle, (3) the duplication of the cube. The great names belonging to this period are Hippias of Elis, Hippocrates of Chios, and Democritus.

Hippias of Elis invented a certain curve described by combining two uniform movements (one angular and the other rectilinear) taking the same time to complete. Hippias himself used his curve for the trisection of any angle or the division of it in any ratio ; but it was afterwards employed by Dinostratus, a brother of Eudoxus's pupil Menaechmus, and by Nicomedes for squaring the circle, whence it got the name τετραγωνίζουσα, *quadratrix*.

Hippocrates of Chios is mentioned by Aristotle as an instance to prove that a man may be a distinguished geometer and, at the same time, a fool in the ordinary affairs of life. He occupies an important place both in elementary geometry and in relation to two of the higher problems above mentioned. He was, so far as is known, the first compiler of a book of Elements; and he was the first to prove the important theorem of Eucl. XII. 2 that circles are to one another as the squares on their diameters, from which he further deduced that similar segments of circles are to one another as the squares on their bases. These propositions were used by him in his tract on the squaring of *lunes*, which was intended to lead up to the squaring of the circle. The essential portions of the tract are preserved in a passage of Simplicius's commentary on Aristotle's *Physics*, which contains substantial extracts from Eudemus's lost *History of Geometry*. Hippocrates showed how to square three particular lunes of different kinds and then, lastly, he squared the sum of a circle and a certain lune. Unfortunately the last-mentioned lune was not one of those which can be squared, so that the attempt to square the circle in this way failed after all.

Hippocrates also attacked the problem of doubling the cube. There are two versions of the origin of this famous problem. According to one story an old tragic poet had represented Minos as having been dissatisfied with the size of a cubical tomb erected for his son Glaucus and having told the architect to make it double the size while retaining the cubical form. The other story says that the Delians, suffering from a pestilence, consulted the oracle and were told to double a certain altar as a means of staying the plague. Hippocrates did not indeed solve the problem of duplication, but reduced it to another, namely that of finding two mean proportionals in continued proportion between two given straight lines; and the problem was ever afterwards attacked in this form. If x, y be the two required mean proportionals between two straight lines a, b, then $a : x = x : y = y : b$, whence $b/a = (x/a)^3$, and, as a particular case, if $b = 2a$, $x^3 = 2a^3$, so that, when x is found, the cube is doubled.

Democritus wrote a large number of mathematical treatises, the titles only of which are preserved. We gather from one of these titles, 'On irrational lines and solids', that he wrote on irrationals. Democritus realized as fully as Zeno, and expressed with no less piquancy, the difficulty connected with the continuous and the infinitesimal. This appears from his dilemma about the circular base of a cone and a parallel section; the section which he means is a section 'indefinitely near' (as the phrase is) to the base, i. e. the *very next* section, as we might say (if there were one). Is it, said Democritus, equal or not equal to the base? If it is equal, so will the very next section to it be, and so on, so that the cone will really be, not a cone, but a cylinder. If it is unequal to the base and in fact less, the surface of the cone will be jagged, like steps, which is very absurd. We may be sure that Democritus's work on 'The contact of a circle or a sphere' discussed a like difficulty.

Lastly, Archimedes tells us that Democritus was the first to state, though he could not give a rigorous proof, that the volume of a cone or a pyramid is one-third of that of the cylinder or prism respectively on the same base and having equal height, theorems first proved by Eudoxus.

We come now to the time of Plato, and here the great names are Archytas, Theodorus of Cyrene, Theaetetus, and Eudoxus.

Archytas (about 430–360 B.C.) wrote on music and the numerical ratios corresponding to the intervals of the tetrachord. He is said to have been the first to write a treatise on mechanics based on mathematical principles; on the practical side he invented a mechanical dove which would fly. In geometry he gave the first solution of the problem of the two mean proportionals, using a wonderful construction in three dimensions which determined a certain point as the intersection of three surfaces, (1) a certain cone, (2) a half-cylinder, (3) an anchorring or *tore* with inner diameter *nil*.

Theodorus, Plato's teacher in mathematics, extended the theory of the irrational by proving incommensurability in certain particular cases other than that of the diagonal of a square in relation to its side, which was already known. He proved that the side of a square containing 3 square feet, or 5 square feet, or any non-square number of square feet up to 17 is incommensurable with one foot, in other words that $\sqrt{3}, \sqrt{5} \ldots \sqrt{17}$ are all incommensurable with 1. Theodorus's proof was evidently not general; and it was reserved for Theaetetus to comprehend all these irrationals in one definition, and to prove the property generally as it is proved in Eucl. X. 9. Much of the content of the rest of Euclid's Book X (dealing with compound irrationals), as also of Book XIII on the five regular solids, was due to Theaetetus, who is even said to have discovered two of those solids (the octahedron and icosahedron).

Plato (427–347 B.C.) was probably not an original mathematician, but he 'caused mathematics in general and geometry in particular to make a great advance by reason of his enthusiasm for them'. He encouraged the members of his school to specialize in mathematics and astronomy; e. g. we are told that in astronomy he set it as a problem to all earnest students to find 'what are the uniform and ordered movements by the assumption of which the apparent motions of the planets may be accounted for '. In Plato's own writings are found certain definitions, e. g. that of a straight line as ' that of which the middle covers the ends ', and some interesting mathematical illustrations, especially that in the second geometrical passage in the *Meno* (86E − 87C). To Plato himself are attributed (1) a formula $(n^2 - 1)^2 + (2n)^2 = (n^2 + 1)^2$ for finding two square numbers the sum of which is a square number, (2) the invention of the method of analysis, which he is said to have explained to Leodamas of Thasos (*mathematical* analysis was, however, certainly, in practice, employed long before). The solution, attributed to Plato, of the problem of the two mean proportionals by means of a frame resembling that which a shoemaker uses to measure a foot, can hardly be his.

Eudoxus (408–355 B.C.), an original genius second to none (unless it be Archimedes) in the history of our subject, made two discoveries of supreme importance for the further development of Greek geometry.

(1) As we have seen, the discovery of the incommensurable rendered inadequate the Pythagorean theory of proportion, which applied to commensurable magnitudes only. It would no doubt be possible, in most cases, to replace proofs depending on proportions by others; but this involved great inconvenience, and a slur was cast on geometry generally. The trouble was remedied once for all by Eudoxus's discovery of the great theory of proportion, applicable to commensurable and incommensurable magnitudes alike, which is expounded in Euclid's Book V. Well might Barrow say of this theory that ' there is nothing in the whole body of the elements of a more subtle invention, nothing more solidly established '. The keystone of the structure is the definition of equal ratios (Eucl. V, Def. 5) ; and twenty-three centuries have not abated a jot from its value, as is plain from the facts that Weierstrass repeats it word for word as his definition of equal

numbers, and it corresponds almost to the point of coincidence with the modern treatment of irrationals due to Dedekind.

(2) Eudoxus discovered the method of exhaustion for measuring curvilinear areas and solids, to which, with the extensions given to it by Archimedes, Greek geometry owes its greatest triumphs. Antiphon the Sophist, in connexion with attempts to square the circle, had asserted that, if we inscribe successive regular polygons in a circle, continually doubling the number of sides, we shall sometime arrive at a polygon the sides of which will coincide with the circumference of the circle. Warned by the unanswerable arguments of Zeno against infinitesimals, mathematicians substituted for this the statement that, by continuing the construction, we can inscribe a polygon approaching equality with the circle *as nearly as we please*. The method of exhaustion used, for the purpose of proof by *reductio ad absurdum*, the lemma proved in Eucl. X. 1 (to the effect that, if from any magnitude we subtract not less than half, and then from the remainder not less than half, and so on continually, there will sometime be left a magnitude less than any assigned magnitude of the same kind, however small) : and this again depends on an assumption which is practically contained in Eucl. V, Def. 4, but is generally known as the Axiom of Archimedes, stating that, if we have two unequal magnitudes, their difference (however small) can, if continually added to itself, be made to exceed any magnitude of the same kind (however great).

The method of exhaustion is seen in operation in Eucl. XII. 1–2, 3–7 Cor., 10, 16–18. Props. 3–7 Cor. and Prop. 10 prove that the volumes of a pyramid and a cone are one-third of the prism and cylinder respectively on the same base and of equal height ; and Archimedes expressly says that these facts were first proved by Eudoxus.

In astronomy Eudoxus is famous for the beautiful theory of concentric spheres which he invented to explain the apparent motions of the planets and, particularly, their apparent stationary points and retrogradations. The theory applied also to the sun and moon, for each of which Eudoxus employed three spheres. He represented the motion of each planet as produced by the rotations of four spheres concentric with the earth, one within the other, and connected in the following way. Each of the inner spheres revolves about a diameter the ends of which (poles) are fixed on the next sphere enclosing it. The outermost sphere represents the daily rotation, the second a motion along the zodiac circle ; the poles of the third sphere are fixed on the latter circle ; the poles of the fourth sphere (carrying the planet fixed on its equator) are so fixed on the third sphere, and the speeds and directions of rotation so arranged, that the planet describes on the second sphere a curve called the *hippopede* (horse-fetter), or a figure of eight, lying along and longitudinally bisected by the zodiac circle. The whole arrangement is a marvel of geometrical ingenuity.

Heraclides of Pontus (about 388–315 B.C.), a pupil of Plato, made a great step forward in astronomy by his declaration that the earth rotates on its own axis once in 24 hours, and by his discovery that Mercury and Venus revolve about the sun like satellites.

Menaechmus, a pupil of Eudoxus, was the discoverer of the conic sections, two of which, the parabola and the hyperbola, he used for solving the problem of the two mean proportionals. If $a : x = x : y = y : b$, then $x^2 = ay$, $y^2 = bx$ and $xy = ab$. These equations represent, in Cartesian co-ordinates, and with rectangular axes, the conics by the intersection of which two and two Menaechmus solved the problem ; in the case of the rectangular hyperbola it was the asymptote-property which he used.

We pass to Euclid's times. A little older than Euclid, Autolycus of Pitane wrote two books, *On the Moving Sphere*, a work on Sphaeric for use in astronomy, and *On Risings and*

Settings. The former work is the earliest Greek textbook
which has reached us intact. It was before Euclid when he
wrote his *Phaenomena*, and there are many points of contact
between the two books.

Euclid flourished about 300 B. C. or a little earlier. His
great work, the *Elements* in thirteen Books, is too well known
to need description. No work presumably, except the Bible,
has had such a reign ; and future generations will come back
to it again and again as they tire of the variegated substitutes
for it and the confusion resulting from their bewildering
multiplicity. After what has been said above of the growth
of the Elements, we can appreciate the remark of Proclus
about Euclid, ' who put together the Elements, collecting
many of Eudoxus's theorems, perfecting many of Theaetetus's
and also bringing to irrefragable demonstration the things
which were only somewhat loosely proved by his predecessors '.
Though a large portion of the subject-matter had been
investigated by those predecessors, everything goes to show
that the whole arrangement was Euclid's own ; it is certain
that he made great changes in the order of propositions and
in the proofs, and that his innovations began at the very
beginning of Book I.

Euclid wrote other books on both elementary and higher
geometry, and on the other mathematical subjects known in
his day. The elementary geometrical works include the *Data*
and *On Divisions* (*of figures*), the first of which survives in
Greek and the second in Arabic only ; also the *Pseudaria*,
now lost, which was a sort of guide to fallacies in geometrical
reasoning. The treatises on higher geometry are all lost ;
they include (1) the *Conics* in four Books, which covered almost
the same ground as the first three Books of Apollonius's *Conics*,
although no doubt, for Euclid, the conics were still, as with his
predecessors, sections of a right-angled, an obtuse-angled, and
an acute-angled cone respectively made by a plane perpen-

dicular to a generator in each case; (2) the *Porisms* in three Books, the importance and difficulty of which can be inferred from Pappus's account of it and the lemmas which he gives for use with it; (3) the *Surface-Loci*, to which again Pappus furnishes lemmas; one of these implies that Euclid assumed as known the focus-directrix property of the three conics, which is absent from Apollonius's *Conics*.

In applied mathematics Euclid wrote (1) the *Phaenomena*, a work on spherical astronomy in which ὁ ὁρίζων (without κύκλος or any qualifying words) appears for the first time in the sense of *horizon*; (2) the *Optics*, a kind of elementary treatise on perspective: these two treatises are extant in Greek; (3) a work on the Elements of Music. The *Sectio Canonis*, which has come down under the name of Euclid, can, however, hardly be his in its present form.

In the period between Euclid and Archimedes comes Aristarchus of Samos (about 310–230 B.C.), famous for having anticipated Copernicus. Accepting Heraclides's view that the earth rotates about its own axis, Aristarchus went further and put forward the hypothesis that the sun itself is at rest, and that the earth, as well as Mercury, Venus, and the other planets, revolve in circles about the sun. We have this on the unquestionable authority of Archimedes, who was only some twenty-five years later, and who must have seen the book containing the hypothesis in question. We are told too that Cleanthes the Stoic thought that Aristarchus ought to be indicted on the charge of impiety for setting the Hearth of the Universe in motion.

One work of Aristarchus, *On the sizes and distances of the Sun and Moon*, which is extant in Greek, is highly interesting in itself, though it contains no word of the heliocentric hypothesis. Thoroughly classical in form and style, it lays down certain hypotheses and then deduces therefrom, by rigorous geometry, the sizes and distances of the sun and

moon. If the hypotheses had been exact, the results would
have been correct too ; but Aristarchus in fact assumed a certain angle to be 87° which is really 89° 50′, and the angle
subtended at the centre of the earth by the diameter of either
the sun or the moon to be 2°, whereas we know from Archimedes that Aristarchus himself discovered that the latter
angle is only $\frac{1}{2}$°. The effect of Aristarchus's geometry is to
find arithmetical limits to the values of what are really
trigonometrical ratios of certain small angles, namely

$$\tfrac{1}{18} > \sin 3° > \tfrac{1}{20}, \quad \tfrac{1}{45} > \sin 1° > \tfrac{1}{60}, \quad 1 > \cos 1° > \tfrac{89}{90}.$$

The main results obtained are (1) that the diameter of the sun
is between 18 and 20 times the diameter of the moon, (2) that
the diameter of the moon is between 2/45ths and 1/30th of the
distance of the centre of the moon from our eye, and (3) that
the diameter of the sun is between 19/3rds and 43/6ths of
the diameter of the earth. The book contains a good deal of
arithmetical calculation.

Archimedes was born about 287 B.C. and was killed at the
sack of Syracuse by Marcellus's army in 212 B.C. The stories
about him are well known, how he said ' Give me a place to
stand on, and I will move the earth ' (πᾶ βῶ καὶ κινῶ τὰν γᾶν);
how, having thought of the solution of the problem of the
crown when in the bath, he ran home naked shouting εὕρηκα,
εὕρηκα ; and how, the capture of Syracuse having found him
intent on a figure drawn on the ground, he said to a Roman
soldier who came up, ' Stand away, fellow, from my diagram.'
Of his work few people know more than that he invented
a tubular screw which is still used for pumping water, and that
for a long time he foiled the attacks of the Romans on Syracuse
by the mechanical devices and engines which he used against
them. But he thought meanly of these things, and his real
interest was in pure mathematical speculation ; he caused to
be engraved on his tomb a representation of a cylinder circum-

scribing a sphere, with the ratio 3/2 which the cylinder bears to the sphere : from which we infer that he regarded this as his greatest discovery.

Archimedes's works are all original, and are perfect models of mathematical exposition ; their wide range will be seen from the list of those which survive : *On the Sphere and Cylinder* I, II, *Measurement of a Circle, On Conoids and Spheroids, On Spirals, On Plane Equilibriums* I, II, the *Sandreckoner, Quadrature of the Parabola, On Floating Bodies* I, II, and lastly the *Method* (only discovered in 1906). The difficult Cattle-Problem is also attributed to him, and a *Liber Assumptorum* which has reached us through the Arabic, but which cannot be his in its present form, although some of the propositions in it (notably that about the ' Salinon ', salt-cellar, and others about circles inscribed in the ἀρβηλος, shoemaker's knife) are quite likely to be of Archimedean origin. Among lost works were the *Catoptrica, On Sphere-making,* and investigations into polyhedra, including thirteen semi-regular solids, the discovery of which is attributed by Pappus to Archimedes.

Speaking generally, the geometrical works are directed to the measurement of curvilinear areas and volumes ; and Archimedes employs a method which is a development of Eudoxus's method of exhaustion. Eudoxus apparently approached the figure to be measured from below only, i. e. by means of figures successively inscribed to it. Archimedes approaches it from both sides by successively inscribing figures and circumscribing others also, thereby compressing them, as it were, until they coincide as nearly as we please with the figure to be measured. In many cases his procedure is, when the analytical equivalents are set down, seen to amount to real *integration* ; this is so with his investigation of the areas of a parabolic segment and a spiral, the surface and volume of a sphere, and the volume of any segments of the conoids and spheroids.

The newly-discovered *Method* is especially interesting as showing how Archimedes originally obtained his results; this was by a clever mechanical method of (theoretically) *weighing* infinitesimal elements of the figure to be measured against elements of another figure the area or content of which (as the case may be) is known; it amounts to an *avoidance* of integration. Archimedes, however, would only admit that the mechanical method is useful for finding results; he did not consider them proved until they were established geometrically.

In the *Measurement of a Circle*, after proving by exhaustion that the area of a circle is equal to a right-angled triangle with the perpendicular sides equal respectively to the radius and the circumference of the circle, Archimedes finds, by sheer calculation, upper and lower limits to the ratio of the circumference of a circle to its diameter (what we call π). This he does by inscribing and circumscribing regular polygons of 96 sides and calculating approximately their respective perimeters. He begins by assuming as known certain approximate values for $\sqrt{3}$, namely $\frac{1351}{780} > \sqrt{3} > \frac{265}{153}$, and his calculations involve approximating to the square roots of several large numbers (up to seven digits). The text only gives the results, but it is evident that the extraction of square roots presented no difficulty, notwithstanding the comparative inconvenience of the alphabetic system of numerals. The result obtained is well known, namely $3\frac{1}{7} > \pi > 3\frac{10}{71}$.

The *Plane Equilibriums* is the first scientific treatise on the first principles of mechanics, which are established by pure geometry. The most important result established in Book I is the principle of the lever. This was known to Plato and Aristotle, but they had no real proof. The Aristotelian *Mechanics* merely ' refers ' the lever ' to the circle ', asserting that the force which acts at the greater distance from the fulcrum moves the system more easily, because it describes a greater circle. Archimedes also finds the centre of gravity of a parallelogram, a triangle, a trapezium and finally (in Book II) of a parabolic segment and of a portion of it cut off by a straight line parallel to the base.

The *Sandreckoner* is remarkable for the development in it of a system for expressing very large numbers by *orders* and *periods* based on powers of myriad-myriads (10,000^2). It also contains the important reference to the heliocentric theory of the universe put forward by Aristarchus of Samos in a book of ' hypotheses', as well as historical details of previous attempts to measure the size of the earth and to give the sizes and distances of the sun and moon.

Lastly, Archimedes invented the whole science of hydro-statics. Beginning the treatise *On Floating Bodies* with an assumption about uniform pressure in a fluid, he first proves that the surface of a fluid at rest is a sphere with its centre at the centre of the earth. Other propositions show that, if a solid floats in a fluid, the weight of the solid is equal to that of the fluid displaced, and, if a solid heavier than a fluid is weighed in it, it will be lighter than its true weight by the weight of the fluid displaced. Then, after a second assumption that bodies which are forced upwards in a fluid are forced upwards along the perpendiculars to the surface which pass through their centres of gravity, Archi-medes deals with the position of rest and stability of a segment of a sphere floating in a fluid with its base entirely above or entirely below the surface. Book II is an extraordinary *tour de force*, investigating fully all the positions of rest and stability of a right segment of a paraboloid floating in a fluid according (1) to the relation between the axis of the solid and the para-meter of the generating parabola, and (2) to the specific gravity of the solid in relation to the fluid ; the term ' specific gravity' is not used, but the idea is fully expressed in other words.

Almost contemporary with Archimedes was Eratosthenes of Cyrene, to whom Archimedes dedicated the *Method* ; the preface to this work shows that Archimedes thought highly of his mathematical ability. He was indeed recognized by his contemporaries as a man of great distinction in all branches, though the names Beta and Pentathlos[1] applied to him indicate that he just fell below the first rank in each subject. Ptolemy Euergetes appointed him to be tutor to his son (Philopator), and he became librarian at Alexandria; he recognized his obligation to Ptolemy by erecting a column with a graceful epigram. In this epigram he referred to the earlier solutions of the problem of duplicating the cube or finding the two mean proportionals, and advocated his own in preference, because it would give any number of means; on the column was fixed a bronze representation of his appliance, a frame with right-angled triangles (or rectangles) movable along two parallel grooves and over one another, together with a condensed proof. The *Platonicus* of Eratosthenes evidently dealt with the fundamental notions of mathematics in connexion with Plato's philosophy, and seems to have begun with the story of the origin of the duplication problem.

The most famous achievement of Eratosthenes was his measurement of the earth. Archimedes quotes an earlier measurement which made the circumference of the earth 300,000 stades. Eratosthenes improved upon this. He observed that at the summer solstice at Syene, at noon, the sun cast no shadow, while at the same moment the upright gnomon at Alexandria cast a shadow corresponding to an angle between the gnomon and the sun's rays of 1/50th of four right angles. The distance between Syene and Alexandria being known to be 5,000 stades, this gave for the circumference of the earth 250,000 stades, which Eratosthenes seems later, for some reason, to have changed to 252,000 stades. On the

---

[1] This word primarily means an all-round athlete, a winner in all five of the sports constituting the πένταθλον, namely jumping, discus-throwing, running, wrestling, and boxing (or javelin-throwing).

most probable assumption as to the length of the stade used, the 252,000 stades give about 7,850 miles, only 50 miles less than the true polar diameter.

In the work *On the Measurement of the Earth* Eratosthenes is said to have discussed other astronomical matters, the distance of the tropic and polar circles, the sizes and distances of the sun and moon, total and partial eclipses, &c. Besides other works on astronomy and chronology, Eratosthenes wrote a *Geographica* in three books, in which he first gave a history of geography up to date and then passed on to mathematical geography, the spherical shape of the earth, &c., &c.

Apollonius of Perga was with justice called by his contemporaries the 'Great Geometer', on the strength of his great treatise, the *Conics*. He is mentioned as a famous astronomer of the reign of Ptolemy Euergetes (247–222 B.C.); and he dedicated the fourth and later Books of the *Conics* to King Attalus I of Pergamum (241–197 B.C.).

The *Conics*, a colossal work, originally in eight Books, survives as to the first four Books in Greek and as to three more in Arabic, the eighth being lost. From Apollonius's prefaces we can judge of the relation of his work to Euclid's *Conics*, the content of which answered to the first three Books of Apollonius. Although Euclid knew that an ellipse could be otherwise produced, e. g. as an oblique section of a right cylinder, there is no doubt that he produced all three conics from right cones like his predecessors. Apollonius, however, obtains them in the most general way by cutting any oblique cone, and his original axes of reference, a diameter and the tangent at its extremity, are in general oblique; the fundamental properties are found with reference to these axes by 'application of areas', the three varieties of which, *application* (παραβολή), application with an *excess* (ὑπερβολή) and application with a *deficiency* (ἔλλειψις), give the properties of the three curves respectively and account for the names *parabola, hyperbola,* and *ellipse,* by which Apollonius called them for the first time. The principal axes only appear, as a particular case, after it has been shown that the curves have a like property when referred to any other diameter and the tangent at its extremity, instead of those arising out of the original construction. The first four Books constitute what Apollonius calls an elementary introduction ; the remaining Books are specialized investigations, the most important being Book V (on normals) and Book VII (mainly on conjugate diameters). Normals are treated, not in connexion with tangents, but as *minimum* or *maximum* straight lines drawn to the curves from different points or classes of points. Apollonius discusses such questions as the number of normals that can be drawn from one point (according to its position) and the construction of all such normals. Certain propositions of great difficulty enable us to deduce quite easily the Cartesian equations to the *evolutes* of the three conics.

Several other works of Apollonius are described by Pappus as forming part of the ' Treasury of Analysis '. All are lost except the *Sectio Rationis* in two Books, which survives in Arabic and was published in a Latin translation by Halley in 1706. It deals with all possible cases of the general problem ' given two straight lines either parallel or intersecting, and a fixed point on each, to draw through any given point a straight line which shall cut off intercepts from the two lines (measured from the fixed points) bearing a given ratio to one another '. The lost treatise *Sectio Spatii* dealt similarly with the like problem in which the intercepts cut off have to contain a given rectangle.

The other treatises included in Pappus's account are (1) On *Determinate Section* ; (2) *Contacts* or *Tangencies,* Book II of which is entirely devoted to the problem of drawing a circle to touch three given circles (Apollonius's solution can, with the aid of Pappus's auxiliary propositions, be satisfactorily restored) ;　(3) *Plane Loci*, i. e. loci which are straight lines or circles ;　(4) Νεύσεις, *Inclinationes* (the general problem called a νεῦσις being to insert between two lines, straight or curved, a straight line of given length *verging* to a given point, i. e. so that, if produced, it passes through the point, Apollonius restricted himself to cases which could be solved by 'plane' methods, i.e. by the straight line and circle only).

Apollonius is also said to have written (5) a *Comparison of the dodecahedron with the icosahedron* (inscribed in the same sphere), in which he proved that their surfaces are in the same ratio as their volumes ;　(6) *On the cochlias* or cylindrical helix ; (7) a 'General Treatise', which apparently dealt with the fundamental assumptions, &c., of elementary geometry ; (8) a work on *unordered irrationals*, i. e. irrationals of more complicated form than those of Eucl. Book X ;　(9) *On the burning-mirror*, dealing with spherical mirrors and probably with mirrors of parabolic section also ;　(10) ὠκυτόκιον ('quick delivery'). In the last-named work Apollonius found an approximation to π closer than that in Archimedes's *Measurement of a Circle ;* and possibly the book also contained Apollonius's exposition of his notation for large numbers according to 'tetrads' (successive powers of the myriad).

In astronomy Apollonius is said to have made special researches regarding the moon, and to have been called ε (Epsilon) because the form of that letter is associated with the moon. He was also a master of the theory of epicycles and eccentrics.

With Archimedes and Apollonius Greek geometry reached its culminating point ; indeed, without some more elastic notation and machinery such as algebra provides, geometry was practically at the end of its resources. For some time, however, there were capable geometers who kept up the tradition, filling in details, devising alternative solutions of problems, or discovering new curves for use or investigation.

Nicomedes, probably intermediate in date between Eratosthenes and Apollonius, was the inventor of the *conchoid* or *cochloid*, of which, according to Pappus, there were three varieties. Diocles (about the end of the second century B.C.) is known as the discoverer of the *cissoid* which was used for duplicating the cube. He also wrote a book περὶ πυρείων, *On burning-mirrors*, which probably discussed, among other forms of mirror, surfaces of parabolic or elliptic section, and used the focal properties of the two conics; it was in this work that Diocles gave an independent and clever solution (by means of an ellipse and a rectangular hyperbola) of Archimedes's problem of cutting a sphere into two segments in a given ratio. Dionysodorus gave a solution by means of conics of the auxiliary cubic equation to which Archimedes reduced this problem; he also found the solid content of a *tore* or anchor-ring.

Perseus is known as the discoverer and investigator of the *spiric sections*, i. e. certain sections of the σπεῖρα, one variety of which is the *tore*. The *spire* is generated by the revolution of a circle about a straight line in its plane, which straight line may either be external to the circle (in which case the figure produced is the tore), or may cut or touch the circle.

Zenodorus was the author of a treatise on *Isometric figures*, the problem in which was to compare the content of different figures, plane or solid, having equal contours or surfaces respectively.

Hypsicles (second half of second century B.C.) wrote what became known as 'Book XIV' of the *Elements* containing supplementary propositions on the regular solids (partly drawn from Aristaeus and Apollonius); he seems also to have written on polygonal numbers. A mediocre astronomical work (Ἀναφορικός) attributed to him is the first Greek book in which we find the division of the zodiac circle into 360 parts or degrees.

Posidonius the Stoic (about 135–51 B.C.) wrote on geography

and astronomy under the titles *On the Ocean* and περὶ μετεώρων. He made a new but faulty calculation of the circumference of the earth (240,000 stades). *Per contra*, in a separate tract on the size of the sun (in refutation of the Epicurean view that it is as big as it *looks*), he made assumptions (partly guess-work) which give for the diameter of the sun a figure of 3,000,000 stades (39¼ times the diameter of the earth), a result much nearer the truth than those obtained by Aristarchus, Hipparchus, and Ptolemy. In elementary geometry Posidonius gave certain definitions (notably of parallels, based on the idea of equidistance).

Geminus of Rhodes, a pupil of Posidonius, wrote (about 70 B.C.) an encyclopaedic work on the classification and content of mathematics, including the history of each subject, from which Proclus and others have preserved notable extracts. An-Nairīzī (an Arabian commentator on Euclid) reproduces an attempt by one ' Aganis ', who appears to be Geminus, to prove the parallel-postulate.

But from this time onwards the study of higher geometry (except sphaeric) seems to have languished, until that admirable mathematician, Pappus, arose (towards the end of the third century A.D.) to revive interest in the subject. From the way in which, in his great *Collection*, Pappus thinks it necessary to describe in detail the contents of the classical works belonging to the ' Treasury of Analysis ' we gather that by his time many of them had been lost or forgotten, and that he aimed at nothing less than re-establishing geometry at its former level. No one could have been better qualified for the task. Presumably such interest as Pappus was able to arouse soon flickered out; but his *Collection* remains, after the original works of the great mathematicians, the most comprehensive and valuable of all our sources, being a handbook or guide to Greek geometry and covering practically the whole field. Among the original things in Pappus's *Collection* is an enunciation which amounts to an anticipation of what is known as Guldin's Theorem.

It remains to speak of three subjects, trigonometry (represented by Hipparchus, Menelaus, and Ptolemy), mensuration (in Heron of Alexandria), and algebra (Diophantus).

Although, in a sense, the beginnings of trigonometry go back to Archimedes (*Measurement of a Circle*), Hipparchus was the first person who can be proved to have used trigonometry systematically. Hipparchus, the greatest astronomer of antiquity, whose observations were made between 161 and 126 B.C., discovered the precession of the equinoxes, calculated the mean lunar month at 29 days, 12 hours, 44 minutes, 2½ seconds (which differs by less than a second from the present accepted figure !), made more correct estimates of the sizes and distances of the sun and moon, introduced great improvements in the instruments used for observations, and compiled a catalogue of some 850 stars ; he seems to have been the first to state the position of these stars in terms of latitude and longitude (in relation to the ecliptic). He wrote a treatise in twelve Books on Chords in a Circle, equivalent to a table of trigonometrical sines. For calculating arcs in astronomy from other arcs given by means of tables he used propositions in spherical trigonometry.

The *Sphaerica* of Theodosius of Bithynia (written, say, 20 B.C.) contains no trigonometry. It is otherwise with the *Sphaerica* of Menelaus (fl. A.D. 100) extant in Arabic ; Book I of this work contains propositions about spherical triangles corresponding to the main propositions of Euclid about plane triangles (e.g. congruence theorems and the proposition that in a spherical triangle the three angles are together greater than two right angles), while Book III contains genuine spherical trigonometry, consisting of ' Menelaus's Theorem ' with reference to the sphere and deductions therefrom.

Ptolemy's great work, the *Syntaxis*, written about A.D. 150

and originally called Μαθηματικὴ σύνταξις, came to be known as Μεγάλη σύνταξις; the Arabs made up from the superlative μέγιστος the word al-Majisti which became *Almagest*.

Book I, containing the necessary preliminaries to the study of the Ptolemaic system, gives a Table of Chords in a circle subtended by angles at the centre of ½° increasing by half-degrees to 180°. The circle is divided into 360 μοῖραι, parts or degrees, and the diameter into 120 parts (τμήματα); the chords are given in terms of the latter with sexagesimal fractions (e. g. the chord subtended by an angle of 120° is 103ᵖ 53′ 23″). The Table of Chords is equivalent to a table of the *sines* of the halves of the angles in the table, for, if (crd. 2 a) represents the chord subtended by an angle of 2 a (crd. 2 a)/120 = sin a. Ptolemy first gives the minimum number of geometrical propositions required for the calculation of the chords. The first of these finds (crd. 36°) and (crd. 72°) from the geometry of the inscribed pentagon and decagon; the second ('Ptolemy's Theorem' about a quadrilateral in a circle) is equivalent to the formula for sin $(\theta - \phi)$, the third to that for sin ½ θ. From (crd. 72°) and (crd. 60°) Ptolemy, by using these propositions successively, deduces (crd. 1½°) and (crd. ¾°), from which he obtains (crd. 1°) by a clever interpolation. To complete the table he only needs his fourth proposition, which is equivalent to the formula for cos $(\theta + \phi)$.

Ptolemy wrote other minor astronomical works, most of which survive in Greek or Arabic, an *Optics* in five Books (four Books almost complete were translated into Latin in the twelfth century), and an attempted proof of the parallel-postulate which is reproduced by Proclus.

Heron of Alexandria (date uncertain; he may have lived as late as the third century A. D.) was an almost encyclopaedic writer on mathematical and physical subjects. He aimed at practical utility rather than theoretical completeness; hence, apart from the interesting collection of *Definitions* which has

come down under his name, and his commentary on Euclid
which is represented only by extracts in Proclus and an-Nairīzī,
his geometry is mostly mensuration in the shape of numerical
examples worked out. As these could be indefinitely multiplied, there was a temptation to add to them and to use
Heron's name. However much of the separate works edited
by Hultsch (the *Geometrica, Geodaesia, Stereometrica, Mensurae,
Liber geëponicus*) is genuine, we must now regard as more
authoritative the genuine *Metrica* discovered at Constantinople
in 1896 and edited by H. Schöne in 1903 (Teubner). Book I
on the measurement of areas is specially interesting for (1) its
statement of the formula used by Heron for finding approximations to surds, (2) the elegant geometrical proof of the formula
for the area of a triangle $\Delta = \sqrt{\{s\ (s-a)\ (s-b)\ (s-c)\}}$, a formula
now known to be due to Archimedes, (3) an allusion to limits
to the value of π found by Archimedes and more exact than
the $3\frac{1}{7}$ and $3\frac{10}{71}$ obtained in the *Measurement of a Circle*.

Book I of the *Metrica* calculates the areas of triangles,
quadrilaterals, the regular polygons up to the dodecagon (the
areas even of the heptagon, enneagon, and hendecagon are
approximately evaluated), the circle and a segment of it, the
ellipse, a parabolic segment, and the surfaces of a cylinder,
a right cone, a sphere and a segment thereof. Book II deals
with the measurement of solids, the cylinder, prisms, pyramids
and cones and frusta thereof, the sphere and a segment of it,
the anchor-ring or tore, the five regular solids, and finally the
two special solids of Archimedes's *Method* ; full use is made
of all Archimedes's results. Book III is on the division of
figures. The plane portion is much on the lines of Euclid's
Divisions (of figures). The solids divided in given ratios are
the sphere, the pyramid, the cone and a frustum thereof.
Incidentally Heron shows how he obtained an approximation
to the cube root of a non-cube number (100). Quadratic
equations are solved by Heron by a regular rule not unlike our

method, and the *Geometrica* contains two interesting indeterminate problems.

Heron also wrote *Pneumatica* (where the reader will find such things as siphons, Heron's Fountain, penny-in-the-slot machines, a fire-engine, a water-organ, and many arrangements employing the force of steam), *Automaton-making*, *Belopoeïca* (on engines of war), *Catoptrica*, and *Mechanics*. The *Mechanics* has been edited from the Arabic; it is (except for considerable fragments) lost in Greek. It deals with the puzzle of 'Aristotle's Wheel', the parallelogram of velocities, definitions of, and problems on, the centre of gravity, the distribution of weights between several supports, the five mechanical powers, mechanics in daily life (queries and answers). Pappus covers much the same ground in Book VIII of his *Collection*.

We come, lastly, to Algebra. Problems involving simple equations are found in the Papyrus Rhind, in the *Epanthema* of Thymaridas already referred to, and in the arithmetical epigrams in the Greek Anthology (Plato alludes to this class of problem in the *Laws*, 819 B, C); the Anthology even includes two cases of indeterminate equations of the first degree. The Pythagoreans gave general solutions in rational numbers of the equations $x^2 + y^2 = z^2$ and $2x^2 - y^2 = \pm 1$, which are indeterminate equations of the second degree.

The first to make systematic use of symbols in algebraical work was Diophantus of Alexandria (fl. about A.D. 250). He used (1) a sign for the unknown quantity, which he calls ἀριθμός, and compendia for its powers up to the sixth; (2) a sign (⋀) with the effect of our *minus*. The latter sign probably represents ΛI, an abbreviation for the root of the word λείπειν (to be wanting); the sign for ἀριθμός (ς) is most likely an abbreviation for the letters αρ; the compendia for the powers of the unknown are Δ^Υ for δύναμις, the square, Κ^Υ for κύβος, the cube, and so on. Diophantus shows that he solved quadratic equations by rule, like Heron. His *Arithmetica*, of

which six books only (out of thirteen) survive, contains a certain
number of problems leading to simple equations, but is mostly
devoted to indeterminate or semi-determinate analysis, mainly
of the second degree. The collection is extraordinarily varied,
and the devices resorted to are highly ingenious. The problems
solved are such as the following (fractional as well as integral
solutions being admitted) : ' Given a number, to find three
others such that the sum of the three, or of any pair of them,
together with the given number is a square ', ' To find four
numbers such that the square of the sum *plus* or *minus* any one
of the numbers is a square', ' To find three numbers such that the
product of any two *plus* or *minus* the sum of the three is a square'.
Diophantus assumes as known certain theorems about numbers
which are the sums of two and three squares respectively, and
other propositions in the Theory of Numbers. He also wrote a
book *On Polygonal Numbers* of which only a fragment survives.

With Pappus and Diophantus the list of original writers on
mathematics comes to an end. After them came the commentators whose names only can be mentioned here. Theon
of Alexandria, the editor of Euclid, lived towards the end of
the fourth century A. D. To the fifth and sixth centuries belong
Proclus, Simplicius, and Eutocius, to whom we can never be
grateful enough for the precious fragments which they have
preserved from works now lost, and particularly the *History
of Geometry* and the *History of Astronomy* by Aristotle's pupil
Eudemus.

Such is the story of Greek mathematical science. If anything could enhance the marvel of it, it would be the consideration of the shortness of the time (about 350 years) within
which the Greeks, starting from the very beginning, brought
geometry to the point of performing operations equivalent to
the integral calculus and, in the realm of astronomy, actually
anticipated Copernicus.

T. L. Heath.

NATURAL SCIENCE

Aristotle

THERE is a little essay of Goethe's called, simply, *Die Natur*. It comes among those tracts on Natural Science in which the poet and philosopher turned his restless mind to problems of light and colour, of leaf and flower, of bony skull and kindred vertebra ; and it sounds like a prose-poem, a noble paean, eulogizing the love and glorifying the study of Nature. Some twenty-five hundred years before, Anaximander had written a book with the same title, *Concerning Nature*, περὶ φύσεως : but its subject was not the same. It was a variant of the old traditional cosmogonies. It told of how in the beginning the earth was without form and void. It sought to trace all things back to the Infinite, τὸ ἄπειρον—to That which knows no bounds of space or time but is before all worlds, and to whose bosom again all things, all worlds, return. For Goethe Nature meant the beauty, the all but sensuous beauty of the world ; for the older philosopher it was the mystery of the Creative Spirit.

Than Nature, in Goethe's sense, no theme is more familiar to us, for whom many a poet tells the story and many a lesser poet echoes the conceit ; but if there be anywhere in Greek such overt praise and worship of Nature's beauty, I cannot call it to mind. Yet in Latin the *divini gloria ruris* is praised and *Natura daedala rerum* worshipped, as we are wont to praise and worship them, for their own sweet sakes. It is one of the ways, one of the simpler ways, in which the Roman world seems nearer to us than the Greek : and not only seems, but is so. For compared with the great early civilizations, Rome is modern and of the West; while, draw her close as we may to our hearts, Greece brings along with her a breath of the East and a whisper of remote antiquity. A Tuscan gentleman of to-day, like a Roman gentleman of yesterday, is at heart a husbandman, like Cato; he is *ruris amator*, like Horace; he gets him to his little farm or vineyard (*O rus, quando te aspiciam !*), like Atticus or the younger Pliny. As Bacon praised his garden, so does Pliny praise his farm, with its cornfields and meadowland, vineyard and woodland, orchard and pasture, bee-hives and flowers. That God made the country and man made the town was (long before Cowper) a saying of Varro's; but in Greek I can think of no such apophthegm.

As Schiller puts it, the Greeks looked on Nature with their minds more than with their hearts, nor ever clung to her with outspoken admiration and affection. And Humboldt, asserting (as I would do) that the portrayal of nature, for her own sake and in all her manifold diversity, was foreign to the Greek idea, declares that the landscape is always the mere background of their picture, while their foreground is filled with the affairs and actions and thoughts of men. But all the while, as in some old Italian picture—of Domenichino or Albani or Leonardo himself—the subordinated background is delicately traced and exquisitely beautiful; and sometimes we come to value it in the end more than all the rest of the composition.

Deep down in the love of Nature, whether it be of the sensual or intellectual kind, and in the art of observation which is its outcome and first expression, lie the roots of all our Natural Science. All the world over these are the heritage of all men, though the inheritance be richer or poorer here and there : they are shown forth in the lore and wisdom of hunter and fisherman, of shepherd and husbandman, of artist and poet. The natural history of the ancients is not enshrined in Aristotle and Pliny. It pervades the vast literature of classical antiquity.

For all we may say of the reticence with which the Greeks proclaim it, it greets us nobly in Homer, it sings to us in Anacreon, Sicilian shepherds tune their pipes to it in Theocritus : and anon in Virgil we dream of it to the coo of doves and the sound of bees' industrious murmur.

Not only from such great names as these do we reach the letter and the spirit of ancient Natural History. We must go a-wandering into the by-ways of literature. We must eke out the scientific treatises of Aristotle and Pliny by help of the fragments which remain of the works of such naturalists as Speusippus or Alexander the Myndian ; add to the familiar stories of Herodotus the Indian tales of Ctesias and Megasthenes ; sit with Athenaeus and his friends at the supper table, gleaning from cook and epicure, listening to the merry idle troop of convivial gentlemen capping verses and spinning yarns ; read Xenophon's treatise on Hunting, study the didactic poems, the Cynegetica and Halieutica, of Oppian and of Ovid. And then again we may hark back to the greater world of letters, wherein poet and scholar, from petty fabulist to the great dramatists, from Homer's majesty to Lucian's wit, share in the love of Nature and enliven the delicate background of their story with allusions to beast and bird.

Such allusions, refined at first by art and hallowed at last by familiar memory, lie treasured in men's hearts and enshrine themselves in our noblest literature. Take, of a thousand crowding instances, that great passage in the *Iliad* where the Greek host, disembarking on the plains of the Scamander, is likened to a migrating flock of cranes or geese or long-necked swans, as they fly proudly over the Asian meadows and alight screaming by Cayster's stream—and Virgil echoes more than once the familiar lines. The crane was a well-known bird. Its lofty flight brings it, again in Homer, to the very gates of heaven. Hesiod and Pindar speak of its far-off cry, heard from above the clouds : and that it ' observed the time of its coming ', ' intelligent of seasons ', was a proverb old in Hesiod's day—when the crane signalled the approach of winter, and when it bade the husbandman make ready to plough. It follows the plough, in Theocritus, as persistently as the wolf the kid and the peasant-lad his sweetheart. The discipline of the migrating cranes, the serried wedge of their ranks in flight, the good order of the resting flock, are often, and often fancifully, described. Aristotle records how they have an appointed leader, who keeps watch by night and in flight keeps calling to the laggards ; and all this old story Euripides, the most naturalistic of the great tragedians, puts into verse :

> The ordered host of Libyan birds avoids
> The wintry storm, obedient to the call
> Of their old leader, piping to his flock.

Lastly, Milton gathers up the spirit and the letter of these and many another ancient allusion to the migrating cranes :

> Part loosely wing the region ; part more wise,
> In common ranged in figure, wedge their way
> Intelligent of seasons, and set forth
> Their aery caravan, high over seas
> Flying, and over lands ; with mutual wing
> Easing their flight ; so steers the prudent crane.

But the natural history of the poets is a story without an end, and in our estimation, however brief it be, of ancient knowledge, there are other matters to be considered, and other points of view where we must take our stand.

When we consider the science of the Greeks, and come quickly to love it and slowly to see how great it was, we likewise see that it was restricted as compared with our own, curiously partial or particular in its limitations. The practical and ' useful ' sciences of chemistry, mechanics, and engineering, which in our modern world crowd the others to the wall, are absent altogether, or so concealed that we forget and pass them by. Mathematics is enthroned high over all, as it is meet she should be ; and of uncontested right she occupies her throne century after century, from Pythagoras to Proclus, from the scattered schools of early Hellenic civilization to the rise and fall of the great Alexandrine University. Near beside her sits, from of old, the daughter-science of Astronomy ; and these twain were worshipped by the greatest scientific intellects of the Greeks. But though we do not hear of them nor read of them, we must not suppose for a moment that the practical or technical sciences were lacking in so rich and complex a civilization. China, that most glorious of all living monuments of Antiquity, tells us nothing of her own chemistry, but we know that it is there. Peep into a Chinese town, walk through its narrow streets, thronged but quiet, wherein there is neither rumbling of coaches nor rattling of wheels, and you shall see the nearest thing on earth to what we hear of Sybaris. To the production of those glowing silks and delicate porcelains and fine metal-work has gone a vast store of chemical know-ledge, traditional and empirical. So was it, precisely, in ancient Greece ; and Plato knew that it was so—that the dyer, the perfumer, and the apothecary had subtle arts, a subtle science of their own, a science not to be belittled nor despised. We may pass here and there by diligent search from conjecture to assurance; analyse a pigment, an alloy or a slag; discover from an older record than the Greeks', the chemical pre-scription wherewith an Egyptian princess darkened her eyes, or study the pictured hearth, bellows, oven, crucibles with which the followers of Tubal-Cain smelted their ore. Once in a way, but seldom, do we meet with ancient chemistry even in Greek literature. There is a curious passage (its text is faulty and the translation hard) in the story of the Argonauts, where Medea concocts a magic brew. She put divers herbs in it, herbs yielding coloured juices such as safflower and alkanet, and soapwort and fleawort to give consistency or 'body' to the lye; she put in alum and blue vitriol (or sulphate of copper), and she put in blood. The magic brew was no more and no less than a dye, a red or purple dye, and a prodigious deal of chemistry had gone to the making of it. For the copper was there to produce a 'lake' or copper-salt of the vegetable alkaloids, which copper-lakes are among the most brilliant and most permanent of colouring matters; the alum was there as a 'mordant'; and even the blood was doubtless there incorporated for better reasons than super-stitious ones, in all probability for the purpose of clarifying (by means of its coagulating albumen) the seething and turbid brew.

The 'Orphic' version of the story, in which this passage occurs, is probably an Alexandrine compilation, and whether the ingredients of the brew had been part of the ancient legend or were merely suggested to the poet by the knowledge of his own day we cannot tell; in either case the prescription is old enough, and is at least pre-Byzantine by a few centuries. Such as it is, it does not stand alone. Other fragments of ancient chemistry, more or less akin to it, have been gathered together; in Galen's book on *The making of Simples*, in Pliny, in Paulus Aegineta, and for that matter in certain Egyptian papyri (especially a certain very famous one, still extant, of which Clement of Alexandria speaks as a secret or 'hermetic' book), we can trace the broken and scattered stones of a great edifice of ancient chemistry.

Nevertheless, all this weight of chemical learning figures scantily in literature, and is conspicuously absent from our conception of the natural genius of the Greeks. We have no reason to suppose that ancient chemistry, or any part of it, was ever peculiarly Greek, or that this science was the especial property of any nation whatsoever; moreover it was a trade, or a bundle of trades, whose trade-secrets were too precious to be revealed, and so constituted not a science but a mystery.

So has it always been with chemistry, the most cosmopolitan of sciences, the most secret of arts. Quietly and stealthily it crept through the world ; the tinker brought it with his solder and his flux ; the African tribes who were the first workers in iron passed it on to the great metallurgists who forged Damascan and Toledan steel.

This ' trade ' of Chemistry was never a science for a Gentleman, as philosophy and mathematics were ; and Plato, greatest of philosophers, was one of the greatest of gentlemen. Long, long afterwards, Oxford said the same thing to Robert Boyle— that Chemistry was no proper avocation for a gentleman ; but he thought otherwise, and the ' brother of the Earl of Cork ' became the Father of scientific Chemistry.

Now I take it that in regard to biology Aristotle did much the same thing as Boyle, breaking through a similar tradition ; and herein one of the greatest of his great services is to be found. There was a wealth of natural history before his time ; but it belonged to the farmer, the huntsman, and the fisherman. —with something over (doubtless) for the schoolboy, the idler, and the poet. But Aristotle made it a science, and won a place for it in Philosophy. He did for it just what Pythagoras had done (as Proclus tells us) for mathematics in an earlier age, when he discerned the philosophy underlying the old empirical art of ' geometry ', and made it the basis of ' a liberal education '.[1]

The Mediterranean fisherman, like the Chinese fisherman or the Japanese, has still, and always has had, a wide knowledge of all that pertains to and accompanies his craft. Our Scottish fishermen have a limited vocabulary, which scarce extends beyond the names of the few common fishes with which the market is supplied. But at Marseilles or Genoa or in the Levant

---

[1] ἐπὶ δὲ τούτοις Πυθαγόρας τὴν περὶ αὐτὴν φιλοσοφίαν εἰς σχῆμα παιδείας ἐλευθέρου μετέστησεν. *Procli Comment. Euclidis lib. I, Prolegom. II* (p. 65, ed. Friedlein).

they have names for many hundreds of species, of fish and shell-fish and cuttle-fish and worms and corallines, and all manner of swimming and creeping things; they know a vast deal about the habits of their lives, far more, sometimes, than do we 'scientific men'; they are naturalists by tradition and by trade. Neither, by the way, must we forget the ancient medical and anatomical learning of the great Aesculapian guild, nor the still more recondite knowledge possessed by various priesthoods (again like their brethren of to-day in China and Japan) of the several creatures, sacred fish, pigeons, guinea-fowl, snakes, cuttlefish, and what not, which time out of mind they had reared, tended, and venerated.

Of what new facts Aristotle actually discovered it is impossible to be sure. Could it ever be proved that he discovered many, or could it even be shown that of his own hand he discovered nothing at all, it would affect but little our estimate of his greatness and our admiration of his learning. He was the first of Greek philosophers and gentlemen to see that all these things were good to know and worthy to be told. This was his great discovery.

I have sought elsewhere to show that Aristotle spent two years, the happiest years perhaps of all his life—a long honeymoon—by the sea-side in the island of Mytilene, after he had married the little Princess, and before he began the hard work of his life: before he taught Alexander in Macedon, and long before he spoke *urbi et orbi* in the Lyceum. Here it was that he learned the great bulk of his natural history, in which, wide and general as it is, the things of the sea have from first to last a notable predominance.

I have tried to illustrate elsewhere (as many another writer has done) something of the variety and the depth of Aristotle's knowledge of animals—choosing an example here and there, but only drawing a little water from an inexhaustible well.

A famous case is that of the 'molluscs', where either

Aristotle's knowledge was exceptionally minute, or where it has come down to us with unusual completeness.

These are the cuttle-fish, which have now surrendered their Aristotelian name of ' molluscs ' to that greater group which is seen to include them, together with the shell-fish or 'ostraco-derma' of Aristotle. These cuttle-fishes are creatures that we seldom see, but in the Mediterranean they are an article of food and many kinds are known to the fishermen. All or wellnigh all of these many kinds were known to Aristotle. He described their form and their anatomy, their habits, their development, all with such faithful accuracy that what we can add to-day seems of secondary importance. He begins with a methodical description of the general form, tells us of the body and fins, of the eight arms with their rows of suckers, of the abnormal position of the head. He points out the two long arms of Sepia and of the calamaries, and their absence in the octopus ; and he tells us, what was only confirmed of late, that with these two long arms the creature clings to the rock and sways about like a ship at anchor. He describes the great eyes, the two big teeth forming the beak ; and he dissects the whole structure of the gut, with its long gullet, its round crop, its stomach and the little coiled coecal diverticulum : dissecting not only one but several species, and noting differences that were not observed again till Cuvier re-dissected them. He describes the funnel and its relation to the mantle-sac, and the ink-bag, which he shows to be largest in Sepia of all others. And here, by the way, he seems to make one of those apparent errors that, as it happens, turn out to be justified : for he tells us that in Octopus, unlike the rest, the funnel is on the upper side ; the fact being that when the creature lies prone upon the ground, with all its arms outspread, the funnel-tube (instead of being flattened out beneath the creature's prostrate body) is long enough to pro-trude upwards between arms and head, and to appear on one side or other thereof, in a position apparently the reverse of its natural one. He describes the character of the cuttle-bone in Sepia, and of the horny pen which takes its place in the various calamaries, and notes the lack of any similar structure in Octopus. He dissects in both sexes the reproductive organs, noting without exception all their essential and complicated parts ; and he had figured these in his lost volume of anatomical diagrams. He describes the various kinds of eggs, and, with still more surprising knowledge, shows us the little embryo cuttle-fish, with its great yolk-sac attached, in apparent contrast to the chick's, to the little creature's developing head.

But there is one other remarkable feature that he knew ages before it was rediscovered, almost in our own time. In certain male cuttle-fishes, in the breeding season, one of the arms develops in a curious fashion into a long coiled whip-lash, and in the act of breeding may then be transferred to the mantle-cavity of the female. Cuvier himself knew nothing of the nature or the function of this separated arm, and indeed, if I am not mistaken, it was he who mistook it for a parasitic worm. But Aristotle tells us of its use and its temporary development, and of its structure in detail, and his description tallies closely with the accounts of the most recent writers.

A scarcely less minute account follows of the ' Malacostraca ' or crustaceans, the lobsters and the crabs, the shrimps and the prawns, and others of their kind, a chapter to which Cuvier devoted a celebrated essay. There be many kinds of crabs— the common kind, the big ' granny ' crabs, the little horsemen-crabs, that scamper over the sand and which are for the most part empty, that is to say, whose respiratory cavities are exceptionally large ; and there are the freshwater crabs. There are the little shrimps and the big hump-backed fellows, or prawns ; there are the ' crangons ' or squillae ; and the big lobsters and the crawfish or ' langoustes ', their spiny cousins. We read about their beady eyes, which turn every way ; about their

big rough antennae and the smaller, smoother pair between ;
the great teeth, or mandibles ; the carapace with its projecting
rostrum, the jointed abdomen with the tail-fins at the end,
and the little flaps below on which the female drops her spawn.
In more or less detail these things are severally described, and
the many limbs severally enumerated, in one kind after another.
The descriptions of the lobster and the langouste are particularly minute, and the comparison or contrast between the
two is drawn with elaborate precision. In the former, besides
other differences between male and female, the female is said
to have the ' first foot ' (or leg) bifurcate, while in the male
it is undivided. It seems a trifling matter, but it is true ; it
is so small a point that I searched long before at last I found
mention made of it in a German monograph. The puzzling
thing is that it is (as we should say) the last and not the first
leg which is so distinguished ; but after all, it is only a convention of our own to count the limbs from before backwards.
To inspect a lobster's limbs, we lay it on its back (as Aristotle
did), and see the legs overlapping, each hinder one above the
one before ; the hindmost is the first we see, and the one we
must first lift up to inspect the others.

Aristotle's account of fishes is a prodigious history of habits,
food, migrations, modes of capture, times and ways of spawning,
and anatomical details ; but it is not here that we can elucidate
or even illustrate this astonishing Ichthyology. It is not always
easy to understand—but the obstacle lies often, I take it, in
our own ignorance. The identification of species is not always
plain, for here as elsewhere Aristotle did not reckon with a time
or place where the familiar words of Greek should be unknown
or their homely significance forgotten. Among the great host
of fish-names there are several referring, somehow or other, to
the Grey Mullet, which puzzle both naturalist and lexico-
grapher. A young officer told me the other day how he had
watched an Arab fisherman emptying out his creel of Grey

Mullet on some Syrian beach, and the Arab gave four if not five names to as many different kinds, betwixt which my friend could see no difference whatsoever. Had my friend been an ichthyologist he would doubtless have noticed that one had eyelids and the others none ; that one had little brushes on its lips, another a small but wide-open slit under the jaw, another a yellow spot on its gill-covers, and so on. The Mullets are a difficult group, but Aristotle, like the Arab fisherman, evidently recognized their fine distinctions and employed the appropriate names. Again, Aristotle speaks of a certain nest-building fish, the ' phycis ', and regarding this Cuvier fell into error (where once upon a time I followed him). In Cuvier's time there was but one nest-building fish known such as to suit, apparently, the passage, namely the little black goby ; but after Cuvier's day the nest-building habits of the ' wrasses ' became known to naturalists, as they had doubtless been known ages before to the fishermen—and to Aristotle.

Like almost every other little point on which we happen to touch, we might make this one the starting-point (here comes in the delight and fascination of the interpreter's task !) for other stories.

Speusippus, Plato's successor in the Academy, was both philosopher and naturalist, and we may take it, if we please, that his leaning towards biology, and the biological trend which at this time became more and more marked in Athenian philosophy, were not unconnected with the great impulse which Aristotle had given. However this may be, Speusippus wrote a book περὶ Ὁμοίων, 'Concerning Resemblances'; and this, of which we only possess a few fragmentary sentences, must have been a very curious and an interesting book. He mentions, among other similar cases, that our little fish *phycis* has a close outward semblance to the sea-perch ; and this is enough to clinch the proof that Aristotle's nest-building fish was not a goby but a wrasse. The whole purport of

Speusippus's book seems to have been to discuss how, or why, with all Nature's apparently infinite variety, certain animals have a singularly close resemblance to certain others, though they be quite distinct in kind. It is a problem which perplexes us still, when we are astonished and even deluded by the likeness between a wasp and a hover-fly, a merlin and a cuckoo. In certain extreme cases we call it ' mimicry ', and invoke hypotheses to account for this ' mimetic ' resemblance ; and those of us who reject these hypotheses must fain take refuge in others, as far-reaching in their way. This at least we know, that Speusippus seized upon a real problem of biology, of lasting interest and even of fundamental importance.

To come back to Aristotle and his fishes, let us glance at one little point more. The reproduction of the eel is an ancient puzzle, which has found its full solution only in our own day. While the salmon, for instance, comes up the river to breed and goes down again to the sea, the eel goes down to the ocean to spawn, and the old eels come back no more but perish in the great waters. The eel's egg develops into a little flattened, transparent fish, altogether different in outward appearance from an eel, which turns afterwards into a young eel or ' elver ' ; and Professor Grassi, who had a big share in elucidating the whole matter, tells us the curious fact that he found the Sicilian fishermen well acquainted with the little transparent larva (the *Leptocephalus* of modern naturalists), that they knew well what it was, and that they had a name for it—*Casentula*. Now Aristotle, in a passage which I think has been much misunderstood (and which we must admit to be in part erroneous), tells us that the eel develops from what he calls γῆς ἔντερα, a word which we translate, literally, the ' guts of the earth ', and which commentators interpret as ' earthworms ' ! But in Sicilian Doric, γῆς ἔντερα would at once become γᾶς ἔντερα ; and between ' Gasentera ' and the modern Sicilian ' Casentula ' there is scarce a hairbreadth's difference. So we may be permitted to suppose that here again Aristotle was singularly and accurately informed; and that he knew by sight and name the little larva of the eel, whose discovery and identification is one of the modest triumphs of recent investigation.

Aristotle's many pages on fishes are delightful reading. The anatomist may read of such recondite matters as the *placenta vitellina* of the smooth dog-fish, whereby the viviparous embryo is nourished within the womb, after a fashion analogous to that of mammalian embryology—a phenomenon brought to light anew by Johannes Müller, and which excited him to enthusiastic admiration of Aristotle's minute and faithful anatomy. Again we may read of the periodic migration of the tunnies, of the great net or 'madrague' in which they are captured, and of the watchmen, the θυννοσκόποι, the 'hooers' of our ancient Cornish fishery, who give warning from tower or headland of the approaching shoal. The student may learn what manner of fish it was (the great Eagle-ray) with whose barbed fin-spine—most primitive of spear-heads—Ulysses was slain; and again, he may learn not a little about that νάρκη, or torpedo, to which Meno compared his master Socrates, in a somewhat ambiguous compliment.

In rambling fashion Aristotle has a deal to tell us about insects, and he has left us a sort of treatise on the whole natural history of the bee. He knew the several inmates of the hive, though like others of his day (save, perhaps, only Xenophon), and like Shakespeare too, he took the queen-bee for a king. He describes the building of the comb, the laying of the eggs, the provision of the larvae with food. He discusses the various qualities of honey and the flowers from which these are drawn. He is learned in the diseases and the enemies of bees. He tells us many curious things about the economy of the hive and the arts of the bee-keeper, some of which things have a very modern and familiar look about them : for instance, the use of a net or screen to keep out the drones, a net so nicely contrived that these sturdy fellows are just kept out, while the leaner, slenderer workers are just let in. But it would be a long, long story to tell of Aristotle's knowledge of the bee, and to compare it with what is, haply, the still deeper skill and learning of that master of bee-craft, Virgil.

Then, having perfect freedom to go whithersoever we chose and to follow the bees across the boundless fields of ancient literature, we might read of the wild bees and of their honey out of a rock, and of the hive-bees too, in Homer; follow them to their first legendary home in Crete, where the infant Jupiter was fed on honey—as a baby's lips are touched with it even unto this day; trace their association with Proserpine and her mother, or their subtler connexion with Ephesian Diana; find in the poets, from Hesiod to the later Anthology, a hundred sweet references—to the bee-tree in the oak-wood, to the flowery hill Hymettus. Perhaps, at last, we might even happen on the place where Origen seems so strangely to foreshadow Shakespeare—speaking of the king of the bees with his retinue of courtiers (his officers of sorts), the relays of workmen (the poor mechanic porters crowding in), the punishment of the idle (where some, like magistrates, correct at home), the wars, the vanquished, and the plunder (which pillage they with merry march bring home To the tent-royal of their Emperor).

Go back to Aristotle, and we may listen to him again while he talks of many other kindred insects: of the humble-bee and its kind, of the mason-bee with its hard round nest of clay, of the robber-bees, and of the various wasps and hornets; or (still more curiously and unexpectedly) of the hunter-wasp or 'ichneumon', and how it kills the spider, carries it home to its nest, and lays its eggs in its poor body, that the little wasp-grubs may afterwards be fed. Or again of the great wasps which he calls Anthrenae, and how they chase the big flies, and cut off their heads, and fly away with the rest of the carcass—all agreeing to the very letter with what Henri Fabre tells us of a certain large wasp of Southern Europe, and how it captures the big ' taons ' or horse-flies : ' Pour donner le coup de grâce à leurs Taons mal sacrifiés, et se débattants encore entre les pattes du ravisseur, j'ai vu des Bembex mâchonner la tête et le thorax des victimes.' Verily, there is nothing new under the sun.

With the metamorphoses of various insects Aristotle was well acquainted. He knew how the house-fly passes its early stages in a dung-hill, and how the grubs of the big horse-flies and Tabanids live in decayed wood ; how certain little flies or gnats are engendered (as he calls it) in the slime of vinegar. He relates with great care and accuracy the life-history of the common gnat, from its aquatic larva, the little red ' blood-worm ' of our pools ; he describes them wriggling about like tiny bits of red weed, in the water of some half-empty well ; and he explains, finally, the change by which they become stiff and motionless and hard, until a husk breaks away and the little gnat is seen sitting upon it ; and by and by the sun's heat or a puff of wind starts it off, and away it flies.

Some of these stories are indeed remarkable, for the events related are more or less hidden and obscure ; and so, with all this knowledge at hand, it is not a little strange that Aristotle has very little indeed to tell us about the far more obvious phenomena of the life-history of the butterfly, and of the several kinds of butterflies and moths. He does tell us briefly that the butterfly comes from a caterpillar, which lives on cabbage-leaves and feeds voraciously, then turns into a chrysalis and eats no more, nor has it a mouth to eat withal ; it is hard and, as it were, dead, but yet it moves and wriggles when you touch it, and after a while the husk bursts and out comes the butterfly. The account is good enough, so far as it goes, but nevertheless Aristotle shows no affection for the butterfly, does not linger and dally over it, tells no stories about it. This is all of a piece with the rest of Greek literature, and poetry in particular, where allusions to the butterfly are scanty and rare. I think the Greeks found something ominous or uncanny, something not to be lightly spoken of, in that all but disembodied spirit which we call a butterfly, and they called by the name of ψυχή, the Soul. They had a curious name (νεκύδαλλος) for the pupa. It sounds like a 'little corpse' (νέκυς), and like a little corpse within its shroud or coffin the pupa sleeps in its cocoon. A late poet describes the butterfly ' coming back from the grave to the light of day '; and certain of the Fathers of the Church, St. Basil in particular, point the moral accordingly, and draw a doubtless time-honoured allegory of the Resurrection and the Life from the grub which is not dead but sleepeth, and the butterfly which (as it were) is raised in glory.

Of one large moth, Aristotle gives us an account which has been a puzzle to many. This begins as a great grub or caterpillar, with (as it were) horns ; and, growing by easy stages, it spins at length a cocoon. There is a class of women who unwind and reel off the cocoons, and afterwards weave a fabric with the thread ; and a certain woman of Cos is credited with the invention of this fabric. This is, at first sight, a plain and straightforward description of the silkworm ; but we know that it was not till long afterwards, nearly a thousand years after, in Justinian's reign, that the silkworm and the mulberry-tree which is its food were brought out of the East into Byzantine Greece. We learn something of this Coan silkworm from Pliny, who tells us that it lived on the ash and oak and cypress tree ; and from Clement of Alexandria and other of the Fathers we glean a little more—for instance, that the larva was covered with thick-set hairs, and that the cocoon was of a loose material something like a spider's web. All this agrees in every particular with a certain large moth (*Lasiocampa otus*), which spins a rough cocoon not unlike that of our Emperor moth, and lives in south-eastern Europe, feeding on the cypress and the oak.

Many other silkworms besides the true or common one are still employed, worms which yield the Tussore silks of India and other kindred silks in Japan; and so likewise was this rough silky fabric spun and woven in Hellas, until in course of time it was surpassed and superseded by the finer produce of the 'Seric worm', and the older industry died out and was utterly forgotten.

Ere we leave the subject of insects let us linger a moment over one which the Greeks loved, and loved most of all. When as schoolboys we first began to read our Thucydides, we met in the very beginning with the story of how rich Athenians wore Golden Grasshoppers (as the schoolmaster calls them) in their hair. These golden ornaments were, of course, no common grasshoppers, but the little Cicadas, whose sharp chirrup seemed delightful music to the Greeks. It is unpleasant to our ears, as Browning found it; but in a multitude of Greek poets, in Alcaeus and Anacreon and all through the whole Anthology, we hear its praise. We have it, for instance, in the *Birds*:

> Though the hot sun be shining in the sky
> In the deep flowery meadow-grass I lie:
> To listen to the shrill melodious tune
> Of crickets, thrilled to ecstasy at noon.

Of this familiar and beloved insect Aristotle gives a copious account. He describes two separate species, which we still recognize easily; a larger one and the better singer, the other smaller and the first to come and last to go with the summer season. He recognized the curious vocal organ, or vibratory drum, at the cicada's waist, and saw that some cicadas possessed it and others not; and he knew, as the poets also knew, that it was the males who sang, while their wives listened and were silent. He tells how the cicada is absent from tree-less countries, as, for instance, from Cyrene (and why, I wonder, does he go all the way to Cyrene for his illustration?), neither is it heard in deep and sunless woods; but in the olive-groves you hear it at its best, for an olive-grove is sparse and the sun comes through. Then he tells us briefly, but with remarkable accuracy, the story of the creature's life : how the female, with her long ovipositor, lays her eggs deep down in dead, hollow twigs, such as the canes on which the vines are propped ; how the brood, when they escape from the egg, burrow underground ; how later on they emerge, especially in rainy weather, when the rains have softened the soil ; how then the larva changes into another form, the so-called ' nymph ' ; and how at last, when summer comes, the skin of the nymph breaks and the perfect insect issues forth, changes colour, and begins to sing. In Aristophanes, in Theocritus, in Lucretius, Virgil, Martial, and in the Anthology, we may gather up a host of poetical allusions to the natural history thus simply epitomized.

The Book about Animals, the *Historia Animalium* as we say, from which I have quoted these few examples of Aristotle's store of information, may be taken to represent the first necessary stage of scientific inquiry. There is a kind of *manual* philosophy (as old Lord Monboddo called it) which investigates facts which escape the vulgar, and may be called the *anecdotes* or *secret history* of nature. In this fascinating pursuit Gilbert White excelled, and John Ray and many another—the whole brotherhood of simple naturalists. But such accumulated knowledge of facts is but the foundation of a philosophy ; and ' nothing deserves the name of philosophy, except what explains the causes and principles of things '. Aristotle would have done much had he merely shown (as Gilbert White showed to the country gentlemen of his day) that the minute observation of nature was something worth the scholar and the gentleman's while ; but, far more than this, he made a Science of natural knowledge, and set it once for all within the realm of Philosophy. He set it side by side with the more ancient science of Astronomy, which for many hundred years in Egypt and the East, and for some few centuries in Hellas, had occupied the mind of philosophers and the attention of educated men. I have quoted before a great sentence in which he explains his purpose, and makes excuse for his temerity. 'The glory, doubtless, of the heavenly bodies fills us with more delight than the contemplation of these lowly things; for the sun and stars are born not, neither do they decay, but are eternal and divine. But the heavens are high and afar off, and of celestial things the knowledge that our senses give us is scanty and dim. The living creatures, on the other hand, are at our door, and if we so desire it we may gain ample and certain knowledge of each and all. We take pleasure in the beauty of a statue, shall not then the living fill us with delight; and all the more if in the spirit of philosophy we search for causes and recognize the evidences of design. Then will nature's purpose and her deep-seated laws be everywhere revealed, all tending in her multitudinous work to one form or another of the Beautiful.'

Aristotle's voluminous writings have come down to us through many grave vicissitudes. The greatest of them all are happily intact, or very nearly so; but some are lost and others have suffered disorder and corruption. The work known as the 'Parts of Animals' opens (as our text has it) with a chapter which seems meant for a general exordium to the whole series of biological treatises; and I know no chapter in all Aristotle's books which better shows (in plainer English or easier Greek) the master-hand of the great Teacher and Philosopher. He begins by telling us (it has ever since been a common saying) that every science, every branch of knowledge, admits of two sorts of proficiency—that which may properly be termed scientific knowledge, and that which is within the reach of ordinary educated men. He proceeds to discuss the 'method' of scientific inquiry, whether we should begin with the specific and proceed to the general, or whether we are to deal first with common or generical characters and thereafterward with special peculiarities. Are we entitled to treat of animals, as is done in mathematical astronomy, by dealing first with facts or phenomena and then proceeding to discover and relate their several causes? At once this leads to a brief discussion (elaborated elsewhere) of the two great Causes, or aspects of cause—the final cause and the ' moving ' or efficient cause—the *reason why* or the purpose for which, and the antecedent cause which, *of necessity*, brings a thing to be such as it is. Here is one of the great crucial questions of philosophy, and Aristotle's leaning to the side of the Final Cause has been a dominant influence upon the minds of men throughout the whole history of learning. Empedocles had taken another view : he held that the rain comes when it listeth, or ' of necessity '; that we have no right to suppose it comes to make the corn grow in spring, any more than to spoil the autumn sheaves : that the teeth grow by the operation of some natural (or physical) law, and that their apparent and undoubted fitness for cutting and grinding is not purposeful but coincident ; that the backbone is divided into vertebrae because of the antecedent forces, or flexions, which act upon it in the womb. And Empedocles proceeds to the great evolutionary deduction, the clear prevision of Darwin's philosophy, that fit and unfit arise alike, but that what is fit to survive does survive and what is unfit perishes.

The story is far too long and the theme involved too grave and difficult for treatment here. But I would venture to suggest that Aristotle inclined to slur over the physical and lean the more to the final cause, for this simple reason (whatever other reasons there may be), that he was a better biologist than a physicist : that he lacked somewhat the mathematical turn of mind which was intrinsic to the older schools of philosophy. For better for worse the course he took, the choice he made, was of incalculable import, and had power for centuries to guide (dare we say, to bias) the teaching of the schools, the progress of learning, and the innermost beliefs of men.

In this one short but pregnant chapter of Aristotle's there is far more than we can hope even to epitomize. He has much

to say in it of ' classification ', an important matter indeed,
and he discusses it as a great logician should, in all its rigour.
Many commentators have sought for Aristotle's ' classification
of animals ' ; for my part I have never found it, and, in our
sense of the word, I am certain it is not there. An unbending,
unchanging classification of animals would have been something
foreign to all his logic ; it is all very well, it becomes practically
necessary, when we have to arrange our animals on the shelves
of a museum or in the arid pages of a ' systematic ' catalogue ;
and it takes a new complexion when, or if, we can attain to
a real or historical classification, following lines of actual descent
and based on proven facts of historical evolution. But Aristotle
(as it seems to me) neither was bound to a museum catalogue
nor indulged in visions either of a complete *scala naturae* or of
an hypothetical phylogeny. He classified animals as he found
them ; and, as a logician, he had a dichotomy for every
difference which presented itself to his mind. At one time
he divided animals into those with blood and those without,
at another into the air-breathers and the water-breathers ;
into the wild and the tame, the social and the solitary, and
so on in endless ways besides. At the same time he had a
quick eye for the great natural groups, such ' genera ' (as he
called them) as Fish or Bird, Insect or Mollusc. So it comes
to pass that, while he fashioned no hard and fast scheme of
classification, and would undoubtedly (I hold) have thought it
vain to do so, the threads of his several partial or temporary
classifications come together after all, though in a somewhat
hazy pattern, yet in a very beautiful and coherent parti-
coloured web. And though his order is not always our order,
yet a certain exquisite orderliness is of the very essence of his
thought and style. It is the characteristic which Molière hits
upon in *Les Femmes savantes*,—' Je m'attache *pour l'ordre* au
péripatétisme '.

Before he finishes the great chapter of which we have begun
to speak he indicates that there are more ways than one of

relating, or classifying, our facts ; that, for instance, it may be equally proper and necessary to deal now with the animals and their several parts or properties, and at another time with the parts or properties as such, explaining and illustrating them in turn by the several animals which display or possess them. The 'Parts of Animals' is, then, a corollary, a necessary corollary, to the more anecdotal *Historia Animalium*. And yet again, there is a third alternative—to discuss the great functions or actions or potentialities of the organism, as it were first of all in the abstract, and then to correlate them with the parts which in this or that creature are provided and are 'designed' to effect them. This involves the conception and the writing of separate physiological treatises on such themes as Respiration, Locomotion, on Sleeping and Waking, and lastly (and in some respects the most ambitious, most erudite, and most astonishing of them all) the great account of the Generation of Animals.

So the whole range, we might say the whole conceivable range, of biological science is sketched out, and the greater part of the great canvas is painted in. But to bring it into touch with human life, and to make good its claim to the high places of philosophy, we must go yet farther and study Life itself, and what men call the Soul. So grows the great conception. We begin with trivial anecdote, with the things that fisherman, huntsman, peasant know ; the sciences of zoology, anatomy, physiology take shape before our very eyes ; and by evening we sit humbly at the feet of the great teacher of Life itself, the historian of the Soul. It is not for us to attempt to show that even here the story does not end, but the highest chapters of philosophy begin. Then, when we remember that this short narrative of ours is but the faintest adumbration of one side only of the philosopher's many-sided task and enterprise, we begin to rise towards a comprehension of Roger Bacon's saying, that 'although Aristotle did not arrive at the end of knowledge, he set in order all parts of philosophy'. In the same spirit a modern critic declares : 'Il n'a seulement défini et constitué chacune des parties de la science ; il en a de plus montré le lien et l'unité '.

Aristotle, like Shakespeare, is full of old saws, tags of wisdom, jewels five words long. Here is such a one, good for teacher and pupil alike—Δεῖ πιστεύειν τὸν μανθάνοντα. It tells us that the road to Learning lies through Faith ; and it means that to be a scholar one should have a heart as well as brains.

By reason partly of extraneous interpolation, but doubtless also through a lingering credulity from which even philosophers are not immune, we find in Aristotle many a strange story. The goats that breathe through their ears, the vulture impregnated by the wind, the eagle that dies of hunger, the stag caught by music, the salamander which walks through fire, the unicorn, the mantichore, are but a few of the 'Vulgar Errors ' or 'Received Tenents ' (as Sir Thomas Browne has it) which are perpetuated, not originated, in the *Historia Animalium*. Some of them come, through Persia, from the farther East : and others (we meet with them once more in Horapollo the Egyptian priest) are but the exoteric or allegorical expression of the arcana of ancient Egyptian religion.

So it comes to pass that for two thousand years and throughout all lands men have come to Aristotle, and found in him information and instruction—that which they desired. Arab and Moor and Syrian and Jew treasured his books while the western world sat in darkness ; the great centuries of Scholasticism hung upon his words ; the oldest of our Universities, Bologna, Paris, Oxford, were based upon his teaching, yea, all but established for his study. Where he has been, there, seen or unseen, his influence remains ; even the Moor and the Arab find in him, to this day, a teacher after their own hearts : a teacher of eternal verities, telling of sleep and dreams, of youth and age, of life and death, of generation and corruption, of growth and of decay : a guide to the book of Nature, a revealer of the Spirit, a prophet of the works of God.

The purpose of these little essays, I have been told (though I had half forgotten it), is to help though ever so little to defend and justify the study of the language and the vast literature of Greece. It is a task for which I am unfitted and unprepared. When Oliver Goldsmith proposed to teach Greek at Leyden, where he 'had been told it was a desideratum', the Principal of that celebrated University met him (as we all know) with weighty objections. 'I never learned Greek', said the Principal, 'and I don't find that I have ever missed it. I have had a Doctor's cap and gown without Greek. I have ten thousand florins a year without Greek; and, in short', continued he, 'as I don't know Greek, I do not believe there is any good in it.'—I have heard or read the story again and again, for is it not written in the *Vicar of Wakefield* ? But I never heard that any man, not Goldsmith himself, attempted to confute the argument. I agree for the most part with the Principal, and can see clearly that all the Greek that Goldsmith knew, and all the Greek in all the world, would have meant nothing and done nothing for him. But there is and will be many another who finds in Greek wisdom and sweet Hellenic speech something which he needs must have, and lacking which he would be poor indeed : something which is as a staff in his hand, a light upon his path, a lantern to his feet.

In this workaday world we may still easily possess ourselves, as Gibbon says the subjects of the Byzantine Throne, even in their lowest servitude and depression, were still possessed, ' of a golden key that could unlock the treasures of antiquity, of a musical and prolific language that gives a soul to the objects of sense, and a body to the abstractions of philosophy '.

Our very lives seem prolonged by the recollection of antiquity ; for, as Cicero says, not to know what has been transacted in former times is to continue always a child. I borrow the citation from Dr. Johnson, who reminds us also of a saying of Aristotle himself, that as students we ought first to examine and understand what has been written by the ancients, and then cast our eyes round upon the world. And Johnson prefaces both quotations by another :

> Tibi res antiquae laudis et artis
> ingredior, sanctos ausus recludere fontes.

But now I, who have dared to draw my tiny draft from Aristotle's great well, seem after all to be seeking an excuse, seeking it in example and precept. Precept, at least, I know to be of no avail. My father spent all the many days of his life in the study of Greek ; you might suppose it was for Wisdom's sake,—but my father was a modest man. The fact is, he did it for a simpler reason still, a very curious reason, to be whispered rather than told : he did it *for love*.

Nigh forty years ago, I first stepped out on the east-windy streets of a certain lean and hungry town (lean, I mean, as regards scholarship) where it was to be my lot to spend thereafter many and many a year. And the very first thing I saw there was an inscription over a very humble doorway, ' *Hic mecum habitant Dante, Cervantes, Molière* '. It was the home of a poor schoolmaster, who as a teacher of languages eked out the scanty profits of his school. I was not a little comforted by the announcement. So the poor scholar, looking on the ragged regiment of his few books, is helped, consoled, exalted by the reflection : *Hic mecum habitant . . . Homerus, Plato, Aristoteles*. And were one in a moment of inadvertence to inquire of him why he occupied himself with Greek, he might perchance stammer (like Dominie Sampson) an almost inarticulate reply ; but more probably he would be stricken speechless by the enormous outrage of the request, and the reason of his devotion would be hidden from the questioner for ever.

D'ARCY WENTWORTH THOMPSON.

BIOLOGY

Before Aristotle

WHAT is science? It is a question that cannot be answered easily, nor perhaps answered at all. None of the definitions seem to cover the field exactly; they are either too wide or too narrow. But we can see science in its growth and we can say that being a process it can exist only as growth. Where does the science of biology begin? Again we cannot say, but we can watch its evolution and its progress. Among the Greeks the accurate observation of living forms, which is at least one of the essentials of biological science, goes back very far. The word *Biology*, used in our sense, would, it is true, have been an impossibility among them, for *bios* refers to the life of man and could not be applied, except in a strained or metaphorical sense, to that of other living things.[1] But the *ideas* we associate with the word are clearly developed in Greek philosophy and the foundations of biology are of great antiquity.

The Greek people had many roots, racial, cultural, and spiritual, and from them all they inherited various powers and qualities and derived various ideas and traditions. The most suggestive source for our purpose is that of the Minoan race whom they dispossessed and whose lands they occupied. That highly gifted people exhibited in all stages of its development a marvellous power of graphically representing animal forms, of which the famous Cretan friezes, Vaphio cups (Fig. 5), and

---

[1] The word *Biology* was introduced by Gottfried Reinhold Treviranus (1776–1837) in his *Biologie oder die Philosophie der lebenden Natur*, 6 vols., Göttingen, 1802–22, and was adopted by J.-B. de Lamarck (1744–1829) in his *Hydrogéologie*, Paris, 1802. It is probable that the first English use of the word in its modern sense is by Sir William Lawrence (1783–1867) in his work *On the Physiology, Zoology, and Natural History of Man*, London, 1819; there are earlier English uses of the word, however, contrasted with *biography*.

Mycenean lions provide well-known examples. It is difficult not to believe that the Minoan element, entering into the mosaic of peoples that we call the Greeks, was in part at least responsible for the like graphic power developed in the Hellenic world, though little contact has yet been demonstrated between Minoan and archaic Greek Art.

For the earliest biological achievements of Greek peoples we have to rely largely on information gleaned from artistic remains. It is true that we have a few fragments of the works of both Ionian and Italo-Sicilian philosophers, and in them we read of theoretical speculation as to the nature of life and of the soul, and we can thus form some idea of the first attempts of such workers as Alcmaeon of Croton (*c.* 500 B.C.) to lay bare the structure of animals by dissection.[1] The pharmacopœia also of some of the earliest works of the Hippocratic collection betrays considerable knowledge of both native and foreign plants.[2] Moreover, scattered through the pages of Herodotus and other early writers is a good deal of casual information concerning animals and plants, though such material is second-hand and gives us little information concerning the habit of exact observation that is the necessary basis of science.

Something more is, however, revealed by early Greek Art. We are in possession of a series of vases of the seventh and sixth centuries before the Christian era showing a closeness of observation of animal forms that tells of a people awake to the study of nature. We have thus portrayed for us a number of animals— plants seldom or never appear—and among the best rendered are wild creatures; we see antelopes quietly feeding or startled at a sound, birds flying or picking worms from the ground, fallow

[1] The remains of Alcmaeon are given in H. Diel's *Die Fragmente der Vorsokratiker*, Berlin, 1903, p. 103. Alcmaeon is considered in the companion chapter on *Greek Medicine*.

[2] Especially the περὶ γυναικείης φύσιος, *On the nature of woman*, and the περὶ γυναικείων, *On the diseases of women*.

deer forcing their way through thickets, browsing peacefully, or galloping away, boars facing the hounds and dogs chasing hares, wild cattle forming their defensive circle, hawks seizing

Fig. 1. Lioness and young from an Ionian vase of the sixth century B.C. found at Caere in Southern Etruria (Louvre, Salle E, No. 298), from *Le Dessin des Animaux en Grèce d'après les vases peints*, by J. Morin, Paris (Renouard), 1911. The animal is drawing itself up to attack its hunters. The scanty mane, the form of the paws, the udders, and the dentition are all heavily though accurately represented.

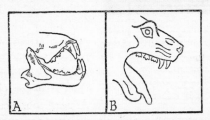

Fig. 2. A, Jaw bones of lion; B, head of lioness from Caere vase (Fig. 1), after Morin. Note the careful way in which the artist has distinguished the molar from the cutting teeth.

their prey. Many of these exhibit minutely accurate observation. The very direction of the hairs on the animals' coats has sometimes been closely studied, and often the muscles are well rendered. In some cases even the dentition has been found accurately portrayed, as in a sixth-century representation on an Ionian vase of a lioness—an animal then very rare on the Eastern Mediterranean littoral, but still known in Babylonia, Syria, and Asia Minor. The details of the work show that the artist must have examined the animal in captivity (Figs. 1 and 2).

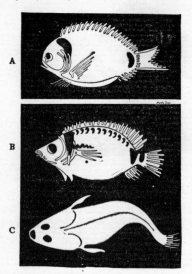

Fig. 3. Paintings of fish on plates. Italo-Greek work of the fourth century B.C. From Morin.

A. Sargus vulgaris.

B. Crenilabrus mediterraneus.

C. Uranoscopus scaber ?

Animal paintings of this order are found scattered over the Greek world with special centres or schools in such places as Cyprus, Boeotia, or Chalcis. The very name for a painter in Greek, *zoographos*, recalls the attention paid to living forms. By the fifth century, in painting them as in other departments of Art, the supremacy of Attica had asserted itself, and there are many beautiful Attic vase-paintings of animals to place by the side of the magnificent horses' heads of the Parthenon (Fig. 6). In Attica, too, was early developed a characteristic and closely accurate type of representation of marine forms, and this attained a wider vogue in Southern Italy in the fourth century. From the latter period a number of dishes and vases have come down to us bearing a large variety of fish forms, portrayed with an exactness that is interesting in view of the attention to marine creatures in the surviving literature of Aristotelian origin (Fig. 3).

These artistic products are more than a mere reflex of the

daily life of the people. The habits and positions of animals
are observed by the hunter, as are the forms and colours of
fish by the fisherman ; but the methods of huntsman and
fisher do not account for the accurate portrayal of a lion's
dentition, the correct numbering of a fish's scales or the close
study of the lie of the feathers on the head, and the pads on
the feet, of a bird of prey (Fig. 4). With observations such as
these we are in the presence of something worthy of the name
Biology. Though but little literature on that topic earlier

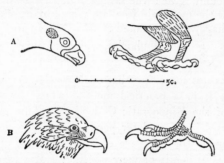

FIG. 4. Head and talons of the Sea-eagle, *Haliaëtus albicilla*:
  A, From an Ionic vase of the sixth century B. C.
  B, Drawn from the object.
From Morin.

than the writings of Aristotle has come down to us, yet both
the character of his writings and such paintings and pictures
as these, suggest the existence of a strong interest and a wide
literature, biological in the modern sense, antecedent to the
fourth century.

Greek science, however, exhibits throughout its history
a peculiar characteristic differentiating it from the modern
scientific standpoint. Most of the work of the Greek scientist
was done in relation to man. Nature interested him mainly
in relation to himself. The Greek scientific and philosophic
world was an anthropocentric world, and this comes out in

the overwhelming mass of medical as distinct from biological writings that have come down to us. Such, too, is the sentiment expressed by the poets in their descriptions of the animal creation :

Many wonders there be, but naught more wondrous than man :

. . . .

The light-witted birds of the air, the beasts of the weald and
    the wood
He traps with his woven snare, and the brood of the briny flood.
Master of cunning he : the savage bull, and the hart
Who roams the mountain free, are tamed by his infinite art.
And the shaggy rough-maned steed is broken to bear the bit.

Sophocles, *Antigone*, verses 342 ff.
(Translation of F. Storr.)

It is thus not surprising that our first systematic treatment of animals is in a practical medical work, the περὶ διαίτης, *On diet*, of the Hippocratic Collection. This very peculiar treatise dates from the later part of the fifth century. It is strongly under the influence of Heracleitus (*c.* 540–475) and contains many points of view which reappear in later philosophy. All animals, according to it, are formed of fire and water, nothing is born and nothing dies, but there is a perpetual and eternal revolution of things, so that change itself is the only reality. Man's nature is but a parallel to that of the universal nature, and the arts of man are but an imitation or reflex of the natural arts or, again, of the bodily functions. The soul, a mixture of water and fire, consumes itself in infancy and old age, and increases during adult life. Here, too, we meet with that singular doctrine, not without bearing on the course of later biological thought, that in the foetus all parts are formed simultaneously. On the proportion of fire and water in the body all depends, sex, temper, temperament, intellect. Such speculative ideas separate this book from the sober method of the more typical Hippocratic medical works with which indeed it has little in common.

After having discussed these theoretical matters the work turns to its own practical concerns, and in the course of setting out the natures of foods gives in effect a rough classification of animals. These are set forth in groups, and from among the larger groups only the reptiles and insects are missing. The list has been described, perhaps hardly with justification, as the *Coan classificatory system*. We have here, indeed, no *system* in the sense in which that word is now applied to the animal kingdom, but we have yet some sort of definite arrangement of animals according to their supposed natures. The passage opens with mammals, which are divided into domesticated and wild, the latter being mentioned in order according to size, next follow the land-birds, then the water-fowl, and then the fishes. These fish are divided into (1) the haunters of the shore, (2) the free-swimming forms, (3) the cartilaginous fishes or Selachii, which are not so named but are placed together, (4) the mud-loving forms, and (5) the fresh-water fish. Finally come invertebrates arranged in some sort of order according to their structure. The characteristic feature of the ' classification ' is the separation of the fish from the remaining vertebrates and of the invertebrates from both. Of the fifty animals named no less than twenty are fish, about a fifth of the number studied by Aristotle, but we must remember that here only edible species are mentioned. The existence of the work shows at least that in the fifth century there was already a close and accurate study of animal forms, a study that may justly be called scientific. The predominance of fish and their classification in greater detail than the other groups is not an unexpected feature. The Mediterranean is especially rich in these forms, the Greeks were a maritime people, and Greek literature is full of imagery drawn from the fisher's craft. From Minoan to Byzantine times the variety, beauty, and colour of fish made a deep impression on Greek minds as reflected in their art.

Much more important, however, for subsequent biological

development than such observations on the nature and habits of animals, is the service that the Hippocratic physicians rendered to Anatomy and to Physiology, departments in which the structure of man and of the domesticated animals stands apart from that of the rest of the animal kingdom. It is with the nature and constitution of man that most of the surviving early biological writings are concerned, and in these departments are unmistakable tendencies towards systematic arrangement of the material. Thus we have division and description of the body in sevens from the periphery to the centre and from the vertex to the sole of the foot,[1] or a division into four regions or zones.[2] The teaching concerning the four elements and four humours too became of great importance and some of it was later adopted by Aristotle. We also meet numerous mechanical explanations of bodily structures, comparisons between anatomical conditions encountered in related animals, experiments on living creatures,[3] systematic incubation of hen's eggs for the study of their development, parallels drawn between the development of plants and of human and animal embryos, theories of generation, among which is that which was afterwards called ' pangenesis '—discussion of the survival of the stronger over the weaker—almost our survival of the fittest—and a theory of inheritance of acquired characters.[4] All these things show not only extensive knowledge but also an attempt to apply such knowledge to human needs. When we consider how even in later centuries biology was linked with medicine, and how powerful and fundamental was the influence of the Hippocratic writings, not only on their immediate successors in antiquity, but also on the Middle Ages and right into the nineteenth century, we shall recognize the significance of these developments.

[1] περὶ ἑβδομάδων. The Greek text is lost. We have, however, an early and barbarous Latin translation, and there has recently been printed an Arabic commentary. G. Bergsträsser, *Pseudogaleni in Hippocratis de septimanis commentarium ab Hunnino Q. F. arabice versum*, Leipzig, 1914.

[2] περὶ νούσων δ'.   [3] περὶ καρδίης.   [4] Especially in the περὶ γονῆς.

Fig. 5. MINOAN GOLD CUP. SIXTEENTH CENTURY B.C.

Fig. 6. HORSE'S HEAD. FROM PARTHENON. 440 B.C.

Such was the character of biological thought within the fifth century, and a generation inspired by this movement produced some noteworthy works in the period which immediately followed. In the treatise περὶ τροφῆς, *On nourishment*, which may perhaps be dated about 400 b. c., we learn of the pulse for the first time in Greek medical literature, and read of a physiological system which lasted until the time of Harvey, with the arteries arising from the heart and the veins from the liver. Of about the same date is a work περὶ καρδίης, *On the heart*, which describes the ventricles as well as the great vessels and their valves, and compares the heart of animals with that of man.

A little later, perhaps 390 b. c., is the treatise περὶ σαρκῶν, *On muscles*, which contains much more than its title suggests. It has the old system of sevens and, inspired perhaps by the philosophy of Heracleitus (*c.* 540–475), describes the heart as sending air, fire, and movement to the different parts of the body through the vessels which are themselves constantly in movement. The infant in its mother's womb is believed to draw in air and fire through its mouth and to eat *in utero*. The action of air on the blood is compared to its action on fire. In contrast to some of the other Hippocratic treatises the central nervous system is in the background ; much attention, however, is given to the special senses. The brain resounds during audition. The olfactory nerves are hollow, lead to the brain, and convey volatile substances to it which cause it to secrete mucus. The eyes also have been examined, and their coats and humours roughly described; an allusion, the first in literature, is perhaps made to the crystalline lens, and the eyes of animals are compared with those of man. There is evidence not only of dissection but of experiment, and in efforts to compare the resistance of various tissues to such processes as boiling, we may see the small beginning of chemical physiology.

An abler work than any of these, but exhibiting less power of observation is a treatise, περὶ γονῆς, *On generation*, that may perhaps be dated about 380 B. C.[1] It exhibits a writer of much philosophic power, very anxious for physiological explanations, but hampered by ignorance of physics. He has, in fact, the weaknesses and in a minor degree the strength of his successor Aristotle, of whose great work on generation he gives us a foretaste. He sets forth in considerable detail a doctrine of pangenesis, not wholly unlike that of Darwin. In order to explain the phenomena of inheritance he supposes that vessels reach the seed, carrying with them samples from all parts of the body. He believes that channels pass from all the organs to the brain and then to the spinal marrow (or to the marrow direct), thence to the kidneys and on to the genital organs ; he believes, too, that he knows the actual location of one such channel, for he observes, wrongly, that incision behind the ears, by interrupting the passage, leads to impotence. As an outcome of this theory he is prepared to accept inheritance of acquired characters. The embryo develops and breathes by material transmitted from the mother through the umbilical cord. We encounter here also a very detailed description of a specimen of exfoliated *membrana mucosa uteri* which our author mistakes for an embryo, but his remarks at least exhibit the most eager curiosity.[2]

The author of this work on generation is thus a ' biologist ' in the modern sense, and among the passages exhibiting him in this light is his comparison of the human embryo with the chick. ' The embryo is in a membrane in the centre of which is the navel through which it draws and gives its breath, and the

---

[1] The three works περὶ γονῆς, περὶ φύσιος παιδίου, περὶ νούσων δ', *On generation, on the nature of the embryo, on diseases, book IV*, form really one treatise on generation.

[2] περὶ φύσιος παιδίου, *On the nature of the embryo*, § 13. The same experience is described in the περὶ σαρκῶν, *On the muscles*.

membranes arise from the umbilical cord. . . . The structure of the child you will find from first to last as I have already described. . . . If you wish, try this experiment : take twenty or more eggs and let them be incubated by two or more hens. Then each day from the second to that of hatching remove an egg, break it, and examine it. You will find exactly as I say, for the nature of the bird can be likened to that of man. The membranes [you will see] proceed from the umbilical cord, and all that I have said on the subject of the infant you will find in a bird's egg, and one who has made these observations will be surprised to find an umbilical cord in a bird's egg.' [1]

The same interest that he exhibits for the development of man and animals he shows also for plants.

' A seed laid in the ground fills itself with the juices there contained, for the soil contains in itself juices of every nature for the nourishment of plants. Thus filled with juice the seed is distended and swells, and thereby the power (=faculty ἡ δύναμις) diffused in the seed is compressed by pneuma and juice, and bursting the seed becomes the first leaves. But a time comes when these leaves can no longer get nourished from the juices in the seed. Then the seed and the leaves erupt below, for urged by the leaves the seed sends down that part of its power which is yet concentrated within it and so the roots are produced as an extension of the leaves. When at last the plant is well rooted below and is drawing its nutriment from the earth, then the whole grain disappears, being absorbed, save for the husk, which is the most solid part ; and even that, decomposing in the earth, ultimately becomes invisible. In time some of the leaves put forth branches. The plant being thus produced by humidity from the seed is still soft and moist. Growing actively both above and below, it cannot as yet bear fruit, for it has not the quality of force and reserve (δύναμις ἰσχυρὴ καὶ πιαρά) from which a seed can be precipitated. But when, with time, the plant becomes firmer and better rooted, it develops veins as passages both

---

[1] περὶ φύσιος παιδίου, *On the nature of the embryo*, § 29.

upwards and downwards, and it draws from the soil not only water but more abundantly also substances that are denser and fatter. Warmed, too, by the sun, these act as a ferment to the extremities and give rise to fruit after its kind. The fruit thus develops much from little, for every plant draws from the earth a power more abundant than that with which it started, and the fermentation takes place not at one place but at many.'[1]

Nor does our author hesitate to draw an analogy between the plant and the mammalian embryo. ' In the same way the infant lives within its mother's womb and in a state corresponding to the health of the mother . . . and you will find a complete similitude between the products of the soil and the products of the womb.'

The early Greek literature is so scantily provided with illustrations drawn from botanical study, that it is worth considering the remarkable comparison of generation of plants from cuttings and from seeds in the same work.

' As regards plants generated from cuttings . . . that part of a branch where it was cut from a tree is placed in the earth and there rootlets are sent out. This is how it happens : The part of the plant within the soil draws up juices, swells, and develops a pneuma ($\pi\nu\epsilon\hat{v}\mu\alpha$ $\check{\iota}\sigma\chi\epsilon\iota$), but not so the part without. The pneuma and the juice concentrate the power of the plant below so that it becomes denser. Then the lower end erupts and gives forth tender roots. Then the plant, taking from below, draws juices from the roots and transmits them to the part above the soil which thus also swells and develops pneuma ; thus the power from being diffused in the plant becomes concentrated and budding, gives forth leaves. . . . Cuttings, then, differ from seeds. With a seed the leaves are borne first, then the roots are sent down ; with a cutting the roots form first and then the leaves.'[2]

But with these works of the early part of the fourth century the first stage of Greek biology reaches its finest development.

[1] $\pi\epsilon\rho\grave{\iota}$ $\phi\acute{v}\sigma\iota\sigma$ $\pi\alpha\iota\delta\acute{\iota}\sigma\nu$, *On the nature of the embryo*, § 22.
[2] Ibid. § 23.

Later Hippocratic treatises which deal with physiological topics are on a lower plane, and we must seek some external cause for the failure. Nor have we far to seek. This period saw the rise of a movement that had the most profound influence on every department of thought. We see the advent into the Greek world of a great intellectual movement as a result of which the department of philosophy that dealt with nature receded before Ethics. Of that intellectual revolution—perhaps the greatest the world has seen—Athens was the site and Socrates (470–399) the protagonist. With the movement itself and its characteristic fruit we are not concerned. But the great successor and pupil of its founder gives us in the *Timaeus* a picture of the depth to which natural science can be degraded in the effort to give a specific teleological meaning to all parts of the visible Universe. The book and the picture which it draws, dark and repulsive to the mind trained in modern scientific method, enthralled the imagination of a large part of mankind for wellnigh two thousand years. Organic nature appears in this work of Plato (427–347) as the degeneration of man whom the Creator has made most perfect. The school that held this view ultimately decayed as a result of its failure to advance positive knowledge. As the centuries went by its views became further and further divorced from phenomena, and the bizarre developments of later Neoplatonism stand to this day as a warning against any system which shall neglect the investigation of nature. But in its decay Platonism dragged science down and destroyed by neglect nearly all earlier bio-logical material. Mathematics, not being a phenomenal study, suited better the Neoplatonic mood and continued to advance, carrying astronomy with it for a while—astronomy that affected the life of man and that soon became the handmaid of astrology; medicine, too, that determined the conditions of man's life was also cherished, though often mistakenly, but pure science was doomed.

But though the ethical view of nature overwhelmed science in the end, the advent of the mighty figure of Aristotle (384–322) stayed the tide for a time. Yet the writer on Greek Biology remains at a disadvantage in contrast with the Historian of Greek Mathematics, of Greek Astronomy, or of Greek Medicine, in the scantiness of the materials for presenting an account of the development of his studies before Aristotle. The huge form of that magnificent naturalist completely overshadows Greek as it does much of later Biology.

CHARLES SINGER.

After Aristotle

ALL Aristotle's surviving biological works refer primarily to the animal creation. His work on plants is lost or rather has survived as the merest corrupted fragment. We are fortunate, however, in the possession of a couple of complete works by his pupil and successor Theophrastus (372–287), which may not only be taken to represent the Aristotelian attitude towards the plant world, but also give us an inkling of the general state of biological science in the generation which succeeded the master.

These treatises of Theophrastus are in many respects the most complete and orderly of all ancient biological works that have reached our time. They give an idea of the kind of interest that the working scientist of that day could develop when inspired rather by the genius of a great teacher than by the power of his own thoughts. Theophrastus is a pedestrian where Aristotle is a creature of wings, he is in a relation to the master of the same order that the morphologists of the second half of the nineteenth century were to Darwin. For a couple of generations after the appearance of the *Origin of Species* in 1859 the industry and ability of naturalists all over the world were occupied in working out in detail the structure

Fig. 7.   A R I S T O T L E

From HERCULANEUM
Probably work of fourth century B. C.

and mode of life of living things on the basis of the Evolutionary philosophy. Nearly all the work on morphology and much of that on physiology since his time might be treated as a commentary on the works of Darwin. These volumes of Theophrastus give the same impression. They represent the remains—alas, almost the only biological remains—of a school working under the impulse of a great idea and spurred by the memory of a great teacher. As such they afford a parallel to much scientific work of our own day, produced by men without genius save that provided by a vision and a hope and an ideal. Of such men it is impossible to write as of Aristotle. Their lives are summed up by their actual achievement, and since Theophrastus is an orderly writer whose works have descended to us in good state, he is a very suitable instance of the actual standard of achievement of ancient biology. 'Without vision the people perish' and the very breath of life of science is drawn, and can only be drawn, from that very small band of prophets who from time to time, during the ages, have provided the great generalizations and the great ideals. In this light let us examine the work of Theophrastus.

In the absence of any adequate system of classification, almost all botany until the seventeenth century consisted mainly of descriptions of species. To describe accurately a leaf or a root in the language in ordinary use would often take pages. Modern botanists have invented an elaborate terminology which, however hideous to eye and ear, has the crowning merit of helping to abbreviate scientific literature. Botanical writers previous to the seventeenth century were substantially without this special mode of expression. It is partly to this lack that we owe the persistent attempts throughout the centuries to represent plants pictorially in herbals, manuscript and printed, and thus the possibility of an adequate history of plant illustration.

Theophrastus seems to have felt acutely the need of botanical terms, and there are cases in which he seeks to give a special technical meaning to words in more or less current use. Among such words are *carpos* = fruit, *pericarpion* = seed vessel = pericarp, and *metra*, the word used by him for the central core of any stem whether formed of wood, pith, or other substance. It is from the usage of Theophrastus that the exact definition of fruit and pericarp has come down to us.[1] We may easily discern also the purpose for which he introduces into botany the term *metra*, a word meaning primarily the *womb*, and the vacancy in the Greek language which it was made to fill. ' *Metra*,' he says, ' is that which is in the middle of the wood, being third in order from the bark and [thus] like to the marrow in bones. Some call it the *heart* (καρδίαν), others the *inside* (ἐντεριώνην), yet others call only the innermost part of the metra itself the heart, while others again call this *marrow*.'[2] He is thus inventing a word to cover all the different kinds of core and importing it from another study. This is the method of modern scientific nomenclature which hardly existed for botanists even as late as the sixteenth century of our era. The real foundations of our modern nomenclature were laid in the later sixteenth and in the seventeenth century by Cesalpino and Joachim Jung.

Theophrastus understood the value of developmental study, a conception derived from his master. ' A plant ', he says, ' has power of germination in all its parts, for it has life in them all, wherefore we should regard them not for what they are but for what they are becoming.'[3] The various modes of plant reproduction are correctly distinguished in a way that passes beyond the only surviving earlier treatise that deals in

---

[1] It is possible that Theophrastus derived the word pericarp from Aristotle. Cp. *De anima*, ii. 1, 412 b 2. In the passage τὸ φύλλον περικαρπίου σκέπασμα, τὸ δὲ περικάρπιον καρποῦ, in the *De anima* the word does not, however, seem to have the full technical force that Theophrastus gives to it.

[2] *Historia plantarum*, i. 2, vi.   [3] *Ibid*. i. 1, iv.

detail with the subject, the Hippocratic work *On genera-tion.* ' The manner of generation of trees and plants are these : spontaneous, from a seed, from a root, from a piece torn off, from a branch or twig, from the trunk itself, or from pieces of the wood cut up small.' [1] The marvel of germination must have awakened admiration from a very early date. We have already seen it occupying a more ancient author, and it had also been one of the chief preoccupations of Aristotle. It is thus not remarkable that the process should impress Theophrastus, who has left on record his views on the forma-tion of the plant from the seed.

' Some germinate, root and leaves, from the same point, some separately from either end of the seed. Thus wheat, barley, spelt, and all such cereals [germinate] from either end, corresponding to the position [of the seed] in the ear, the root from the stout lower part, the shoot from the upper ; but the two, root and stem, form a single continuous whole. The bean and other leguminous plants are not so, but in them root and stem are from the same point, namely, their place of attachment to the pod, where, it is plain, they have their origin. In some cases there is a process, as in beans, chick peas, and especially lupines, from which the root grows downward, the leaf and stem upward. . . . In certain trees the bud first germinates within the seed, and, as it increases in size, the seeds split—all such seeds are, as it were, in two halves ; again, all those of leguminous plants have plainly two lobes and are double—and then the root is immediately thrust out. But in cereals, the seeds being in one piece, this does not happen, but the root grows a little before [the shoot].

' Barley and wheat come up monophyllous, but peas, beans, and chick peas polyphyllous. All leguminous plants have a single woody root, from which grow slender side roots . . . but wheat, barley, and the other cereals have numerous slender roots by which they are matted together. . . . There is a con-trast between these two kinds ; the leguminous plants have

[1] *Historia plantarum,* ii. 1, i.

a single root and have many side-growths above from the
[single] stem . . . while the cereals have many roots and send
up many shoots, but these have no side-shoots.'[1]

There can be no doubt that here is a piece of minute
observation on the behaviour of germinating seeds. The distinction between dicotyledons and monocotyledons is accurately
set forth, though the stress is laid not so much on the coty-
ledonous character of the seed as on the relation of root and
shoot. In the dicotyledons root and shoot are represented as
springing from the same point, and in monocotyledons from
opposite poles in the seed.

No further effective work was done on the germinating seed
until the invention of the microscope, and the appearance of
the work of Highmore (1613–85),[2] and the much more searching
investigations of Malpighi (1628–94)[3] and Grew (1641–1712)[4]
after the middle of the seventeenth century. The observations
of Theophrastus are, however, so accurate, so lucid, and so
complete that they might well be used as legends for the plates
of these writers two thousand years after him.

Much has been written as to the knowledge of the sex of
plants among the ancients. It may be stated that of the sexual
elements of the flower no ancient writer had any clear idea.
Nevertheless, sex is often attributed to plants, and the simile
of the *Loves of Plants* enters into works of the poets. Plants
are frequently described as male and female in ancient biological writings also, and Pliny goes so far as to say that some
students considered that all herbs and trees were sexual.[5] Yet
when such passages can be tested it will be found that these
so-called males and females are usually different species. In

[1] *Historia plantarum*, viii. 1, i.
[2] Nathaniel Highmore, *A History of Generation*, London, 1651.
[3] Marcello Malpighi, *Anatome plantarum*, London, 1675.
[4] Nehemiah Grew, *Anatomy of Vegetables begun*, London, 1672.
[5] Pliny, *Naturalis historia*, xiii. 4.

a few cases a sterile variety is described as the male and a fertile as the female. In a small residuum of cases diœcious plants or flowers are regarded as male and female, but with no real comprehension of the sexual nature of the flowers. There remain the palms, in which the knowledge of plant sex had advanced a trifle farther. ' With dates ', says Theophrastus, ' the males should be brought to the females ; for the males make the fruit persist and ripen, and this some call by analogy *to use the wild fig* (ὀλυνθάζειν).[1] The process is thus : when the male is in the flower they at once cut off the spathe with the flower and shake the bloom, with its flower and dust, over the fruit of the female, and, if it is thus treated, it retains the fruit and does not shed it.'[2] The fertilizing character of the spathe of the male date palm was familiar in Babylon from a very early date. It is recorded by Herodotus[3] and is represented by a frequent symbol on the Assyrian monuments.

The comparison of the fertilization of the date palm to the use of the wild fig refers to the practice of Caprification. Theophrastus tells us that there are certain trees, the fig among them, which are apt to shed their fruit prematurely. To remedy this ' the device adopted is caprification. Gall insects come out of the wild figs which are hanging there, eat the tops of the cultivated figs, and so make them swell '.[4] These gall-insects ' are engendered from the seeds '.[5] Theophrastus distinguished between the process as applied to the fig and the date, observing that ' in both [fig and date] the

[1] The curious word ὀλυνθάζειν, here translated *to use the wild fig*, is from ὄλυνθος, a kind of wild fig which seldom ripens. The special meaning here given to the word is explained in another work of Theophrastus, *De causis plantarum*, ii. 9, xv. After describing caprification in figs, he says τὸ δὲ ἐπὶ τῶν φοινίκων συμβαῖνον οὐ ταὐτὸν μέν, ἔχει δέ τινα ὁμοιότητα τούτῳ δι' ὃ καλοῦσιν ὀλυνθάζειν αὐτούς ' The same thing is not done with dates, but something analogous to it, whence this is called ὀλυνθάζειν '.

[2] *Historia plantarum*, ii. 8, iv.   [3] Herodotus i. 193.
[4] *Historia plantarum*, ii. 8, i.   [5] *Ibid.* ii. 8, ii.

male aids the female—for they call the fruit-bearing [palm] *female*—but whilst in the one there is a union of the two sexes, in the other things are different '.[1]

Theophrastus was not very successful in distinguishing the nature of the primary elements of plants, though he was able to separate root, stem, leaf, stipule, and flower on morphological as well as to a limited extent on physiological grounds. For the root he adopts the familiar definition, the only one possible before the rise of chemistry, that it ' is that by which the plant draws up nourishment ',[2] a description that applies to the account given by the pre-Aristotelian author of the work περὶ γονῆς, *On generation.* But Theophrastus shows by many examples that he is capable of following out morphological homologies. Thus he knows that the ivy regularly puts forth roots from the shoots between the leaves, by means of which it gets hold of trees and walls,[3] that the mistletoe will not sprout except on the bark of living trees into which it strikes its roots, and that the very peculiar formation of the mangrove tree is to be explained by the fact that ' this plant sends out roots from the shoots till it has hold on the ground and roots again : and so there comes to be a continuous circle of roots round the tree, not connected with the main stem, but at a distance from it '.[4] He does not succeed, however, in distinguishing the real nature of such structures as bulbs, rhizomes, and tubers, but regards them all as roots. Nor is he more successful in his discussion of the nature of stems. As to leaves, he is more definite and satisfactory, though wholly in the dark as to their function ; he is quite clear that the pinnate leaf of the rowan tree, for instance, is a leaf and not a branch.

Notwithstanding his lack of insight as to the nature of sex in flowers, he attains to an approximately correct idea of the

[1] *Historia plantarum,* ii. 8, iv. [2] *Ibid.* i. 1, ix.
[3] *Ibid.* iii. 18, x. [4] *De causis plantarum,* ii. 23.

Fig. 8.   THEOPHRASTUS

From VILLA ALBANI
Copy (second century A. D.?) of earlier work

relation of flower and fruit. Some plants, he says, 'have [the flower] around the fruit itself as vine and olive; [the flowers] of the latter, when they drop, look as though they had a hole through them, and this is taken for a sign that it has blossomed well; for if [the flower] is burnt up or sodden, the fruit falls with it, and so it does not become pierced. Most flowers have the fruit case in the middle, or it may be the flower is on the top of the pericarp as in pomegranate, apple, pear, plum, and myrtle . . . for these have their seeds below the flower. . . . In some cases again the flower is on top of the seeds themselves as in . . . all thistle-like plants'.[1] Thus Theophrastus has succeeded in distinguishing between the hypogynous, perigynous, and epigynous types of flower, and has almost come to regard its relation to the fruit as the essential floral element.

Theophrastus has a perfectly clear idea of plant distribution as dependent on soil and climate, and at times seems to be on the point of passing from a statement of climatic distribution into one of real geographical regions. The general question of plant distribution long remained at, if it did not recede from, the position where he left it. The usefulness of the manuscript and early printed herbals in the West was for centuries marred by the retention of plant descriptions prepared for the Greek East and Latin South, and these works were saved from complete ineffectiveness only by an occasional appeal to nature.

With the death of Theophrastus about 287 B.C. pure biological science substantially disappears from the Greek world, and we get the same type of deterioration that is later encountered in other scientific departments. Science ceases to have the motive of the desire to know, and becomes an applied study, subservient to the practical arts. It is an attitude from which in the end applied science itself must suffer also. Yet the centuries that

[1] *Historia plantarum*, i. 13, iii.

follow were not without biological writers of very great ability. In the medical school of Alexandria anatomy and physiology became placed on a firm basis from about 300 B.C., but always in the position subordinate to medicine that they have since occupied. Two great names of that school, Herophilus and Erasistratus, we must consider elsewhere.[1] Their works have disappeared and we have the merest fragments of them. In the last pre-Christian and the first two post-Christian centuries, however, there were several writers, portions of whose works have survived and are of great biological importance. Among them we include Crateuas, a botanical writer and illustrator, who greatly developed, if he did not actually introduce, the method of representing plants systematically by illustration rather than by description. This method, important still, was even more important when there was no proper system of botanical nomenclature. Crateuas by his paintings of plants, copies of which have not improbably descended to our time, began a tradition which, fixed about the fifth century, remained almost rigid until the re-discovery of nature in the sixteenth. He was physician to Mithridates VI Eupator (120–63 B.C.), but his work was well known and appreciated at Rome, which became the place of resort for Greek talent.[2]

Celsus, who flourished about 20 B.C., wrote an excellent work on medicine, but gives all too little glimpse of anatomy and physiology. Rufus of Ephesus, however, in the next century practised dissection of apes and other animals. He described the decussation of the optic nerves and the capsule of the crystalline lens, and gave the first clear description that has survived of the structure of the eye. He regarded the nerves

[1] See the companion chapter on *Greek Medicine*.

[2] The surviving fragments of the works of Crateuas have recently been printed by M. Wellmann as an appendix to the text of Dioscorides, *De materia medica*, 3 vols., Berlin, 1906–17, iii. pp. 144–6. The source and fate of his plant drawings are discussed in the same author's *Krateuas*, Berlin, 1897.

as originating from the brain, and distinguished between nerves of motion and of sensation. He described the oviduct of the sheep and rightly held that life was possible without the spleen.

The second Christian century brings us two writers who, while scientifically inconsiderable, acted as the main carriers of such tradition of Greek biology as reached the Middle Ages, Pliny and Dioscorides. Pliny (A.D. 23–79), though a Latin, owes almost everything of value in his encyclopaedia to Greek writings. In his *Natural History* we have a collection of current views on the nature, origin, and uses of plants and animals such as we might expect from an intelligent, industrious, and honest member of the landed class who was devoid of critical or special scientific skill. Scientifically the work is contemptible, but it demands mention in any study of the legacy of Greece, since it was, for centuries, a main conduit of the ancient teaching and observations on natural history. Read throughout the ages, alike in the darkest as in the more enlightened periods, copied and recopied, translated, commented on, extracted and abridged, a large part of Pliny's work has gradually passed into folk-keeping, so that through its agency the gipsy fortune-teller of to-day is still reciting garbled versions of the formulae of Aristotle and Hippocrates of two and a half millennia ago.

The fate of Dioscorides (flourished A.D. 60) has been not dissimilar. His work *On Materia Medica* consists of a series of short accounts of plants, arranged almost without reference to the nature of the plants themselves, but quite invaluable for its terse and striking descriptions which often include habits and habitats. Its history has shown it to be one of the most influential botanical treatises ever penned. It provided most of the little botanical knowledge that reached the Middle Ages. It furnished the chief stimulus to botanical research at the time of the Renaissance. It has decided the general form of every modern pharmacopœia. It has practically determined modern plant nomenclature both popular and scientific.

Translated into nearly every language from Anglo-Saxon and Bohemian to Arabic and Hebrew, appearing both abstracted and in full in innumerable beautifully illuminated manuscripts, some of which are still among the fairest treasures of the great national libraries, Dioscorides, the drug-monger, appealed to scholasticized minds for centuries. The frequency with which fragments of him are encountered in papyri shows how popular his work was in Egypt in the third and fourth centuries. One of the earliest datable Greek codices in existence is a glorious volume of Dioscorides written in capitals,[1] thought worthy to form a wedding gift for a lady who was the daughter of one Roman emperor and the betrothed of a second.[2] The illustrations of this fifth-century manuscript are a very valuable monument for the history of art and the chief adornment of what was once the Royal Library at Vienna[3] (figs. 9–10). Illustrated Latin translations of Dioscorides were in use in the time of Cassiodorus (490–585). A work based on it, similarly illustrated, but bearing the name of Apuleius, is among the most frequent of mediaeval botanical documents and the earliest surviving specimen is contemporary with Cassiodorus himself.[4] After the

[1] The manuscript in question is Med. Graec. 1 at what was the Royal Library at Vienna. It is known as the *Constantinopolitanus*. After the war it was taken to St. Mark's at Venice, but either has been or is about to be restored to Vienna. A facsimile of this grand manuscript was published by Sijthoff, Leyden, 1906.

[2] The lady in question was Juliana Anicia, daughter of Anicius Olybrius, Emperor of the West in 472, and his wife Placidia, daughter of Valentinian III. Juliana was betrothed in 479 by the Eastern Emperor Zeno to Theodoric the Ostrogoth, but was married, probably in 487 when the manuscript was presented to her, to Areobindus, a high military officer under the Byzantine Emperor Anastasius.

[3] The importance of this manuscript as well as the position of Dioscorides as medical botanist is discussed by Charles Singer in an article ' Greek Biology and the Rise of Modern Biology ', *Studies in the History and Method of Science*, vol. ii, Oxford, 1921.

[4] This manuscript is at the University Library at Leyden, where it is numbered Voss Q 9.

Fifth-century drawings from JULIANA ANICIA MS., copied from originals of first century B.C. (?)

Fig. 10

ΓΕΡΑΝΙΟΝ = *Geranium pyrenaicum, L.*

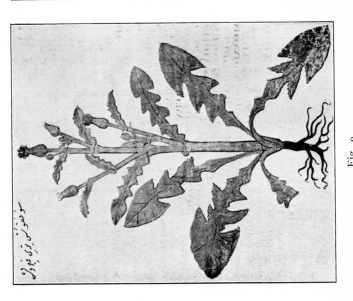

Fig. 9

ΣΟΓΚΟΣ ΤΡΥΦΕΡΟΣ = *Crepis paludosa, Mœn.*

revival of learning Dioscorides continued to attract an immense amount of philological and botanical ability, and scores of editions of his works, many of them nobly illustrated, poured out of the presses of the sixteenth and seventeenth centuries.

But the greatest biologist of the late Greek period, and indeed one of the greatest biologists of all time, was Claudius Galen of Pergamon (A.D. 131–201). Galen devoted himself to medicine from an early age, and in his twenty-first year we hear of him studying anatomy at Smyrna under Pelops. With the object of extending his knowledge of drugs he early made long journeys to Asia Minor. Later he proceeded to Alexandria, where he improved his anatomical equipment, and here, he tells us, he examined a human skeleton. It is indeed probable that his direct practical acquaintance with human anatomy was limited to the skeleton and that dissection of the human body was no longer carried on at Alexandria in his time. Thus his physiology and anatomy had to be derived mainly from animal sources. He is the most voluminous of all ancient scientific writers and one of the most voluminous writers of antiquity in any department. We are not here concerned with the medical material which mainly fills these huge volumes, but only with the physiological views which not only prevailed in medicine until Harvey and after, but also governed for fifteen hundred years alike the scientific and the popular ideas on the nature and workings of the animal body, and have for centuries been embedded in our speech. A knowledge of these physiological views of Galen is necessary for any understanding of the history of biology and illuminates many literary allusions of the Middle Ages and Renaissance.

Between the foundation of the Alexandrian school and the time of Galen, medicine was divided among a great number of sects. Galen was an eclectic and took portions of his teaching from many of these schools, but he was also a naturalist of great ability and industry, and knew well the value of the

experimental way. Yet he was a somewhat windy philosopher
and, priding himself on his philosophic powers, did not hesitate
to draw conclusions from evidence which was by no means
always adequate. The physiological system that he thus succeeded in building up we may now briefly consider (fig. 11).

The basic principle of life, in the Galenic physiology, is
a *spirit*, *anima* or *pneuma*, drawn from the general world-soul
in the act of respiration. It enters the body through the
rough artery (τραχεῖα ἀρτηρία, *arteria aspera* of mediaeval
notation), the organ known to our nomenclature as the trachea.
From this trachea the pneuma passes to the lung and then,
through the *vein-like artery* (ἀρτηρία φλεβώδης, *arteria venalis*
of mediaeval writers, the pulmonary vein of our nomenclature),
to the left ventricle. Here it will be best to leave it for
a moment and trace the vascular system along a different
route.

Ingested food, passing down the alimentary tract, was
absorbed as chyle from the intestine, collected by the portal
vessel, and conveyed by it to the liver. That organ, the site
of the innate heat in Galen's view, had the power of elaborating
the chyle into venous blood and of imbuing it with a spirit
or pneuma which is innate in all living substance, so long as
it remains alive, the *natural spirits* (πνεῦμα φυσικόν, *spiritus
naturalis* of the mediaevals). Charged with this, and also with
the nutritive material derived from the food, the venous blood
is distributed by the liver through the veins which arise from
it in the same way as the arteries from the heart. These veins
carry nourishment and *natural spirits* to all parts of the body.
Iecur fons venarum, the liver as the source of the veins, remained
through the centuries the watchword of the Galenic physiology.
The blood was held to ebb and flow continuously in the veins
during life.

Now from the liver arose one great vessel, the hepatic vein,
from division of which the others were held to come off as

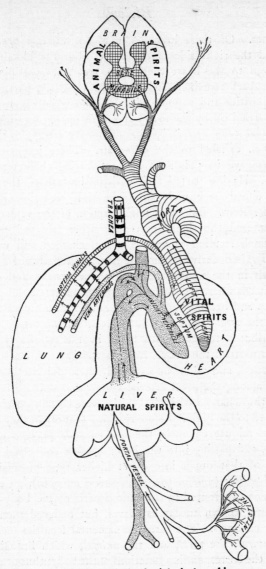

FIG. 11. Illustrating Galen's physiological teaching.

branches. Of these branches, one, our *common vena cava*, entered the right side of the heart. For the blood that it conveyed to the heart there were two fates possible. The greater part remained awhile in the ventricle, parting with its impurities and vapours, exhalations of the organs, which were carried off by the *artery-like vein* (φλὲψ ἀρτηριώδης, the mediaeval *vena arterialis*, our pulmonary artery) to the lung and then exhaled to the outer air. These impurities and vapours gave its poisonous and suffocating character to the breath. Having parted thus with its impurities, the venous blood ebbed back again from the right ventricle into the venous system. But for a small fraction of the venous blood that entered the right ventricle another fate was reserved. This small fraction of venous blood, charged still with the *natural spirits* derived from the liver, passed through minute channels in the septum between the ventricles and entered the left chamber. Arrived there, it encountered the external pneuma and became thereby elaborated into a higher form of spirit, the *vital spirits* (πνεῦμα ζωτικόν, *spiritus vitalis*), which is distributed together with blood by the arterial system to various parts of the body. In the arterial system it also ebbed and flowed, and might be seen and felt to pulsate there.

But among the great arterial vessels that sent forth arterial blood thus charged with vital spirits were certain vessels which ascended to the brain. Before reaching that organ they divided up into minute channels, the *rete mirabile* (πλέγμα μέγιστον θαῦμα), and passing into the brain became converted by the action of that organ into a yet higher type of spirits, the *animal spirits* (πνεῦμα ψυχικόν, *spiritus animalis*), an ethereal substance distributed to the various parts of the body by the structures known to-day as nerves, but believed then to be hollow channels. The three fundamental faculties (δυνάμεις), the *natural*, the *vital*, and the *animal*, which brought into action the corresponding functions of the body, thus originated as an expression of the primal force or pneuma.

This physiology, we may emphasize, is not derived from an investigation of human anatomy. In the human brain there is no *rete mirabile*, though such an organ is found in the calf. In the human liver there is no *hepatic vein*, though such an organ is found in the dog. Dogs, calves, pigs, bears, and, above all, Barbary apes were freely dissected by Galen and were the creatures from which he derived his physiological ideas. Many of Galen's anatomical and physiological errors are due to his attributing to one creature the structures found in another, a fact that only very gradually dawned on the Renaissance anatomists.

The whole knowledge possessed by the world in the department of physiology from the third to the seventeenth century, nearly all the biological conceptions till the thirteenth, and most of the anatomy and much of the botany until the sixteenth century, all the ideas of the physical structure of living things throughout the Middle Ages, were contained in a small number of these works of Galen. The biological works of Aristotle and Theophrastus lingered precariously in a few rare manuscripts in the monasteries of the East ; the total output of hundreds of years of Alexandrian and Pergamenian activities was utterly destroyed ; the Ionian biological works, of which a sample has by a miracle survived, were forgotten ; but these vast, windy, ill-arranged treatises of Galen lingered on. Translated into Latin, Syriac, Arabic, and Hebrew, they saturated the intellectual world of the Middle Ages. Commented on by later Greek writers, who were themselves in turn translated into the same list of languages, they were yet again served up under the names of such Greek writers as Oribasius, Paul of Aegina, or Alexander of Tralles.

What is the secret of the vitality of these Galenic biological conceptions? The answer can be given in four words. *Galen is a teleologist* ; and a teleologist of a kind whose views happened to fit in with the prevailing theological attitude of the Middle Ages, whether Christian, Moslem, or Jewish. Accord-

ing to him everything which exists and displays activity in the
human body originates in and is formed by an intelligent being
and on an intelligent plan, so that the organ in structure and
function is the result of that plan. 'It was the Creator's infinite
wisdom which selected the best means to attain his beneficent
ends, and it is a proof of His omnipotence that he created every
good thing according to His design, and thereby fulfilled
His will.' [1]

After Galen there is a thousand years of darkness, and biology
ceases to have a history. The mind of the Dark Ages turned
towards theology, and such remains of Neoplatonic philosophy
as were absorbed into the religious system were little likely to
be of aid to the scientific attitude. One department of positive
knowledge must of course persist. Men still suffered from the
infirmities of the flesh and still sought relief from them. But
the books from which that advice was sought had nothing to
do with general principles nor with knowledge as such. They
were the most wretched of the treatises that still masqueraded
under the names of Hippocrates and Galen, mostly mere
formularies, antidotaries, or perhaps at best symptom lists.
And, when the depression of the western intellect had passed
its worst, there was still no biological material on which it
could be nourished.

The prevailing interest of the barbarian world, at last
beginning to settle into its heritage of antiquity, was with
Logic. Of Aristotle there survived in Latin dress only the
Categories and the *De interpretatione*, the merciful legacy of
Boethius, the last of the philosophers. Had a translation of
Aristotle's *Historia animalium* or *De generatione animalium*
survived, had a Latin version of the Hippocratic work *On
generation* or of the treatises of Theophrastus *On plants*
reached the earlier Middle Ages, the whole mental history

[1] A good instance of Galen's teleological point of view is afforded by his
classical description of *the hand* in the περὶ χρείας τῶν ἐν ἀνθρώπου σώματι
μορίων, *On the uses of the parts of the body of man*, i. 1.   This passage is
available in English in a tract by Thomas Bellott, London, 1840.

of Europe might have been different and the rediscovery of nature might have been antedated by centuries. But this was a change of heart for which the world had long to wait; something much less was the earliest biological gift of Greece. The gift, when it came, came in two forms, one of which has not been adequately recognized, but both are equally her legacy. These two forms are, firstly, the well-known work of the early translators and, secondly, the tardily recognized work of certain schools of minor art.

The earliest biological treatises to become accessible in the west were rendered not from Greek but from Arabic.[1] The first of them was perhaps the treatise περὶ μυῶν κινήσεως, *On movement of muscles* of Galen, a work which contains more than its title suggests and indeed sets forth much of the Galenic physiological system. It was rendered into Latin from the Arabic of Joannitius (Hunain ibn Ishaq, 809–73), probably about the year 1200, by one Mark of Toledo. It attracted little attention, but very soon after biological works of Aristotle began to become accessible. The first was probably the fragment *On plants*. The Greek original of this is lost, and besides the Latin, only an Arabic version of a former Arabic translation of a Syriac rendering of a Greek commentary is now known! Such a work appeared from the hand of a translator known as Alfred the Englishman about 1220 or a little later. Neither it nor another work from the same translator, *On the motion of the heart*, which sought to establish the primacy of that organ on Aristotelian grounds, can be said to contain any of the spirit of the master.[2]

[1] The early European translations from the Arabic are tabulated with unparalleled learning by M. Steinschneider, 'Die Europäischen Ueberset zungen aus dem Arabischen bis Mitte des 17. Jahrhunderts', in the *Sitzungsberichte der kais. Akad. der Wissenschaften in Wien*, cxlix and cli, Vienna, 1904 and 1905.

[2] C. H. Haskins, 'The reception of Arabic science in England,' *English Historical Review*, London, 1915, p. 56.

A little better than these is the work of the wizard Michael the Scot (1175?–1234?). Roger Bacon tells us that Michael in 1230 ' appeared [at Oxford], bringing with him the works of Aristotle in natural history and mathematics, with wise expositors, so that the philosophy of Aristotle was magnified among the Latins '.[1] Scott produced his work *De animalibus* about this date and he included in it the three great biological works of Aristotle, all rendered from an inferior Arabic version.[2] Albertus Magnus (1206–80) had not as yet a translation direct from the Greek to go upon for his great commentary on the *History of animals*, but he depended on Scott. The biological works of Aristotle were rendered into Latin direct from the Greek in the year 1260 probably by William of Moerbeke.[3] Such translations, appearing in the full scholastic age when everything was against direct observation, cannot be said to have fallen on a fertile ground. They presented an ordered account of nature and a good method of investigation, but those were gifts to a society that knew little of their real value.[4]

Yet the advent of these texts was coincident with a returning desire to observe nature. Albert, with all his scholasticism, was no contemptible naturalist. He may be said to have begun first-hand plant study in modern times so far as literary records are concerned. His book *De vegetabilibus*

[1] Roger Bacon, *Opus majus*, edited by J. H. Bridges, 3 vols., London, 1897–1900. Vol. iii, p. 66.

[2] On the Aristotelian translations of Scott see A. H. Querfeld, *Michael Scottus und seine Schrift, De secretis naturae,* Leipzig, 1919; and C. H. Haskins, ' Michael Scot and Frederick II ' in *Isis*, ii. 250, Brussels, 1922.

[3] J. G. Schneider, *Aristotelis de animalibus historiae*, Leipzig, 1811, p. cxxvi. L. Dittmeyer, *Guilelmi Moerbekensis translatio commentationis Aristotelicae de generatione animalium*, Dillingen, 1915. L. Dittmeyer, *De animalibus historia*, Leipzig, 1907.

[4] The subject of the Latin translations of Aristotle is traversed by A. and C. Jourdain, *Recherches critiques sur l'âge des traductions latines d'Aristote*, 2nd ed., Paris, 1843; M. Grabmann, *Forschungen uber die lateinischen Aristoteles Ubersetzungen des XIII. Jahrhunderts*, Münster i/W., 1916; and F. Wüstenfeld, *Die Ubersetzungen arabischer Werke in das Lateinische seit dem XI. Jahrhundert*, Göttingen, 1877.

contains excellent observations, and he is worthy of inclusion among the fathers of botany. In his vast treatise *De animalibus*, hampered as he is by his learning and verbosity, he shows himself a true observer and one who has absorbed something of the spirit of the great naturalist to whose works he had devoted a lifetime of study and on which he professes to be commenting. We see clearly the leaven of the Aristotelian spirit working, though Albert is still a schoolman. We may select for quotation a passage on the generation of fish, a subject on which some of Aristotle's most remarkable descriptions remained unconfirmed till modern times. These descriptions impressed Albert in the same way as they do the modern naturalist. To those who know nothing of the stimulating power of the Aristotelian biological works, Albert's description of the embryos of fish and his accurate distinction of their mode of development from that of birds, by the absence of an allantoic membrane in the one and its presence in the other, must surely be startling. Albert depends on Aristotle—a third-hand version of Aristotle—but does not slavishly follow him.

'Between the mode of development (*anathomiam generationis*) of birds' and fishes' eggs there is this difference : during the development of the fish the second of the two veins which extend from the heart [as described by Aristotle in birds] does not exist. For we do not find the vein which extends to the outer covering in the eggs of birds which some wrongly call the navel because it carries the blood to the exterior parts ; but we do find the vein that corresponds to the yolk vein of birds, for this vein imbibes the nourishment by which the limbs increase. . . . In fishes as in birds, channels extend from the heart first to the head and the eyes, and first in them appear the great upper parts. As the growth of the young fish increases the albumen decreases, being incorporated into the members of the young fish, and it disappears entirely when development and

formation are complete.   The beating of the heart . . . is conveyed to the lower part of the belly, carrying pulse and life to
the inferior members.

' While the young [fish] are small and not yet fully developed
they have veins of great length which take the place of the
navel-string, but as they grow and develop, these shorten
and contract into the body towards the heart, as we have
said about birds.   The young fish and the eggs are enclosed
and in a covering, as are the eggs and young of birds.   This
covering resembles the dura mater [of the brain], and beneath
it is another [corresponding therefore to the pia mater of the
brain] which contains the young animal and nothing else.' [1]

In the next century Conrad von Megenberg (1309–98) produced his *Book of Nature*, a complete work on natural history,
the first of the kind in the vernacular, founded on Latin
versions, now rendered direct from the Greek, of the Aristotelian and Galenic biological works.   It is well ordered and
opens with a systematic account of the structure and physiology of man as a type of the animal creation, which is then
systematically described and followed by an account of plants.
Conrad, though guided by Aristotle, uses his own eyes and ears,
and with him and Albert the era of direct observation has
begun.[2]

But there was another department in which the legacy of
Greece found an even earlier appreciation.   For centuries the
illustrations to herbals and bestiaries had been copied from
hand to hand, continuing a tradition that had its rise with

[1] The enormous *De Animalibus* of Albert of Cologne is now available in
an edition by H. Stadler, *Albertus Magnus De Animalibus Libri XXVI nach
der cölner Urschrift*, 2 vols., Münster i/W., 1916–21.   The quotation is
translated from vol. i, pp. 465–6.

[2] Conrad's work is conveniently edited by H. Schultz, *Das Buch der Natur
von Conrad von Megenberg, die erste Naturgeschichte in deutscher Sprache, in
Neu-Hochdeutsche Sprache bearbeitet*, Greifswald, 1897.   Conrad's work is
based on that of Thomas of Cantimpré (1201–70).

Greek artists of the first century B. C. But their work, copied at each stage without reference to the object, moved constantly farther from resemblance to the original. At last the illustrations became little but formal patterns, a state in which they remained in some late copies prepared as recently as the sixteenth century. But at a certain period a change set in, and the artist, no longer content to rely on tradition, appeals at last to nature. This new stirring in art corresponds with the new stirring in letters, the Arabian revival—itself a legacy of Greece, though sadly deteriorated in transit—that gave rise to scholasticism. In much of the beautiful carved and sculptured work of the French cathedrals the new movement appears in the earlier part of the thirteenth century. At such a place as Chartres we see the attempt to render plants and animals faithfully in stone as early as 1240 or before. In the easier medium of parchment the same tendency appears even earlier. When once it begins the process progresses slowly until the great recovery of the Greek texts in the fifteenth century, when it is again accelerated.

During the sixteenth century the energy of botanists and zoologists was largely absorbed in producing most carefully annotated and illustrated editions of Dioscorides and Theophrastus and accounts of animals, habits, and structure that were intended to illustrate the writings of Aristotle, while the anatomists explored the bodies of man and beast to confirm or refute Galen. The great monographs on birds, fishes, and plants of this period, ostensibly little but commentaries on Pliny, Aristotle, and Dioscorides, represent really the first important efforts of modern times at a natural history. They pass naturally into the encyclopaedias of the later sixteenth century, and these into the physiological works of the seventeenth. Aristotle was never a dead hand in Biology as he was in Physics, and this for the reason that he was a great biologist but was not a great physicist.

With the advance of the sixteenth century the works of Aristotle, and to a less extent those of Dioscorides and Galen, became the great stimulus to the foundation of a new biological science. Matthioli (1520–77), in his commentary on Dioscorides (first edition 1544), which was one of the first works of its type to appear in the vernacular, made a number of first-hand observations on the habits and structure of plants that is startling even to a modern botanist. About the same time Galenic physiology, expressed also in numerous works in the vulgar tongue and rousing the curiosity of the physicians, became the clear parent of modern physiology and comparative anatomy. But, above all, the Aristotelian biological works were fertilizers of the mind. It is very interesting to watch a fine observer such as Fabricius ab Acquapendente (1537–1619) laying the foundations of modern embryology in a splendid series of first-hand observations, treating his own great researches almost as a commentary on Aristotle. What an impressive contrast to the arid physics of the time based also on Aristotle ! ' My purpose ', says Fabricius, ' is to treat of the formation of the foetus in every animal, setting out from that which proceeds from the egg : for this ought to take precedence of all other discussion of the subject, both because it is not difficult to make out Aristotle's view of the matter, and because his treatise on the Formation of the Foetus from the egg is by far the fullest, and the subject is by much the most extensive and difficult.' [1]

The industrious and careful Fabricius, with a wonderful talent for observation lit not by his own lamp but by that of Aristotle, bears a relation to the master much like that held by Aristotle's pupil in the flesh, Theophrastus. The works of the two men, Fabricius and Theophrastus, bear indeed a resemblance to each other. Both rely on the same group of general ideas, both progress in much the same ordered calm from observation to observation, both have an inspiration which

[1] Hieronimo Fabrizio of Acquapendente, *De formato foetu*, Padua, 1604.

is efficient and stimulating but below the greatest, both are enthusiastic and effective as investigators of fact, but timid and ineffective in drawing conclusions.

But Fabricius was more happy in his pupils than Theophrastus, for we may watch the same Aristotelian ideas fermenting in the mind of Fabricius's successor, the greatest biologist since Aristotle himself, William Harvey (1578–1657).[1] This writer's work *On generation* is a careful commentary on Aristotle's work on the same topic, but it is a commentary not in the old sense but in the spirit of Aristotle himself. Each statement is weighed and tested in the light of experience, and the younger naturalist, with all his reverence for Aristotle, does not hesitate to criticize his conclusions. He exhibits an independence of thought, an ingenuity in experiment, and a power of deduction that places his treatise as the middle term of the three great works on embryology of which the other members are those of Aristotle and Karl Ernst von Baer (1796–1876).[2]

With the second half of the seventeenth century and during a large part of the eighteenth the biological works of Aristotle attracted less attention. The battle against the Aristotelian physics had been fought and won, but with them the biological works of Aristotle unjustly passed into the shadow that overhung all the idols of the Middle Ages.

The rediscovery of the Aristotelian biology is a modern thing. The collection of the vast wealth of living forms absorbed the energies of the generations of naturalists from Ray (1627–1705) and Willoughby (1635–72) to Réaumur (1683–1757) and Linnaeus (1707–1778) and beyond to the nineteenth century. The magnitude and fascination of the work seems almost to have excluded general ideas. With the end of this period and the advent of a more philosophical type of naturalist,

---

[1] William Harvey, *Exercitationes de generatione animalium*, London, 1651.
[2] Karl Ernst von Baer, *Ueber die Entwickelungsgeschichte der Thiere*, Königsberg, 1828–37.

such as Cuvier (1769–1832) and members of the Saint-Hilaire family, Aristotle came again to his own. Since the dawn of the nineteenth century, and since naturalists have been in a position to verify the work of Aristotle, his reputation as a naturalist has continuously risen. Johannes Müller (1801–58), Richard Owen (1804–92), George Henry Lewes (1817–78), William Ogle (1827–1912) are a few of the long line of those who have derived direct inspiration from his biological work. With improved modern methods of investigation the problems of generation have absorbed a large amount of biological attention, and interest has become specially concentrated on Aristotle's work on that topic which is perhaps, at the moment, more widely read than any biological treatise, ancient or modern, except the works of Darwin. That great naturalist wrote to Ogle in 1882 : ' From quotations I had seen I had a high notion of Aristotle's merits, but I had not the most remote notion what a wonderful man he was. Linnaeus and Cuvier have been my two gods, though in very different ways, but they were mere schoolboys to old Aristotle.'

CHARLES SINGER.

MEDICINE

Ἡρόφιλος δὲ ἐν τῷ Διαιτητικῷ καὶ σοφίαν φησὶν ἀνεπίδεικτον καὶ τέχνην ἄδηλον καὶ ἰσχὺν ἀναγώνιστον καὶ πλοῦτον ἀχρεῖον καὶ λόγον ἀδύνατον, ὑγιείας ἀπούσης.

HEROPHILOS, a Greek philosopher and physician (*c.* 300 B.C.), has truly written ' that Science and Art have equally nothing to show, that Strength is incapable of effort, Wealth useless, and Eloquence powerless if Health be wanting '.[1] All peoples therefore have had their methods of treating those departures from health that we call disease, and among peoples of higher culture such methods have been reduced in most cases to something resembling a system. In antiquity, as now, a variety of such systems were in vogue, and those nations who practised the art of writing from an early date have left considerable records of their medical methods and doctrines. We may thus form a fairly good idea of the medical principles of the Mesopotamian, the Egyptian, the Iranian, the Indian, and the Chinese civilizations. Much in these systems, as in the medical procedure of more primitive tribes, was based upon some theory of disease which fitted in with a larger theory of the nature of evil. Of these theories the commonest was and is the demonic, the view that regards deviation from the normal state of health as due either to the attacks of supernatural beings or to their actual entry into the body of the sufferer. A medical system based on such a view is susceptible of great elaboration in a higher civilization, but not being founded on

---

[1] The works of Herophilus are lost. This fine passage has been preserved for us by Sextus Empiricus, a third-century physician, in his πρὸς τοὺς μαθηματικοὺς ἀντιρρητικοί, which is in essence an attack on all positive philosophy. It is an entertaining fact that we should have to go to such a work for remains of the greatest anatomist of antiquity. The passage is in the section directed against ethical writers, xi. 50.

observation is hardly capable of indefinite development, for a point must ultimately be reached at which the mind recoils from complex conclusions far remote from observed phenomena. The medicine of the ancient and settled civilization of such a people as the Assyro-Babylonians, for instance, of which substantial traces have been recovered, is hardly, if at all, more effective, though far more systematized, than that of many a wild and unlettered tribe that may be observed to-day. Of such medicine as this we may give an account, but we can hardly write a *history*. We cannot establish those elements of continuity and of development from which alone history can be constructed.

It is the distinction of the Greeks alone among the nations of antiquity that they practised a system of medicine based not on theory but on observation accumulated systematically as time went on. The claim can be made for the Greeks that some at least among them were deflected by no theory, were deceived by no theurgy, were hampered by no tradition in their search for the facts of disease and in their attempts at interpreting its phenomena. Only the Greeks among the ancients could look on their healers as *physicians* (=naturalists, φύσις=nature), and that word itself stands as a lasting reminder of their achievement.[1]

At a certain stage in the history of the Western world—the exact point in time may be disputed but the event is admitted by all—men turned to explore the treasures of the ancient wisdom and the whole mass of Greek medical learning was gradually laid before the student. That mass contained much dross, material that survived from early as

[1] The word φυσικός, though it passed over into Latin (Cicero) with the meaning *naturalist*, acquired the connotation of *sorcerer* among the later Greek writers. Perhaps the word *physicianus* was introduced to make a distinction from the charm-mongering *physicus*. In later Latin *physicus* and *medicus* are almost always interchangeable.

from late Greek times which was hardly, if at all, superior to the debased compositions that circulated in the name of medicine in the middle centuries. But the recovered Greek medical writings also contained some material of the purest and most scientific type, and that material and the spirit in which it was written, form the debt of modern medicine to antiquity.

It is a debt the value of which cannot be exaggerated. The physicians of the revival of learning, and for long after, doubtless pinned their faith too much to the written word of their Greek forbears and sought to imprison the free spirit of Hippocrates and Galen in the rigid wall of their own rediscovered texts. The great medical pioneers of a somewhat later age, enraged by this attempt, the real nature of which was largely hidden from them, not infrequently revolted and rightly revolted against the bondage to the Greeks in which they had been brought up. Yet it is sure that these modern discoverers were the true inheritors of the Greeks. Without Herophilus we should have had no Harvey and the rise of physiology might have been delayed for centuries; had Galen's works not survived, Vesalius would never have reconstructed Anatomy, and Surgery too might have stayed behind with her laggard sister, Medicine; the Hippocratic collection was the necessary and acknowledged basis for the work of the greatest of modern clinical observers, Thomas Sydenham, and the teaching of Hippocrates and of his school is the substantial basis of instruction in the wards of a modern hospital. In the pages which follow we propose therefore to review the general character of medical knowledge in the best Greek period and to consider briefly how much of that great heritage remained accessible to the earlier modern physicians. The reader will thus be able to form some estimate of the degree to which the legacy has been passed on to our own times.

It is evident that among such a group of peoples as the Greeks, varying in state of civilization, in mental power, in geographical and economic position and in general outlook, the practice of medicine can have been by no means uniform. Without any method of centralizing medical education and standardizing teaching there was a great variety of doctrines and of practice in vogue among them, and much of this was on a low level of folk custom. Such lower grade material of Greek origin has come down to us in abundance, though much of it, curiously enough, from a later time. But the overwhelming mass of earlier Greek medical literature sets forth for us a pure scientific effort to observe and to classify disease, to make generalizations from carefully collected data, to explain the origin of disease on rational grounds, and to apply remedies, when possible, on a reasoned basis. We may thus rest fairly well assured that, despite serious and irreparable losses, we are still in possession of some of the very finest products of the Greek medical intellect.

There is ample evidence that the Greeks inherited, in common with many other peoples of Mediterranean and Asiatic origin, a whole system of magical or at least non-rational pharmacy and medicine from a remoter ancestry. Striking parallels can be drawn between these folk elements among the Greeks and the medical systems of the early Romans, as well as with the medicine of the Indian Vedas, of the ancient Egyptians, and of the earliest European barbarian writings. It is thus reasonable to suppose that these elements, when they appear in later Greek writings, represent more primitive folk elements working up, under the influence of social disintegration and consequent mental deterioration, through the upper strata of the literate Greek world. But with these elements, intensely interesting to the anthropologist, the psychologist, the ethnologist, and to the historian of religion, we are not here greatly concerned. Important as they are, they constitute no part of the special claim of the Greek people to distinction, but rather aid us in uniting the Greek mentality with that of other kindred peoples. Here we shall rather discuss the course of Greek scientific medicine proper, the type of medical doctrine and practice, capable of development in the proper sense of the word, that forms the basis of our modern system. We are concerned, in fact, with the earliest evolutionary medicine.

We need hardly discuss the first origins of Greek Medicine. The material is scanty and the conclusions somewhat doubtful and perhaps premature, for the discovery of a considerable fragment of the historical work of Menon, a pupil of Aristotle, containing a description of the views of some of the precursors of the Hippocratic school, renews a hope that more extended investigation may yield further information as to the sources and nature of the earliest Greek medical writings.[1] The study of Mesopotamian star-lore has linked it up with early Greek astronomical science. The efforts of cuneiform scholars have not, however, been equally successful for medicine, and on the whole the general tendency of modern research is to give less weight to Mesopotamian and more to Egyptian sources than had previously been admitted ; thus very recently an Egyptian medical papyrus of about 1700 B. c. has been described which bears a distinct resemblance to some of the Hippocratic treatises.[2] A number of drugs, too, habitually used by the Greeks, such as *Andropogon*, *Cardamoms*, and *Sesame orientalis*, are of Indian origin. There are also the Minoan cultures to be considered, and though our knowledge is not yet sufficient to speak of the heritage that Greek medicine may or may not have derived from that source, it seems not improbable that Greek hygiene may here owe a debt.[3] Omitting, therefore, this early epoch, we pass

---

[1] This fragment has been published in vol. iii, part 1, of the *Supplementum Aristotelicum* by H. Diels as *Anonymi Londinensis ex Aristotelis Iatricis Menonis et Aliis Medicis Eclogae*, Berlin, 1893. See also H. Bekh and F. Spät, *Anonymus Londinensis, Auszuge eines Unbekannten aus Aristoteles-Menons Handbuch der Medizin*, Berlin, 1896.

[2] As we go to press there appears a preliminary account of the very remarkable Edwin Smith papyrus, see J. H. Breasted in *Recueil d'études egyptologiques dédiées à la mémoire de Champollion*, Paris 1922, and *New York Historical Society Bulletin*, 1922.

[3] It is tempting, also, to connect the Asclepian snake cult with the prominence of the serpent in Minoan religion.

direct to the later period, between the sixth and fourth centuries, from which documents have actually come down to us.

The earliest medical school of which we have definite
information is that of Cnidus, a Lacedaemonian colony in
Asiatic Doris. Its origin may perhaps reach back to the seventh
century B.C. We have actual records that the teachers of
Cnidus were accustomed to collect systematically the phenomena of disease, of which they had produced a very complex
classification, and we probably possess also several of their
actual works. The physicians of Cos, their only contemporary
critics whose writings have survived, considered that the
Cnidian physicians paid too much attention to the actual
sensations of the patient and to the physical signs of the
disease. The most important of the Cnidian doctrines were
drawn up in a series of *Sentences* or Aphorisms, and these, it
appears, inculcated a treatment along Egyptian lines of the
symptom or at most the disease, rather than the patient,
a statement borne out by the contents of the gynaecological
works of probable Cnidian origin included in the so-called
' Hippocratic Collection '. A few names of Cnidian physicians
have, moreover, come down to us with titles of their works, and
a later statement that they practised anatomy. There can be
little doubt too that the Cnidian school drew also on Persian
and Indian Medicine.

The origin of the school of the neighbouring island of Cos
was a little later than that of Cnidus and probably dates from
the sixth century B.C. Of the Coan school, or at least of the
general tendencies that it represented, we have a magnificent
and copious literary monument in the Corpus Hippocraticum,
a collection which was probably put together in the early part
of the third century B.C. by a commission of Alexandrian
scholars at the order of the book-loving Ptolemy Soter (reigned
323–285 B.C.). The elements of which this collection is composed are of varying dates from the sixth to the fourth century
B.C., and of varying value and origin, but they mainly represent

the point of view of physicians of the eastern part of the Greek world in the fifth and fourth centuries.

The most obvious feature, the outstanding element that at once strikes the modern observer in these 'Coan' writings, is the enormous emphasis laid on the actual course of disease. 'It appears to me a most excellent thing', so opens one of the greatest of the Hippocratic works, 'for a physician to cultivate *pronoia*.[1] Foreknowing and foretelling in the presence of the sick the past, present, and future (of their symptoms) and explaining all that the patients are neglecting, he would be believed to understand their condition, so that men would have confidence to entrust themselves to his care. . . . Thus he would win just respect and be a good physician. By an earlier forecast in each case he would be more able to tend those aright who have a chance of surviving, and by foreseeing and stating who will die, and who will survive, he will escape blame . . .'[2]

Just as the Cnidians by dividing up diseases according to symptoms over-emphasized diagnosis and over-elaborated treatment, so the Coans laid very great force on prognosis and adopted therefore a largely expectant attitude towards diseases. Both Cnidian and Coan physicians were held together by a common bond which was, historically if not actually, related to temple worship. Physicians leagued together in the name of a god, as were the Asclepiadae, might escape, and did escape, the baser theurgic elements of temple medicine. Of these they were as devoid as a modern Catholic physician might be

---

[1] This word *pronoia*, as Galen explains (εἰς τὸ Ἱπποκράτους προγνωστικόν, K. xviii, B. p. 10), is not used in the philosophic sense, as when we ask whether the universe was made by chance or by *pronoia*, nor is it used quite in the modern sense of *prognosis*, though it includes that too. *Pronoia* in Hippocrates means knowing things about a patient before you are told them. See E. T. Withington, ' Some Greek medical terms with reference to Luke and Liddell and Scott,' *Proceedings of the Royal Society of Medicine* (*Section of the History of Medicine*), xiii, p. 124, London, 1920.

[2] *Prognostics* I.

expected to be free from the absurdities of Lourdes. But the extreme cult of prognosis among the Coans may not improbably be traced back to the medical lore of the temple soothsayers whose divine omens were replaced by indications of a physical nature in the patient himself.[1] We are tempted too to link it with that process of astronomical and astrological prognosis practised in the Mesopotamian civilizations from which Ionia imitated and derived so much. Religion had thus the same relation to medicine that it would have with a modern 'religious' medical man as suggesting the motive and determining the general direction of his practice though without influence on the details and method.

During the development of the Coan medical school along these lines in the sixth and fifth centuries, there was going on a most remarkable movement at the very other extreme of the Greek world. Into the course and general importance of Sicilian philosophy it is not our place to enter, but that extraordinary movement was not without its repercussion on medical theory and practice. Very important in this direction was Empedocles of Agrigentum (*c.* 500–*c.* 430 B.C.). His view that the blood is the seat of the 'innate heat', ἔμφυτον θερμόν, he took from folk belief—'the blood is the life'—and this innate heat he closely identified with soul. More profitable was his doctrine that breathing takes place not only through what are now known as the respiratory passages but also through the pores of the skin. His teaching led to a belief in the heart as the centre of the vascular system and the chief organ of the 'pneuma' which was distributed by the blood vessels. This pneuma was equivalent to both soul and life, but it was something more. It was identified with air and breath, and the pneuma could be seen to rise as shimmering steam from the shed blood of the

---

[1] There is a discussion of the relation of the Asclepiadae to temple practice in an article by E. T. Withington, 'The Asclepiadae and the Priest of Asclepius,' in *Studies in the History and Method of Science*, edited by Charles Singer, vol. ii, Oxford, 1921.

sacrificial victim—for was not the blood its natural home?
There was a pneuma, too, that interpenetrated the universe
around us and gave it those qualities of life that it was felt to
possess. Anaximenes (*c.* 610–*c.* 545 B.C.), an Ionian predecessor
of Empedocles, may be said to have defined for us these functions of the pneuma; οἷον ἡ ψυχὴ ἡ ἡμετέρα ἀὴρ οὖσα συγκρατεῖ
ἡμᾶς, ὅλον τὸν κόσμον πνεῦμα καὶ ἀὴρ περιέχει, 'As our soul,
being air, sustains us, so pneuma and air pervade the whole
universe';[1] but it is the speculation of Empedocles himself
that came to be regarded as the basis of the Pneumatic School
in Medicine which had later very important developments.

Another early member of the Western school who made
important contributions to medical doctrine—in which relation
alone we need consider him—was Pythagoras of Samos (*c.* 580–
c. 490 B.C.). For him number, as the purest conception, formed
the basis of philosophy. Unity was the symbol of perfection
and corresponded to God Himself. The material universe was
represented by 2, and was divided by the number 12, whence
we have 3 worlds and 4 spheres. These in turn, according at
least to the later Pythagoreans, give rise to the four elements,
earth, air, fire, and water—a primary doctrine of medicine and
of science derived perhaps from ancient Egypt and surviving
for more than two millennia. The Pythagoreans taught, too,
of the existence of an animal soul, an emanation of the soul
of the universe. In all this we may distinguish the germ of
that doctrine of the relation of man and universe, microcosm
and macrocosm, which, suppressed as irrelevant in the Hippocratic works, reappears in the Platonic and especially in the
Neoplatonic writings, and forms a very important dogma in
later medicine.

A pupil of Pythagoras and an older contemporary of
Empedocles was Alcmaeon of Croton (*c.* 500 B. C.), who began
to construct a positive basis for medical science by the practice

[1] The works of Anaximenes are lost. This phrase of his, however, is
preserved by the later writer Aetios.

of dissection of animals, and discovered the optic nerves and
the Eustachian tubes. He even extended his researches to
Embryology, describing the head of the foetus as the first
part to be developed—a justifiable deduction from appearances.
Alcmaeon introduced also the doctrine that health depends
on harmony, disease on discord of the elements within the
body. Curiosity as to the distribution of the vessels was
excited by Empedocles and Alcmaeon and led to further
dissection, and Alcmaeon's pupils Acron (*c.* 480 B. C.) and
Pausanias (*c.* 480 B. C.), and the later Philistion of Lokri,[1] the
contemporary of Plato, all made anatomical investigations.

The views of Empedocles, and especially his doctrine that
regarded the heart as the main site of the pneuma, though
rejected by the Coan school as a whole, were not without
influence on Ionia. Diogenes of Apollonia, the philosopher of
pneumatism, a late fifth-century writer who must have been
contemporary with Hippocrates the Great, himself made an
investigation of the blood vessels ; and the influence of the
same school may be traced in a little work περὶ καρδίης, *On the
heart*, which is the best anatomical treatise of the Hippocratic
Collection. This work describes the aorta and the pulmonary
artery as well as the three valves at the root of each of the
great vessels, and it speaks of experiments to test their validity.
It treats of the pericardium and of the pericardial fluid and
perhaps of the musculi papillares, and contrasts the thickness
of the walls of right and left ventricles. The author considers
that the left ventricle is empty of blood—as indeed it is after
death—and is the source of the innate heat and of the absolute
intelligence. These views fit in with the doctrines of Empedocles, so that we may perhaps even venture to regard this work
as a surviving document of the Sicilian school. It is interesting
to observe that we have here the first hint of human dissection,
for the author tells us that the hearts of animals may be

---

[1] For the work of these physicians see especially M. Wellmann, *Fragment-
sammlung der griechischen Aerzte*, Bd. I, Berlin, 1901.

compared to that of man. The distinction of having been the first to write on human anatomy, as such, belongs however, probably to a later writer, Diocles, son of Archidamus of Carystus, who lived in the fourth century B. c.[1]

We may now turn to the Hippocratic Corpus as a whole. This collection consists of about 60 or 70 separate works, written at various periods and in various states of preservation. At best only a very small proportion of them can be attributed to Hippocrates, but the discussion of the general question of the ' genuineness ' of the works is now admitted to be futile, for it is certain that we have no criteria whatever to determine whether or no a particular work be from the pen of the Father of Medicine, and the most we can ever say of such a treatise is that it appears to be of his school and in his spirit. Yet among the great gifts of this collection to our time and to all time are two which stand out above all others, the picture of a man, and the picture of a method.

The man is Hippocrates himself. Of the actual details of his life we know next to nothing. His period of greatest activity falls about 400 B.c. He seems to have led a wandering life. Born of a long line of physicians in the island of Cos, he exerted his activities in Thrace, Abdera, Delos, the Propontis (Cyzicus), Thasos, Thessaly (notably at Larissa and Meliboea), Athens, and elsewhere, dying at Larissa in extreme old age about the year 377 B.c. He had many pupils, among whom were his two sons Thessalus and Dracon, who also undertook journeys, his son-in-law Polybus, of whose works a fragment has been preserved for us by Aristotle,[2] together with three other Coans bearing the names Apollonius, Dexippus, and Praxagoras. This

---

[1] Galen, περὶ ἀνατομικῶν ἐγχειρήσεων, *On anatomical preparations*, § 1, K. II, p. 282.

[2] *Historia animalium*, iii. 3, where it is ascribed to Polybus. The same passage is, however, repeated twice in the Hippocratic writings, viz. in the περὶ φύσιος ἀνθρώπου, *On the nature of man*, Littré, vi. 58, and in the περὶ ὀστέων φύσιος, *On the nature of bones*, Littré, ix. 174.

is practically all we know of him with certainty. But though this glimpse is very dim and distant, yet we cannot exaggerate the influence on the course of medicine and the value for physicians of all time of the traditional picture that was early formed of him and that may indeed well be drawn again from the works bearing his name. In beauty and dignity that figure is beyond praise. Perhaps gaining in stateliness what he loses in clearness, Hippocrates will ever remain the type of the perfect physician. Learned, observant, humane, with a profound reverence for the claims of his patients, but an overmastering desire that his experience shall benefit others, orderly and calm, disturbed only by anxiety to record his knowledge for the use of his brother physicians and for the relief of suffering, grave, thoughtful and reticent, pure of mind and master of his passions, this is no overdrawn picture of the Father of Medicine as he appeared to his contemporaries and successors. It is a figure of character and virtue which has had an ethical value to medical men of all ages comparable only to the influence exerted on their followers by the founders of the great religions. If one needed a maxim to place upon the statue of Hippocrates, none could be found better than that from the book Παραγγελίαι, *Precepts*:

ἢν γὰρ παρῇ φιλανθρωπίη πάρεστι καὶ φιλοτεχνίη

'Where the love of man is, there also is love of the Art.'[1]

The numerous busts of him which have reached our time are no portraits. But the best of them are something much better and more helpful to us than any portrait. They are idealized representations of the kind of man a physician should be and was in the eyes of the best and wisest of the Greeks.[2]

The method of the Hippocratic writers is that known to-day as the 'inductive'. Without the vast scientific heritage that is in our own hands, with only a comparatively small number of observations drawn from the Coan and neighbouring schools, surrounded by all manner of bizarre oriental religions in which no adequate relation of cause and effect was recognized, and

---

[1] Παραγγελίαι, § 6.   [2] See Fig. 1.

Fig. 2. ASCLEPIUS

British Museum, fourth century B.C.

Fig. 1. HIPPOCRATES

British Museum, second or third century B.C.

above all constantly urged by the exuberant genius for speculation of that Greek people in the midst of whom they lived and
whose intellectual temptations they shared, they remain nevertheless, for the most part, patient observers of fact, sceptical
of the marvellous and the unverifiable, hesitating to theorize
beyond the data, yet eager always to generalize from actual
experience; calm, faithful, effective servants of the sick. There
is almost no type of mental activity known to us that was not
exhibited by the Greeks and cannot be paralleled from their
writings; but careful and constant return to verification from
experience, expressed in a record of actual observations—the
habitual method adopted in modern scientific departments—is
rare among them except in these early medical authors.

The spirit of their practice cannot be better illustrated than
by the words of the so-called ' Hippocratic oath '. That document, though of late date in its present form, throws a flood of
light on the ethics of Greek medicine.

' I swear by Apollo the physician and Asclepius and Hygieia
and Panacea, invoking all the gods and goddesses to be my
witnesses, that I will fulfil this Oath and this written covenant
to the best of my power and of my judgment.

' I will look upon him who shall have taught me this art even
as on mine own parents ; I will share with him my substance,
and supply his necessities if he be in need ; I will regard his
offspring even as my own brethren, and will teach them this
art, if they desire to learn it, without fee or covenant. I will
impart it by precept, by lecture and by all other manner of
teaching, not only to my own sons but also to the sons of him
who has taught me, and to disciples bound by covenant and
oath according to the law of the physicians, but to none other.

' The regimen I adopt shall be for the benefit of the patients
to the best of my power and judgment, not for their injury or
for any wrongful purpose. I will not give a deadly drug to any
one, though it be asked of me, nor will I lead the way in such
counsel ; and likewise I will not give a woman a pessary to
procure abortion. But I will keep my life and my art in purity
and holiness. Whatsoever house I enter, I will enter for the
benefit of the sick, refraining from all voluntary wrongdoing
and corruption, especially seduction of male or female, bond

or free. Whatsoever things I see or hear concerning the life of men, in my attendance on the sick or even apart from my attendance, which ought not to be blabbed abroad, I will keep silence on them, counting such things to be as religious secrets.

' If I fulfil this oath and confound it not, be it mine to enjoy life and art alike, with good repute among all men for all time to come ; but may the contrary befall me if I transgress and violate my oath.' [1]

Respected equally throughout the ages by Arab, Jew, and Christian, the oath remains the watchword of the profession of medicine.[2] The ethical value of such a declaration could not escape the attention even of a Byzantine formalist, and it is interesting to observe that in our oldest Greek manuscript of the Hippocratic text, dating from the tenth century, this magnificent passage is headed by the words ' from the oath of Hippocrates according as it may be sworn by a Christian.'[3]

When we examine the Hippocratic corpus more closely, we discern that not only are the treatises by many hands, but there is not even a uniform opinion and doctrine running through them. This is well brought out by some of the more famous of the phrases of this remarkable collection. Thus a well-known passage from the *Airs, Waters, and Places* tells us that the Scythians attribute a certain physical disability to a god, ' but it appears to me ', says the author, ' that these affections are just as much divine as are all others and that no disease is either more divine or more human than another, but that all are equally divine, for each of them has its own nature, and none of them arise without a natural cause.' But, on the other hand, the author of the great work on *Prognostics* advises us that when the physician is called in he must seek to ascertain the nature of the affections that he is treating, and especially ' if there be anything divine in the disease, and to learn a foreknowledge of

[1] Translation by Professor Arthur Platt.

[2] It must, however, be admitted that in the Hippocratic collection are breaches of the oath, e. g. in the induction of abortion related in περὶ φύσιος παιδίου. There is evidence, however, that the author of this work was not a medical practitioner. [3] Rome Urbinas 64, fo. 116.

this also.'[1] We may note too that this sentence almost immediately precedes what is perhaps the most famous of all the Hippocratic sentences, the description of what has since been termed the *Hippocratic facies*. This wonderful description of the signs of death may be given as an illustration of the habitual attitude of the Hippocratic school towards prognosis and of the very careful way in which they noted details :

' He [the physician] should observe thus in acute diseases : first, the countenance of the patient, if it be like to those who are in health, *and especially if it be like itself, for this would be the best*; but the more unlike to this, the worse it is ; such would be these : *sharp nose, hollow eyes, collapsed temples ; ears cold, contracted, and their lobes turned out ; skin about the forehead rough, distended, and parched ; the colour of the whole face greenish or dusky.* If the countenance be so at the beginning of the disease, and if this cannot be accounted for from the other symptoms, inquiry must be made whether he has passed a sleepless night ; whether his bowels have been very loose ; or whether he is suffering from hunger ; and if any of these be admitted the danger may be reckoned as less ; and it may be judged in the course of a day and night if the appearance of the countenance proceed from these. But if none of these be said to exist, and the symptoms do not subside in that time, be it known for certain that death is at hand.'[2]

Again, in the work *On the Art* [*of Medicine*] we read : ' I hold it to be physicianly to abstain from treating those who are overwhelmed by disease ',[3] a prudent if inhumane procedure among a people who might regard the doctor's powers as partaking of the nature of magic, and perhaps a wise course to follow at this day in some places not very far from Cos. Yet in the book *On Diseases* we are advised even in the presence of an incurable disease ' to give relief with such treatment as is possible '.[4]

Furthermore, works by authors of the Hippocratic school

[1] Kühlewein, i. 79, regards this as an interpolated passage.

[2] Littré, ii. 112 ; Kühlewein, i. 79. The texts vary : Kühlewein is followed except in the last sentence.

[3] Περὶ τέχνης, § 3.   [4] Περὶ νούσων αʹ, § 6.

stand sometimes in a position of direct controversy with each other. Thus in the treatise *On the Heart* an experiment is set forth which is held to prove that a part at least of imbibed fluid passes into the cavity of the lung and thence to the parts of the body, a popular error in antiquity which recurs in Plato's *Timaeus*. This view, however, is specifically held to be fallacious by the author of the work *On Diseases*, who is supported by a polemical section in the surviving Menon fragment.

Passages like these have convinced all students that we have to deal in this collection with a variety of works written at different dates by different authors and under different conditions, a state that may be well understood when we reflect that among the Greeks medicine was a progressive study for a far longer period of time than has yet been the case in the Western world. An account of such a collection can therefore only be given in the most general fashion. The system or systems of medicine that we shall thus attempt to describe was in vogue up to the Alexandrian period, that is, to the beginning of the third century B.C.

Anatomy and physiology, the basis of our modern system, was still a very weak point in the knowledge of the pre-Alexandrians. The surface form of the body was intimately studied in connexion especially with fractures, but there is no evidence in the literature of the period of any closer acquaintance with human anatomical structure.[1] The same fact is well borne out by Greek Art, for in its noblest period the artist betrays no evidence of assistance derived from anatomization. Such evidence is not found until we come to sculpture of Alexandrian date, when the somewhat strained attitudes and exaggerated musculature of certain works of the school of Pergamon suggest that the artist derived hints, if not direct information, from anatomists who, we know, were active at that time. It is not improbable, however, that separate bones, if not complete skeletons, were commonly studied earlier, for the

---

[1] A reference to dissection in the περὶ ἄρθρων, *On the joints*, § 1, appears to the present writer to be of Alexandrian date.

surgical works of the Hippocratic collection, and especially those on fractures and dislocations, give evidence of a knowledge of the relations of bones to each other and of their natural position in the body which could not be obtained, or only obtained with greatest difficulty, without this aid.

There are in the Hippocratic works a certain number of comparisons between human and animal structures that would have been made possible by surgical operations and occasional accidents. The view has been put forward that some anatomical knowledge was derived through the practice of augury from the entrails of sacrificial animals. It appears, however, improbable that a system so scientific and so little related to temple practice would have had much to learn from these sources, and, more-over, since we know that animals were actually dissected as early as the time of Alcmaeon it would be unnecessary to invoke the aid of the priests. The unknown author of the περὶ τόπων τῶν κατὰ ἄνθρωπον, *On the sites of [diseases] in man*, a work written about 400 B.C., declares indeed that ' physical structure is the basis of medicine ', but the formal treatises on anatomy that we possess from Hippocratic times give the general anatomical standard of the corpus, and it is a very disappointing one. The tract *On Anatomy*, though probably of much later date (perhaps *c.* 330 B.C.), is inferior even to the treatise *On the Heart* (per-haps of about 400 B.C.).

Physiology and Pathology are almost as much in the back-ground as anatomy in the Hippocratic collection. As a formal discipline and part of medical education we find no trace of these studies among the pre-Alexandrian physicians. But the meagreness of the number of ascertained facts did not prevent much speculation among a people eager to seek the causes of things. Of that speculation we learn much from the fragments of contemporary medical writers and philosophers, from the medical works of the Alexandrian period, and to some extent from the Hippocratic writings themselves. But the wiser and more sober among the writers of the Hippocratic corpus were bent on something other than the causes of things. Their

pre-occupation was primarily with the suffering patient, and the
best of them therefore excluded—and we may assume consciously—all but the rarest references to such speculation.

The general state of health of the body was considered by
the Hippocratists to depend on the distribution of the four
elements, earth, air, fire, and water, whose mixture (*crasis*) and
cardinal properties, dryness, warmth, coldness, and moistness,
form the body and its constituents. To these correspond the
cardinal fluids, blood, phlegm, yellow bile and back bile. The
fundamental condition of life is the *innate heat*, the abdication
of which is death. This innate heat is greatest in youth when
most fuel is therefore required, but gradually declines with age.
Another necessity for the support of life is the *pneuma* which
circulates in the vessels. All this may seem fanciful enough, but
we may remember that the first half of the nineteenth century
had waned before the doctrine of the humours which had then
lasted for at least twenty-two centuries became obsolete, and
perhaps it still survives in certain modern scientific developments. Moreover, the finest and most characteristic of the
Hippocratic works either do not mention or but casually refer
to these theories which are not essential to their main pre-
occupation. Their task of observation of symptoms, of the
separation of the essentials from the accidents of disease, and of
generalization from experience could go on unaffected by any
view of the nature of man and of the world. Even treatment,
which must almost of necessity be based on *some* theory of
causation, was little deflected by a view of elements and humours
on which it was impossible to act directly, while therapeutics
was further safeguarded from such influence by the doctrine of
Nature as the healer of diseases, νούσων φύσεις ἰητροί, the *vis medi-
catrix naturae* of the later Latin writers and of the present day.

Diseases are to be cured, in the Hippocratic view, by restoring
the disturbed harmony in the relation of the elements and
humours. These, in fact, tend naturally to an equilibrium and
in most cases if left to themselves will be brought to this state

by the natural tendency to recovery. The process is known as *pepsis* or, to give it the Latin form, *coctio*, and the turning-point at which the effects of this process exhibit themselves is the *crisis*, a term which, together with some of its original content, has still a place in medicine. Such a turning-point does in fact occur in many diseases, especially those of a zymotic character, on certain special days, though undue emphasis was laid by the Greek physicians upon the exact numerical character of the event. It was no unimportant duty of the physician to assist nature by bringing his remedies to bear at the critical times. If the crisis is wanting, or if the remedies are applied at the wrong moment, the disease may become incurable. But diseases were only immediately or proximately caused by disturbances in the balance or harmony of the humours. This was a mere hypothesis, as the Hippocratists themselves well knew. There were other more remote causes which came into the actual purview of the physician, conditions which he could and did study. Such conditions were, for instance, injudicious modes of life, exposure to climatic changes, advancing age, and the like. Many of these could be directly corrected. But for those that could not there were various therapeutic measures at hand.

That human bodies are and normally remain in a state of health, and that on the whole they tend to recover from disease, is an attitude so familiar to us to-day that we scarcely need to be reminded of it. We live some twenty-three centuries later than Hippocrates ; for some sixteen of those centuries the civilized world thought that to retain health periodical bleedings and potions were necessary ; for the last century or two we have been gradually returning on the Hippocratic position !

The chief glory of the Hippocratic collection regarded from the clinical point of view is perhaps the actual description of cases. A number of these—forty-two in all—have survived.[1] They are not

[1] They are to be found as an Appendix to Books I and III of the *Epidemics* and embedded in Book III.

only unique as a collection for nearly 2,000 years, but they are still to this day models of what succinct clinical records should be, clear and short, without a superfluous word, yet with all that is most essential, and exhibiting merely a desire to record the most important facts without the least attempt to prejudge the case. They illustrate to the full the Greek genius for seizing on the essential. The writer shows not the least wish to exalt his own skill. He seeks merely to put the data before the reader for his guidance under like circumstances. It is a reflex of the spirit of full honesty in which these men lived and worked that the great majority of the cases are recorded to have died. Two of this remarkable little collection may be given :

' The woman with quinsy, who lodged with Aristion : her complaint began in the tongue ; voice inarticulate ; tongue red and parched. *First day*, shivered, then became heated. *Third day*, rigor, acute fever ; reddish and hard swelling on both sides of neck and chest; extremities cold and livid ; respiration elevated; drink returned by the nose; she could not swallow ; alvine and urinary discharges suppressed. *Fourth day*, all symptoms exacerbated. *Fifth day*, she died.'

We probably have here to do with a case of diphtheria. The quinsy, the paralysis of the palate leading to return of the food through the nose, and the difficulty with speech and swallowing are typical results of this affection which was here complicated by a spread of the septic processes into the neck and chest, a not uncommon sequela of the disease. The rapid onset of the conditions is rather unusual, but may be explained if we regard the case as a mild and unnoticed diphtheria, subsequently complicated by paralysis and by secondary septic infection, for which reasons she came under observation.

' In Thasos, the wife of Delearces who lodged on the plain, through sorrow was seized with an acute and shivering fever. From first to last she always wrapped herself up in her bedclothes ; kept silent, fumbled, picked, bored and gathered hairs [from the clothes] ; tears, and again laughter ; no sleep ; bowels irritable, but passed nothing ; when urged drank a little ; urine thin and scanty ; to the touch the fever was slight ; coldness of the extremities. *Ninth day*, talked much incoherently, and again sank into silence. *Fourteenth day*, breathing rare, large, and spaced, and again hurried. *Seventeenth day*, after stimulation of the bowels she passed even drinks, nor could retain anything ; totally insensible ; skin parched and tense. *Twentieth day*, much talk, and again became composed, then voiceless ; respiration hurried. *Twenty-first day*, died. Her respiration throughout was rare and large ; she was totally insensible ; always wrapped up in her bedclothes ; throughout either much talk, or complete silence.'

This second case is in part a description of low muttering delirium, a common end of continued fevers such as, for instance, typhoid. The description closely resembles the condition known now in medicine as the ' typhoid state '. Incidentally the case contains a reference to a type of breathing common among the dying. The respiration becomes deep and slow, as it sinks gradually into quietude and becomes rarer and rarer until it seems to cease altogether, and then it gradually becomes more rapid and so on alternately. This type of breathing is known to physicians as ' Cheyne-Stokes ' respiration in commemoration of two distinguished Irish physicians of the last century who brought it to the attention of medical men.[1] Recently it has been partially explained on a physiological basis. We may note that there is another and even better pen-picture of Cheyne-Stokes respiration in the Hippocratic collection. It is in the famous case of ' Philescos who lived by the wall and who took to his bed on the first day of acute fever '. About the middle of the sixth day he died and the physician notes that

[1] John Cheyne (1777–1836) described this type of respiration in the *Dublin Hospital Reports*, 1818, ii, p. 216. An extreme case of this condition had been described by Cheyne's namesake George Cheyne (1671–1743) as the famous ' Case of the Hon. Col. Townshend ' in his *English Malady*, London, 1733. William Stokes (1804–78) published his account of Cheyne-Stokes breathing in the *Dublin Quarterly Journal of the Medical Sciences*, 1846, ii, p. 73.

' the respiration throughout was *like that of a person recollecting himself* and was large and rare '. Cheyne-Stokes breathing is admirably described as ' that of a person recollecting himself '.

Such records as these may be contrasted with certain others that have come down from Greek antiquity. We may instance two steles discovered at Epidaurus in 1885, bearing accounts of forty-four temple cures. The following two are fair samples of the cures there described :

'*Aristagora of Troizen.* She had tape-worm, and while she slept in the Temple of Asclepius at Troizen, she saw a vision. She thought that, as the god was not present, but was away in Epidaurus, his sons cut off her head, but were unable to put it back again. Then they sent a messenger to Asclepius asking him to come to Troizen. Meanwhile day came, and the priest actually saw her head cut off from the body. The next night Aristagora had a dream. She thought the god came from Epidaurus and fastened her head on to her neck. Then he cut open her belly, and stitched it up again. So she was cured.'

' A man had an abdominal abscess. He saw a vision, and thought that the god ordered the slaves who accompanied him to lift him up and hold him, so that his abdomen could be cut open. The man tried to get away, but his slaves caught him and bound him. So Asclepius cut him open, rid him of the abscess, and then stitched him up again, releasing him from his bonds. Straightway he departed cured, and the floor of the Abaton was covered with blood.' [1]

In the records of almost all temple cures, a great number of which have survived in a wide variety of documents, an essential element is the process of ἐγκοίμησις, *incubation* or temple sleep, usually in a special sleeping-place or Abaton. The process has a close parallel in certain modern Greek churches and in places of worship much further West ; there are even traces of it in these islands, and it is more than probable that the Christian

[1] The Epidaurian inscriptions are given by M. Fraenkel in the *Corpus Inscriptionum Graecarum* IV, 951-6, and are discussed by Mary Hamilton (Mrs. Guy Dickins), *Incubation*, St. Andrews, 1906, from whose translation I have quoted. Further inscriptions are given by Cavvadias in the *Archaiologike Ephemeris*, 1918, p. 155 (issued 1921).

practice is descended by direct continuity from the pagan.[1] The whole character of the temple treatment was—and is—of a kind to suggest to the patient that he should dream of the god, an event which therefore usually takes place. Such treatment by suggestion is applicable only to certain classes of disease and is always liable to fall into the hands of fanatics and impostors. The difficulty that the honest practitioner encounters is that the sufferer, in the nature of the case, can hardly be brought to believe that his ailment is what in fact it is, a lesion of the mind. It is this which gives the miracle-monger his chance.

Examine for a moment the two cases from Epidaurus, which are quite typical of the series. We observe that the first is described simply as a case of 'tape-worm' without any justification for the diagnosis. It is not unfrequent nowadays for thin and anxious patients to state, similarly without justification, that they suffer from this condition. They attribute certain common gastric experiences to this cause of which perhaps they have learned from sensational advertisements, and then they ask cure for a condition which they themselves have diagnosed, but which has no existence in fact. Such a case is often appropriately treated by suggestion. Though the elaborateness of the suggestion in the temple cure is a little startling, yet it can easily be paralleled from the legends of the Christian saints. Moreover, we must remember that we are not here dealing with an account set down by the patient herself, but with an edificatory inscription put up by the temple officials.

In the second inscription, the man with an abdominal abscess, we have a much simpler state of affairs. It is evident that an operation was actually performed by the priest masquerading as Asclepius, while the patient was held down by the slaves. He is assured that all is a dream and departs cured with the tell-tale comment ' and the floor of the Abaton was covered with blood '.

[1] We are almost told as much in the apocryphal *Gospel of Nicodemus*, § 1, a work probably composed about the end of the fourth century.

These cases might be multiplied indefinitely without great profit for our particular theme, for in such matters there is no development, no evolution, no history. There can be no doubt that a very large part of Greek practice was on this level, as is a small part of modern medicine, but it is not a level with which we are here dealing and we shall therefore pass it by. But a word of caution must be added. Such temple worship has been compared with modern psycho-analysis. That method, like all methods, has doubtless been abused at times; but it is in essence, unlike the temple system, a purely scientific process by which the ultimate basis of the patient's delusions are laid bare and demonstrated to him.

There is indeed another side to these Asclepian temples. They gradually developed along the lines of our health resorts and developed many of the qualities—lovely and unlovely—that we associate with certain continental watering places. On the bad side they became gossiping centres or even something little better than brothels, as we may gather from the *Mimes* of Herondas. On the good side they formed a quiet refuge among beautiful and interesting surroundings where the sick, exhausted, and convalescent might gain the benefits that accrue from pure air, fine scenery, and a regular and regulated mode of life. It is more than probable too that the open air and manner of living benefited many cases of incipient phthisis.

Returning to the Hippocratic collection, the purely surgical treatises will be found no less remarkable than those of clinical observation. A very able surgeon, Francis Adams (1796–1861), who was eminent as a Greek scholar, gave it as his opinion in the middle of the nineteenth century that no systematic writer on surgery up to his time had given so good and so complete an account of certain dislocations, notably of the hip-joint, as that to be found in the Hippocratic collection. Some types of injury to the hip, as described in the Hippocratic writings, were certainly otherwise quite inadequately known until described by Sir Astley Cooper (1768–1841),

From MS. of APOLLONIUS OF KITIUM, of Ninth Century
Copied from a pre-christian original

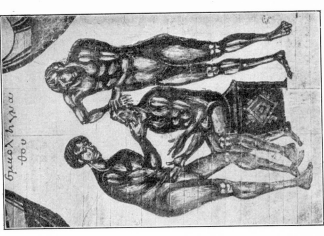

Fig. 3
REDUCING DISLOCATED SHOULDER

Fig. 4
REDUCING DISLOCATED JAW

himself a peculiarly Hippocratic character.[1] The verdict of Adams was probably just, though since his time the surgery of dislocations, aided especially by X-rays, has been enabled to pass very definitely beyond the Hippocratic position. Admirable, too, is the Hippocratic description of dislocation of the shoulder and of the jaw. In dislocation of hip, shoulder, or jaw, as in most similar lesions, there is considerable deformity produced. The nature and meaning of this deformity is described with remarkable exactness by the Hippocratic writer, who also sets forth the resulting disability. The principles and indeed the very details of treatment in these cases are, save for the use of an anaesthetic, practically identical with those of the present day. The processes are unfortunately not suitable for detailed quotation and description here, but they are of special interest since a graphic record of them has come down to us. There exists in the Laurentian Library at Florence a ninth-century Greek surgical manuscript which contains figures of surgeons reducing the dislocations in question. There is good reason to suppose that these miniatures are copied from figures first prepared in pre-Christian times many centuries earlier, and we may here see the actual processes of reduction of such fractures, as conducted by a surgeon of the direct Hippocratic tradition [2] (see Figs. 3, 4).

In keeping with all this is most of the surgical work of the collection. We are almost startled by the modern sound of the whole procedure as we run through the rough note-book κατ᾽ ἰητρεῖον, *Concerning the Surgery*, or the more elaborate treatise περὶ ἰητροῦ, *On the Physician*, where we may read minute directions for the preparation of the operating-room,

---

[1] Astley Paston Cooper, *Treatise on Dislocations and Fractures of the Joints*, London, 1822, and *Observations on Fractures of the Neck and the Thighbone*, &c., London, 1823.

[2] This famous manuscript is known as Laurentian, Plutarch 74, 7, and its figures have been reproduced by H. Schöne, *Apollonius von Kitium*, Leipzig, 1896.

and on such points as the management of light both artificial
and natural, scrupulous cleanliness of the hands, the care and
use of the instruments, with the special precautions needed

FIG. 5.

A GREEK CLINIC OF ABOUT 480–470 B.C. From a vase-painting.

In the centre sits a physician holding a lancet and bleeding a patient
from the median vein at the bend of the right elbow into a large open
basin. Above and behind the physician are suspended three cupping vessels.
To the right sits another patient awaiting his turn; his left arm is bandaged
in the region of the biceps. The figure beyond him smells a flower, perhaps
as a preservative against infection. Behind the physician stands a man
leaning on a staff; he is wounded in the left leg, which is bandaged. By
his side stands a dwarfish figure with disproportionately large head, whose
body exhibits deformities typical of the developmental disease now known
as *Achondroplasia*; in addition to these deformities we note that his body
is hairy and the bridge of his nose sunken; on his back he carries a hare
which is almost as tall as himself. Talking to the dwarf is a man leaning
on a long staff, who has the remains of a bandage round his chest.

See E. Pottier, 'Une Clinique grecque au Vᵉ siècle (vase antique du
collection Peztel)', *Fondation Eugène Piot, Monuments et Mémoires*,
xiii. 149, Paris, 1906. (Some of our interpretations differ from those of
M. Pottier.)

when they are of iron, the decencies to be observed during the
operation, the general method of bandaging, the placing of
the patient, the use and abuse of splints, and the need for
tidiness, order, and cleanliness. Many of these directions are
enlarged upon in other surgical works of the collection, among

FIG. 6. A kylix from the Berlin Museum of about 490 B.C. It bears the
inscription ΣΟΣΙΑΣ ΕΠΟΙΗΣΕΝ, *Sosias made* (*me*), and represents Achilles
bandaging Patroclus, the names of the two heroes being written round the
margin. The painter is Euphronios, and the work is regarded as the masterpiece of that great artist. The left upper arm of Patroclus is injured, and
Achilles is bandaging it with a two-rolled bandage, which he is trying
to bring down to extend over the elbow. The treatment of the hands,
a department in which Euphronios excelled, is particularly fine. Achilles
was not a trained surgeon, and it will be observed, from the position of the
two tails of the bandage, that he will have some difficulty when it comes to
its final fastening!

which we find especially full instructions for bandaging and
for the diagnosis and treatment of fractures and dislocations.
A very fair representation of such a surgery as these works
describe is to be found on a vase-painting of Attic origin of the
earlier part of the fifth century, and, therefore, a generation
before Hippocrates (see fig. 5). There are also several beautiful
representations on vases of the actual processes of bandaging
(fig. 6).

Among the surgical procedures of which descriptions are
to be found in the Hippocratic writings are the opening of
the chest for the condition known as *empyema* (accumulation
of pus within the pleura frequently following pneumonia),
and trephining the skull in cases of fracture of that part—two
fundamental operations of modern surgery. Surgical art has
advanced enormously in our own times, yet a text-book containing much that is useful to this day might be prepared from
these surgical contents of the collection alone.

When we pass to the works on Medicine, in the restricted
sense, we enter into a region more difficult and perhaps even
more fascinating. We are no longer dealing with simple lesions
of known origin, but with the effects of disease and degeneration, of the essential character of which the Hippocratic writers
could in the nature of the case know very little. Rigidly guard-
ing themselves from any attempt to explain disease by more
immediate and hypothetical causes and thus diverting the
reader's energies in the medically useless direction of vague
speculation—the prevalent mental vice of the Greeks—the
best of these physicians are content if they can put forward
generalized conclusions from actually observed cases. Many
of their thoughts have now become household words,
and they have become so, largely as a direct heritage from
these ancient physicians. But it must be remembered that
ideas so familiar to us were with them the result of long and
carefully recorded experience and are like nothing that we
encounter in the medicine of other ancient nations. Such

conclusions are best set forth perhaps in the wonderful book of the *Aphorisms* from which we may permit ourselves a few quotations :

' Life is short, and the Art long ; the opportunity fleeting ; experiment dangerous, and judgement difficult. Yet we must be prepared not only to do our duty ourselves, but also patient, attendants, and external circumstances must co-operate.' ¹

In this one memorable paragraph, so condensed in the original as to be almost untranslatable, he who ' first separated medicine from philosophy ' puts aside at once all speculative interest while in the actual presence of the sick. His whole energy is concentrated on the case in hand with that peculiar attitude, at once impersonal and intensely personal, that has since been the mark of the physician, and that has made of Medicine both a science and an art.

' For extreme diseases, extreme methods of cure.' ²
' The aged endure fasting most easily ; next adults ; next young persons, and least of all children, and especially such as are the most lively.'
' Growing bodies have the most innate heat ; they therefore require the most nourishment, and if they have it not they waste. In the aged there is little heat, and therefore they require little fuel, for it would be extinguished by much. Similarly fevers in the aged are not so acute, because their bodies are cold.'
' In disease sleep that is laborious is a deadly symptom ; but if sleep relieves it is not deadly.'
' Sleep that puts an end to delirium is a good symptom.'

¹ The first lines are the source of the famous lines in Goethe's *Faust* :
> ' Ach Gott ! die Kunst ist lang
> Und kurz ist unser Leben,
> Mir wird bei meinem kritischen Bestreben
> Doch oft um Kopf und Busen bang.'

² The extreme of treatment refers in the original to the extreme restriction of diet, ἐς ἀκριβείην, but the meaning of the Aphorism has always been taken as more generalized.

'If a convalescent eats well, but does not put on flesh, it is a bad symptom.'

'Food or drink which is a little less good but more palatable, is to be preferred to such that is better but less palatable.'

'The old have generally fewer complaints than young; but those chronic diseases which do befall them generally never leave them.'

Here we have a group of observations, some of which have become literally household words, nor is it difficult to understand how such sayings have passed from professional into lay keeping. This magnificent book of *Aphorisms* was very early translated into Latin, probably before and certainly not later than the sixth century of the Christian era, and thus became accessible throughout the West. Manuscripts of this Latin version, dating from the ninth and tenth centuries of our era, have survived in the actual places in which they were written, at Monte Cassino in Southern Italy and at Einsiedeln in Switzerland, and in 991 the book of *Aphorisms* was well known and closely studied at the Cathedral school of Chartres. From France the *Aphorisms* reached England, and they are mentioned in documents of the tenth or eleventh century. By now, too, the book had been translated into Syriac and later into Arabic and Hebrew, so that in the true mediaeval period it was known both East and West, and in the vernacular as well as the classical tongues. From the oriental dialects several further translations were again made into Latin. An enormous number of manuscripts of the work have survived in almost every Western dialect, and these show on the whole that the text has been surprisingly little tampered with. In the middle of the thirteenth century some of the better-known Aphorisms were absorbed into a very popular Latin poem that went forth in the name of the medical school of Salerno, though with a false ascription to a yet earlier date. The Salernitan poem, being itself translated into every European vernacular, further helped to bring Hippocrates into every home.

But by no means all the Aphorisms are of a kind that could well become absorbed into folk medicine. It is only those concerning frequently recurring states to which this fate could befall. The book contains also a number of notes on rare conditions seldom seen or noted save by medical men. Such are the following very acute observations :

'Spasm supervening on a wound is fatal.'

'Those seized with tetanus die within four days, or if they survive so long they recover.'

'A convulsion, or hiccup, supervening on a copious discharge of blood is bad.'

'If after severe and grave wounds no swelling appears, it is very serious.'

These four sentences all concern wounds. The first two refer to the disease *tetanus*, which is very liable to supervene on wounds fouled with earth, especially in hot and moist localities. The disease is characterized by a series of painful muscular contractions which in the more severe and fatal form may become a continuous spasm, a type that is referred to in the first sentence. It is true of tetanus that the later the onset after the wound is sustained the better the chance of recovery. This is brought out by the second sentence. The third and fourth sentences record untoward symptoms following a severe wound, now well recognized and watched for by every surgeon. There were, of course, innumerable illustrations of the truth of these Aphorisms in extensive wounds, especially those involving crushed limbs, in the late war.

'Phthisis occurs most commonly between the ages of eighteen and thirty-five.'

'Diarrhœa supervening on phthisis is mortal.'

The period given by the *Aphorisms* for the maximum frequency of onset of the disease is closely borne out by modern observations. The second Aphorism is equally valid ; continued diarrhœa is a very frequent antecedent of the fatal event in chronic phthisis, and post-mortem examination has shown that secondary involvement of the bowel is an exceedingly common condition in this disease.

No less remarkable is the following saying : ' In jaundice it is a grave matter if the liver becomes indurated.' Jaundice is a common and comparatively trivial symptom following or accompanying a large variety of diseases. In and by itself it is of little importance and almost always disappears spontaneously. There is a small group of pathological conditions, however, in which this is not the case. The commonest and most important of these are the fatal affections of cirrhosis and cancer of the liver in which that organ may be felt to be enlarged and hardened. If therefore the liver can be so felt in a case of jaundice, it is, as the Aphorism says, of gravest import. Representations of such cases have actually come down to us from Greek times. Thus on a monument erected at Athens to the memory of a physician who died in the second century of the Christian era we may see the process of clinical examination (fig. 7). The physician is palpating the liver of a dwarfish figure whose swollen belly, wasted limbs, and anxious look tell of some such condition as that described in the Aphorism. The ridge caused by the enlarged liver can even be detected on the statue.

' We must attend to the appearances of the eyes in sleep as presented from below ; for if a portion of the white be seen between the closing eyelids, and if this be not connected with diarrhœa or severe purging, it is a very bad and mortal symptom.' In this, the last Aphorism which we shall quote, we see the Hippocratic physician actually making his observations. Now during sleep the eyeball is turned upward, so that if the eye be then opened and examined only the white is seen. In the later stages of all wasting and chronic diseases the eyelids tend not to be closed during sleep. Such patients, as is well known, often die with the eyes open and sometimes exhibiting only the whites.

But the Hippocratic physician was not content to make only

passive observation; he also took active measures to elicit the 'physical signs'. In modern times a large, perhaps the chief, task of the student of medicine is to acquire a knowledge of these so-called physical signs of disease, the tradition of which has been gradually rebuilt during the last three centuries. Among the most important measures in which he learns to acquire facility is that of auscultation. This useful process has come specially into vogue since the invention of the stethoscope in 1819 by Laennec, who derived valuable hints for it from the Hippocratic writings. Auscultation is several times mentioned and described by the Hippocratic physicians, who used the direct method of listening and not the mediate method devised by Laennec. There are, however, certain cases in which the modern physician still finds the older non-instrumental Hippocratic method superior. In the Hippocratic work περὶ νούσων, *On diseases*, we read of a case with fluid in the pleura that 'you will place the patient on a seat which does not move, an assistant will hold him by the shoulders, and you will shake him, applying the ear to the chest, so as to recognize on which side the sign occurs'. This sign is still used by physicians and is known as *Hippocratic succussion*. In another passage in the same work the symptoms of pleurisy are described and 'a creak like that of leather may be heard'. This is the well known *pleuritic rub* which the physician is accustomed to seek in such cases, and of which the creak of leather is an excellent representation.

Such quotations give an insight into the general method and attitude of the Hippocratics. Of an art such as medicine, which even in those times had a long and rational tradition behind it, it is impossible to give more than the merest glimpse in such a review as this. The actual practice is far too complex to set down briefly. This is especially the case with the ancient teaching as regards epidemic disease at which we must cursorily glance. The Hippocratic physicians and indeed all antiquity were as yet ignorant of the nature, and were but dimly aware of the existence, of infection.[1] For them acute disease was something imposed on the patient from outside, but how it reached him from outside and what it was that thus reached him they were still admittedly ignorant. In this dilemma they turned to prolonged observation and noted as a result of repeated experience that epidemic diseases in their world had characteristic seasonal and regional distributions. One country was not quite like another, nor was one season like another nor even one year like another. By a series of carefully collated observations as to how regions, seasons, and years differed from each other, they succeeded in laying the basis of a rational study of epidemiology which gave rise to the notion of an ' epidemic constitution ' of the different years, a conception which was very fertile and stimulating to the great clinicians of the seventeenth and eighteenth centuries and is by no means without value even for the modern epidemiologist. The work of the modern fathers of epidemiology was consciously based on Hippocrates.

Before parting with the Hippocratic physician a word must be said as to his therapeutic means. His general armoury may be described as resembling that of the modern physician of about two generations ago. During those two generations we have, it is true, added to our list of effective remedies but, on the other hand, there has been by common consent a return to the Hippocratic simplicity of treatment. After rest and

---

[1] The ancients knew almost nothing of infection *as applied specifically* to disease. All early peoples—including Greeks and Romans—believed in the transmission of qualities from object to object. Thus purity and impurity and good and bad luck were infections, and diseases were held to be infections in that sense. But there is little evidence in the belief of the special infectivity of *disease as such* in antiquity. Some few diseases are, however, unequivocally referred to as infectious in a limited number of passages, e.g. ophthalmia, scabies, and phthisis in the περὶ διαφορᾶς πυρετῶν, *On the differentiae of fevers*, K. vii, p. 279. The references to infection in antiquity are detailed by C. and D. Singer, 'The scientific position of Girolamo Fracastoro', *Annals of Medical History*, vol. i, New York, 1917.

Fig. 7. ATHENIAN FUNERARY MONUMENT

Second century A.D.   British Museum

Inscription reads: 'Jason, also called Dekmos, the Acharnian, a physician', followed by his genealogy.   By side of patient stands a cupping vessel.

quiet the central factor in treatment was Dietetics. This
science regarded the age—'Old persons use less nutriment
than young'; the season—'In winter abundant nourishment
is wholesome, in summer a more frugal diet'; the bodily
condition—'Lean persons should take little food, but this
little should be fat, fat persons on the other hand should
take much food, but it should be lean'. Respect was also paid
to the digestibility of different foods—'white meat is more
easily digestible than dark'—and to their preparation. Water,
barley water, and lime water were recommended as drinks.
The dietetic principles of the Hippocratics, especially in
connexion with fevers, are substantially those of the present
day, and it may be said that the general medical tendency of
the last generation in these matters has been an even closer
approximation to the Hippocratic. 'The more we nourish
unhealthy bodies the more we injure them'; 'The sick
upon whom fever seizes with the greatest severity from the
very outset, must at once subject themselves to a rigid diet';
'Complete abstinence often acts well, if the strength of the
patient can in any way sustain it'; yet 'We should examine the
strength of the sick, to see whether they be in condition to
maintain this spare diet to the crisis of the disease'. 'In the
application of these rules we must always be mindful of the
strength of the patient and of the course of each particular
disease, as well as of the constitution and ordinary mode of
life in each disease.'

Besides diet the Hippocratic physician had at his disposal
a considerable variety of other remedies. Baths, inunctions,
clysters, warm and cold suffusions, massage and gymnastic, as
well as gentler exercise are among them. He probably employed
cupping and bleeding rather too freely, and we have several
representations of the instruments used for these operations
(fig. 8). He was no great user of drugs and seldom names
them except, we may note, in the works on the treatment of
women, which are probably of Cnidian origin and whence

the greater part of the 300 constituents of the Hippocratic pharmacopœia are derived. Thus his list of drugs is small, but several known to him are still used by us.

The work of these men may be summed up by saying that without dissection, without any experimental physiology or pathology, and without any instrumental aid they pushed the knowledge of the course and origin of disease as far as it is conceivable that men in such circumstances could push it. This was done as a process of pure scientific induction. Their surgery, though hardly based on anatomy, was grounded on the most carefully recorded experience. In therapeutics they allowed themselves neither to be deceived by false hopes nor led aside by vain traditions. Yet in diagnosis, prognosis, surgery and therapeutics alike they were in many departments unsurpassed until the nineteenth century, and to some of their methods we have reverted in the twentieth. Persisting throughout the ages as a more or less definite tradition, which attained clearer form during and after the sixteenth century, Hippocratic methods have formed the basis of all departments of modern advance.

But the history of Greek medicine did not end with the Hippocratic collection; in many respects it may indeed be held only to begin there; yet we never get again a glimpse of so high an ethical and professional standard as that which these works convey. From Alexandrian times onwards, too, the history of Greek medicine becomes largely a history of various schools of medical thought, each of which has only a partial view of the course and nature of medical knowledge. The unravelling of the course and teachings of these sects has long been a pre-occupation of professed medical historians, but the general reader can hardly take an interest in differences between the Dogmatists, Empirics, and Methodists whose doctrines are as dead as themselves. In this later Alexandrian and Hellenistic age the Greek intellect is no less active than before, but there is a change in the taste of the material. A general decay of the spirit is reflected in the medical as in the literary products of the time, and we never again feel that elevation of a beautiful and calmly righteous presence that breathes through the Hippocratic collection and gives it a peculiar aroma.

We shall pass over the general course of later Greek medicine with great rapidity. A definite medical school was established at Alexandria and others perhaps at Pergamon and elsewhere. Athens, after the death of Aristotle and his pupils, passes entirely into the background and is of no importance so far as medicine is concerned. At Alexandria, where a great medical library was collected, anatomy began to be studied and two men whose discoveries were of primary importance for the history of that subject, Erasistratus and Herophilus, early practised there. With anatomy as a basis medical education could become much more systematic. It is a very great misfortune that the works of these two eminent men have disappeared. Of Herophilus fragments have survived embedded in the works of Galen (A. D. 130–201), Caelius Aurelianus (fifth century), and others. These fragments have been the subject of one of the earliest, most laborious, and most successful attempts made in modern times to reconstruct the lost work of an ancient author.[1] For Erasistratus our chief source of information are two polemical treatises directed against him by Galen. Recently, too, a little more information concerning the works of both men has become available from the Menon papyrus.

It has been found possible to reconstruct especially a treatise on anatomy by Herophilus with a considerable show of probability. He opened by giving general directions for the process of dissection and followed with detailed descriptions of the various systems, nervous, vascular, glandular, digestive, generative, and osseous. There was a separate section on the liver, a small part of which has survived. It is of his account of the nervous system that we have perhaps the best record,

[1] K. F. H. Marx, *Herophilus, ein Beitrag zur Geschichte der Medizin*, Karlsruhe, 1838.

and it is evident that he has advanced far beyond the Hippocratic position. In the braincase he saw the membranes that
cover the brain and distinguished between the cerebrum and
cerebellum. He attained to some knowledge of the ventricles
of the brain, the cranial and spinal nerves, the nerves of the
heart, and the coats of the eye. He distinguished the blood
sinuses of the skull, and the *torcular Herophili* (winepress of
Herophilus), a sinus described by him, has preserved his
name in modern anatomical nomenclature. He even made out
more minute structures, such as the little depression in the
fourth ventricle of the brain, known to modern anatomists
as the *calamus scriptorius*, which still bears the name which he
gave it (κάλαμος ᾧ γράφομεν), because it seemed to him, as Galen
tells us, to resemble the pens then in use in Alexandria.[1] We still
use, too, his term *duodenum* (δωδεκαδάκτυλος ἔκφυσις = twelve-
finger extension), for as Galen assures us, Herophilus ' so named
the first part of the intestine before it is rolled into folds '.[2]
The duodenum is a U-shaped section of the intestine following immediately on the stomach. Being fixed down behind
the abdominal cavity it cannot be further convoluted, and
this accounts for Galen's description of it. It is about twelve
fingers' breadth long in the animals dissected by Herophilus.

Erasistratus, the slightly younger Alexandrian contemporary
of Herophilus, has the credit of further anatomical discoveries.
He described correctly the action of the epiglottis in preventing
the entrance of food and drink into the windpipe during the
act of swallowing, he saw the lacteal vessels in the mesentery,
and pursued further the anatomy of the brain. He improved
on the anatomy of the heart, and described the auriculo-
ventricular valves and their mode of closure. He distinguished
clearly the motor and sensory nerves. He seems to have

---

[1] Galen, περὶ ἀνατομικῶν ἐγχειρήσεων, *On anatomical preparations*, ix. 5
(last sentence).

[2] Galen, περὶ φλεβῶν καὶ ἀρτηριῶν ἀνατομῆς, *On the anatomy of veins and
arteries*, i.

adopted a definitely experimental attitude—a very rare thing among ancient physicians—and a description of an experiment made by him has recently been recovered. ‘If’, he says, ‘you take an animal, a bird, for example, and keep it for a time in a jar without giving it food and then weigh it together with its excreta you will find that there is a considerable loss of weight.’[1] The experiment is a simple one, but it was about nineteen hundred years before a modern professor, Sanctorio Santorio (1561–1636), thought of repeating it.[2]

The anatomical advances made by the Alexandrian school naturally reacted on surgical efficiency. The improvement so effected may be gathered, for instance, from an account of the anatomical relationships in certain cases of dislocation of the hip given by the Alexandrian surgeon Hegetor, who lived about 100 B.C. In his book περὶ αἰτιῶν, *On causes* [*of disease*], he asks ‘why (certain surgeons) do not seek another way of reducing a luxation of the hip. . . . If the joints of the jaw, shoulder, elbow, knee, finger, &c., can be replaced, the same, they think, must be true of all parts, nor can they give an account of why the femur cannot be put back into its place. . . . They might have known, however, that from the head of the femur arises a ligament which is inserted into the socket of the hip bone . . . and if this ligament is once ruptured the thigh bone cannot be retained in place’.[3] This passage contains the first description of the structure known to modern anatomists as the *ligamentum teres*, a strong fibrous band which unites the head of the femur with the socket into which it fits in the hip bone, like the string that binds the cup and

---

[1] The quotation is from chapter xxxiii, line 44 of the *Anonymus Londinensis*. H. Diels, *Anonymus Londinensis* in the *Supplementum Aristotelicum*, vol. iii, pars 1, Berlin, 1893.

[2] Sanctorio Santorio, *Oratio in archilyceo patavino anno 1612 habita; de medicina statica aphorismi*. Venice, 1614.

[3] This is the only passage of Hegetor's writing that has survived. It has been preserved in the work of Apollonius of Citium.

ball of a child's toy. This ligament is ruptured in certain severe cases of dislocation of the hip.

After the establishment of the school at Alexandria, medical teaching rapidly became organized, but throughout the whole course of antiquity it suffered from the absence of anything in the nature of a state diploma. Any one could practise, with the result that many quacks, cranks, and fanatics were to be found among the ranks of the practitioners who often were or had been slaves. The great Alexandrian school, however, did much to preserve some sort of professional standard, and above all its anatomical discipline helped to this end.

Between the founding of the Alexandrian school and Galen we are not rich in medical writings. Apart from fragments and minor productions, the works of only five authors have survived from this period of over four hundred years, namely, Celsus, Dioscorides, Aretaeus of Cappadocia, and two Ephesian authors bearing the names of Rufus and Soranus.

The work of Celsus of the end of the first century B.C. is a Latin treatise, probably translated from Greek, and is the surviving medical volume of a complete cyclopaedia of knowledge. In spite of its unpromising origin it is an excellent compendium of its subject and shows a good deal of advance in many respects beyond the Hippocratic position. The moral tone too is very high, though without the lofty and detached beauty of Hippocrates. Anatomy has greatly improved, and with it surgical procedure, and the work is probably representative of the best Alexandrian practice. The pharmacopœia is more copious, but has not yet become burdensome. The general line of treatment is sensible and humane and the language concise and clear. Among other items he describes dental practice, with the indications for and methods of tooth extraction, the wiring of teeth, and perhaps a dental mirror. There is an excellent account of what might be thought to be the modern operation for removal of the tonsils. Celsus is still commemorated in modern medicine by the *area Celsi*, a not

Fig. 8. VOTIVE TABLET representing cupping and bleeding instruments from Temple of Asclepius at Athens. In centre is represented a folding case containing scalpels of various forms. On either side are cupping vessels.

uncommon disease of the skin. The *De re medica* is in fact one of the very best medical text-books that have come down to us from antiquity. It has had a romantic history. Forgotten during the Middle Ages, it was brought to light by the classical scholar Guarino of Verona (1374–1460) in 1426, and a better copy was discovered by his friend Lamola in 1427. Another copy was found by Thomas Parentucelli (1397–1455), afterwards Pope Nicholas V in 1443, and the text was later studied by Politian (1454–94). Though one of the latest of the great classical medical texts to be discovered, it was one of the first to be printed (Florence, 1478), and it ran through very many early editions and had great influence on the medical renaissance.

After Celsus comes Dioscorides in the first century A. D. He was a Greek military surgeon of Cilician origin who served under Nero, and in him the Greek intellect is obviously beginning to flag. His work is prodigiously important for the history of botany, yet so far as rational medicine is concerned he is almost negligible. He begins at the wrong end, either giving lists of drugs with the symptoms that they are said to cure or to relieve, or lists of symptoms with a series of named drugs. Clinical observation and record are wholly absent, and the spirit of Hippocrates has departed from this elaborate pharmacopœia.

With the second century of the Christian era we terminate the creative period of Greek medicine. We are provided with the works of four important writers of this century, of whom three, Rufus of Ephesus, Soranus of Ephesus, and Aretaeus of Cappadocia, though valuable for forming a picture of the state of medicine in their day, were without substantial influence on the course of medicine in later ages.

Rufus of Ephesus, a little junior to Dioscorides, has left us the first formal work on human anatomy and is of some importance in the history of comparative anatomy. In medicine he is memorable as the first to have described bubonic plague, and in surgery for his description of the methods of arresting haemorrhage and his knowledge of the anatomy of the eye. A work by him *On gout* was translated into Latin in the sixth century, but remained unknown till modern times.

Soranus of Ephesus (A. D. *c*. 90–*c*. 150), an acute writer on gynaecology, has left a book which illustrates well the anatomy of his day. It exercised an influence for many centuries to come, and a Latin abstract of it prepared about the sixth century by one Moschion has come down to us in an almost contemporary manuscript.[1] It is interesting as opposing the Hippocratic theory that the male embryo is originated in the right and the female in the left half of the womb, a fallacy derived originally from Empedocles and Parmenides, but perpetuated by Latin translations of the Hippocratic treatises until the seventeenth century. His work was adorned by figures, and some of these, naturally greatly altered by copyists, but still not infinitely removed from the facts, have survived in a manuscript of the ninth century, and give us a distant idea of the appearance of ancient anatomical drawings.[2] We may assist our imagination a little further, in forming an idea of what such diagrams were like, with the help of certain other mediaeval figures representing the form and distribution of the various anatomical ' systems ', veins, arteries, nerves, bones, and muscles which are probably traceable to an Alexandrian origin.[3]

Aretaeus of Cappadocia was probably a contemporary of Galen (second half of the second century A. D.). As a clinical author his reputation stands high, perhaps too high, his descriptions of pneumonia, empyema, diabetes, and elephan-

[1] Leyden Voss 4° 9* of the sixth century is a fragment of this work.

[2] V. Rose, *Sorani Ephesii vetus translatio Latina cum additis Graeci textus reliquiis*, Leipzig, 1882; F. Weindler, *Geschichte der gynäkologisch-anatomischen Abbildung*, Dresden, 1908.

[3] The discovery and attribution of these figures is the work of K. Sudhoff. A bibliography of his writings on the subject will be found in a ' Study in Early Renaissance Anatomy ' in C. Singer's *Studies in the History and Method of Science*, vol. i, Oxford, 1917.

tiasis having especially drawn attention. In treatment he uses simple remedies, is not affected by polypharmacy, and suggests many ingenious mechanical devices. It would appear that Aretaeus is not an independent writer, but mainly a compiler. He relies largely on Archigenes, a distinguished physician contemporary with Juvenal, whose works have perished save the fragments preserved in this manner by Aretaeus and Aetius. Aretaeus was a very popular writer among the Greeks in all ages, but he was not translated into Latin, and was unknown in the West until the middle of the sixteenth century.[1] He is philologically interesting as still using the Ionic dialect.

There remains the huge overshadowing figure of Galen. The enormous mass of the surviving work of this man, the dictator of medicine until the revival of learning and beyond, tends to throw out of perspective the whole of Greek medical records. The works of Galen alone form about half of the mass of surviving Greek medical writings, and occupy, in the standard edition, twenty-two thick, closely-printed volumes. These cover every department of medicine, anatomy, physiology, pathology, medical theory, therapeutics, as well as clinical medicine and surgery. In style they are verbose and heavy and very frequently polemical. They are saturated with a teleology which, at times, becomes excessively tedious. In the anatomical works, masses of teleological explanation dilute the account of often imperfectly described structures. Yet to this element we owe the preservation of the mass of Galen's works, for his intensely teleological point of view appealed to the theological bias both of Western Christianity and of Eastern Islam. Intolerable as literature, his works are a valuable treasure house of medical knowledge and experience, custom, tradition, and history.

As in the case of the Hippocratic corpus, so in the case of the Galenic corpus we are dealing to some extent with material

[1] First Latin edition Venice, 1552; first Greek edition Paris, 1554.

from various sources. In the case of Galen, however, we have a good standard of genuineness, for he has left us a list of his books which can be checked off against those which we actually possess. The general standpoint of the Galenic is not unlike that of the Hippocratic writings, but the noble vision of the lofty-minded, pure-souled physician has utterly passed away. In his place we have an acute, honest, very contentious fellow, bristling with energy and of prodigious industry, not unkindly, but loving strife, a thoroughly 'aggressive' character. He loves truth, but he loves argument quite as much. The value of his philosophical writings, of which some have survived, cannot be discussed here, but it is evident that he is frequently satisfied with purely verbal explanations. An ingenious physiologist, a born experimenter, an excellent anatomist and eager to improve, possessing a good knowledge of the human skeleton and an accurate acquaintance with the internal parts so far as this can be derived from a most industrious devotion to dissection of animals, equipped with all the learning of the schools of Pergamon, Smyrna, and Alexandria, and rich with the experience of a vast practice at Rome, Galen is essentially an 'efficient' man. He has the grace to acknowledge constantly and repeatedly his indebtedness to the Hippocratic writings. Such was the man whose remains, along with the Hippocratic collection, formed the main medical legacy of Greece to the Western world.

Some of Galen's works are mere drug lists, little superior to those of Dioscorides ; [1] with the depression of the intelligence that corresponded with the break up of the Roman Empire, it was these that were chiefly seized on and distributed in the West. Attractive too to the debased intellect of the late Roman world were certain spurious, superstitious, and astrological works that circulated in the name of Galen and Hippocrates.[2] The

---

[1] e. g. περὶ κράσεως καὶ δυνάμεως τῶν ἁπάντων φαρμάκων and the φάρμακα.

[2] e. g. *De dinamidiis Galeni*, *Secreta Hippocratis* and many astrological tracts.

Greek medical writers after Galen were but his imitators and abstractors, but through some of them Galen's works reached the West at a very early period in the Middle Ages. Such abstractors who were early translated into Latin were Oribasius (325–403), Paul of Aegina (625–690), and Alexander of Tralles (525–605). Of the best and most scientific of Galen's works the Middle Ages knew little or nothing.

Later Galen and Hippocrates became a little more accessible, not by translation from the Greek, but by translation from the Arabic of a Syriac version. The first work to be so rendered was a version of *Aphorisms* of Hippocrates which, however, as we have seen, were already available in Latin dress, together with the Hippocratic *Regimen in acute diseases*, and certain works of Galen as corruptly interpreted by Isaac Judaeus. These were rendered from Arabic into Latin by Constantine, an African adventurer who became a monk at Monte Cassino and died there in 1087. Constantine was a wretched craftsman with an imperfect knowledge of both Arabic and Latin. More effective was the great twelfth-century translator from the Arabic, Gerard of Cremona (died 1185), who turned many medical works into Latin from Arabic, and who was followed by a whole host of imitators. Yet more important for the advance of medicine, however, was the learned revival of the thirteenth century. In the main that revival was based on translations from Arabic, but a certain number of works were also rendered direct from the Greek. During the thirteenth century Aristotle's scientific works began to be treated in this way, but more important for the course of medicine were those of Galen, and they had to wait till the following century. The long treatise of Galen, περὶ χρείας τῶν ἐν ἀνθρώπου σώματι μορίων, *On the uses of the bodily parts in man*, was translated from the Greek into Latin by Nicholas of Reggio in the earlier part of the fourteenth century. This work, with all its defects, was by far the best account of the human body then available. Many manuscripts of the Latin version have survived, and it was translated into several vernaculars, including

English, and profoundly influenced surgery. The rendering
into Latin of this treatise, and its wide distribution, may be
regarded as the starting-point of modern scientific medicine.
Its appearance is moreover a part of the phenomenon of the
revived interest in dissection which had begun to be practised
in the Universities in the thirteenth century,[1] and was a generally
accepted discipline in the fourteenth and fifteenth.[2]

Until the end of the fifteenth century progress in anatomy
was almost imperceptible. During the fifteenth century
more Galenic and Hippocratic texts were recovered and
gradually turned into Latin, but still without vitally affecting
the course of Anatomy. The actual printing of collected
editions of Hippocrates and Galen came rather late, for the
debased taste of the Renaissance physicians continued to prefer
Dioscorides and the Arabs, of whom numerous editions appeared, so that medicine made no advance corresponding to
the progress of scholarship. The Hippocratic works were first
printed in 1525, and an isolated edition of the inferior Galen
in 1490, but the real advance in Medicine was not made by
direct study of these works. So long as they were treated in
the old scholastic spirit such works were of no more value
than those of the Arabists or others inherited from the Middle
Ages. Even Hippocrates can be spoilt by a commentary, and
it was not until the investigator began actually to compare
his own observations with those of Hippocrates and Galen that
the real value of these works became apparent. The department in which this happened first was Anatomy, and such
revolutionaries as Leonardo da Vinci (1452–1518), who never

[1] Dissection of animals was practised at Salerno as early as the eleventh
century.

[2] The sources of the anatomical knowledge of the Middle Ages are dis-
cussed in detail in the following works : R. R. von Töply, *Studien zur
Geschichte der Anatomie im Mittelalter*, Vienna, 1898 ; K. Sudhoff, *Tradition
und Naturbeobachtung*, Leipzig, 1907 ; and also numerous articles in the
Archiv für Geschichte der Medizin und Naturwissenschaften ; Charles Singer,
' A Study in Early Renaissance Anatomy ', in *Studies in the History and
Method of Science*, vol. i, Oxford, 1917.

published, and Vesalius (1514–1564), whose great work appeared in 1543, were really basing their work on Galen, though they were much occupied in proving Galen's errors. Antonio Benivieni (died 1502), an eager prophet of the new spirit, revived the Hippocratic tradition by actually collecting notes of a few cases with accompanying records of deaths and post-mortem findings, among which it is interesting to observe a case of appendicitis.[1] His example was occasionally followed during the sixteenth century, as for instance, by the Portuguese Jewish physician Amatus Lusitanus (1511–c. 1562), who printed no fewer than seven hundred cases; but the real revival of the Hippocratic tradition came in the next century with Sydenham (1624–1689) and Boerhaave (1668–1738), who were consciously working on the Hippocratic basis and endeavouring to extend the Hippocratic experience.

Lastly surgery came to profit by the revival. The greatest of the sixteenth-century surgeons, the lovable and loving Ambroise Paré (1510–1590), though he was, as he himself humbly confessed, an ignorant man knowing neither Latin nor Greek, can be shown to have derived much from the works of antiquity, which were circulating in translation in his day and were thus filtering down to the unlearned.

Texts of Hippocrates and of Galen had formed an integral part in the medical instruction of the universities from their commencement in the thirteenth century. The first Greek text of the *Aphorisms* of Hippocrates appeared in 1532, edited by no less a hand than that of François Rabelais. With the further recovery of the Greek texts and preparation of better translations, these became almost the sole mode of instruction during the fifteenth and sixteenth centuries. The translators became legion and their competence varied. One highly skilled translator, however, is of special interest to English readers. Thomas Linacre (1460 ?–1524), Physician to Henry VIII, Tutor to the Princess Mary, founder and first president of the College

---

[1] Benivieni's notes were published posthumously. Some of the spurious Greek works of the Hippocratic collection have also case notes.

of Physicians, a benefactor of both the ancient Universities and one of the earliest, ablest, most typical, and most exasperating of the English humanists, spent much energy on this work of translation for which his abilities peculiarly fitted him. He was responsible for no less than six important works of Galen, of which one, the *De temperamentis et de inaequali intemperie*, printed at Cambridge in 1521, was among the earliest books impressed in that town and is said to be the first printed in England for which Greek types were used. It has been honoured by reproduction in facsimile in modern times. Such works as these, purely literary efforts, had great vogue for a century and more, and were much in use in the Universities. These humanistic products sometimes produced, among the advocates of the new scientific method, a degree of fury which was only rivalled by that of some of the humanists themselves towards the translators from the Arabic. But these are now dead fires. As the clinical and scientific methods of teaching gained ground, textual studies receded in medical education, as Hippocrates and Galen themselves would have wished them to recede.

The texts of Hippocrates and Galen have now ceased to occupy a place in any medical curriculum. Yet all who know these writings, know too, not only that their spirit is still with us, but that the works themselves form the background of modern practice, and that their very phraseology is still in use at the bedside. Modern medicine may be truly described as in essence a creation of the Greeks. To realize the nature of our medical system, some knowledge of its Greek sources is essential. It would indeed be a bad day for medicine if ever this debt to the Greeks were forgotten, and the loss would be at least as much ethical as intellectual. But there is happily no fear of this, for the figure and spirit of Hippocrates are more real and living to-day than they have been since the great collapse of the Greek scientific intellect in the third and fourth centuries of the Christian era.

CHARLES SINGER.

The author has to thank Mr. R. W. Livingstone, Dr. E. T. Withington, Prof. A. Platt, and Mr. J. D. Beazley for corrections and suggestions.

LITERATURE

A MAN walking down Shaftesbury Avenue from Piccadilly to Charing Cross Road passes the *Lyric Theatre*. If it is the evening, a *dramatic* performance is probably taking place inside. It may be a *tragedy*, or some form of *comedy*. If it is a *musical comedy* and he enters, he will see elaborate *scenery* and a play which may open with a *prologue* and which is partly composed of *dialogue* between the various *characters*, partly of songs in various *metres* sung by a *chorus* to the accompaniment of an *orchestra*. As the words in italics indicate, our imaginary passer-by will have seen, though he may not have suspected it, a symbol of the indelible mark which the Greeks have set on the aesthetic and intellectual life of Europe, and of the living presence of Greece in the twentieth century. An ancient Athenian might be startled at the sight of a musical comedy and its chorus, but he would be looking at his own child, a descendant, however distant, degenerate, and hard to recognize, of that chorus which with dance and song moved round the altar of Dionysus in the theatre of his home.

The same imprint, clear or faint, is on all our literary forms, except perhaps one. Epic, lyric, elegiac, dramatic, didactic, poetry, history, biography, rhetoric and oratory, the epigram, the essay, the sermon, the novel, letter writing and literary criticism are all Greek by origin, and in nearly every case their name betrays their source. Rome raises a doubtful claim to satire, but the substance of satire is present in the Old Comedy, and the form seems to have existed in writings now lost. There are even one or two *genres*, such as the imaginary speech, which Greece invented and which are not, fortunately, found in modern literature. When the curtain rose on Homer, European literature did not exist : long before it falls on the late Byzantines, the lines were laid on which it has moved up to our own day. This is the entire work of a single people, politically weak, numerically small, materially poor—according to the economy of nature which in things of the mind and the spirit gives a germinating power to few. The Greeks are justly admired for individual poems, plays, and pieces of writing; but it was something even greater to have explored the possibilities of literature so far that posterity, while it has developed Greek *genres*, has not hitherto been able to add to them. This is one part of the Greek Legacy to literature.

Another part are the works themselves. Literature can only be judged by reading it, and certainly it cannot be characterized in a few pages. But a man ignorant of Greek and anxious to estimate its value might form some idea by inquiring the opinions of qualified judges. He would find them unanimous : I suppose it is true that no man of eminence qualified to speak has ever spoken of Greek literature in any tone but one. The first testimony is that of the Romans. It is borne by their literature, starting in translations from Greek, adopting one after another of their *genres*, permeated through and through (and most of all in the greatest writers) by imitations, reminiscences, influences of Greek, confessing and glorying in the debt. 'In learning,' says Cicero, ' and in every branch of literature, the Greeks are our masters.'[1] A Roman boy should begin his studies with Greek, Quintilian thought, ' because Latin learning is derived from Greek.'[2] The same note is repeated in the literature of the Renaissance, and re-echoed by the most various voices of our own century.

'Though one of the Greek tragedians may seem rather greater and more complete than another, their work as a whole has a single pervading quality. It is marked by grandeur,

[1] *Tusc.* I. I. 2.   [2] *Inst. Or.* I. I. 12.

excellence, sanity, complete humanity, a high philosophy of life, a lofty way of thinking, a powerful intuition (*Anschauung*). We find these qualities in their surviving lyric and epic poetry as well as in their drama : we find them in their philosophers, orators, and historians and, to an equally high degree, in their surviving sculpture.' [1]

'Beside the great Attic poets, like Aeschylus and Sophocles, I am absolutely nothing.' [2]

'He spoke with great animation of the advantage of classical study, Greek especially. "Where," he said, "would one look for a greater orator than Demosthenes ; or finer dramatic poetry, next to Shakspere, than that of Aeschylus or Sophocles, not to speak of Euripides." Herodotus he thought "the most interesting and instructive book, next to the Bible, which had ever been written".' [3]

'The period which intervened between the birth of Pericles and the death of Aristotle is undoubtedly, whether considered in itself or with reference to the effects which it has produced upon the subsequent destinies of civilized man, the most memorable in the history of the world. . . . The wrecks and fragments of these subtle and profound minds, like the ruins of a fine statue, obscurely suggest to us the grandeur and perfection of the whole. Their very language . . . in variety, in simplicity, in flexibility, and in copiousness, excels every other language of the western world.' Then, after some words on their sculpture, he adds : 'their poetry seems to maintain a very high, though not so disproportionate a rank, in the comparison' (with other literatures). [4]

'The Greeks are the most remarkable people who have yet existed. . . . They were the beginners of nearly everything, Christianity excepted, of which the modern world makes its

---

[1] Goethe, *Gespräche*, 3. 387.   [2] Ibid., 3. 443.
[3] Wordsworth, *Table-talk*.
[4] Shelley, *On the Manners of the Ancients*.

boast. . . . They were the first people who had a historical
literature ; as perfect of its kind (though not the highest kind),
as their oratory, their sculpture, and their architecture. They
were the founders of mathematics, of physics, of the inductive
study of politics, of the philosophy of human nature and life.
In each they made the indispensable first steps, which are the
foundation of all the rest.' [1]

'I have gone back to Greek literature with a passion quite
astonishing to myself . . . I felt as if I had never known before
what intellectual enjoyment was. Oh that wonderful people !
There is not one art, not one science, about which we may
not use the same expression which Lucretius has employed
about the victory over superstition "*Primum Graius homo*".
I think myself very fortunate in having been able to return
to these great masters while still in the full vigour of life and
when my taste and judgement are mature. Most people read
all the Greek that they ever read before they are five-and-
twenty. . . . A young man, whatever his genius may be, is
no judge of such a writer as Thucydides. I had no high
opinion of him ten years ago. I have now been reading him
with a mind accustomed to historical researches and to political
affairs ; and I am astonished at my own former blindness, and
at his greatness. I could not bear Euripides at college. I now
read my recantation. He has faults undoubtedly. But what
a poet !' [2]

These men—and there is no difficulty in adding to their
number—are not only qualified but unprejudiced witnesses.
They have no *parti pris*. They cannot be accused, as school-
masters and dons are sometimes accused, of holding shares in
a great Trading Bank of Greece and Rome Unlimited, and
having a personal motive for their enthusiasm. Nor can it be
said that they admired Greece because they knew nothing
better. All—Goethe no less than the others—had English

[1] Mill, *Dissertations*, ii. 283 f.   [2] Macaulay, *Life and Letters*, i. 431.

literature in their hands, knew it well and appreciated its greatness. Yet this, given in their own words, is the impression which Greek made on them. *Securus iudicat orbis terrarum* ; and the verdict here is plain. It is clear that we have in Greek a surviving body of poetry and prose which is of unique interest to any one who cares for literature.

I have tried to give a summary answer to the question, What did the Greeks achieve? They invented every literary *genre* which we know, they laid the lines which European literature has followed, they created a body of prose and poetry which has won the homage of the world. The further question, What can the world still learn from them, is less easy to answer. The answer lies in Greek literature, and the essence of a literature cannot be extracted and bottled in a number of abstract formulae. No literature is great in virtue of its qualities, which are always something less than the literature itself, but only in so far as it expands to the breadth of the universe and climbs to its height. This is the final test which must be applied. How far Greek literature satisfies it, can be judged from the testimonies which have been quoted above.

Remembering this let us deliberately narrow our view and talk of qualities : and here, narrowing it again, let us confine the discussion to certain qualities, which are found indeed in all literatures, but are elsewhere neither so universal nor carried to so high a power. No one can think of Greek literature without thinking of them ; they live on the lips of its admirers, and in them the inspiration of Greek literature is chiefly enshrined. These essential qualities are Simplicity, Perfection of Form, Truth and Beauty. Greek literature is much more than these qualities. The *Agamemnon*, the *Oedipus*, the *Bacchae* are not to be explained wholly by them. The greatness of these plays is partly something individual, and partly it is what makes *King Lear* or *Faust* or *Brand* great : and that is neither entirely nor mainly simplicity or beauty or truth or form. But my object is to emphasize qualities for which Greek is exceptional, and though some critics may have talked of the beauty of Greek literature till beauty was absurdly supposed to be its chief or only quality, they were right to recognize the prominence of beauty there, and though truth is a mark of the greatest writing in all languages, it is more universal in Greek than in any other literature.

If a reader turned from Milton to Homer, from Shakespeare to Sophocles, from Plato or Aristotle to some modern work on ethics, politics, or literary criticism, he would find one point of difference between the earlier and the later writers in the greater simplicity of the former. They are briefer : the *Oedipus Tyrannus* has 1530 lines while the first two acts of *Hamlet* alone have more than 1600, and Greek histories and philosophical writings are correspondingly shorter than their modern counterparts. The whole of Thucydides could be printed in a twenty-four page issue of *The Times*, and leave room to spare ; the essay of Aristotle on Poetry, which for generations dictated the principles of dramatic writing, has forty-five short pages ; the *Republic* of Plato, which has influenced thought more than any other philosophic work, has a little over three hundred. Brevity indeed is not always simplicity, and it is possible to be at once simple and lengthy. But any one who examines these Greek writers will find that they are brief, because, avoiding bypaths and by-plots, elaboration or minute detail, they strike out the central features of their picture with an effortless economy of line. Their writing has a double quality. It shows a firm hold on the central and fundamental things : and it presents them unmixed with and unconfused by minor issues, so that they stand out like forest trees which no undergrowth of brushwood masks. It is im-

portant to make this distinction, for all great literature has
the first of these qualities ; the second is largely an accident
of time. As civilization moves further from its origin, it cannot
but receive a thousand tributaries that continually augment its
volume, and colour and confuse its streams : at the sources it
flows clear and untroubled. The interests of an early age are
the primal and essential interests of human nature and the
literature of such an age presents them unalloyed and uncomplicated by lesser issues. In the thinkers the main and fundamental
problems stand clearly out, and Plato and Thucydides take us
straight to them. The poets make their poetry from emotions
and interests that are as old as man, and have none of the
refinements and complications which education and a long
inheritance of culture superadd to the essential stuff of human
nature. ' You Greeks are always children,' said the Egyptian
priest to Solon ; and he spoke the truth in a sense which he
did not mean. The Greeks' feelings were not dulled or sophisticated by the *damnosa hereditas* of the past. Neither their life
nor their mental atmosphere was complicated. They had not
' thought themselves into weariness '. They were the children
of the world, and they united the startling acuteness, directness,
and simplicity of children to the intellects of men.

Pater took *La Gioconda* of Leonardo da Vinci to symbolize
the difference of modern and ancient art, and to illustrate the
intricacy and complication of the former, as compared with
the simplicity of the latter. ' Hers is the head,' he writes of the
Monna Lisa, 'upon which all " the ends of the world are come ",
and the eyelids are a little weary. It is a beauty wrought out
from within upon the flesh, the deposit, little cell by cell, of
strange thoughts and fantastic reveries and exquisite passions.
Set it for a moment beside one of those white goddesses or
beautiful women of antiquity, and how would they be troubled
by this beauty, into which the soul with all its maladies has
passed ! All the thoughts and experience of the world have

etched and moulded there, in that which they have of power to refine and make expressive the outward form. . . . She is older than the rocks among which she sits ; like the vampire, she has been dead many times and learned the secrets of the grave ; and has been a diver in deep seas, and keeps their fallen day about her . . . ; and all this lives only in the delicacy with which it has moulded the changing lineaments, and tinged the eyelids and the hands. The fancy of a perpetual life, sweeping together ten thousand experiences, is an old one ; and modern thought has conceived the idea of humanity as wrought upon by, and summing up in itself, all modes of thought and life. Certainly Lady Lisa might stand as the embodiment of the old fancy, the symbol of the modern idea.' Slightly fanciful and Pateresque as these words are, they are substantially true, as any one who sets Monna Lisa by a piece of fifth-century sculpture can easily see. There is the same contrast between Greek literature and our own. How ' troubled ' would Homer or Sophocles be by the writings of Browning or Meredith, of Henry James or Conrad, in whom so many eddies and cross-currents of thought and experience unite.

Compare the story of Hector and Andromache with some famous passage from any of these writers. ' So spake glorious Hector and stretched out his arm to his boy. But the child shrunk crying to the bosom of his fair-girdled nurse, dismayed at the look of his dear father and in fear of the bronze and the horsehair crest that nodded fiercely from his helmet's top. Then his dear father and his lady mother laughed aloud : forthwith glorious Hector took the helmet from his head and laid it, all gleaming, on the earth ; then kissed he his dear son and danced him in his arms, and spoke in prayer to Zeus and all the gods, " O Zeus and all ye gods, grant that this my son may be as I am, pre-eminent among the Trojans, and as valiant in might, and may he be a great king of Troy." So he spoke and laid his son in his dear wife's arms ; and she took him to her fragrant bosom, smiling through tears. And her husband had pity to see her, and caressed her with his hand, and spoke and called her by her name : "Dear one, I pray thee be not of oversorrowful heart ; no man against my fate shall send me to my death ; but destiny, I ween, no man hath escaped." So spake glorious Hector and took up his horsehair-crested helmet ; and his dear wife departed to her home, often looking back and letting fall great tears. And she came to the well-built house of man-slaying Hector, and found therein her many handmaidens, and stirred lamentation in them all. So they wept for Hector, while he yet lived, in his house ; for they thought that he would no more come back to them from battle.' [1] These are emotions shared by mankind twenty centuries before Christ and twenty centuries after him, common equally to Shakespeare or Napoleon and to the stupidest and least educated of mankind ; and these emotions are expressed with a simplicity as elemental as themselves. Subjects as simple may be found in our literature ; expression as direct would be hard to find. Even a primitive like Chaucer is the heir of dimly apprehended inheritances from Greece and Rome, and is haunted by fancies from lost and living fairylands of literature. It is in our Bible that we find the elemental feelings of Homer and an expression even more direct. 'And she departed and wandered in the wilderness of Beer-sheba. And the water was spent in the bottle, and she cast the child under one of the shrubs. And she went and sat her down over against him a good way off, as it were a bowshot : for she said, Let me not see the death of the child. And she sat down over against him, and lift up her voice, and wept.' [2]

Like the writer of the Pentateuch, Homer lived in a world

[1] Homer, *Iliad*, vi. 466 ff. (with omissions : chiefly from the translation of Lang, Leaf, and Myers). It should be remembered that, of the three figures in this scene, the husband will be dead in a few days, while within a year the wife will be a slave and the child thrown from the city wall.

[2] Genesis xxi. 14 f.

whose emotions were elemental, and writing of this kind came naturally to him. The weight of tradition began to weigh on succeeding ages, but it never became heavy, because the accumulations were small and the world was still comparatively simple. Also its poets and prose writers moved in the fields of action as soldiers and politicians, continually confronting the realities of life, and knowing them as they are, not as they appear in a study. Thus their topics are central, the writing is simple. The subjects of the *Oedipus Tyrannus* or the *Hercules Furens* might be called morbid; but not the handling of them by Sophocles and Euripides. The unnatural element is in the background and almost unnoticed; the interest lies in the spectacle of great men in overwhelming disaster—an elemental theme and belonging to the general life of man. The treatment is as simple as in Homer, the figures few, subordinate interests out of sight, the light thrown full on the central tragedy. Hence comes a rare intensity, an immediacy of impression, a sense of nearness to the thing described, which will strike any one who reads the messenger's speech in the *Hercules Furens*, or the scene where the identity of Oedipus is discovered, or indeed any great passage in Greek Drama. This simplicity of treatment persists, when with Menander and the Alexandrians we pass into a world more like our own and find literature, still simple in form, but more artistic, more intellectual, more literary, less centrally and fundamentally human.

It would be foolish to demand that modern writers should have the simplicity of Homer or the age of Pericles, or to pretend that they cannot be great without it. Every age must and will have its own literature, reflecting the minds and circumstances of those who write it. Nor is the advantage entirely on the side of the Greeks. A drama of Shakespeare or a novel of Tolstoi, with their long roll of *dramatis personae*, are more like life than a Greek tragedy with its absence of byplot and its few, central, characters. A modern historian would have recorded and discussed aspects of the history of fifth-century Greece which Thucydides ignores. Modern literature may claim that, with less intensity, it has greater amplitude and a more faithful presentation of the complexity of life. On the other hand the Greeks are free from that dominance of the abnormal which is one danger of modern literature ; they do not explore sexual and other aberrations or encourage their readers to explore them. They are also free from that dominance of the unessential, which, in life as in literature, is a more innocent but more subtle and perhaps equally ruinous vice. That is why their simplicity is refreshing and salutary. *Porro unum necessarium.* In life human beings return from a distracting variety of interests to a few simple things ; or, if they do not return, run the risk of losing their souls. In literature, which is the shadow of life, they need to do the same.

The simplicity of Greek literature is accompanied by the highest literary art. Nothing could be more surprising. The primitive conditions that preserve simplicity are apparently incompatible with technical perfection, which is a late-born child of literature and the creation of matured taste, long experiment, and patient work. But in Greek, and perhaps only in Greek, *naïveté* and art go hand in hand. There is something almost uncanny in Homer's union of the two : it is a paradox that the character of Achilles, the death of Hector, the primitive cunning of Odysseus, should be portrayed in such a metre and such a vocabulary ; it seems unnatural that so highly wrought and refined a medium should be used to depict the life and ideas of a society which is nearer to savagery than to civilization. But unnatural or not, so it is.

The most obvious quality of Greek literature is its form, the high level of its technique. There are exceptions : the earlier plays of Aeschylus are crude in conception, the prose of Gorgias is as fantastic as that of Lyly, the sentences of Thucydides are often awkward and ungrammatical; Aeschylus stands at the origin of drama, Gorgias and Thucydides are the creators of periodic prose, and they have the weaknesses of pioneers. But in general, Greek work in poetry and prose is highly wrought and finely finished; and so rapidly did their art find itself, that within the lifetime of Aeschylus Sophocles reached the highest level of dramatic and literary technique, and within a generation from Thucydides Plato evolved his unequalled style. An artistic instinct was in the blood of the Greeks, and betrays itself throughout their literature, in the choric odes with their complicated respondencies and subtle variations; in Plato arranging and rearranging the first eight words of his *Republic*; in the interest which the Greeks took in the theory of literary art, seeking here as elsewhere λόγον διδόναι, to give an account of their practice. How much more they reflected on it than we do, the *Rhetoric* of Aristotle, the *De Compositione* of Dionysius and the endless writings of the rhetoricians show.

This is universally admitted, but justice is more rarely done to even clearer evidence of the Greek gift for technique. Other nations have understood the art of writing, and left those monuments in words which are as unsubstantial and fleeting as air, yet more imperishable than brass or stone; but no nation has created literary art in the sense in which the Greeks created it, or developed, as they did, the various literary *genres* out of nothing. They had no models or guides or external help. Rome had Greek literature to follow and herself gave patterns to her successors; but the Greeks made what they made out of nothing, and are thus creators in the true sense of the word, and as no other people have been. Two instances, Homer and the Greek Drama, will serve to show this.

In the dawn of a literature at least, we expect roughness and crudity, an uncertain judgement and a faltering hand; but the first known Greek poem, like Athena in the myth, is born full grown and mature. Yet its makers made the story and the rich language and the elaborate and unrivalled metre for themselves. It does not lessen this achievement that the Homeric poems may have been the fine flower of a period of poetic growth; the work that went to form them was done by Greeks. But it needs imagination to appreciate the difficulty of the task which they undertook unconsciously and performed without theory or deliberate purpose by the mere light of nature.

It is hard to create even a primitive poetic vocabulary, where one does not exist, and there is nothing primitive about

οἱ δ' ὥς τ' αἰγυπιοὶ γαμψώνυχες ἀγκυλοχεῖλαι
πέτρῃ ἐφ' ὑψηλῇ μεγάλα κλάζοντε μάχωνται,

or

ὅσσον δ' ἠεροειδὲς ἀνὴρ ἴδεν ὀφθαλμοῖσιν
ἥμενος ἐν σκοπιῇ, λεύσσων ἐπὶ οἴνοπα πόντον,
τόσσον ἐπιθρῴσκουσι θεῶν ὑψηχέες ἵπποι.[1]

It is hard, as the beginnings of Roman poetry show, to devise a metre which is not rough, unmusical, or even grotesque: yet for richness and strength this first metre of Europe has never been rivalled by the Greeks or by any one else. The same natural technical skill appears in more subtle things even than metre or language. Homer is born knowing by some instinct the profound secret of literary art which Aristotle formulated centuries later as the principle of unity of Action. The plot of a play, he writes in the *Poetics*, 'should have for its subject a single action, whole and complete, with a beginning, a middle, and an end. . . . It will differ in structure from historical compositions, which of necessity present not a single action, but

---

[1] *Iliad*, xvi. 428 f.: 'As vultures with crooked talons and curved beaks that upon some high crag fight, screaming loudly.' *Ibid.* v. 770 f.: 'As far as a man's view ranges in the haze, as he sits on a point of outlook and gazes over the wine-dark sea, so far at a spring leap the loud-neighing horses of the gods.'

a single period, and all that happened within that period to one person or to many, little connected together as the events may be. . . . Such is the practice, we may say, of most poets. Here again the transcendant excellence of Homer appears. He never attempts to make the whole war of Troy the subject of his poem. It would have been too vast a theme, and not easily embraced in a single view : while if he had kept it in moderate limits, it would have been over-complicated by the variety of incidents. As it is, he detaches a single portion.' [1] Once stated, the principle of unity of action becomes a commonplace of literary art. But, as the *Annals* of Ennius or the *Faerie Queen* show, it is not obvious until stated, and the poets from whose practice Aristotle made his induction, must have had a rare technical instinct unconsciously to preserve unity of interest through the complications of a long epic or drama. Such achievements were only possible to a people with a natural genius for literary art. In the hands of the Greeks the various elements of litera-ture found their τέλος and achieved their natural form, almost with the same instinctive evolution by which a seed unfolds to its predestined shape.

This can be illustrated even better from Greek drama. A modern author who wishes to write a play may not find the task easy, but he knows the general form which a drama has to take and the general principles to be followed in writing it. The right length is given him, the division into scenes and acts, the methods of exposition and dialogue, the conception of a *dé-nouement*, the law of unity of action, and the rest. The fathers of Greek tragedy had no such help. They had no drama in our sense of the word, but simply a band of fifty persons dressed like satyrs, and dancing round an altar and singing a song. Out of this anything or nothing might have been made. The Greeks, with the instinctive and unerring motions of genius, developed from it the highest and most elaborate of

[1] *Poetics*, c. 23 (tr. Butcher).

literary forms, and within a hundred years are writing plays which Shelley classes with *King Lear*, and which Swinburne can call, ' probably, on the whole, the greatest spiritual work of man '.

In divining the principles of literary art and evolving the various kinds of literature no people can be compared to the Greeks, and probably none can show a mass of work executed with so uniformly high a finish. But when we compare writer with writer we shall find individual artists to rival them. Though the strength of English literature does not lie in technical perfection, Milton, Pope, and Tennyson—to name no others— have in their different ways as firm a grasp of it as any Greek, and it can be learned from French writers, with whom it is the rule rather than the exception, as well as from the Greeks. This is hardly true of another quality of Greek writing, which may be classed with technical finish, though it is in fact something more. It is one of the most characteristic features of Greek ; yet on first acquaintance, it is often disconcerting and even distasteful. If a reader new to the classics opened Thucydides, his first impression would probably be one of jejuneness, of baldness. If, fresh from Shelley or Tennyson, he came across the epigram of Simonides on the Spartan dead at Thermopylae,

ὦ ξεῖν', ἀγγέλλειν Λακεδαιμονίοις ὅτι τῇδε
κείμεθα, τοῖς κείνων ῥήμασι πειθόμενοι,[1]

he might see little in it but a prosaic want of colour. This exceeding simplicity or economy is a stumbling-block to those who are accustomed to the expansive modern manner. Yet such a reader would have been making the acquaintance of some of the finest things in Greek literature, which is always at its greatest when most simple, and he would have been face to face with a characteristic quality of it.

The contrast with the usual English manner may be illustrated

---

[1] ' Stranger, tell the Spartans that we lie here, obeying their words.'

by quoting a famous epigram—Ben Jonson's epitaph on a boy actor :

> Weep with me, all you that read
>   This little story ;
> And know, for whom a tear you shed,
>   Death's self is sorry.
>
> 'Twas a child that so did thrive
>   In grace and feature,
> As heaven and nature seemed to strive
>   Which owned the creature.
>
> Years he numbered scarce thirteen
>   When Fates turned cruel,
> Yet three filled zodiacs had he been
>   The stage's jewel ;
>
> And did act (what now we moan)
>   Old men so duly,
> As sooth the Parcae thought him one,
>   He played so truly.
>
> So, by error, to his fate
>   They all consented ;
> But, viewing him since, alas, too late !
>   They have repented.

These lines—and they are not the whole of the poem—are enough to illustrate the difference between the Greek method and the English, the latter rich and profuse, following the flow of an opulent fancy, the former reticent and restrained, leaving the reader's imagination room and need to play its part. There are materials for half-a-dozen epigrams in Ben Jonson's poem. Had he been Simonides or Plato, he would have stopped after the fourth line and, in the opinion of some critics, by saving his paper he would have improved his poem.

In their theory and in their practice the Greek writers were true to this principle of Economy. Their proverbs proclaim it :

' the half is greater than the whole ' : ' sow with the hand and not with the whole sack.' The great passages of their literature illustrate it. It is to be found no less in Thucydides' account of the siege of Syracuse and in the close of the *Phaedo* or the *Republic* than in the death of Hector or the meeting of Priam and Achilles. The Greek writers may have emotions that would seem to demand vehement and extended expression, topics to inspire a poet and tempt him to amplify them ; but resisting the temptation they set the facts down quietly and pass on practically without comment. The close of the *Phaedo* exemplifies this restraint. Plato has just related with severe economy of detail the death of his master. His comment on the event which saddened and confounded his whole life is but this : ' Such, Echecrates, was the death of our friend, the best man, I think, that I have ever known, the wisest too and the most just.' [1]

There are noble examples of reticence and economy in English literature, some of the most conspicuous of which can be traced to classical influence ; but no one would contend that these qualities are the rule in our great writers. The English genius is rich and lavish rather than restrained. It is less in its nature to write like Sappho,

Ϝέσπερε, πάντα φέρων ὅσα φαίνολις ἐσκέδασ' αὔως,
φέρεις οἶν, φέρες αἶγα, φέρεις ἄπυ ματέρι παῖδα,[2]

than like Byron,

O Hesperus, thou bringest all good things—
  Home to the weary, to the hungry cheer,
To the young bird the parent's brooding wings,
  The welcome stall to the o'er-laboured steer ;

---

[1] *Phaedo*, 118 B.
[2] fr. 95 : ' Star of evening, bringing all things that bright dawn has scattered, you bring the sheep, you bring the goat, you bring the child back to its mother.'

Whate'er of peace about our hearthstone clings,
  Whate'er our household gods protect of dear,
Are gathered round us by thy look of rest;
Thou bring'st the child too to its mother's breast.

Something may be said in favour of both methods. Amplitude of treatment and fullness of detail enrich the imagination, while economy stimulates it. The latter may become jejune, and is safe only in the hands of great writers : the former is apt to provide too rich a feast and to leave the full-fed mind inert. Everything is done for it and nothing left it to do. Economy on the other hand throws the reader on his own resources. It sets the imagination wandering in the fields of infinity. Some readers find this one of the essential delights of literature, though others prefer that the author should take them by the hand and indicate every detail with the precision of the sign-posts at a German *Kurort*.

Economy is the reflection in literature of that σωφροσύνη, which is the most deeply-rooted of Greek ideals, the most untranslatable of Greek words. But it was helped by an accident. If the art of printing were lost, modern works would contract within narrower limits, and the Greek economy was encouraged by the fact that Fust was not yet born. We, who do not rely on hand-copying for the propagation of our books, naturally write at greater length: and while it loses in conciseness, literature has a compensating gain in amplitude. But the habit of writing for money, which encourages abundant production, and the existence of the printing-press, which makes it easy, expose us to dangers from which the ancients were free. The newspapers are the worst offenders, saying many things which need not be said at all, and saying everything in a superfluous and excessive way. But literature suffers hardly less. The greatest figures of the last fifty years, such as Browning, Meredith, Hardy and Conrad, dilute their pages with unessential, if not inferior, stuff, and produce writing which has not received the *summa*

manus. Had their work been less by a half—a modest reduction
—it would have been more perfect because more time could
have been devoted to it, more powerful because each stroke
would have been precise and strong, more telling because these
strokes would not have been combined with ineffective blows.
This is even truer of lesser men and other forms of literature.
It is because the *Agricola* of Tacitus extends to but thirty pages,
that the biography of a Roman civil servant of no great genius
will outlive those of far greater men. The art of omission is the
art which English writers most need to learn ; the literary *lima*
is their least-handled tool. Both art and tool were perfectly
understood and constantly used by the Greeks.

The third mark of Greek Literature, with which I have to
deal, is perhaps its most important, certainly its most universal
quality. It is truthfulness. The Greeks told no fewer lies
than other races, but they had the desire and the power to see
the world as it is. By this essential quality they gave Europe
the conception of philosophy and science. These we inherit
from them alone ; Palestine and our German ancestors neither
created them, nor show any signs of the temper that creates
them, and Rome received her share from Greece.

The word ' Truthfulness ' may seem to suggest the realism
of some modern writers. But the Greek truthfulness was
different. It should be distinguished from the laboured
detachment and painful impartiality of such a writer as
Flaubert, whose realism conceals him in the same sense as
the walls of the engine-room conceal the panting machines
within. The Greek Truthfulness is spontaneous, natural,
and effortless—the native quality of the artist, who sees, and
forgets himself in the vision. Nor has it anything to do with
photographic realism. It has not the impersonality of that
method or its flat and lifeless effect. A man, and no machine,
makes the picture, feeling intensely what he sees, and though

this intensity does not distort his vision, we are conscious, as we read, of a human personality, and we feel the electric thrill of life.

Nor is it akin to that type of modern realism, which, like a noxious drug, lays hold on the spirits and depresses the heart— the realism which paints so black a picture of human life, that it affects us physically like days of continued fog, and gives us no more complete and truthful a picture of the world. There is hardly any Greek writer, perhaps none at all, of whom this can be said. Many moderns can faithfully describe what is disagreeable, but their effects are often brutal and always depressing. The gift of portraying suffering and evil with unflinching truth, yet of conveying other feelings than those of mere horror, is reserved for few. Its rarity perhaps explains the rarity of great tragedy, of which it seems to be a condition that it shall truthfully show what is darkest in life, without leaving a final and dominant sense of gloom. The great Greek writers possessed this secret. They are as sensitive to evil and suffering as any writer and fully as faithful in recording them. But whereas other men are simply depressed or disgusted or appalled, lose their vital forces, and gaze in paralysed fascination, these writers, in virtue of a sense which is more aesthetic than moral, are aware of tremendous issues, see in sordid suffering the agonies of a labouring universe, and feel awe and wonder, not mere disgust and distress, at what human beings suffer and endure. That is why Homer leaves us with another feeling than depression, when he tells how Priam begged his son's body from the man who killed him. ' So Priam entered unseen of them and stood near and clasped with his hands the knees of Achilles and kissed the terrible murderous hands that had slain so many of his sons. But Achilles was amazed at the sight of Priam, and amazed were the rest, and they looked at each other. And Priam entreated and addressed him. " Remember your own father, godlike Achilles : he is of like years with me, and stands on the hateful road of old age. Perhaps the neighbours round about harry him and there is none to keep misery and ruin from him. Yet when he hears that you are alive, he rejoices and hopes, day in, day out, to see his dear son returning from Troy. But I am utterly wretched, for I begat the best of sons in Troy, and none of them is left. The one I had, who was the stay of Troy and its people, you killed but now as he fought for his country— even Hector. Respect the gods, Achilles, and pity me, and remember your own father. I am more unhappy than he. I have faced what no other mortal man ever yet faced—to stretch my hand to the face of my sons' slayer." '[1] There is suffering and evil enough here, and there is no attempt to disguise or lessen them. Yet most readers, I think, would read this passage with different feelings from those provoked by the close of *Madame Bovary* or of *Jude the Obscure*. Its truthfulness is neither ugly nor depressing.

Nor again is the Greek truthfulness identical with objectivity. An objective writer tells his story and conveys his impressions, as far as possible, by relating facts without commenting upon them. Dramatists and novelists are compelled by the nature of their art to be objective in this sense of the word (though Fielding and Thackeray in the one field, and Ibsen and Shaw in the other, manage to make their comments with their own lips, not those of their characters). But such a writer would not of necessity be more truthful or impartial than any one else. He can distort truth as thoroughly by selecting certain facts and ignoring others as by making misleading comments. He may be violently one-sided and present only the facts that support his view, thus indirectly putting himself into what he writes quite as fully as a confessed partizan, though less openly. Such a writer is objective, but his objectivity with him is no more than a literary method. Now it is true that the Greeks use this method, telling a story without personal comments, not only

[1] *Iliad*, xxiv. 277 f. (with omissions).

in their epics and plays where this method is natural, but also in their histories and elsewhere. Thucydides for instance tells the story of a great war, yet his comments on it are few, and are mainly given in the dramatic and would-be objective form of speeches by leading men of the day. But the Greeks have objectivity in a far more important sense than this. Their objectivity is no literary device but a quality of mind. They have the power of standing aloof from matters in which they are personally interested, and surveying them from outside, like impartial spectators, with the keenest interest, but without bias. As the Delphic priestess in the act of prophecy lost her individuality and became the mouthpiece of the god, so the Greek allowed· facts to speak for themselves, became their mouthpiece and banished the intrusive ego. If therefore we call the Greeks objective, all this must be included in our definition of the word.

We shall understand Greek ' truthfulness ' best, if, dropping philosophical terms, and forgetting modern meanings, we remember a saying of Anaxagoras, who, when asked for what purpose he was born, replied : ' To contemplate the works of nature.' The disinterested passion for contemplating things, which gathered inquiring groups round Socrates to discuss what justice and friendship mean, or whether goodness is knowledge and can be learnt, has its counterpart in literature. The Greeks were fascinated by the spectacle of man and the world, and their fascination is seen not only in their formal philosophy. Of their poets too it may be said that they were born to see the world and human life—not to moralize or to indulge in sentiment or rhetoric or mysticism about it, but to see it. Keats's description of the poetic temperament fits them closely : ' It has no self, it is everything and nothing . . . It enjoys light and shade . . . A poet is the most unpoetical of anything in existence, he is continually in, for, and filling some other body.' In such a mood men will write literature that may justly be called truthful. Avoiding the didactic, they will not distort truth to suit personal bias; avoiding rhetoric, they will not sacrifice it to fine phrases; avoiding sentiment and fancy, they will not gratify their own or their hearer's feelings at the expense of truth; avoiding mysticism, they will not move away from facts into a world of emotions. Their care will be to see things, and their delight will be in the mere vision. They will echo the words of Keats, 'If a sparrow comes before my windows, I take part in its existence and pick about the gravel'[1]: they will not treat it as Shelley treats the skylark, or even as Keats and Wordsworth treat the nightingale. Herein is one of the secrets of Greek poetry, for the Greek poets, more than any others, bring us in a manner entirely simple and natural into immediate contact with what they describe, and thus escape the thousand distortions for which epigram, rhetoric, sentiment, fancy, mysticism and romanticism are responsible. This secret may be called 'directness'. It is the habit of looking straight and steadily at things, and describing them as they are, the very contrary of the habit of didactic comment and of rhetorical or emotional inflation. The 'direct' writer, in the fullest extent that is possible, keeps himself and his feelings in the background. He does not allow the mists which rise from a man's personality to come between him and his subject.

A few instances of directness will give a better idea of it than many definitions. The epigram quoted a few pages back shows how the Greek writer lets his subject speak instead of expressing his own feelings about it. So does the following epitaph, placed by a father on his son's grave.

$$\Delta\omega\delta\epsilon\kappa\epsilon\tau\hat{\eta} \ \tau\grave{o}\nu \ \pi\alpha\hat{\iota}\delta\alpha \ \pi\alpha\tau\grave{\eta}\rho \ \grave{a}\pi\acute{\epsilon}\theta\eta\kappa\epsilon \ \Phi\acute{\iota}\lambda\iota\pi\pi\sigma\varsigma$$
$$\grave{\epsilon}\nu\theta\acute{a}\delta\epsilon \ \tau\grave{\eta}\nu \ \pi\sigma\lambda\lambda\grave{\eta}\nu \ \grave{\epsilon}\lambda\pi\acute{\iota}\delta\alpha \ N\iota\kappa\sigma\tau\acute{\epsilon}\lambda\eta\nu.[2]$$

---

[1] I have taken these quotations of Keats from Bradley, *Oxford Lecture on Poetry*, p. 238.

[2] Callimachus, *Epigr.* 20: 'His father Philip laid here to rest his twelve-year old son, his high hope, Nicoteles.'

The bereaved father says nothing of his sorrow, or the greatness of his loss, but records his son's name and age and says that he was his father's ' high hope ', and so doing gives us everything. Simonides does not express his own feelings about the heroism of the Spartan dead ; their grave speaks for them to the passer-by. Nor is this a mere literary method, a way of writing which states facts and leaves them to make an impression by their own weight, unaided by comment or explanation. A comparison of Ben Jonson's epigram with the Greek epitaph, will show that directness is much more than this. The fancies with which Jonson closes are pretty ; but they are false, for they are really incompatible with deep feeling : the Greek directness never loses from sight the dead child ; it sees only that and the father's sorrow.

The following extract deals with a very different subject, but illustrates directness equally well. The scene is the Athenian colony of Amphipolis on the Struma ; the dramatis personae are the Spartan general Brasidas who wishes to capture it, and the Athenian Thucydides who was then at Thasos, distant half a day's sail from Amphipolis. ' As soon as Thucydides heard the news about Brasidas, he sailed quickly to Amphipolis . . . in order to garrison it if possible before it could capitulate, or at any rate to occupy Eion (its seaport). Meanwhile Brasidas, fearing the arrival of the Athenian fleet at Thasos and hearing that Thucydides . . . was one of the leading men of the country, did his utmost to get possession of the city before he arrived . . . He therefore offered moderate terms. . . . These terms were accepted, and the city was surrendered to him. On the evening of the same day Thucydides and his ships sailed into Eion, but not until Brasidas had taken possession of Amphipolis : another night, and he would have seized Eion.' [1] The gist of the story contained in this extract is plain. The Spartan general Brasidas seized the important town of Amphipolis, and the Athenian

[1] *Thuc.* iv. 104, 105, 106 (tr. Jowett, mainly).

general came too late to save it. But who would guess that the Athenian general Thucydides was the historian Thucydides who wrote these words, and that the episode which he here describes with such detachment and neutrality earned him perpetual exile under pain of death, from the country which he passionately loved? Thucydides has told the bare facts, objectively, as if they related to some one else, without a comment, without a word of protest, excuse, explanation or regret on the crowning disaster of his life. He writes of himself in the third person. This is not the way in which modern generals write of their mishaps, but it is the Greek way. Thucydides has forgotten himself and his feelings; he sees only the disastrous day when he sailed up the Struma with his ships and found the gates of Amphipolis closed against him. He ignores himself so far that he does not call it disastrous, though disastrous it was for himself and his country. With the same detachment he speaks of the enslavement of Melos and the tragedy of Syracuse, though he thinks, and makes us feel, that the one was the crowning crime, the other the crowning disaster of his country. He narrates the plain facts and leaves the reader to draw his inferences. If we did not know that he was an Athenian, we could hardly tell from his history whether he took the side of Athens or Sparta in the war; so entirely are he and his feelings kept in the background. Yet he was an ardent patriot, and he is describing the war in which his country lost supremacy and empire. No historian of the war of 1914–18, whether on the Allied or the German side, is likely to write of it in this way.

The art of Homer has the same quality of detachment. He is a Greek, writing of a ten years' war between Greeks and Asiatics, yet most of his readers sympathize with Hector rather than with Achilles. He himself preferred neither, but saw and felt equally with both; with the hero who fought the losing battle for Troy, and with him who lost his friend, and,

intoxicated with sorrow, could see and feel nothing but a passion
of revenge. It would seem hardly possible to write the close
of the 22nd Book of the *Iliad*, where the heroes meet, without
taking sides ; we, no doubt, should take Hector's side. But
Homer stands apart from the quarrel, and sees both men and
the feelings of both, writing with the pen of the Recording
Angel, not of the Judge. What he or Thucydides thought in
each case can only be guessed at. They have presented the facts
without comment, and the facts tell their own tale, explain
themselves, carry with them the feelings they should evoke,
and shine by their own light, like the phosphorescence of
the sea.

Little thinking is needed to see that the direct, detached,
objective temper is the generative principle of the Greek
achievement, for it is the parent of science and philosophy,
which are the children of a desire to see things in themselves as
they are, and not as the seer might wish them to be. The effects
of this temper in poetry can be appreciated by a comparison of
certain phenomena of our own literature which are absent
from Greek. The comparison will indicate, too, what modern
writers can learn from the Greeks, and enable us to judge
whether the lessons are needed.

The habit of keeping the eye on the subject, which is the
essence of directness, discourages, and indeed excludes, conventionality, sentimentalism, fancifulness, which prevent a
writer from seeing and recording life as it is. These failings
are always with us, and as I have given one instance of
their working in Ben Jonson's epigram and have discussed
the matter elsewhere,[1] I shall pass to diseases which are more
particularly modern, and with which directness is equally
at war.

The richness of the English language is in itself a danger.
English, like Latin, lends itself superbly to ranting, a capacity

[1] *The Greek Genius and its Meaning to us*, pp. 74 ff.

discovered by the Elizabethans. Modern writers tend to more delicate excess, and have exploited the musical quality of English. This is clear from such a collection as the *Oxford Book of Victorian Verse*, which faithfully represents the output of the age, and contains some fine poetry, but also a very large percentage of what Horace called, *Versus inopes rerum nugaeque canorae*. There is an intolerable deal of sack to a very little bread among the imitators of Tennyson. To such rhetorical or musical trifles no better antidote can be found than Greek literature, for there is no rhetoric in it, and what melodious nothings it contained, were parodied in its own age and have scantily survived to ours. In general it avoided both by its directness. The rhetoric of Lucan or Byron, the predominance of sound over sense in some of Shelley and much of Swinburne arise because those poets shut their eyes to the real world and become lost in the music of words. The Greek, starting with facts, not with sounds or with feelings about facts, could not easily become the victim of words. The temptation did not arise for him, or if it did, his sin was easily detected. Herein he is a good model, especially for poets who are apt to lose sight of the earth and pass into an unearthly paradise of vague feelings. For the greatest poetry is the poetry of things, not of words, and to whatever regions the Muse may take her flight, she can only be safe if she starts from Earth, and keeps her communication with it open.

Directness is also a protection against that literature of egotism which is the excess into which subjective poetry easily falls. Legitimate when kept within bounds, the habit of putting oneself into what one writes can become an offence, and from this offence English literature is not free. No one can complain because Milton and Wordsworth are less detached than Shakespeare or Sophocles ; but the subjectivity of Byron or Carlyle is very different. Their subject is continually darkened by the shadow of their personality ; it suffers a partial, at times a total, eclipse. Childe Harold sees himself in all that he sees, projects himself into Belgium, Athens and Rome, and colours the bluest skies with the jaundiced hues of his temperament. This is almost equally true of Carlyle's pupils, Ruskin and Froude, and, among the moderns, of a swarm of minor poets and novelists, who display before the public the pageant of their indignant or bleeding hearts. Egotism is a fault of manners as much as of morals, and has its peculiar effect and its appropriate penalty. Its effect is to distract a man's attention from major to minor issues, from the large world to the small self; its penalty is that it wearies its audience, and the next generation, if not its own, dislikes the continual obtrusion of an element in which it has no interest. Hence oblivion, often unjust, is the punishment which the egotist suffers. Even our age, interested as it is in personalities, has little time to spare for those of Byron or Carlyle; it is too busy with the characters of its own contemporaries to trouble about those of its predecessors. But no Greek writer is forgotten for this cause. Whatever their other offences, the Greeks are free from literary egotism. Directness turned their eyes to the external world, and taught them to see even themselves from without.

Egotism is a minor defect in English literature. To some it may even seem to be a virtue. A more serious weakness, which our literature shares with other modern literatures, is one-sidedness or incompleteness of view, which reveals itself by a series of reactions, and in England has taken the form of an oscillation between sentimentalism and a rather cruel realism, the latter being dominant at the present time. These two schools represent excesses of temperament, the one of generosity and kindliness, the other of truth; and among our writers of genius Dickens and Hardy typify them well. The one school desire in fiction to reward their good characters and punish the bad, just as they would wish that life should do;

and truth is not allowed to thwart their benevolence or their indignation. In defiance of all probability Micawber and Mr. Mell make a success of life in Australia, though truth cries out that they were born to be failures; while the foot of punishment moves more swiftly and visibly in the pages of Dickens than it does in fact. Then comes the veracious person, who, growing indignant at a travesty of life that misleads the reader and insults truth, gives us the opposite extreme in an imagined world where the shadows are deepened and the high lights carefully blocked out. Scott and Dickens picture a world in which at the end vice finds itself in the gutter while virtue marries the heroine. Later, Thomas Hardy has given us *Jude the Obscure* and *Tess of the D'Urbervilles*.[1] Here is a protest, a redressing of the balance, by an advocate who rises to supply a side of the case which has been ignored. Yet once again Truth is violated, and by her sworn servant; for the world that Hardy portrays is not the world as it is. When Dickens makes Mr. Micawber the District Magistrate of Port Middlebay, he is not representing life, but saying what he and his audience would like to believe in order to feel comfortable when they close the book. As a protest therefore against him in the next generation comes Thomas Hardy, who after recording the miserable end of Tess, writes ' The President of the immortals had ended his sport with Tess '. In so writing he is no true recorder any more than was Dickens, but the self-appointed Judge of a universe which he conceives to be cruel.

Neither Dickens nor Hardy can be called unveracious writers; both give a picture of life that is true up to a point. Hardy, in particular, errs less by distortion than by omission; he sees

[1] In these novels and in *The Dynasts* Mr. Hardy allows his personal views to depress one side of the scales: in his lesser novels he has often shown that he can hold the balance even. This distinction should be borne in mind in all the criticisms of his work, which I have ventured to make.

one side of life, but at the expense of another side ; he fails to hold the balance fairly, and lacks the large charity of the universe. Both writers are incomplete. No one could say of them, what is completely true of most Greek writers and largely true of all, that they see life steadily and see it whole. Still less can this be said of their followers, who, after the fashion of disciples, imitate and develop their defects, and oscillate between sentimental falsity, and the starkness and brutality which have been familiar in English literature during the last twenty years and in French literature for a much longer period. None of these writers, not even the best, is direct. Like Dickens, they consult their generous hearts, or, worse, ask : ' Can truth be told without making the public angry ? ' Or, like Hardy, they veil a didactic purpose under the name of realism, and register a bitter personal protest against the cruelty of life. In either case they narrow their view, and see the world through a mist of temperament.

This point may be illustrated by examining a famous passage from Homer, and then asking how a sentimental and a realistic writer might have treated it. Imagine the death of Hector in the hands of Dickens or Hardy. The first most probably would not have permitted it to occur, or, if he had, would have made Achilles the villain of the piece and emphasized and developed the tragedy in the manner of his death scenes, till he had wearied the reader with pathos. Confronted with such a tragedy he would have given the rein to emotion. Mr. Hardy, we may guess, would be impressed less by the pathos of the scene, than by the savagery of Achilles and the misgovernment of a universe in which such things were possible, and he would not have let these morals escape his readers. By small touches, by stressing suitable incidents, he would have made the tragedy more tragic, and the brutality more brutal. It is thus that he has treated the death of Jude. By so doing, both Dickens and Hardy in their different ways, would have been allowing their own personalities rather than the facts to speak, and, seeing only one side of the story, would have made it less complicated than life and less complete. But in the *Iliad* we see nothing of Homer's personality and hear no voice but that of the facts. The story tells itself without the heightening of artifice. The two men are brought before our eyes— Hector, the last hope of Troy, with his wife and child waiting for him at home—Achilles, mad with the memory of his dead friend. There is no judgement and no comment, but only the thing as it was.

To those who would maintain that Dickens or Hardy give an accurate picture of the world, there are two answers. First, their world is not the world as Shakespeare or Meredith sees it ; this for many persons will be a sufficient disproof of its reality. Second, the history of English and French literatures has been for the last 150 years a history of successive reactions. The classical school was followed by the romantics, the romantics by the realists ; each was a protest and a reaction against its predecessor. These swerving movements must have a cause. Now there are no reactions in literature unless there is some excess to provoke them. The existence of a reaction is a symptom of disease, and not only would it never take place apart from disease, but there is always a chance that it may go too far ; for as in the body, so in the world of letters, a balance once disturbed is difficult to restore. But Greek literature, unlike our own and unlike French, at no stage developed by reaction. Its epic poets are followed by the lyrists and these by the tragedians : tragedy passes into the New Comedy, which is followed by the learned and artistic poetry of Alexandria. In prose the unperiodic style of Herodotus is succeeded by the style of Thucydides ; while Plato and the various orators develop different types of writing. None of these styles, however, and none of these writers, are in reaction against one another. Some traces of reaction against the Homeric outlook of Sophocles may perhaps be found in Euripides. But this contrast lies between two individual writers and not between two literary schools, and has no analogy with the relation of the romantic to the classical or to the realist movements. It is far less marked, for instance, than the contrast between Voltaire and Victor Hugo or that between Victor Hugo and Flaubert. There is no reaction in the development of Greek literature, because at no stage is there any excess to react from ; and there is no excess, because the Greek writers are direct and objective, because they are mirrors that reflect life, not imperfect lenses that distort it each according to its own imperfection.

The literature of the Elizabethans here resembles Greek. It is indeed more wayward, more fanciful, more personal, more luxuriant than the Greek ; but it is on the whole more disinterested, freer from any didactic bent, more inclined to contemplate life for its own sake than the literature of any succeeding epoch in England. Since the Puritans a didactic strain has continually appeared in our writers. We have had revolts and protests, and then, by reaction, more protests and revolts. However admirable in morals, this Protestantism is injurious in literature, for, like all rebellions, it ends in excess and destroys the even-balanced temper which is essential to the creation of the greatest literature. This didactic temper, often disguised as realism, has never been stronger than in our own age, when many who might have found their profession in the Churches are diverted to other paths and seek in literature an outlet that in the past would have been found in the pulpit. Messrs. Wells, Shaw, Galsworthy—to mention no others—are parsons *manqués*, who were designed by nature to write not plays or novels but sermons. Or rather they are dual personalities : clergyman and creative writer have been combined in them and the clergyman has corrupted the poet. The unsatisfied appetite for preaching which a hundred years ago would have been quieted by writing an evangelical tract, to-day issues in a novel or a play. The moral differs, the form changes, the intention and temper are the same.

It is ungrateful to cavil at this moralizing and didactic temper, which animates a large part of the nation and is responsible for much of the British achievement. But its place is in the world of action not in that of letters, and it does not produce the greatest literature or the truest thought. The Greeks might have gained by a greater infusion of it : we, on the other hand, can learn something from their intellectual disinterestedness which in political and social controversies would make opposing views more intelligible and the path to truth easier and plainer, in literature would free us from excesses that are followed by reaction to a contrary excess, and in national life would guard us from the materialism which besets an industrial and commercial age. It is not confined to the Greeks ; but by no people is the ideal of intellectual truth more clearly and universally exhibited than by those who first brought it into an indifferent world, and who built upon it their literature and art no less than their science and philosophy.

The last quality of Greek literature of which I wish to speak is not one which we should expect to find in combination with truthfulness ; it is certainly very rare in modern realists. Yet the Greek instinct for beauty is beyond question. There is the evidence of Winckelmann, who, living in a world that had forgotten Greek, rediscovered it ; or of Keats, who was not brought up to the familiarity with Greek that breeds obtuseness and indifference, but made acquaintance with it when he was of an age to judge. The impression made both on Keats and Winckelmann is that of a new and surpassing beauty. There is the evidence of ' the beautiful mythology of Greece ',[1] the offspring of an untaught folk-imagination, and so far

[1] Keats, *Preface to Endymion.*

richer in the quality of beauty than the mythology of the North.
Even in the sawdust of a mythological dictionary the stories
of Atalanta, Narcissus, Pygmalion, Orpheus and Eurydice,
Phaethon, Medusa keep their magic.

The following extract from the hymn of Demeter may
illustrate this beauty, though it is not one of the greatest
passages of Greek literature and its writer is unknown.   It is
the story of the Earth Mother and her daughter Persephone :

> ἣν 'Αϊδωνεὺς
> ἥρπαξεν, δῶκεν δὲ βαρύκτυπος εὐρυόπα Ζεύς,
> παίζουσαν κούρῃσι σὺν 'Ωκεανοῦ βαθυκόλποις
> ἄνθεά τ' αἰνυμένην, ῥόδα καὶ κρόκον ἠδ' ἴα καλὰ
> λειμῶν' ἂμ μαλακὸν καὶ ἀγαλλίδας ἠδ' ὑάκινθον
> νάρκισσόν θ', ὃν φῦσε δόλον καλυκώπιδι κούρῃ
> Γαῖα Διὸς βουλῇσι χαριζομένη Πολυδέκτῃ,
> θαυμαστὸν γανόωντα· σέβας τό γε πᾶσιν ἰδέσθαι
> ἀθανάτοις τε θεοῖς ἠδὲ θνητοῖς ἀνθρώποις·
> τοῦ καὶ ἀπὸ ῥίζης ἑκατὸν κάρα ἐξεπεφύκει,
> κῶζ' ἥδιστ' ὀδμή, πᾶς δ' οὐρανὸς εὐρὺς ὕπερθε
> γαῖά τε πᾶσ' ἐγέλασσε καὶ ἁλμυρὸν οἶδμα θαλάσσης.
> ἡ δ' ἄρα θαμβήσασ' ὠρέξατο χερσὶν ἄμ' ἄμφω
> καλὸν ἄθυρμα λαβεῖν· χάνε δὲ χθὼν εὐρυάγυια
> Νύσιον ἂμ πεδίον, τῇ ὄρουσεν ἄναξ Πολυδέγμων
> ἵπποις ἀθανάτοισι.[1]

Turn from this to some parallel poem in English literature,

[1] *Hymn to Demeter*, l. 2 ff.   The translation is mainly from Pater, *Greek
Studies.*   'Whom, by the consent of far-seeing, deep-thundering Zeus,
Aidoneus carried away, as she played with the deep-bosomed daughters
of Ocean, gathering flowers in a meadow of soft grass and roses and crocus
and fair violets and iris and hyacinths and the strange glory of the narcissus
which the Earth, favouring the desire of Aidoneus, brought forth to snare
the flower-like girl.   A wonder it was to all, immortal gods and mortal men.
A hundred blossoms grew up from the roots of it, and very sweet was its scent,
and the broad sky above, and all the earth and the salt wave of the sea laughed
to see it.   She in wonder stretched out her two hands to take the lovely play-
thing : thereupon the wide-wayed earth opened in the Nysian plain and the
king of the great nation of the dead sprang out with his immortal horses.'

such as *Oenone* or *Tithonus*. Beautiful as Tennyson is, the
Greek has a better beauty, a beauty not of words or metaphors
or highly-wrought art, but simpler, more spontaneous and more
instinctive, as though not man but nature herself was speaking.
Two writers, who are qualified to judge by being themselves
among the great poets of the world, and who knew and appreciated other literatures, but speak in this way about Greek
alone, have testified to the uniqueness of this beauty. Goethe
says stiffly but precisely : ' in the presence of antiquity the
mind feels itself placed in the most ideal state of nature ; and
even to this day the Homeric hymns have the power of freeing
us, at any rate, for moments, from the terrible burden which
the tradition of many hundreds of years has rolled upon us.'
In these words Goethe has touched on the simplicity and the
naturalness of Greek beauty, in contrast to the more exotic
and elaborate beauty of which mediaeval and modern art and
literature are full. Keats writing about the Grecian urn also
had in his mind the liberating power of Greek beauty :

> Thou, silent form, dost tease us out of thought
> As doth eternity ; Cold Pastoral !
> When old age shall this generation waste
>   Thou shalt remain, in midst of other woe
> Than ours, a friend to man, to whom thou sayst,
> ' Beauty is truth, truth beauty '—that is all
>   Ye know on earth and all ye need to know.

These words point to another trait of Greek beauty, which
any one who has seen Greek statues must have felt : it does
not provoke speculation just as it does not excite desire, because
no elements are mingled with it that might stir such feelings.
It has no admixture, but is mere beauty, sought for itself.

Not only is Greek beauty different in quality from our own,
but it is more abundant. This surely would be the verdict
of an impartial critic who compared Homer, the lyrists, the
tragedians, Plato, Theocritus, the epigrammatists, with the

corresponding names in modern literatures. It amounts to a different way of viewing the world; the Greeks were more sensitive to beauty than we are, just as some people are more sensitive than others to colours or sounds, to moral or intellectual issues. This is curiously illustrated in their treatment of tragic themes. There is no want of tragedy in Homer or the dramatists—their view of life is probably darker than our own—and they have been praised for a pessimism that faced and admitted the black truth. Yet the cloud of evil is continually broken by rays of beauty. Thus Homer lights up the tragic parting of Hector and Andromache by the story of the child and the nodding plumes, yet does not use the incident, as many writers would have used it, to heighten the tragedy, which indeed it neither emphasizes nor diminishes: it is merely a gratuitous touch of delight in children, as accidental and natural as the brighter moments which, in life if not in realistic novels, diversify the darkest hours. Thus too Aeschylus preludes the bloody slaughter of Salamis with the white horses of the dawn, the echoes in the cliffs, the foam whitening beneath the oars, and when he speaks of the island where the Persians are butchered, does not forget the dances in which Pan rejoiced there of old. Thus, again, one of the most tragic moments in the *Hippolytus* is followed by the song,

> Could I take me to some cavern for mine hiding,
> 　In the hill-tops where the Sun scarce hath trod ;
> Or a cloud make the home of mine abiding,
> 　As a bird among the bird-droves of God !
> 　　Could I wing me to my rest amid the roar
> 　　Of the deep Adriatic on the shore,
> Where the water of Eridanus is clear,
> 　And Phaëthon's sad sisters by his grave
> Weep into the river, and each tear
> 　Gleams, a drop of amber, in the wave.[1]

[1] ll. 732 f. (tr. Murray).

The union of beauty and tragedy may be a paradox, but no reader can miss its power. The mere story of Hector's death as told by Homer is poignant, even when read in an English translation : the magic of the original language and metre doubles the effect. The combination of these two apparently inconsistent things, which is one of the marks of Greek poetry, is, of course, found in other literatures ; the description of Ophelia's death in *Hamlet* is an instance of it. But no drama except Greek has that regular interweaving of tragedy with exquisite lyrics by which some of its most powerful effects are secured.

Effect is the wrong word to use, for we have here no literary trick, but a view of life, which is naturally complete and clear-sighted, which is sensitive to the beauty that no evil can destroy, which sees the splendour in tragedy itself, and remembers that though the days of darkness are many it is a pleasant thing for the eyes to behold the sun. This philosophy, implied throughout Greek literature, commends it to many people. Those who disagree with the philosophy will not quarrel with the beauty itself. Hellenism is one of the forces which are continually being buried and re-found, and which, like talismans, have a disturbing power when they fall afresh into human hands. Those who read the literature of the age which rediscovered Greek will see that it brought above all a sense of liberation and expansion. At the Renaissance as in the eighteenth century, Greece found the world in chains, and broke them and threw down the prison walls. The fetters of the two epochs were different, but freedom was brought, at the Renaissance partly, and in the age of Winckelmann entirely, by the vision of beauty which Greece exhibited. Our own age has many chains and knows well the burden of which Goethe spoke. It has multiplied ugliness far faster than beauty, and its writers, prolific, interesting, and thoughtful as they are, do not help it here. It may well find, as other ages have found, in this quality of Greek literature a healing and liberating power.

English literature is surpassed by none, but its defects or dangers are at points where Greek is strong. Greek simplicity recalls us to the central interests of the human heart. Greek truthfulness is a challenge to see the world as it is and shun the emptiness of mere music, the falsities of rhetoric or sentiment, the incompleteness of writers who, instead of seeing life as a whole, ignore or emphasize a part of it as their own sympathies dictate. Greek beauty is a memorial of an aspect of the universe to which ages of thought are often blind. Greek technique is a lesson in ' form ' and a reminder of its place in literature.

Nor is the study of Greek a danger to our national genius. Contact with highly developed foreign models may warp or cramp a literature in its infancy, but cannot harm it when full grown and robust. The native character is then too firmly established to be corrupted, and it is pure gain to have another standard for comparison, for detection of weaknesses and their cure. A reference to English literature will support this view and show that though the influence of Greek there has often been great, it has not been distorting. Consider the English poets who owe most to Greece—Milton, Gray, Shelley, Keats, Landor, Tennyson, Matthew Arnold, Swinburne, Bridges. It would puzzle any critic to find a common denominator between these men, or to trace back to Greece any universal feature in their poetry, except perhaps perfection of form. Technical perfection is not so serious or frequent a vice in English writers, that it can be complained of, and even this common element vanishes, if we add to the poets already quoted the Brownings, who prized and understood Greek and the Greek spirit as well as any of them.

At first sight it may seem strange that Shelley and Keats, Arnold and Swinburne, who were not merely passionate admirers

of Greece but drew their chief inspiration from her, should be
so different in style and matter. The explanation is simple.
Some influences are tyrannous ; they impose themselves, they
dominate, they enslave. But there is a better and rarer type of
influence, which stimulates and inspires yet leaves the poet free
to develop his own genius with enlarged horizons and quickened
sensibilities. Greek influence on our writers has been of this
kind ; perhaps because its literature is singularly free from the
artifice and mannerism which lend themselves to mimicry and
seems like Nature with her many voices speaking.

R. W. LIVINGSTONE.

HISTORY

I

The Relationship between Ancient Greek and Modern Western Civilization

ANCIENT Greek society perished at least as long ago as the seventh century A.D. Many historians would date its death a good many centuries earlier, and all would agree that even if there are symptoms that life still lingered in the body down to this time, its mental and physical energies had long failed, and that the change from lethargy to death was hardly perceptible when it came. Thus even on the most cautious reckoning, there is an interval of thirteen centuries between the close of Greek history and our own times, and the great age of Greek history—the time when Ancient Greek society was in its prime, when it was shaping its own destiny and deflecting the destiny of its neighbours—is separated from our generation by more than two thousand years. What legacy has come down, through these great periods of time, from Ancient Greek society to the contemporary world ? Before trying to answer this big question, let us consider a smaller one : What is the legacy of Ancient Greek History to our own society ? That portion of contemporary humanity which inhabits Western Europe and America constitutes a specific society, for which the most convenient name is ' Western Civilization ', and this society has a relationship with Ancient Greek society which other contemporary societies—for instance, those of Islam, India, and China—have not. It is its child.

This description of the relationship between Ancient Greece

U

and the modern Western world may be something more than a metaphor, for societies like individuals are living creatures, and may therefore be expected to exhibit the same phenomena. At any rate the metaphor illustrates the facts. To begin with, the histories of the two societies overlap. The origins of modern Western society may be traced back a century or two before the Christian era, when the lands and races of Western Europe came into contact with the Levant, where Greek society had grown up and was then in its maturity. The germ of Western society first developed in the body of Greek society, like a child in the womb. The Roman Empire was the period of pregnancy during which the new life was sheltered and nurtured by the old. The 'Dark Age' was the crisis of birth, in which the child broke away from its parent and emerged as a separate, though naked and helpless, individual. The Middle Ages were the period of childhood, in which the new creature, though immature, found itself able to live and grow independently. The fourteenth and fifteenth centuries, with their marked characteristics of transition, may stand for puberty, and the centuries since the year 1500 for our prime. The metaphor works out sufficiently well to throw light on our particular problem : the legacy bequeathed to the Modern West by Ancient Greece.

Children 'inherit' from their parents in several senses of the word. There are features and instincts physically transmitted from the one to the other. There are imitations in early childhood of the parent's speech and gesture which are not perhaps strictly predetermined by the relationship, but which are yet performed subconsciously and are in fact so inevitable that the child is never aware that it is exercising choice in the matter. And there is deliberate and conscious imitation at a later stage when the child is sufficiently mature to appreciate its parent's character. These several forms of 'legacy' from parent to child differ primarily in the extent to which the acceptance and use of them depends upon the child's own will, and it will probably be admitted that the legacies which are the less certain to be transmitted are also the more important if the transmission happens to take place. For example, a child's life and character are more affected by deliberate imitation of its parent at a relatively advanced age than by the unchosen inheritance of some particular colour of hair and eye or shape of chin or pitch of temperament. On the other hand, while the inheritance of these latter characteristics from one among a limited number of ancestral strains is inevitable, the voluntary legacy may never be transmitted at all. The child will not claim it unless he knows his parent and admires or respects him. The parent's premature death or removal or the lack of sufficient sympathy between the parent and the child can in this case inhibit the transmission, and the potential legacy, with its momentous possibilities of influence upon the child's career, will never in fact be bequeathed.

These considerations may guide us in an analysis of the legacy which we have received from our parent society— the civilization of Ancient Greece. First, has Ancient Greece transmitted to us anything comparable to the physical and psychological legacy of an individual human parent to her child? This is a difficult question for us to answer, just as it is difficult for members of the same family to appreciate the 'family likeness' between them. A Moslem or Hindu or Chinaman could judge better than we. But it is certainly possible that the comparative similarity of climatic conditions and the comparative unity of racial stock has created a closer relationship between these two societies than between either one of them and any other. The poetry and philosophy and social life and political institutions of Ancient Greece and the Modern West may conceivably constitute a single species when contrasted with the institutions of other civilizations.

A modern West European or American may have a greater innate appreciation for Homer than for the Old Testament or for Sokrates than for Buddha or Confucius. The parallel which historians so often draw, or imply, between the conflict of Ancient Greece with the Ancient East and that of the Modern West with the Modern East may rest on a real kinship between the two Occidental civilizations as contrasted with their respective Oriental neighbours. But this is uncertain and on the whole unprofitable ground. When we come to the 'subconsciously chosen' type of legacy, the analogy with the relationship between parent and child becomes more evident.

Legacies of this type from Ancient Greek society are prominent in the Middle Ages—the childhood of modern Western civilization which followed the 'Dark Age' crisis of birth. One of the first needs of our young Western society as it struggled to its feet was a symbol of its unity—something corresponding to the attainment of self-consciousness by the individual human being—and for this it borrowed the last constructive idea of the Ancient Greek world. The mediaeval 'Holy Roman Empire' had quite a different purpose and function, in the childhood of modern Western civilization, from the purpose and function of the Roman Empire in the old age of Ancient Greece. But the young civilization did not think of inventing a new institution for its individual needs. In its subconscious pursuit of its own development it conceived itself to be reviving one of the customs of its venerable parent. The political thinkers of Charlemagne's day never imagined that the idea of world unity could be embodied in any other form.

Again, a century or so later, certain portions of Western society, especially the populations of North and Central Italy and the Low Countries, had outdistanced the rest in economic development and needed institutions of local self-government to give their economic vitality free play. In this case, again, Western civilization reverted to an Ancient Greek institution

and revived the 'city-state'. A little later still, the rapidly
growing and differentiating body of Western civilization was
impelled towards territorial expansion, and sought it, like
Ancient Greece in a similar period, round the shores of the
Mediterranean. This mediaeval movement of expansion, which
is commonly called the Crusades, but which made itself felt
in Spain and Sicily and the Aegean as well as in the 'Holy
Land', is a remarkable parallel to the propagation of Ancient
Greek city-states round the same shores between about 750
and 600 B.C. In drifting back upon the Mediterranean, the
mediaeval West was searching for new realms to conquer, but
it was really captured by the romance of its ancestral home.

Here, then, are three prominent features in mediaeval
Western history—the Holy Roman Empire, the Flemish and
Italian communes, and the Crusades—which were legacies from
Ancient Greek history in the sense of being subconscious
reversions to the habits of the parent society. But have these
mediaeval legacies from Ancient Greece been really important
constituents in our history viewed as a whole? Have they not
rather been false growths which led to little or nothing? The
Holy Roman Empire was never more than a mirage. The sense
of unity in the modern Western world is derived not from
this but from a really original institution, the early Papal
Church, in which any legacy from Ancient Greece would be
hard to discern. The national states of modern Europe and
America are derived not from mediaeval Ghent or Bruges or
Florence or Venice but from the new, though clumsy, feudal
communities of mediaeval England and France. And the
expansion of Western society has not followed the direction
indicated by the Crusades. The false trail of the Mediterranean was practically abandoned after less than three centuries'
trial. The true domain of modern Western civilization has
been found in regions which Ancient Greece hardly explored:
Northern Germany and Scandinavia and the British Isles, the

North Sea and the Baltic, the Atlantic and the continent of America. Thus our mediaeval legacies from Ancient Greece —the subconscious reversions of childhood—are historical curiosities rather than vital links between the two civilizations. Our really important legacy from Ancient Greece was adopted with full consciousness and deliberation when we stood on the threshold of our own maturity.

The legacy of this third type which we have received from Ancient Greece has been given the general name of the Renaissance. It was a determined and successful attempt, on the part of our society, to learn everything that the literary and artistic remains of our great predecessor could teach us. It lay within our choice to study these remains or to pass them by, and the fact that we chose to study them has been one of the greatest and the most fortunate decisions in the career of our civilization. The several aspects of this acceptance of what Ancient Greece had to offer have been treated already in the other chapters in this volume. Here it is merely necessary to point out that the Renaissance was a study and assimilation not only of Ancient Greek literature and art, but of architecture, natural science, mathematics, philosophy, political ideas, and all the other higher expressions of a great society. The absorption of this vast current of life largely accounts for the wonderful impetus which has revealed itself in Western civilization during the last four centuries.

Has the current now spent its force? Has the legacy adopted four centuries ago been used up and exhausted? Under the inspiration of Ancient Greece, has the modern West now created a literature, art, architecture, science, mathematics, philosophy, and political thought which equal or surpass the Ancient patterns and turn them from an inspiration into an encumbrance? That seems to be the fundamental question behind the controversy about the study of Ancient Greek life in England to-day. Perhaps the answer may be found—if we may go back to our metaphor—in the uniqueness of the individual personality.

If one considers the relations of a parent and child, or indeed of any two human beings, it is evident that the one could never exhaust all that could be learnt from the personality of the other. The one might acquire every physical, mental, and moral attainment that the other could display, and yet the other's unique individuality would remain—an inexhaustible subject of study, throwing perpetual new light upon the life of the observer himself and of his fellow human beings. This is true of any two human beings, but if the two happen to be people of commanding character and genius it becomes a truism which it would be almost ludicrous to question. Let us apply this to the study not of one individual but of one society by another, and let us take the case in point, in which the two societies happen to be great civilizations. The study of a great civilization has a unique value, not merely for members of another civilization which stands to it in the relation of child to parent, but for every seeker after knowledge who has a civilization of his own. This ultimate and most precious legacy of Ancient Greece is at the disposal of Moslems, Hindus, and Chinese, as well as Westerners. For receiving it there are two qualifications : a good understanding and an open mind.

II

Ancient Greek Civilization as a Work of Art

Civilizations are the greatest and the rarest achievements of human society. Innumerable societies have been coming into being and perishing during many hundreds of thousands of years, and hardly any of them have created civilizations. One can count the civilizations on one's fingers. We have had perhaps three in Europe : the Minoan in the Aegean Islands (the dates 4000–1100 B.C. roughly cover its history) ; the

Greek or Graeco-Roman round the coasts of the Mediterranean
(its history extends between the eleventh century B.C. and the
seventh century A.D.) ; and our modern Western civilization
round the coasts of the Atlantic, which began to emerge from
twilight in the eighth century A.D. and is still in existence.
Then there are the ancient civilizations of Egypt and Lower
Mesopotamia, which were first dominated by Ancient Greece
and then amalgamated into the single Middle Eastern civilization of Islam ; and there are the civilizations of India and
China. Even if we count as civilizations the societies existing
in Mexico and Peru before the Spanish Conquest, the total
number of known independent civilizations, compared with the
total number of known human societies, is very small. And
it is so because the achievement is astonishingly difficult.
There are two constant factors in social life—the spirit of man
and its environment. Social life is the relation between them,
and life only rises to the height of civilization when the spirit
of man is the dominant partner in the relationship—when
instead of being moulded by the environment (as it is in the
tropical forests of Central Africa and Brazil), or simply holding
its own against the environment in a kind of equilibrium (as
it does on the steppes of Central Asia or Arabia, among the
nomads), it moulds the environment to its own purpose, or
' expresses ' itself by ' impressing ' itself upon the world. The
study of a civilization is not different in kind from the study
of a literature. In both cases one is studying a creation of the
spirit of man, or, in more familiar terms, a work of art.

Civilization is a work of art—in the literal meaning of the
phrase and not merely by a metaphor. It is true that works
of art are made by individuals, civilization by a society. But
what work of art is there in which the individual artist owes
nothing to others? And a civilization, the work of countless
individuals and many generations, differs in this respect from
a poem or a statue not in kind but only in degree. It is a social

work of art, expressed in social action, like a ritual or a play. One cannot describe it better than by calling it a tragedy with a plot, and history is the plot of the tragedy of civilization.

Students of the drama, from Aristotle onwards, seem to agree that nearly all the great tragedies in literature are expositions of quite a few fundamental plots. And it is possible that the great tragedies of history—that is, the great civilizations that have been created by the spirit of man—may all reveal the same plot, if we analyse them rightly. Each civilization—for instance, the civilization of Mediaeval and Modern Europe and again that of Ancient Greece—is probably a variant of a single theme. And to study the plot of civilization in a great exposition of it—like the Hellenic exposition or our own Western exposition—is surely the right goal of a humane education.

But of course one asks : Why study Ancient Hellenic civilization rather than ours? The study of any one civilization is so complex, it demands so many preliminary and subordinate studies—linguistic, institutional, economic, psychological—that it is likely to absorb all one's energies. The greatest historians have generally confined themselves to the study of a single civilization, and the great Greek historians—Herodotus, Thucydides, and Polybius—concentrated on their own, and only studied others in so far as their own came into contact with them. Clearly, people who are going to be historians, not for life, but as an education for life, must make their choice. They must practically confine themselves to studying one civilization if they are to reap the fruits of study at all, and in this case it is natural to ask : Why study Hellenism rather than our own history? There are two obvious arguments in favour of studying modern history. It seems more familiar and it seems more useful. And it would be a mistake to misrepresent these arguments by stating them only in their cruder forms. 'Familiar' does not mean 'easy', and to say that modern history seems more useful than ancient does not mean that the study of it is a closer approximation to a Pelman course. There is an exceedingly crude view of education among some people just now—perhaps it is largely due to the war, and may disappear like other ugly effects of the war—which inclines to concentrate education on applied chemistry, say, or engineering, with a vague idea that people whose education has been devoted to these subjects will be more capable of competing with foreigners in the dye industry or of working in munition factories in the next emergency. In the same way, conceivably, concentration on modern history might be supposed to equip a student for securing concessions abroad for a firm, or for winning a parliamentary election. Of course, this attitude, though it is rather widespread just now, is absurd. The fallacy lies in confusing the general theoretical knowledge of a subject acquired through being educated in it with the technical knowledge and personal experience which one must have to turn the same subject to practical account in after life. There is no difference of opinion on this point between ' humanists ' and ' scientists '. The issue is between people who do not appreciate the value of the pursuit of knowledge as an end in itself, and those who do appreciate it and who therefore understand what education means. True lovers of knowledge and true believers in education will be found on the same side in this controversy, whether the subject of their study happens to be the spirit of man or the laws of its environment. But apart from that crude utilitarianism, which is as unscientific as it is un-humane, a serious argument for studying modern rather than ancient history can also be stated from the humane and the scientific point of view. It may be argued that the direct experience we have of our own civilization makes it possible for us to have a deeper, and therefore a more humane and scientific, understanding of it than we can ever have of Ancient Greece. And one might go on to argue, on grounds of humanism alone, that such a comprehension of the character and origins of our civilization would have a more profound humanizing influence upon its development than a less intimate study of a different civilization could produce. This argument is bound to appeal to the generation which has experienced the war. The war is obviously one of the great crises of our civilization. It is like a conflagration lighting up the dim past and throwing it into perspective. The war makes it impossible for us to take our own history for granted. We are bound to inquire into the causes of such an astonishing catastrophe, and as soon as we do that we find ourselves inquiring into the evolution of Western Civilization since it emerged from the Dark Age. The shock of the Peloponnesian War gave just the same intellectual stimulus to Thucydides, and made him preface his history of that war with a critical analysis, brief but unsurpassed, of the origins of Hellenic civilization—the famous introductory chapters of Book I. May not these chapters point the road for us and counsel us to concentrate upon the study of our own history?

This question deserves very serious consideration, not merely from the utilitarian, but from the scientific and humane point of view. But the answer is not a foregone conclusion. There is a case for studying the civilization of Ancient Greece which can be summed up in four points, as follows :

(i) In Greek history the plot of civilization has been worked out to its conclusion. We can sit as spectators through the whole play ; we can say : ' This or that is the crisis ; from this point onwards the end is inevitable ; or if this actor had acted otherwise in those circumstances the issue would not have been the same.' We can grasp the structure of the tragedy and divide it into acts. But in our own history we are like players in the middle of the piece, and though we may be able to say ' This is the third act or the fourth act ', we cannot say ' This is the last act or the last but one '. We

cannot foretell the future ; the work of art we are studying
is incomplete, and therefore we cannot possibly apprehend it
as an artistic whole, however vivid may be our experience of
isolated scenes and situations. The first point in favour of
Greek history is its completeness and its true perspective from
our point of view.

(ii) The second is that the historical experience of the Greeks
has been more finely expressed than ours. Its expression is in
all Greek art and literature—for it is a great mistake to suppose
that historical experience is expressed in so-called historical
records alone. The great poets of Greece are of as much
assistance in understanding the mental history of Greece (which
is after all the essential element in any history) as the philosophers and historians. And Greek historical experience or
mental history is better expressed in Greek literature than ours
is in the literature of modern Europe. Without attempting
to compare the two literatures as literatures it can be said with
some confidence that the surviving masterpieces of Greek
literature give a better insight into the subjective side of
Greek history—into the emotions and speculations which arose
out of the vicissitudes of Greek society and were its most
splendid creations—than any insight into the subjective side
of modern history which we can obtain by studying it through
modern literature.

(iii) The third point is expressed in the concluding phrase of
Aristotle's definition of tragedy (*Poetics*, vi. 2). ' Tragedy ', he
says, ' is an imitation of an action that is serious, complete, and
of a certain magnitude . . . through pity and fear effecting the
proper κάθαρσις, or purgation, of these emotions.' (Butcher's
translation.) This word κάθαρσις—purgation, purification,
cleansing, discharge—has been the subject of interminable
controversy among scholars, but any one acquainted with
Ancient Greek literature who has lived through the war will
understand what it means. Certainly the writer found, in the

worst moments of the war, that passages from the classics—
some line of Aeschylus or Lucretius or Virgil, or the sense
of some speech in Thucydides, or the impression of some mood
of bitterness or serenity in a dialogue of Plato—would come
into his mind and give him relief. These men had travelled
along the road on which our feet were set ; they had travelled
it farther than we, travelled it to the end ; and the wisdom
of greater experience and the poignancy of greater suffering
than ours was expressed in the beauty of their words. In the
writer's personal experience that relief was obtained from
acquaintance with Greek civilization as expressed in Greek
literature. It put one in communication with a different
civilization from our own—with people who had experienced
all and more than we had experienced, and who were now at
peace beyond the world of time and change. Κάθαρσις, then,
is the emotional value which is peculiar to the study of a
different civilization, and which one cannot get, at any rate
with the same intensity, by the study of his own.

(iv) This emotional value has its intellectual counterpart in
the comparative method of study, which one gets by studying,
not his own circumstances, but circumstances comparable to,
without being identical with, his own. This is a commonplace
in the field of language. The study of Ancient Greek is
generally admitted to have more educative value for an Englishman than the study of modern French or German, because
Greek and English embody the fundamental principles of
human language in entirely independent forms of expression,
while French and English, in addition to the elements common
to all language, share the special background of the Bible and
the Classics, which have given them an extensive common
stock of phraseology and imagery. This applies equally to the
study of civilization. One learns more by studying Ancient
Greek religion and comparing it with Christianity than by
studying Christianity in ignorance of other religious pheno-

mena ; and one learns more about institutions by studying the Greek city-state and comparing it with the modern national state than by merely studying the evolution of the national state in modern Europe. If we take utility to mean intellectual and not practical utility—and as humanists and scientists we do—we may claim without paradox that the study of Greek civilization is valuable just because it is not our own.

These, then, are four points in favour of Greek history : we possess the whole tragedy, it is a magnificent expression of the plot, and it has a peculiar emotional value and a peculiar intellectual value which the drama in which we ourselves are actors cannot have for us.

At this point it is necessary to give a sketch of the plot of Greek history—every one must make his own sketch ; the writer offers his to provoke the reader to make his own—and then to illustrate the second point, the beauty of the expression, by quoting half a dozen passages from ancient authors. The other two points—the cathartic and the comparative value of Greek history—are matters of personal experience. I have little doubt that the reader will experience them himself if he takes up this study seriously and from a broad point of view.

III

The Plot of Ancient Greek Civilization

The genesis of Ancient Greek civilization is certainly later than the twelfth century B.C., when Minoan civilization, its predecessor, was still in process of dissolution ; and the termination of Ancient Greek civilization must certainly be placed before the eighth century A.D., when modern Western civilization, its successor, had already come into being. Between these extreme points we cannot exactly date its beginning and end, but we can see that it covers a period of seventeen or eighteen centuries.

It is easier to divide the tragedy into acts. We can at once discern two dramatic crises—the outbreak of the Peloponnesian War and the foundation of the Roman Empire. We can for convenience take precise dates—431 B.C. and 31 B.C.—and group the action into three acts or phases, one before, one between, and one after these critical moments.

It is best to give the analysis in tabular form :

Act I (11th cent.–431 B.C.).

1. Synoikismos (formation of the city-state, the cell of Greek society), 11th cent.–750 B.C.
2. Colonization (propagation of the city-state round the Mediterranean), 750–600 B.C.
3. Economic revolution (change from extensive to intensive growth), 600–500 B.C.
4. Confederation (repulse of Oriental universal empire and creation of an inter-state federation, the Delian League), 500–431 B.C.

Act II (431 B.C.–31 B.C.).

1. The Greek wars (failure of inter-state federation), 431–355 B.C.
2. The Oriental wars (the superman, conquest of the East, struggle for the spoils, barbarian invasion), 355–272 B.C.
3. The first rally (change of scale and fresh experiments in federation—Seleucid Asia, Roman Italy, Aetolian and Achaean ' United States '), 272–218 B.C.
4. The Roman wars (destruction of four great powers by one; devastation of the Mediterranean world), 218–146 B.C.
5. The class wars (capitalism, bolshevism, Napoleonism), 146–31 B.C.

Act III (31 B.C.–7th cent. A.D.).

1. The second rally (final experiment in federation—compromise between city-state autonomy and capitalistic centralization), 31 B.C.–A.D. 180.

2. The first dissolution (external front broken by tribesmen, internal by Christianity), A.D. 180–284.
3. The final rally (Constantine τὸν δῆμον προσεταιρίζεται—tribesmen on to the land, bishops into the bureaucracy), A.D. 284–378.
4. The final dissolution (break of tradition), A.D. 378–7th cent.

This analysis is and must be subjective. Every one has to make his own, just as every one has to apprehend for himself the form of a work of art. But however the historian may analyse the plot and group it into acts, it must be borne in mind that the action is continuous, and that the first emergence of the Greek city-state in the Aegean and the last traces of municipal self-government in the Roman Empire are phases in the history of a single civilization. It may seem a paradox to call this civilization a unity. But the study of Greek and Latin literature leaves no doubt in one's mind that the difference of language there is less significant than the unity of form, and that one is really dealing with a single literature, the Hellenic, which in many of its branches was imitated and propagated in the Latin language, just as it was to a lesser extent in Hebrew, or later on in Syriac and Arabic. The unity is even more apparent when, instead of confining our attention to literature, we regard the whole field of civilization. It is not really possible to draw a distinction between Greek history and Roman history. At most one can say that at some point Greek history enters on a phase which it may be convenient to distinguish verbally by connecting it with the name of Rome. To take the case of the Roman Empire—the reader may possibly have been surprised to find the Roman Empire treated as the third act in the tragedy of Greece; yet when one studies the Empire one finds that it was essentially a Greek institution. Institutionally it was at bottom a federation of city-states, a solution of the political problem with which Greek society had been wrestling since the fifth century B.C. And even the non-municipal element, the centralized bureaucratic organization which Augustus spread like a fine, almost impalpable net to hold his federation of municipalities together, was largely a fruit of Greek administrative experience. As papyrology reveals the administrative system of the Ptolemaic Dynasty—the Greek successors of Alexander who preceded the Caesars in the government of Egypt—we are learning that even those institutions of the Empire which have been regarded as most un-Greek may have been borrowed through a Greek intermediary. Imperial jurisprudence, again, interpreted Roman municipal law into the law of a civilization by reading into it the principles of Greek moral philosophy. And Greek, not Latin, was still the language in which most of the greatest literature of the Imperial period was written. One need only mention works which are still widely read and which have influenced our own civilization—Plutarch's *Lives*, Marcus Aurelius' *Meditations*, and the New Testament. They are all written in Greek, and who will venture to assert that the age in which they were written falls outside Greek history, or that the social experience which produced them was not an act in the tragedy of Hellenic civilization? Even statistically the Empire was more Greek than anything else. Probably a considerable majority of its inhabitants spoke Greek as a lingua franca, if not as their mother-tongue. Nearly all the great industrial and commercial centres were in the Greek or Hellenized provinces. Possibly, during the first two centuries of the Empire, more Greek was spoken than Latin by the proletariat of Rome itself. The Greek core of the Roman Empire played the part of Western Europe in the modern world. The Latinized provinces were thinly populated, backward, and only superficially initiated into the fraternity of civilization. Latinized Spain and Africa were the South America, Latinized Gaul and Britain the Russia of the Ancient Greek world. The pulse of the Empire was driven by a Greek heart, and it beat comparatively feebly in the non-Greek extremities.

IV

The Literary Expression of the Plot

And now, after having suggested a reading of the plot, it is time to let the actors speak for themselves. There is only space to quote half a dozen passages, but they have been chosen to illustrate the critical scenes and situations in the drama as it has been sketched out, and they may persuade the reader that there is something to be said for the present interpretation.

We shall not dwell on the period I have called the first act—that is, the period before 431 B.C. But the reader is recommended, again, not to lay aside the Greek poets when he takes up the Greek historians. Homer will reveal more of the opening scenes than Herodotus; and the exaltation of spirit produced by the repulse of the Persians, and expressed institutionally in the foundation of the Delian League, can hardly be realized emotionally without the poetry of Aeschylus. But the philosophers and scientists are indispensable too. Professor Burnet's *Early Greek Philosophy*, or his *Greek Philosophy from Thales to Plato*, throws light on history and not merely on the Greek theory of knowledge. And the reader should make acquaintance with the little work on 'Atmospheres, Waters, and Localities' emanating from the Hippokratean school of medicine. It is only thirty-eight pages in the Teubner text (Hippocratis *Opera*, vol. i), and it gives clearer expression than Herodotus to the fifth-century scientific point of view. Here is one passage which might have been written in Victorian England. The writer is describing a peculiar disease prevalent among the nomads of southern Russia. 'The natives', he remarks, 'believe that this disease is sent by God, and they reverence and worship its victims, in fear of being stricken by it themselves. I too am quite ready to admit that these phenomena are caused by God, but I take the same view about all phenomena and hold that no single phenomenon is more or less divine in origin than any other. All are uniform and all may be divine, but each phenomenon obeys a law, and natural law knows no exceptions.'

It is hard to leave this first act of the tragedy. It is a triumph of youth, and the phrase in which Herodotus sums up the early history of Sparta expresses the prevailing spirit of early Hellenic civilization. Ἀνά τε ἔδραμον καὶ εὐθενήθησαν : 'They shot up and throve.' But there is another phrase in Herodotus which announces the second act—an ominous phrase which came so natural to him that one may notice about a dozen instances of it in his history. Ἔδει γὰρ τῷ δεῖνι γενέσθαι κακῶς : 'Evil had to befall so-and-so, and therefore'—the story of a catastrophe follows in each case. The thought behind the phrase is expressed in Solon's words to Croesus (Herodotus, Bk. I, ch. 32) : 'Croesus, I know that God is ever envious and disordering' (ταραχῶδες), 'and you ask me about the destiny of man ! '

Note the epithet translated ' disordering ' ; we shall meet the word ταραχή again. It is the bitter phrase of a man who lived on from the great age into the war, but not so bitter as the truth which the writer could not bring himself wholly to express. ' No single phenomenon ', as contemporary Greek science realized, ' is more or less divine than any other ', and the ' envious and disordering ' power, which wrecked Greek civilization, was not an external force, but the very spirit of man by which that civilization had been created. There is a puzzling line in Homer which is applied once or twice to features in a landscape—for instance, to a river : ' The gods call it Xanthos, mankind Skamandros.' So we might say of the downfall of Greece : the Greeks attributed it to the malignity of God, but the divine oracles gave a different answer.

Why did the Confederacy of Delos break down and Greece lose her youth in a ruinous war? Because of the evil in the hearts of men—the envy aroused by the political and commercial greatness of Athens in the governing classes of Sparta and Corinth ; and the covetousness aroused by sudden greatness in the Athenians, tempting their statesmen to degrade the presidency of a free confederacy into a dominion of Athens over Greece, and tempting the Athenian proletariat, and the proletariat in the confederate states, to misuse democracy for the exploitation of the rich by the poor. Envy and covetousness begat injustice, and injustice disloyalty. The city-states, in their rivalry for dominion or their resentment against the domineering of one state over another, forgot their loyalty to the common weal of Greece and fought each other for empire or liberty. And the wealthy and well-born citizens forgot their loyalty to the city in their blind, rancorous feud against the proletariat that was stripping them of property and power, and betrayed their community to foreign enemies.

' Strange how mortals blame the gods. They say that evil is our handiwork, when in truth they bring their sufferings on themselves. By their own folly they force the hand of fate. See, now, how Aigisthos forced it in taking the wedded wife of Atreides and slaying her lord when he returned, yet he had sheer destruction before his eyes, for we ourselves had forewarned him not to slay the king nor wed his wife, or vengeance would come by Atreides' son Orestes, whene'er he should grow to manhood and long for his home. So spake our messenger, but with all his wisdom he did not soften the heart of Aigisthos, and now he has paid in full' (*Odyssey*, a 32–43).

These lines from the first canto of the *Odyssey* were imagined by a generation which could still afford to err, but as Greece approached her hour of destiny, her prophetic inspiration grew clearer. The poets of the sixth century were haunted more insistently than the Homeridai by the possibilities of disaster

inherent in success of every kind—in personal prosperity, in
military victory, and in the social triumph of civilization.
They traced the mischief to an aberration of the human spirit
under the shock of sudden, unexpected attainment, and they
realized that both the accumulated achievement of generations
and the greater promise of the future might be lost irretrievably
by failure at this critical moment. ' Surfeit (κόρος) breeds sin
(ὕβρις) when prosperity visits unbalanced minds.' In slightly
different words, the proverb recurs in the collections of verses
attributed to Theognis and to Solon. Its maker refrained
from adding what was in his and his hearers' thoughts, that
ὕβρις, once engendered, breeds ἄτη—the complete and certain
destruction into which the sinner walks with unseeing eyes.
But the whole moral mystery, to its remorseless end, was
uttered again and again in passionate words by Aeschylus, who
consciously discarded the primitive magical determinism in
which Herodotus afterwards vainly sought relief.

> Φιλεῖ δὲ τίκτειν ὕβρις
> μὲν παλαιὰ νεά-
> ζουσαν ἐν κακοῖς βροτῶν
> ὕβριν τότ' ἢ τόθ', ὅτε τὸ κύριον μόλῃ
> φάος τόκου,
> δαίμονά τ' ἔταν, ἄμαχον, ἀπόλεμον,
> ἀνίερον θράσος, μελαί-
> νας μελάθροισιν Ἄτας,
> εἰδομένας τοκεῦσιν.

But Old Sin loves, when comes the hour again,
   To bring forth New,
Which laugheth lusty amid the tears of men ;
Yea, and Unruth, his comrade, wherewith none
May plead nor strive, which dareth on and on,
   Knowing not fear nor any holy thing ;
Two fires of darkness in a house, born true,
   Like to their ancient spring.

            (*Agamemnon*, vv. 763–71, Murray's transl.)

The poet of the crowning victory over Persia was filled with awe, as well as exultation, at the possibilities for good or evil which his triumphant generation held in their hands. Were they true metal or base? The times would test them, but he had no doubt about the inexorable law.

> Οὐ γὰρ ἔστιν ἔπαλξις
> πλούτου πρὸς κόρον ἀνδρὶ
> λακτίσαντι μέγαν δίκης
> βωμὸν εἰς ἀφάνειαν.

> Never shall state nor gold
>   Shelter his heart from aching
> Whoso the Altar of Justice old
>   Spurneth to night unwaking.

> (*Agamemnon*, vv. 381–4, Murray's transl.)

The *Agamemnon* was written when Athens stood at the height of her glory and her power, and before her sons, following the devices of their hearts, ' like a boy chasing a wingèd bird ', had set a fatal stumbling-block in the way of their city, or smirched her with an intolerable stain. The generation of Marathon foreboded the catastrophe of the Peloponnesian War, yet the shock, when it came, was beyond their powers of imagination, and the effect of it on the mind of Greece was first expressed by the generation which was smitten by the war in early manhood. This is how it was felt by Thucydides (iii. 82):

' So the class-war at Korkyra grew more and more savage, and it made a particular impression because it was the first outbreak of an upheaval that spread in time through almost the whole of Greek society. In every state there were conflicts of class, and the leaders of the respective parties now procured the intervention of the Athenians or the Lakedaimonians on their side. In peace-time they would have had neither the opportunity nor the inclination to call in the foreigner, but now there was the war, and it was easy for any party of violence to get their opponents crushed and themselves into power by an alliance with one of the belligerents. This recrudescence of class-war brought one calamity after another upon the states of Greece—calamities that occur and will continue to occur as long as human nature remains what it is, however they may be modified or occasionally mitigated by changes of circumstance. Under the favourable conditions of peace-time, communities and individuals do not have their hands forced by the logic of events, and can therefore act up to a higher standard. But war strips away all the margins of ordinary life and breaks in character to circumstance by its brutal training. So the states were torn by the class-war, and the sensation made by each outbreak had a sinister effect on the next—in fact, there was something like a competition in perfecting the fine art of conspiracies and atrocities. . . .

(iii. 83) 'Thus the class-war plunged Greek society into every kind of moral evil, and honesty, which is the chief constituent of idealism, was laughed out of existence in the prevailing atmosphere of hostility and suspicion. No argument was cogent enough and no pledge solemn enough to reconcile opponents. The only argument that appealed to the party momentarily in power was the unlikelihood of their remaining there long and the consequent advisability of taking no risks with their enemies. And the stupider the combatants, the greater their chances of survival, just because they were terrified at their deficiencies, expected to be outwitted and outmanœuvred, and therefore plunged recklessly into action, while their superiors in intellect, who trusted to their wits to protect them and disdained practical precautions, were often caught defenceless and brought to destruction.'

There is the effect of the great Greek war upon the first generation. Thucydides, of course, had a sensitive and emotional temperament. He is always controlling himself and reining himself in. But one is struck by an outburst of the

same feeling in a younger man, Xenophon, who was ordinarily
in harmony with his age and was probably rather unimaginative
and self-complacent by nature. The war had given Xenophon
his opportunity as a soldier and a writer. He was not inclined
to quarrel with the 'envious and disordering' powers that
had ruined Greek civilization. But in the last paragraph of
the History of his Own Times he is carried away, for he has
just been describing the battle of Mantinea (362 B.C.), in which
he had lost his son.

'The result of the battle', he writes, 'disappointed every
one's expectations. Almost the whole of Greece had mobilized
on one side or the other, and it was taken for granted that if
it came to an action, the victors would be able to do what
they liked and the vanquished would be at their mercy. But
Providence so disposed it that both sides . . . claimed the
victory and yet neither had gained a foot of territory, a single
city or a particle of power beyond what they had possessed
before the battle. On the contrary, there was more unsettle-
ment and disorder (ταραχή) in Greece after the battle than
before it. But I do not propose to carry my narrative further
and will leave the sequel to any other historian who cares to
record it.' (*Hellenica*, vii. 5 fin.)

Space forbids quotation from Plato, but the reader is recommended, while studying his metaphysics for his philosophy, to
note his moods and emotions for the light they throw upon
the history of his lifetime. Plato's long life—427 to 347 B.C.—
practically coincided with the first phase of the second act of
the tragedy—the series of wars that began in 431 B.C., and
that had reduced the Greek city-states to complete disunion
and exhaustion by 355. Plato belonged to the cultured
governing class which was hit hardest by these first disasters.
At the age of twenty-nine, after witnessing the downfall of
Athens, he had to witness the judicial murder of Sokrates—
the greatest man of the older generation, who had been appre-

ciated and loved by Plato and his friends. Plato's own most promising pupil, whom he had marked out for his successor, was killed in action in a particularly aimless recrudescence of the war. Plato's political disillusionment and perversity are easy to understand. But it is curious and interesting to watch the clash between his political bitterness and his intellectual serenity. In the intellectual and artistic sphere—as a writer, musician, mathematician, metaphysician—he stood consciously at the zenith of Greek history; but whenever he turned to politics he seems to have felt that the spring had gone out of the year. He instinctively antedated the setting of his dialogues. The characters nearly all belong to the generation of Sokrates, which had grown to manhood before the war and whose memories conjured up the glory that the war had extinguished. Note, also, his 'other-worldliness', for it is a feature that comes into Greek civilization with him and gradually permeates it. He turns from science to theology, from the world of time and change to the world of archetypes or ideas. He turns from the social religion of the city-state to a personal religion for which he takes symbols from primitive mythology. He turns from politics to utopias. But Plato only lived to see the first phase of the catastrophe. As we watch the remainder of this second act—those four terrible centuries that followed the year 431 B.C.—there come tidings of calamity after calamity, like the messages of disaster in the Book of Job, and as the world crumbles, people tend more and more to lay up their treasure elsewhere. In the *Laws*, Plato places his utopia no farther away than Crete. Two centuries later the followers of Aristonikos the Bolshevik, outlawed by the cities of Greece and Asia, proclaim themselves citizens of the City of the Sun. Two centuries later still, the followers of Jesus of Nazareth, despairing of this world, pray for its destruction by fire to make way for the Kingdom of Heaven.

Plato's state of mind gives the atmosphere of the first phase

after the catastrophe. For the second phase—the conquest of
the East and the struggle for the spoils—the reader may be
referred to Mr. Edwyn Bevan's *Lectures on the Stoics and
Sceptics* and to Professor Gilbert Murray's Conway Memorial
lecture on *The Stoic Philosophy*. They will show him a system
of philosophy which is no longer a pure product of speculation
but is primarily a moral shelter erected hastily to meet the
storms of life. The third phase—the rally of civilization in
the middle of the third century B.C.—is mirrored in Plutarch's
lives of the Spartan kings Agis and Kleomenes. Any one who
reads them will feel the gallantry of this rally and the pathos
of its failure. And then comes the fourth phase—the Roman
wars against the other great powers of the Mediterranean
world. The Hannibalic war in Italy was, very probably, the
most terrible war that there has ever been, not excepting
the recent war in Europe. The horror of that war haunted
later generations, and its mere memory made oblivion seem
a desirable release from an intolerable world.

> Nil igitur mors est ad nos neque pertinet hilum,
> quandoquidem natura animi mortalis habetur.
> et velut anteacto nil tempore sensimus aegri,
> ad confligendum venientibus undique Poenis,
> omnia cum belli trepido concussa tumultu
> horrida contremuere sub altis aetheris oris,
> in dubioque fuere utrorum ad regna cadendum
> omnibus humanis esset terraque marique,
> sic, ubi non erimus, cum corporis atque animai
> discidium fuerit quibus e sumus uniter apti,
> scilicet haud nobis quicquam, qui non erimus tum,
> accidere omnino poterit sensumque movere,
> non si terra mari miscebitur et mare caelo.

That is a passage of Lucretius (iii. 830–842) which follows
upon an elaborate argument to prove that death destroys
personality and that the soul is not immortal. Here is an
attempt at a translation :

' So death is nothing to us and matters nothing to us, since we have proved that the soul is not immortal. And as in time past we felt no ill, when the Phoenicians were pouring in to battle on every front, when the world rocked with the shock and tumult of war and shivered from centre to firmament, when all mankind on sea and land must fall under the victor's empire and victory was in doubt—so, when we have ceased to be, when body and soul, whose union is our being, have been parted, then nothing can touch us—we shall not be— and nothing can make us feel, no, not if earth is confounded with sea and sea with heaven.'

Lucretius wrote that about a hundred and fifty years after Hannibal evacuated Italy, but the horror is still vivid in his mind, and his poetry arouses it in our minds as we listen. The writer will never forget how those lines kept running in his head during the spring of 1918.

But the victors suffered with the vanquished in the common ruin of civilization. The whole Mediterranean world, and the devastated area in Italy most of all, was shaken by the economic and social revolutions which the Roman wars brought in their train. The proletariat was oppressed to such a degree that the unity of society was permanently destroyed and Greek civilization, after being threatened with a violent extinction by Bolshevik outbreaks—the slave wars in Sicily, the insurrection of Aristonikos and the massacres of Mithradates in Anatolia, the outbreaks of Spartakos and Catilina in Italy— was eventually supplanted by a rival civilization of the proletariat—the Christian Church. The revolutionary last phase in the second act—the final phase before the foundation of the Empire—has left its expression in the cry of the Son of Man : ' The foxes have holes and the birds of the air have nests, but the Son of Man hath not where to lay his head.' It was one of those anonymous phrases that are in all men's mouths because they express what is in all men's hearts.

Tiberius Gracchus used it in his public speeches at Rome; two centuries later it reappears in the discourses of Jesus of Nazareth.

> Ergo inter sese paribus concurrere telis
> Romanas acies iterum videre Philippi,
> nec fuit indignum superis bis sanguine nostro
> Emathiam et latos Haemi pinguescere campos . . .
> Di patrii, Indigetes, et Romule, Vestaque mater
> quae Tuscum Tiberim et Romana Palatia servas,
> hunc saltem everso iuvenem succurrere saeclo
> ne prohibete. satis iam pridem sanguine nostro
> Laomedonteae luimus periuria Troiae . . .
> vicinae ruptis inter se legibus urbes
> arma ferunt ; saevit toto Mars impius orbe ;
> ut cum carceribus sese effudere quadrigae,
> addunt in spatio, et frustra retinacula tendens
> fertur equis auriga neque audit currus habenas.
>
> (*Georgics*, i. 489 seqq.)

'Therefore Philippi saw Roman armies turn their swords against each other a second time in battle, and the gods felt no pity that Emathia and the broad plains of Haemus should twice be fattened with our blood. . . .

'Gods of our fathers, gods of our country, god of our city, goddess of our hearths who watchest over Tuscan Tiber and Roman Palatine, forbid not this last saviour to succour our fallen generation. Our blood has flowed too long. We have paid in full for the sins of our forefathers—the broken faith of ancient Troy. . . .

'The bonds are broken between neighbour cities and they meet in arms. Ungodly war rages the world over. The chariots launched on the race gather speed as they go ; vainly dragging on the reins the driver is swept away by his steeds and the team heeds not the bridle.'

It is a prayer for the lifting of the curse, and this time the 'envious and disordering' powers gave ear. The charioteer regained control, and we are carried on to the third act of the tragedy, in which no small part of its beauty and a very great part of its significance is to be found. The imperial peace could not save the body of Greek civilization—the four centuries of war had inflicted mortal wounds ; but possibly it saved its soul. Although Augustus had not the abilities of Caesar, he felt and pitied the sorrows of the world, and he succeeded in expressing the pity and repentance, the ruthfulness for and piety towards the past, which were astir in the spirits of his generation. But what phrase is adequate to characterize the Empire? The words 'Decline and Fall' suggest themselves, but how should they be applied ? Gibbon took the second century of the Empire, the age of the Antonines, as the Golden Age of the Ancient World, and traced the decline and fall of the Empire from the death of Marcus Aurelius. On the other hand, if the present reading of the plot is right, the fatal catastrophe occurred six centuries earlier, in the year 431 B.C., and the Empire itself was the decline and fall of Greek civilization. But was it only that? One is apt to think so when one reads the diary of Marcus Aurelius, and pictures him in his quarters at Carnuntum, fighting finely but hopelessly on two fronts—against the barbarians on the Danube and the sadness in his own soul.

'Human life ! Its duration is momentary, its substance in perpetual flux, its senses dim, its physical organism perishable, its consciousness a vortex, its destiny dark, its repute uncertain —in fact, the material element is a rolling stream, the spiritual element dreams and vapour, life a war and a sojourning in a far country, fame oblivion. What can see us through? One thing and one only—philosophy, and that means keeping the spirit within us unspoiled and undishonoured, not giving way to pleasure or pain, never acting unthinkingly or deceitfully or insincerely, and never being dependent on the moral support of others. It also means taking what comes contentedly as all part of the process to which we owe our own being; and, above all, it means facing death calmly—taking it simply as a dissolution of the atoms of which every living organism is composed. Their perpetual transformation does not hurt the atoms, so why should one mind the whole organism being transformed and dissolved? It is a law of nature, and natural law can never be wrong.' (Μάρκος Ἀντωνῖνος εἰς ἑαυτόν, ii fin.)

But after quoting Marcus Aurelius, the first citizen of the Empire, it is necessary to add a quotation from Paul of Tarsos, a citizen who has as good a claim as any other to be heard:

' " How are the dead raised up? With what body do they come? " Thou fool, that which thou sowest is not quickened, except it die. . . . It is sown in corruption, it is raised in incorruption; it is sown in dishonour, it is raised in glory; it is sown in weakness, it is raised in power.' . . .

It startles us to be reminded that these two actors appeared on the stage in the same act of the drama, and that Paul actually played his part a century before Marcus played his. Paul's voice suggests not only a younger generation but quite a different play. His thought in the lines just quoted is inspired by a predecessor whom Marcus regarded as one of the innumerable prophets of the proletariat. 'Except a corn of wheat fall into the ground and die, it abideth alone, but if it die, it bringeth forth much fruit.' The saying was included in the miscellaneous traditions about Jesus of Nazareth which were passing from mouth to mouth among the illiterate masses, but which had not begun to excite the curiosity of the educated classes in Marcus's day. What would the scholar have made of it if a collection of these traditions had fallen under his eye, scrawled on bad paper in barbarous Greek? Little enough, for he would have missed the whole background of his own sentiment and thought, which was nothing less than the background of Greek civilization. Great literary memories crowd the brief passage of his diary quoted above—Epiktetos and Lucretius and the Stoa, Plato and Sokrates, Demokritos and the Hippokratean school of medicine from which we took our first quotation, and simpler minds and more primitive artists in the dim generations behind. We are carried right back through the tragedy at which we have been looking on. The two men are worlds apart, in spite of the fact that their propositions, when we strip them naked, are much the same. ' The organism is transformed and dissolved.'—' That which thou sowest is not quickened except it die.' They are both representing death as a phase in the process of nature, but it is not till we grasp the similarity of the thought that we fully realize the difference in the outlook and the emotion.

Under the smooth surface of the Empire there was a great gulf fixed between the ' bourgeois ' society of the city-states and the descendants of the slaves imported during the Roman Wars ; but the Empire, by gradually alleviating the material condition of the proletariat, insensibly affected their point of view. The development of their religion—the one inalienable possession carried by the slaves from their Oriental homes— is an index of the psychological change. In the last phase of the Second Act, the ' Red Guards ' of Sicily and Anatolia had been led by prophets and preachers of their Oriental gods. Their religion had lent itself to their revolutionary state of mind. But under the Empire, as descendants of the plantation-slaves succeeded in purchasing their freedom and forming a new class of shopkeepers and clerks, their religion correspondingly reflected their rise in the world. They remained indifferent, if not hostile, to the Imperial Hellenic tradition, but they began to aspire to a kingdom of their own in this world as well as in the next. The force which had broken out desperately in the crazy wonder-working of Eunous of Enna and had then inspired the ' other-worldly ' exaltation of Paul of Tarsos, was soon conducted into the walls of chapels, and the local associations of Christian chapel-goers were steadily linked up into a federation so powerfully organized that the Imperial federation of city-states had eventually to choose between going into partnership with it or being supplanted. Thus the empire of which Marcus and Paul were citizens was more than the third act in the tragedy of Ancient Greece. While it retarded the inevitable dissolution of one civilization it conceived its successor, and when, after Marcus's death, imperial statesmanship failed, and the ancient organism long preserved by its skill at last broke down, the shock did not extinguish new and old together, but brought the new life to birth. By the seventh century after Christ, when Ancient Greek civilization may be said finally to have dissolved, our own civilization was ready to ' shoot up and thrive ' and repeat the tragedy of mankind.

The writer can best express his personal feeling about the Empire in a parable. It was like the sea round whose shores its network of city-states was strung. The Mediterranean seems at first sight a poor substitute for the rivers that have given their waters to make it. Those were living waters, whether they ran muddy or clear ; the sea seems just salt and still and dead. But as soon as we study the sea, we find movement and life there also. There are silent currents circulating perpetually from one part to another, and the surface-water that seems to be lost by evaporation is not really lost, but will descend in distant places and seasons, with its bitterness all distilled away, as life-giving rain. And as these surface-waters are drawn off into the clouds, their place is taken by lower layers continually rising from the depths. The sea itself is in constant and creative motion, but the influence of this great body of water extends far beyond its shores. One finds it softening the extremes of temperature, quickening the vegetation, and prospering the life of animals and men, in the distant heart of continents and among peoples that have never heard its name.　　　　　　　　ARNOLD TOYNBEE.

POLITICAL THOUGHT

In a survey of the legacy of Ancient Greece to our modern civilization and its problems, it might well seem at first sight as though the political contribution of Greece could be ignored. Greek art, Greek literature, Greek philosophy are among the world's abiding possessions, for the human passions and questionings which gave them birth and the human needs to which they minister will last as long as human life itself. But Greek political thinking is so much bound up with the peculiar and evanescent external conditions of fifth and fourth century Greece, centres indeed so exclusively round the special problems of its intellectual metropolis, Athens, that its interest might appear to have passed away with the régime to which it owes its existence. The *Agamemnon* and the *Antigone*, with their teachings of destiny and duty, the Hermes of Olympia and the Parthenon frieze, with their ever-irresistible charm of youthfulness, the *Phaedo* with its discussion of immortality, the *Metaphysics* of Aristotle with their still subtler and more abstruse speculations, source of so much of our Christian doctrine and apologetic—all these require little defence against the Philistine of to-day, if only he can be induced to gaze at his intended victim before he delivers his blow. But Thucydides with his long and detailed account of an inter-tribal or inter-municipal war, decked out with sham speeches which were never delivered : Plato with his imaginary Utopia, half a small Greek provincial town, half an impossible and unendurably regimented socialist model community, based on a fine-drawn and fallacious comparison between the qualities of the human soul and the class-divisions which happened to prevail in the Greek society of the time : Aristotle with his laborious investigations

into the municipal pathology of his day and his detailed
prescriptions for the betterment of his fellow-provincials
and their institutions—what have we to do with all this in
an age of world problems and conflicts and of not merely
continent-wide but international ideas and projects of
organization? The first duty of any one who seeks to interest
the modern reader in Greek political discussion is to be
perfectly frank and lucid about its limitations. He need have
no cause to be afraid that, when these have been written off
from his prospectus, there will be too little of value remaining.

These limitations can be summarized under two main heads.
They arise, firstly, from a *difference of scale*, and secondly,
from a *difference of outlook*, between ancient and modern
political thought.

The difference of scale leaps to the eye at once, although its
consequences are not all of them so obvious. Ancient Greece
was, for political purposes, a congeries of sovereign states,
generally centring round the urban metropolis of a rural
district smaller than that of an average English county. The
material upon which Greek political thought worked was,
therefore, from our modern point of view not only small-
scale but almost Lilliputian. This can best be appreciated
when we consider how many gradations of scale are interposed
in the modern world between the government of a town or
district of the size of fifth-century Athens and the government
of our own sovereign state, the British Commonwealth.
Athens was far smaller than Leeds, Johannesburg, or Chicago:
yet to be Mayor of any of these is not to fill a position of
commanding responsibility, as political responsibility is understood in the large-scale world of to-day. The American
State, the South African province and Dominion and (for
certain purposes) the English County stand between the
giant municipality and the sovereign parliament. To a
British Premier passing from a coal strike which reacts upon
the trade of the entire world to an Imperial Conference

engaged in tracing out an agreed line of policy on the Pacific Question, the problems of a Pericles, or even of an Alexander, would seem but child's play.

Let us see what results from this difference of scale. In the first place, Greek political thought although (as we shall see) it aimed at *universality*, at arriving at certain definite laws or conclusions about politics, never succeeded in divesting itself of a certain element of local or national individuality. When Plato and Thucydides think and write of ' the State ' they are also thinking of the City—the same word, *polis*, serves indeed for the two—and not merely of the City, i. e., of any municipality, but of a particular city. There are elements in Greek political thought which, just because they owe their inspiration to Athens, can never be universalized. A treatise on education in which general psychological conclusions were intermingled with conclusions based on experience at some English school with a very unique tradition, would require to be carefully examined and applied with caution to the problems of adolescent life in Japan or Nigeria. Similarly, in so far as Greek political thought is Athenian or (to use a much disputed term in what I hold to be its proper sense) *national*, it is not truly political.

The distinction that I am trying to draw is a difficult one and cannot be understood without a short digression about the nature of the study of politics. Politics is the study or activity of government, of the management of the public or common affairs of men. We need ' politicians ', men who will devote themselves to meeting the demand for the management of our common affairs—we need them not because we are Englishmen, Irishmen, or Americans, but because we are human beings living together in society, and because our co-operative relations and activities require to be guided and controlled. Whether the ' politician ' is a tyrant or a Minister of the people is not here to the point ; the point is that he is the manager of what the Romans called *res publica*, the Latin for the good old English word 'Commonwealth'. Politics is therefore primarily concerned with the practical problems arising out of the fact that a number of different human beings are living together, and the more different they are, and the smaller their greatest common measure, the more truly political do such problems become. The first business of the politician or governor is, as Aristotle said, to see that men shall live (the twin problems of supply and defence), his second to see that they shall live well (in the first instance the problems of health and physical development and well-being). In the last analysis *pure politics*, as our great grand-children may discover if ever the World-State becomes a reality, is mainly concerned with *administration*, administration of the affairs common to all in the interests of all.

Now ancient Greek politics were entangled, and modern politics also are still too largely entangled, with the discussion of matters which are not *common* at all, and do not constitute the material of politics in the true sense of the word—with questions arising, not out of the common need for a common law, but out of the inner ultimate and ineradicable differences between the various nations and other groupings of mankind. When the League of Nations or the Dublin City Council is discussing an epidemic of small-pox or the improvement of some dock or wharf, or schools for mothers, or the problem of juvenile employment it is dealing with common interests which affect human beings as human beings : it is on the plane of politics proper. But when the Dublin City Council, following in the wake of the nineteenth century democratic movement throughout Europe, puts forward some proposal in order to give satisfaction to the sentiment that Ireland being the home of a nation ought to be a sovereign state, and when the League of Nations is asked to deal with the political situation created by the clash of contending nationalisms in the British Isles or elsewhere, both bodies, as governing bodies, are out of their depth : for they are faced with an impossible task. Established to deal with politics proper, with the common affairs of men as men, they are bound to flounder helplessly when they are cajoled into the thorny intimate and (let it be added) far more fascinating region of national and individual personality—to a region where, the deeper you penetrate, the less common, uniform, standardized or standardizable are the interests involved, and the less susceptible of being ' settled ', or even understood, by the rough and ready politician accustomed to deal with matters in the bulk and to measure up the results on a quantitative reckoning in the cold and cosmopolitan language of statistics.

In reading the Greek political writers then, we must be careful to distinguish the universal from the local and ephemeral element. The latter is indeed of great interest and value ; but we shall tend to miss the really precious and permanent elements in their thought if we do not take pains to disentangle Thucydides the disillusioned Athenian patriot from Thucydides the scientific historian and psychologist, and Plato the aristocrat born out of due season from Plato the unrivalled student of human nature and of the permanent needs of human society.

The failure to recognize this distinction has led to much misunderstanding and shallow thinking in attempts to apply Greek ideas and maxims too literally to modern life. It is only too common to hear Englishmen, whose knowledge of politics and history, outside the newspapers, is confined to stray reminiscences from a not very ardent pursuit of the classics in their school and college days, basing confident predictions of the failure of modern democracy on some *obiter dictum* of Thucydides or Plato and assessing the fate of the British Commonwealth in terms borrowed from some judgement of Sallust or Tacitus on its wholly different Roman prototype. It is flippancy or pedantry like this which gives rise to the onslaughts of a Cobden or Herbert Spencer or an H. G. Wells and to the practical man's suspicion of a classical education. One might as well go to last year's market reports for guidance in a business deal of to-day as have recourse to Plato, or, for that matter, to Macchiavelli, in an existing political emergency. If a classical education, designed as it is in England to promote 'character' rather than 'intellect' (a vicious distinction which leaves no room for such a quality as intellectual integrity) often leaves behind it but a meagre residuum of knowledge and ideas, it should at least cause the public school man of yesterday and the London clubman of to-day to realize the limitations of his field of study and to abstain from confident political generalization. The Labour M.P. who once remarked to the writer, *à propos* of an Indian debate, that he had been in the House just long enough to know that all he knew about India was that he knew nothing about it, had been brought up, if not in a better at least in a cannier school. There is no sounder training for the student of politics and history, or indeed of any serious subject, than to know everything about something, whether it be the chronological order of Plato's dialogues or the problem of humidity in weaving-sheds, or about placing a field or keeping a wicket. That is why the Duke of Wellington who, if he lacked the intellectuality of a Foch, at least knew both his England and his own job of military science, selected the playing fields rather than the classical classrooms of Eton as the home and training-ground of that concentrated and disinterested endeavour of mind and spirit which had carried his army through patient years of effort to victory. It is all to the good that our classical devotees, faced with criticism and competition from many quarters, should be acquiring both a greater humility and a greater seriousness.

Our first caution then, is that Greek political thought is both national and universal, and that we must learn to distinguish what pertains to nationality from what pertains to government.

A second result which flows from the small-scale character of Greek politics is that we nowhere find an adequate treatment of the problem of *foreign relations*. Foreign policy is one of the weak spots of modern democracy; it is, perhaps, the element in our political technique which is most in need of thoroughgoing revision. We have yet to induce the modern citizen to pay continuous attention to issues which, although they are seemingly remote from his purview, may at any moment shake the whole fabric of his everyday existence; and, when we have done this, we have to persuade him to approach these world-problems not in the spirit of a competitive aggrandizement but with a view to discovering what is the best line of policy in the interests of the world as a whole. So long as the peoples remain self-absorbed, the governments will continue to conduct their mutual relations on a basis of individual self-interest, and the meetings of the Assembly of the League of Nations will remain what they are at present, not gatherings of statesmen solely bent, each from his own angle and upbringing, on the welfare of humanity, but barterings of politicians who (with rare exceptions) have come to the fair to do the best business they can for their own clients. Now Thucydides and Plato give us no help for the League of Nations. Such a phrase as 'the interests of humanity as a whole' would have been politically meaningless to them. They did not think of humanity as a whole; they thought of it as divided sharply into two sections, Greeks and Barbarians, and of the Greek world as a small oasis of intelligence and culture ringed round by a wide and indefinite expanse of barbarism. We also, it is true, speak of 'advanced' and 'backward' peoples: but the latter are not, as they were to the Greeks, a formidable mass, tribe upon tribe, of military power extending up to and beyond the known or legendary confines of the world; they are child-races under our watchful care and control. We have explored and surveyed the whole earth, and where we find weakness or inferiority, we establish a trusteeship. To the Greeks, ever on their guard against barbarian inroads from north, south, east and west, from

Scythians and Libyans, Persians and Carthaginians, the mandate clause of the Covenant would have seemed both theoretically undesirable and practically impossible. No Greek writer ever dreamed of a system of international co-operation between the governments of the world as men then knew it. All of them thought in terms of competition and ever-recurrent warfare or, at best, of a precarious balance of power. Even Plato's Utopia had its soldier class ; and they were real soldiers, not merely police. In this respect, at any rate, vanquished Germany, with practically the whole of her population relieved from military duty and available for productive tasks, has the advantage over the most ideal construction of ancient Greece.

There is a further point to be noted under this head. If Greek thought gives us no guidance in foreign policy, it is no more helpful, except very indirectly, in another difficult region, that of *industrial policy*. The problem of industrial policy, or what is sometimes roughly described as the Labour problem, may perhaps be thus stated : how to secure or maintain for civilized mankind (or for our own particular section of it) the goods and services it needs, whilst at the same time providing justice and freedom for those who produce them. To put it more shortly, how to secure that a good life for the consumer shall be compatible with a good life for the producer. It is a problem which goes to the root of democracy : for the world has never yet known a time when the increase of wealth and the consequent growth of refinement and civilization in the upper section of the community did not lead to degradation and injustice in the lower. Here too the Greeks can give us no help. They did not even face the problem but fail to solve it, like the Romans. Their material civilization was so simple that the problem hardly arose for them at all—except in certain cases, such as that of the mine-slaves. But the fact that they acquiesced, without a twinge of conscience or a trace of repining, in the institution of slavery indicates how they would probably have faced it had it arisen. Confront Plato with the complexity of modern industry, prove to him, as any modern lecturer could, that, for Northern man at any rate, life can only be maintained without degradation on a basis of widespread industrialism and with our familiar equipment of railways, steamships, telephones, *et hoc genus omne*, and it is safe to predict that he would fail to give the reply which the modern reformer would expect from him. Instead of embracing one of the many current varieties of socialism which masquerade as his bastard progeny, he would either accept his interlocutor's premises and tell him to build up his precious northern civilization on a basis of slavery; or he would reject them and advise him, with Samuel Butler, to make a bonfire of the machines. The latter is, indeed, the more probable alternative; for it is that to which the more thoughtful and prophetic (perhaps one can add also, the more Hellenic) of our modern guides are turning. When men so diverse as Tagore the Indian sage and Rathenau the German Trust magnate tell us that the disease from which we are suffering is 'mechanization', and that our crying need is for greater simplicity, it seems safe to predict that Plato would not reject the possibility of providing a 'good life' for the modern man in a world divested of most of the rattling and tinkling paraphernalia of which the nineteenth century so plumed itself as the inventor.

Let us pass now to our second limitation, that arising not from the difference of scale but from the difference of outlook between Greek and modern speculation. We can best sum this up by saying that whereas modern political thought, like modern thought generally, works from the inner to the outer, from the individual to the state and society, the ancient thinkers habitually work in the opposite direction, setting the interests of the community or state above those of the individual. This is what Fustel de Coulanges intended to

convey when he declared that ancient man had no conception
of the meaning of liberty. Liberty is no doubt a somewhat
confusing and ambiguous term; it is hard to cut it loose
from its political associations, from national independence
and democratic self-government. We can perhaps therefore
improve upon the French writer by saying that the Greek
political thinkers do not recognize, or do not make proper
allowance for, the rights and responsibilities of the individual
soul. Just as they failed to distinguish between Nationality
and Government, so they failed also to distinguish between
Conscience and Public duty. Socrates, indeed, meeting his
death in obedience both to Conscience and Law, had a glimpse
of the higher truth; but his followers did not take up this
side of his message or, in so far as they did so in their study
of individual morality, they did not relate it to their theories
of politics. It was a greater than Socrates who summed up
and put the problem with his incomparable directness and
irony: *Render unto Caesar the things which are Caesar's and
unto God the things which are God's.* If this had been said in
the presence of Thucydides, the keenest practical brain that
applied itself to Greek political thinking, he simply would
not have known what it meant. To him Caesar and God,
or, to translate them into his own language, Athens and Athena,
were not opposing but practically identical terms. When the
Athenian, as he described him, 'spent his body, as a mere
external tool, in the city's service and counted his mind as
most truly his own when employed on her behalf,' he was,
according to the universal Greek belief, serving both his God
and his neighbour, both his own highest good and the noblest
of the world's causes. His life was a unity: for he had not yet
learned to disentangle his soul from the soul of the City or
the herd, or his God from the god of Israel or of Athens.
The Greek thinkers, as we shall see, sincerely endeavoured
to distinguish between the 'good citizen' and 'the good
man' and to base the State on foundations of the spirit; but

their work was vitiated by their failure to realize the extent and urgency of the claim of the individual soul. Men must be spiritually free before they can co-operate politically on the highest terms. In the last analysis the weakness of Greek political speculation can be traced back to the weakness of Greek religion. Even Plato played with Pagan orthodoxy and gave the Delphic Apollo a titular place in his Utopia, proving himself as timid in touching Greek superstitions as English thinkers to-day are in touching the Monarchy. It is this basis of insincerity which reveals itself throughout the super-structure. Greek political thought contains already the germs of the disease which, centuries later, led men, plebeians first, later patricians also, to turn away from the outworn symbols that stood for the union of Church and State and to seek comfort in a religion which, if it undermined and eventually overturned the last and greatest of the ancient Empires, established the City of the Soul upon a firm and enduring basis. Julian's *Vicisti Galilaee* marked the end of one strain or tradition in ancient political thought which, originating in the local worships of the City-State, had lasted on, with gathering momentum, until, all over the known world, men bowed the knee before the altar of Caesar, the God-Emperor. From this there was no way forward except through revolution; and mankind paid, in the night of the Dark Ages, for sins of compromise and insincerity committed during long centuries of enlightenment.

The liabilities thus frankly stated, let us turn to the assets.

The first valuable contribution the Greeks made to political study was that they invented it. It is not too much to say that, before fifth-century Greece, politics did not exist. There were powers and principalities, governments and subjects, but politics no more existed than chemistry existed in the age of alchemy. An imitation of an idea, as Plato has taught us, is not the same as an idea ; nor is the imitation of a science the same as a science. Rameses and Nebuchadnezzar, Croesus

the Lydian and Cyrus the Persian, ruled over great empires ;
but within their dominions there were no politics because there
were no public affairs. There were only the private affairs
of the sovereign and his ruling class. Government and all
that pertained to it, from military service and taxation to
the supply of women for the royal harem, was simply the
expression of the power and desire of the ruler. The great
advance made by Greece was to have recognized that public
or common interests exist and to have provided, first for their
management, and secondly for their study. In other words,
the Greeks were the first to rescue the body politic from
charlatans and to hand it over to physicians.

How great an achievement this was we can best recognize
when we consider how large a place the true study of politics,
and the terms and ideas to which it has given rise, fills in the
life of the modern man—especially of the modern Englishman.
Justice and liberty, law and democracy, parliament and public
opinion—all these and many more we owe to the peasants
and craftsmen of the small Greek republics who, having felt
the need for a better management of their humble concerns,
set to work to provide it, with the same inventiveness, the
same adaptation of means to end, which led them, in other
fields, to the invention of the classic temple or of the drama.
If it is going too far to say that every modern politician owes
his stock-in-trade of general ideas to the Greeks, there are
certainly few who do not owe them their perorations.

This is not the place to enlarge on the features of Greek
political organization or to point out the various elements
in Greek political theory or practice which have proved of
permanent value. Only a very summary appreciation can
be attempted. But certain points can be picked out as being
of special interest to the citizen of to-day.

In the first place, the Greeks, having made clear to
themselves that public or common affairs existed, sat down
resolutely to study them. Convinced believers in reason,

they did not fall into the convenient English fallacy of believing that institutions are not made but ' grow ', or that difficulties which seem too thorny for timid fingers to touch will settle themselves by being left alone. Political problems, they felt, were caused by men, by the interaction of human wills and desires, and by men, by the conscious and deliberate application of human intelligence, they could and must be solved. In spite of their belief in mysterious powers which control the destinies of men and nations, they did not think it decent to abandon public affairs to Providence; nor did they avert their gaze from them as too mundane for the squeamish intellectual to handle and turn them over to the tender mercies of the ignorant and less scrupulous demagogue or doctrinaire. Their public affairs were no more interesting than ours : they were indeed considerably less interesting— unless we are prepared to argue that the election of generals to command an army far smaller than the Swiss is a more arresting issue than the choice of a government to bear rule over 400 millions of men on five continents, or that the question of peace or war between two small neighbouring mountain territories outweighs in interest the discussion of the relations between the white and yellow races of mankind. And, if Greek politics were not interesting in themselves, they suffered still further by comparison with the other topics which lay ready to claim the Greek citizen's attention. The modern voter who is too idle to cast his ballot, will give up to business or to pleasure, to motor-car and music-hall, the time and the trouble that he owes to humanity. When the Athenian spent a hot and exhausting day (for why should we think their nerves less susceptible to glare than ours?) listening to a parliamentary debate or to a lawsuit on a hard stone seat in the open air, he was postponing till to-morrow, or till his crops and fruit-trees permitted him the leisure, the discussion of some masterpiece of drama or some new issue of human thought which had leapt during the last few days

or months from the brain of a fellow citizen into immortality.
If it is hard for the citizen of New York to spare the time to
dethrone Tammany, or for the electors of Great Britain to
uproot its more outwardly respectable analogue on this side
of the Atlantic, when his life, and his newspapers, are full of
vulgar and ephemeral distractions, how much harder must
it have been for a Euripidean enthusiast, or a student of
Socrates or Protagoras, to descend for long days to solid earth
in order to strike a bargain with a Thracian chieftain or to
assess some poor devil's damages in drachmae! Let us honour,
not pity or despise them, for having thought it right to do so,
for having deliberately determined to infuse into public
affairs, in themselves so drab and dull, so deficient in the
fineness and subtlety which characterize men's more intimate
concerns, the interest derived from the very fact that honest,
sincere, and able minds devoted themselves to their study.
As Huxley could make the geological procession of the ages
revolve round a piece of chalk, and Sir Richard Owen reconstruct primitive man from the bone of his great toe, so the
citizen of Athens, as we see him depicted for us in the pages of
Thucydides, could raise the great permanent issues of politics,
and cause them to remain living for us two thousand years
later, in debates which were ostensibly concerned with mere
provincial trivialities. When such was the atmosphere created,
no wonder that those who stayed away were held up to obloquy
in an expression (ἰδιώτης) of which our English 'idiot' is the
exact transcription.

Let us dwell for a moment on the attitude of mind in which
the Greek citizen approached political problems. He was
both a Conservative and a Radical; or rather, he brought
to politics the best of Conservatism together with the best
of Radicalism. He was a Conservative because he reverenced
tradition and recognized the power and value of custom.
None of our modern Conservative writers and defenders of
the existing order, not Burke himself or Bismarck or Chateau-

briand, had a deeper sense than the Athenian for 'those unwritten ordinances whose transgression brings admitted shame'. Athens was a Conservative democracy. Most democracies, despite the labels of their politicians, are in reality Conservative; for the common man whose régime they represent is Conservative from the very nature of his life and occupation; it takes leisure and travel, or a wider education than any democracy has as yet bestowed on its young people, to lift the minds of the mass of men out of the rut of habit. But Athens was far more Conservative than the modern democracies with whom we are acquainted. Where the British public rebukes an awkward writer by conspiring to boycott his books, so that, unless he has private means, he is eventually silenced, where the United States, going a step farther, deny his works the privilege of the mails, Athens does not scruple to administer hemlock, and, if an *élite* is indignant or sorrowful, the democracy applauds. Even at the height of the recent Red Terror the United States never went so Conservative as this. This should help us to realize the rock-firm basis of tradition, of use and wont, of patriarchal sanctities, which underlay the working of fifth-century Athenian democracy as we watch its apparent vicissitudes. The citizen could use his mind as freely as he would on the material presented to him for his consideration; but there was a point at which the State, and his own instincts, cried 'Halt'; and, except in rare cases, he obeyed. It is only fair to add that the most enlightened modern opinion would entirely support the Athenian view against the discussion of 'unwritten laws' in Parliament. The difference between the Conservative Athenian democrat and the modern Liberal in such matters is, not that the one refuses, while the other demands, the discussion of life's sanctities in Parliament and law-court, but that the one appeals to custom and the other to conscience as the sanction of the unwritten law itself. Whether it be the gods or man, the law of the hearth or of the heart, that is at issue, both agree that what is private and holy has no place in the forum of common debate.

But, within these well-recognized limits, the Greek citizen was a Radical; that is to say, he was ready to apply his reason to public affairs without fear or prejudice. He loved straight and sincere thinking; he tried hard to face the real situation before him and not to be clouded or led astray by side-issues or inhibitions. There is many a lesson in common honesty to be learnt by our politicians and public in the speeches of Thucydides. Shallow critics have been known to dub them cynical, an adjective which the English, adepts in self-deception, are fond of applying to nations sincerer in self-analysis than themselves. When we refuse formally to reopen an issue on which action is in fact being taken daily, because it is a party question and a Coalition government is in power, when we leave to the healing mercies of time a problem with regard to which inaction itself constitutes a policy, when we deliberately invent party labels or election cries designed to confuse the mind of the voter and to distract him from the real issue, when our politicians have become professionals in the art of what Thucydides described as 'the use of fair phrases to arrive at guilty ends' and a British Premier, more euphemistically, as 'political strategy', we might do worse than sit down to read, mark, learn, digest, and apply to our modern situations, the immortal speeches or essays in which Thucydides lays bare for us the heart of the political life of his day, and to let them act as a purge of some of our own too sugary diet. The bitter-sweet of truth is not always popular on the hustings; but it is good feeding for the plain citizen, whether ancient or modern.

This leads on to a further reflection. The Greeks, in their political thinking, were essentially realists, rather than idealists. This is true of all the Greek writers, even those who, like Plato, starting from the market-place of Athens, lead us up to a Utopia in the clouds. They were realists in that they based their political studies on the world as it is and human nature as it is, rather than on some personal and fanciful conception of what man and the world ought to be. To put it in other words, they are realists because they are psychologists, because they applied the psychological method to political problems. That they were the first to do so goes without saying : for no one before them had applied any method at all, except in the most rough-and-ready manner. But they did it so perfectly, with such utter and artistic simplicity, that those who followed them accepted or criticized their results without observing the basis of human study on which they were built up, and it is only in quite recent years, through the work of patient inquirers who, like Graham Wallas, have laboured systematically in both fields, that politics and psychology have once more been drawn together.

It may perhaps seem strange to a modern reader to be told that, in this very important respect, Thucydides, Plato, and Aristotle are sounder in their method than the whole long line of political thinkers and statesmen up to our own day. Let the reader who doubts it turn to the texts. He will find that all the three writers whom I have named toiled at the study of human nature before they set pen to paper. The *Republic* opens with several books of psychological analysis, no doubt at times a little fantastic in its attempts at premature classification, but full of life and reality, and not only Greek reality but human reality. Aristotle precedes his work on *Politics*, in which he embodied the results of a study of all the available political and constitutional material of his day—for a Greek could work like a modern German or American thesis-grubber when he tried—with a book on *Ethics* which is still regarded, quite rightly, as a standard work for the modern student. As for Thucydides, his knowledge of men, the fruit of patient experience deepened by disappointment, is felt behind every line of his book, as one descries it in the features of his undegenerate descendant Venizelos. Turn now to the moderns. Where

2486   z

in Hobbes or in Bentham, in Locke or Burke or Rousseau, in the individualists or the Socialists, the Hegelians or the anarchists, do we find, until quite recently, a really wide and open-minded attempt to see man as he is ? Our ears are assailed by a chorus of catchwords, based on some arbitrary and ephemeral estimate of men's reactions to outward events and institutions. Men argue backwards and forwards as to whether ' human nature can be changed ', whether man is guided solely by self-interest, or is only waiting to be set free from sordid cares to be guided solely by his love for his fellows, whether fear or hope, custom or the sense of adventure, form his natural and most compelling spur to action. Meanwhile in the great debate, in Burke's *Reflections* as in Marx's *Capital*, in Maine and Mill and Mazzini, as among the hacks who vulgarize their results in text-books and election literature, man as he is has vanished behind a cloud of doctrine or verbiage. We need the simplicity, or cynicism, of the Greeks to recall us to realities.

Let us for a moment imagine Thucydides face to face with the problems of our post-war world of to-day. We have only to read his immortal analysis of the war-mood of Greece, and of the nervous and emotional phenomena which accompanied it, to realize that his first effort would have been to explain us to ourselves. He would not allow us to acquiesce idly in our vague disillusionment, our impatience of foreigners, our suspicion of the idealisms of the Wilson brand. He would trace our discontent ruthlessly to its sources and hold up to our eyes the strange compound of sorrow and fatigue, impatience and disappointment, aspiration and helplessness which makes us what we are. ' The war-mood brought with it many and terrible symptoms such as have occurred and will always continue to occur, so long as human nature remains what it is ; though in a severer or milder form, according to the variety of the particular cases.' Thucydides would have had eyes for it in all its forms, mild or severe, simple or complex, pitiful or repulsive. He would show us the English upper and middle class, shaken out of its comfort and complacency, its easy and patronizing security, by the shock of war and bereavement, facing a future of unknown and terrifying ideas and forces, with the brutal tax-gatherer administering the *coup de grâce* to its equanimity : the working class, called to fight for a cause which it but dimly understood, in the hope of a new world which victory was to call into being, exhorted by the nation's leaders to be as daring in its home policies as in the trenches, and then confronted with a world of failing markets and impoverished customers and with the full rigour of the merciless laws of supply and demand which, just because it had wished them out of existence, it had grown accustomed to believe could be ignored, oscillating, according to age, temperament or experience, between resignation and impotent fury, between old-fashioned trade-unionism and the latest fashion in extremism : France, emerging nerve-racked from a fifty years' obsession and a five years' nightmare, half-dead with sorrow and suspense, yet too proud in victory to own her weakness, looking round, half-defiant, half-wistful, among her allies for one who can understand her unspoken need, and longing, with all the intensity of her sensitive nature, to be able to resume, in security and quietness of mind, the arts and activities of normal life in which she has been, and will be again, the Athens of the modern world : Germany, tougher in fibre than her western neighbour yet equally shaken and exhausted : a land of sheep without a shepherd, rushing hither and thither seeking for a direction and a *Weltanschauung*, her amazing powers of industry and concentration and her rich and turbid life of feeling running to waste for lack of channelled guidance : Belgium, self-confident, industrious and rejuvenated : Italy, made one at last and measuring her strength to face the tasks of a new epoch in her history : and, behind, the great new surging world of the Slav, from the disciplined enthusiasm of Prague, under her philosopher-president, to the birth-agonies of a new Russia in the grip of the rough tyrant-physicians of the Kremlin. All this a modern Thucydides would attempt to set before us, not forgetting the conservative forces and the gods of the older generation, the great Catholic and Protestant, Moslem and Socialist traditions, the power of the bankers and the merchants, the universities and the press, and all the various types of humanity produced and hall-marked by their activity. And then, and not till then, having shown us what we are, each of us in his niche and all of us together in our little corner in the vast Temple of mankind, having made us see our pettyisms and orthodoxies against a universal background of time and space, he would have broken silence and allowed himself to speak to us of remedies. *Know yourself* is the first, perhaps the only, message of the scientific historian to our bewildered age.

But by what right, it will be asked, in this age of *Wissenschaft* and *Fachmenschen*, of specialism and research-institutes and organized intellectual production, do you speak of Thucydides as a scientific historian? Here is a man who, without a university degree or any university training at all, after a brief military career for which he took no staff college course (as witness his generalship), sits down to write a chronicle of the war in which he played a part, basing his account simply on his own experience and on the testimony of such eye-witnesses as he was able to meet. Any tiro on the history staff at a modern college or university could predict the result—one of those bulky volumes, full of detail and post-prandial reminiscence, in which splenetic elderly gentlemen have so often sought to justify their own existence, and to call down damnation on the War Office, before an indifferent public. How can anything better be expected from a mere soldier, a rough practical man, untrained in the arts of research, in collecting facts on slips of paper and arranging and re-arranging them till an induction emerges, in looking up reference books in

libraries and 'listing' them in a neat alphabetical bibliography, totally ignorant of the *Hilfswissenschaften,* the
laborious subsidiary studies on the basis of which scientific
history is built up, ignorant even of foreign languages, who has
read no sociology, and is not even aware of its existence, whose
geographical studies are limited to his own journeys and the
tales of his friends, who, finally, has the impertinence to
intersperse his narrative with fictitious speeches, thus destroying any pretence at a scientific character for his treatise, and
revealing it in its true nature as a mere work of art or imagination? It may indeed be doubted whether a modern trained
librarian, working according to the classification laid down by
the standard Congress library at Washington, would, when
his attention was drawn to it, admit so offending a writer
on to his history shelves at all. His place, he would probably
say, is with the prose-poets, or with the writers of historical
fiction next door to them.

Yet turn to the opening chapters of Thucydides' book. You
will find most of the sciences on which long modern treatises
are written : but you will find something more : you will
find them blended into a unity. Let those who deny that
Thucydides was a sociologist, who continue to claim that
Herbert Spencer, inventor of the horrid word, invented also
the science, re-read Thucydides' account of the evolution
(for it was as an evolution that he saw and depicted it) of
Greek society from the earliest times to his own day. Let
those who cry up anthropology examine into his treatment
of legend and custom and his power, untrained in Seminar or
institute, to use it as sociological evidence. Let the geo-
graphers, too forgetful sometimes that man is not the creature
of environment alone, refresh their minds by recalling those
brilliant sallies in geographical thinking in which he explains
some of the features of early Greek settlement and city-
building. It is not only orthodox history, of the school of
Ranke, of which Thucydides is the father and inspirer : there

is not one of the many movements which have sought to broaden
out historical study in recent years, from Buckle and Leplay
and Vidal de la Blache down to the psycho-analysts of our own
day and of to-morrow who will not find in Thucydides some
gleaming anticipation along the path of their own thought.

Here we touch upon what is perhaps the cardinal merit of
the Greek political thinkers, as it is of the Greek contribution
as a whole. They saw all the problems : but saw each in its
place within the larger whole. They ' saw life steadily and saw
it whole '. Matthew Arnold's line is hackneyed enough ; but
it cannot be bettered. To put the same thought in another
way, the Greeks were natural Catholics, while we of to-day,
especially on the political field, are constantly relapsing into
an unhelpful Protestantism. By Catholicism I mean nothing
doctrinal, or indeed religious at all, but simply the habit of
mind which insists on looking at the whole before the parts,
at setting the common before the sectional interest, and in
sweetening and harmonizing the inevitable contrarieties and
antagonisms of life by remaining steadily conscious of its
major and reconciling interests. A Catholic is one whose
intellect, to use the words of Newman, himself, despite his
religious label, one of the greatest of the tribe, ' cannot be
partial, cannot be exclusive, cannot be impetuous, cannot be
at a loss, cannot but be patient, collected and majestically
calm, because it discerns the end in every beginning, the
origin in each end, the law in every interruption, the limit in
each delay, because it ever knows where it stands and how its
path lies from one point to another '. Protestantism, on the
other hand, is the attitude of protest, of revolt, of indignation :
the spirit which is conscious only of what it is *against*, and is
too ignorant, or too angry, to survey the whole field of problems involved in its protest or to think out an alternative
scheme. If the Greeks can render us no other service in our
discontents they can at least lift us, by the example of their
wide and fearless vision, out of our petty Protestant rebellious-

ness and recrimination and plant our feet solidly on the rock
of steady Catholic thinking.

Take a few instances, drawn from Plato, of what I call the
Catholic spirit. Perhaps the most difficult and unsettling of
all our modern problems is that of the relations between men
and women in a society which has granted or is about to grant
to women complete equality of rights and opportunities
without having effected the corresponding inner revolution
of thought and sentiment. Masculine society, in other words,
despite a multitude of professions, has not yet admitted, still
less assimilated, the educated woman into its ranks. Here is
a problem with far reaching and most difficult implications
which Plato discussed more than two thousand years ago, but
in how different a spirit from so many of the 'feminists' of
to-day. Not that he was less 'advanced' in his speculations:
he was ready to face all that there was to face and to go a good
deal farther in his suggestions of policy than would be regarded
as printable in a modern English or American review. But his
spirit is throughout perfectly serene and, in the best sense of
the word, scientific, so that he can work out his argument to
the end without a trace of squeamishness or false modesty.
Where shall we find in our modern discussions of women's
employment, equal work for equal pay, and the like, the
central point so simply and clearly stated as in the following
sentence: 'Then, if we find either the male or the female
sex excelling the other in any art or other pursuit, we shall
say that this particular pursuit must be assigned to one and not
to the other; but if we find that the difference simply consists
in this, that the female conceives and the male begets, we shall
not allow that that goes any way to prove that a woman
differs from a man with reference to the subject of which we
are speaking, and we shall still consider that our guardians
and their wives should follow the same pursuits.' If all our
modern discussion were as clean and direct as this, we should
have made greater progress in this subject by now. Greek

intellectual integrity, and clarity of thought and expression, were not hampered by a festering and obstructive legacy of what it is a libel on a great movement to describe as Puritanism.

Take a second example—the influence of occupation on character. This is a subject which goes to the root of many of our social problems for, till we have studied the reactions of different classes of employment, not only on the body but on the mind, and perfected our methods of vocational guidance, we shall still have left open one of the greatest avenues to unhappiness. The modern inquirer will find a very interesting adumbration of this line of thought in the *Republic*; and if here, as in the problem of the relations between men and women, he finds Plato's remedies somewhat drastic, and is inclined to dissent from his veto on actors and acrobats, let him consider the appalling extent to which, during recent generations, the consumer has been pampered at the expense of the producer, and ask himself how often, when he attends a music-hall as a narcotic after a distracting day, or when he rings up on the telephone or books a ticket at a railway office, he considers the kind of life to which he is an accomplice in condemning those who minister to his needs and desires. Plato believed in the value of beauty and, being more than a mere modern aesthete, held no skindeep creed. He knew and understood the vital significance of rhythm and harmony, of grace and freedom, in the outward order of life as in the soul; and if he found himself plunged down in the centre of one of our modern hives of progress he would have some searching questions to ask. For ' absence of grace ' he tells us ' and bad rhythm and bad harmony are sisters to bad words and bad nature ' and ' we would not have our guardians reared among images of evil as in a foul pasture and there day by day, and little by little, gather impressions from all that surrounds them, until at last a great mass of evil gathers in their inmost souls and they know it not '. Has the most widespread malady of our time ever been better diagnosed; and do not our capitalist and socialist physicians, with their merely material remedies, look very small by the side of this commanding and convincing simplicity of statement?

We have dwelt upon some of the special directions in which Thucydides and Plato can be of help to us. Let us now turn briefly to the third of the great triad. Aristotle is, of course, the most systematic thinker of the three : and it is just for that very reason that the two elements already noted in Greek political thought, the local and ephemeral and the universal, are most closely interwoven and most baffling to disentangle. Tutor of Alexander though he was, his mind is incapable of stepping outside the city-state framework. His *Ethics* is half a treatise on human nature, half a book, akin to the *Characters* of Theophrastus, on deportment for a Greek citizen. No wonder that successive generations of English undergraduates have failed to respond to the human excellence or social charm, of his hero or paragon, described as ' the big-souled ' or ' magnificent man '. Similarly the *Politics* is a book in which it needs a trained reader, already familiar with Greek life, to pick out the universal from the particular and draw his own modern conclusions. But when you have read, say, the first book of the *Politics* in this spirit, when you have ruled out from what is said of the State all that pertains solely to the City, when you have made allowance for the hazardous biological, psychological, and sociological generalizations (' man is more of a political animal than bees or other gregarious animals', 'he who is by nature not his own but another's and not a man is by nature a slave', 'the state is by nature clearly prior to the family and to the individual, since the whole is of necessity prior to the part '), based, as the examples show, on the embryonic condition of those sciences at the time, you have a large residuum of practical wisdom that is and will remain of value to the modern world.

Let us look for a moment at one element in this legacy, for it has recently become a subject of much controversy— Aristotle's conception of the State, and of its relation to other social and political groupings. As has already been said, Greek political thought is open to criticism for unduly neglecting the claim of the individual. Aristotle is less open to this indictment than either of his great compeers : he does indeed allow, for certain favoured individuals, an inner or ' theoretical ' life, as he calls it, remote from the concerns of the City-State and almost, except for its excessive intellectuality, recalling the monastic ideal of the Middle Age. But this is only for the fewest. Nevertheless it involved the admission that behind the citizen remained the man, who might conceivably on occasion have his rights, that ' political science ', as he says, ' does not make men ', as Thucydides regarded Athens as making Athenians, ' but receives them from nature and uses them '. And the justification for this taking over of human nature by the state, this subjection of man over the whole or part of his nature, is clearly set forth. It is that ' man when perfected [i.e. taken over and educated by the State] is the best of animals, but, when separated from law and justice, he is the worst of all ', or, as he puts it in another place, the man who does not participate in State or city life is ' either a beast or a god '—more likely (as the order of the words indicates) the former. In other words, it is law and justice, not, as Thucydides would have it, an exaltation of the spirit to its highest power, nor, as Plato preaches, some organic identification between the inner life of the soul and the outward order of society, which is the basis and justification of politics. ' It is justice ', he says, using the word in a strict, not a platonic or metaphysical sense, ' which is the bond of men in states, and the administration of justice, i.e. the determination of what is just, which is the principle of order in political society.'

Now, with this principle clearly laid down, and with the claim of the individual thus partially or at least implicitly recognized, it is easier to understand Aristotle's *intransigeant* attitude towards the claims of associations other than the state, a point on which much recent controversy has turned. ' Every state ', so his *Politics* open, ' is an association of some kind, and every association is established with a view to some good. . . . But if all associations aim at some good, the state, or political association, *which is the highest of all and which embraces all the rest,* aims, and in a greater degree than any other, at the highest good.' In other words, in cases of conflict of allegiance between the state or political association and some other form of grouping, whether Church or Trade Union or professional or humanitarian organization, the claim of the state must take precedence.

This doctrine has been much attacked as involving an indefensible ' State absolutism ', a denial of ' personality ' to lesser groups, even as a negation of the right to lesser loyalties. Mr. Figgis, in a number of suggestive, if unconvincing, writings, has recalled the theories of the Jesuits and other anti-state minorities and protestants on this subject, reinforcing them from the Nonconformist and Trade Union theories or inclinations of our own day : and a whole school of younger ' progressive ' intellectuals made bold to follow him. The assault on state-sovereignty has, however, already been brought to a standstill by the impact of fact. Strange as it may appear in an age of sectarianism and rebel theorizing, the war revealed the truth that the mass of mankind, now as in ancient Greece, respond at need to the call of citizenship : that when the cry goes up summoning each and all to the tents, it is not this or that little tabernacle but the protecting shelter of the larger and more truly representative state organizations to which men flock; that the sects and conventicles which have fed the enthusiasm and provided the activity of leisure hours cannot maintain their appeal when the whole fabric of our society is in danger. Exclusive of those who refused allegiance on true grounds of conscience, and the despicable remnant who shammed a similar conviction, the number of Englishmen who definitely set allegiance to some other political or social grouping before allegiance to the state was surprisingly small. So little are fundamental loyalties, or the dictates of an un-analysed common sense, affected, in this country, by fine-spun theories and arguments.

But what we called commonsense views, after all, can be analysed and ought to be analysed. And there is a very sound and practical reason, as Aristotle knew, why men prefer the state to lesser associations. It is because the state leaves them more free. Those who talk of state-absolutism are ignoring the simple truth that there is no tyranny like the tyranny of near neighbours. The smaller the group the tighter its stranglehold over your life and activities. Groups and lesser loyalties are highly necessary, and indeed desirable, in our modern large-scale society; but they involve men, and especially weak-willed and thoughtless men, in far greater dangers than their larger citizenship. What the confessional at its worst may be to a woman, professional or business or other loyalty may be to a man. The modern world is full of men who have bartered away their integrity of soul to preserve the unity of the party or the unbroken tradition of the organization or the interests of the trade or even the existence of the business. If the secrets of all hearts could be revealed, how many high officials and dignitaries in Church and Party, in Trade Union and employers' federation, would be discovered to be thinking and even saying in private what their lesser loyalties forbid them to proclaim in public to their fellow-guildsmen. The state, in its larger field, may sometimes commit terrible blunders and even crimes; but at least, in these days of large-scale government, it does not expose its citizens to the daily falsehoods and hypocrisies, to the insidious clogging of the wheels of progress with the grit of petty personal considerations, which seem inevitable in the life of the smaller groupings of men and women. Seen in this light, the state stands out as the guardian not only of justice but of freedom, of an inner freedom of soul and spirit with which the professional and syndicalist attitude of mind is so often in flagrant, if unavowed, contradiction. If all this was not visible to Aristotle when he penned his immortal opening paragraph of the *Politics*, he is at least entitled to the credit of having laid his doctrine of state-sovereignty on a foundation

so sure that over twenty centuries of discussion from the
Stoics and Cynics, through Augustine and Dante, down to
Rousseau and Lenin, have not been able to shake it. Against
Church and Soviet, as against sage and hermit and anarchist,
the territorial state still holds its own over the whole civilized
world; and the latest construction of idealism at Geneva,
misnamed though it is, is but an association of such states, far
larger indeed in average size, but of the same kind and composition as those upon which the Greek philosopher fixed as
the true object of political study and the most effective and
enduring agency for securing a good life for civilized mankind.

What are the chief and most enduring thoughts which
contact with the Greek political thinkers leaves with us?
They are surely twofold, the first concerning the material
of politics, the second concerning the men and women
of to-day who are called to be citizens. Public affairs, we
feel, so far from being a tiresome preoccupation or 'a dirty
business' are one of the great permanent interests of the race :
if they were not too trivial or too debasing for great artists
like Thucydides and Plato, we need not fear lest they be too
trivial or debasing for ourselves. And if they are not beneath
our study, neither should they elude it by being enwrapped
in clouds of rhetoric or in the cotton-wool of sentimentality.
The Greeks should teach us, once and for all, that the common
affairs of mankind are matter to think about as well as to feel
about. What distinguishes what we call a 'good' statesman
and a 'public-spirited' citizen from their less truly political
colleagues is not that they have warmer feelings—there are
as many affectionate sons and loving husbands among the tools
of politics as among the elect—but the fact that by a resolute
use of the related powers of intellect and imagination they
have been able to raise their feelings on to a higher plane and
to face great issues with a mind attuned, not to the familiar
appeal of hearth and home, but to the grander and more
difficult music of humanity. The psychologists are teaching
us, in the individual life, how we can 'sublimate' our emotions,

when life denies them an outlet on the level of our desire, by raising them to a higher and more rarified range of feeling and action. As we can sublimate our love of individuals, so we can sublimate our love of country, not quenching or denying our patriotism, but consciously dividing and apportioning it. We must learn to preserve for our blood and nation that precious part of our gift of service which, just because it is intimate and of the family, cannot be offered directly to humanity ; but we must learn also the more difficult lesson of transferring to the international stage, the arena where men, because they are men, labour at common tasks and seek a greatest common measure of co-operation, all these interests and loyalties which safely and rightly belong there. This is the claim and call of the modern Caesar, whether his separate capitals remain, as they are to-day, in London, Paris, Washington, and the other centres of state-sovereignty, or whether mankind can rise, if not in our own day, to the level of a single allegiance. We shall neglect that call at our peril. For, unless we render unto Caesar that which is properly his, unless we discard our un-thinking and divisive nationalisms, our noble sentiments will avail us nothing and, in the civil war of the angels, patriotism against patriotism, Mammon and Beelzebub will come into their own. In these days of large-scale organization and mammoth syndicates, it takes a Caesar, a multi-national government, to keep a giant trust at bay. Had the land of Washington and Lincoln been broken up into separate govern-ments instead of drawn together into a single territory of United States, private interests would have taken and defeated each government in detail, and freedom would have vanished from the land—unless indeed, in some conflict of devil with devil, of bank and railroad against oil and lumber, the angels crept once more into their own. The same reasoning applies to the smaller governments in other continents to-day. Local patriotism is but a stripling David in face of the Goliaths of modern commercialism. More and more men will be driven, if not by reason, then by exploitation and suffering, to learn the lesson of what is still mistakenly thought of as imperialism until they find themselves crying out, with the apostle of the Gentiles, who fought his own battle against nationalism, ' I appeal unto Caesar.'

But the Greeks have a message for us not only as regards the material of our politics but as regards ourselves. What can we do to help humanity forward in these problems of its common affairs? The age of Utopia-dreams is over. We know now that modern science has made the world one place and that social salvation is not to be found, as the early socialists imagined, by fleeing from the haunts of men and founding some model city in a wilderness. We must make our contribution here and now, in the drab world in which fate has set us. If we cannot hope to turn it into Utopia, let us at least make it as much like Utopia as we can. This, after all, is Plato's message, even in the most idealistic and visionary of his books. The famous passage is worth quoting in detail :

' Then do you think any less of our argument because we cannot prove that it is possible to found a state of the kind we have described?'

' Surely not,' he said . . .

' Then do not compel me to show that what we have decided in our argument could in all respects be reproduced in experience. If we manage to discover how a state could be organized in any close correspondence to our description, then you must allow that we have discovered that your commands could be realized. Will you not be content with that ? I certainly should be.'

' Yes, I will,' he said.

' Then next apparently we must try to discover . . . what is the smallest change by which a state might arrive at this manner of constitution. . . .'

' Most certainly,' he said.

' Well, there is one change,' I said, ' which I think we could certainly prove would bring about the revolution. It is certainly neither a small nor an easy change, but it is possible.'

' What is it ? ' he said.

' Now,' I said, ' I am at the very topic which we likened to the greatest wave. Spoken, however, it shall be, even though it is likely to deluge me with laughter and ridicule. . . . Consider then what I am about to say.'

' Say on,' he said.

' Unless,' I said, ' lovers of wisdom bear sovereign rule in states, or those who are now called sovereigns and governors become sincere and capable lovers of wisdom, and government and love of wisdom be brought together, and unless the numerous natures who at present pursue either government or wisdom, the one to the exclusion of the other, be forcibly debarred from this behaviour, there will be no respite from evil, my dear Glaucon, for states, nor, I fancy, for humanity; nor will this constitution, which we have just described in our argument, come to that realization which is possible for it and see the light of day. It is this which has for so long made me hesitate to speak. I saw how paradoxical it would sound. For it is given to few to perceive that no other constitution could ever bring happiness either to states or individuals.'

Thus far the philosopher of antiquity. His words are sometimes interpreted as a cry for some philosopher-genius to take the task of government out of our too feeble grasp. But that is not his message for us. The age in which philosopher-emperors were possible has passed beyond recall. To us Plato's words are an appeal to become, each and all of us, in our own sphere, lovers of wisdom according to the measure of our ability. If we would amend the world around us—and it is in sore need of amendment—our first duty is to eschew falsehood and to follow truth in our own lives, in our thoughts and actions. Revolutions spring not from without inwards but from within outwards ; and it is often when the external world seems most sick and sorrowful, when selfishness and irresponsibility sit enthroned in the world's seats of government, that the power of truth is most active in the silent region of the soul, strengthening it in order that it may issue forth once again to impress man's unconquerable purpose of order, justice and freedom upon the recalcitrant material which forms the stuff of men's common problems on this small globe of ours.   A. E. ZIMMERN.

THE LAMPS OF GREEK ART

AMID the superficialities and struggles of the world around us, it is refreshing to turn back for a moment to the mellow wisdom of Matthew Arnold ; and I will start with a quotation from *Literature and Dogma*: 'As well imagine a man with a sense for sculpture not cultivating it by the help of the remains of Greek art, or a man with a sense for poetry not cultivating it by the help of Homer and Shakespeare, as a man with a sense for conduct not cultivating it by the help of the Bible.' To Arnold the Bible, Homer, Shakespeare, Greek art, are the great and eternal classics, which for all time must be the stimulus and the models for the greatest of human achievements. Beyond doubt in the fifty years since Arnold wrote there has been a marked drift away from classics of every kind. To acknowledge classics at all seems a survival of the spirit of aristocracy. We are convinced that we are better than our fathers, and must break away from their tutelage. In some degree this arises out of the unrest and nervous strain produced by the great war. But it does not come only from nervous tension. It is a definite tendency of society, which has to be considered on its merits by all who feel called on to take a share in the world movement. We cannot ignore those who are drifting away from the settled anchorages, or we run the risk of being ignored ourselves.

The task has fallen to me to try to give reasons why Greek art has still a claim on our attention. Among Englishmen the appreciation of art never has been and never can be as keen as the appreciation of poetry and philosophy. But on the other hand I think it can be shown that in the field of art our

A a

debt to Greece is even greater than in the field of philosophy and poetry. For in these latter we have a certain national genius, and have produced classics recognized through Europe. But in art our achievements have been but moderate; and at the present time a living sense of art is probably rarer among us than in any highly civilized country except America.

I will begin with a bold assertion, which I hope to justify as we proceed. But for ancient Greece, the art of Europe would to-day be on much the same level as the fantastic and degraded art of India. And but for the continued influence of Greek art, that of Europe would continually be in danger of drifting into chaotic extravagance.

In the century before the Persian wars of 500–480 B.C., Greece, both Ionian and Dorian, was throwing out fresh shoots of life in every direction, breaking through the crust of archaic convention, producing a new standard of excellence, in poetry, in philosophy, in history, and in art. In every province, morals, intellect, imagination, Greece was striking out, to the right and the left. And in the century after the Persian wars, she reaped the full harvest of her splendid sowing, and produced the masterpieces which have remained ever since memorable, to the study of which each generation recurs, and whence it learns of what human nature is capable.

After 400 B.C. there was not, as many suppose, a sudden decline in the quality of artistic production. Many of the works of the later centuries were in their way almost unsurpassable. The philosophy of Aristotle, the poetry of Theocritus, such statues as the Aphrodite of Melos and the Victory of Samothrace, are great lights for all time. But the works of maturity have seldom the charm which marks those which are full of the optimism and promise of youth.

Ruskin has written an admirable work on the Seven Lamps of Architecture, a work which, though it sometimes passes into extravagance, is full of suggestion and even inspiration.

It seems to me strange that while the economic views of Ruskin, full of generosity, but also wanting in measure and any basis of fact, should still be current among us, his writings on art, in which his genius had full course, should be comparatively neglected. However that may be, as one who has been greatly stimulated by those writings, I propose to try to produce a faint echo of one of them by speaking successively of the lamps of Greek art, lamps which give us light and serve to show our way. I find in Greek art eight notable features: (1) Humanism, (2) Simplicity, (3) Balance and Measure, (4) Naturalism, (5) Idealism, (6) Patience, (7) Joy, (8) Fellowship.

As my space is closely limited I cannot attempt to develop the subject of Greek art in all its provinces and in all its bearings. I must limit myself to the art of sculpture, the most characteristic branch, and the only branch which has left us sufficient materials for the formation of a satisfactory notion. And I must limit myself further to such of the sculpture as represents the human form. In the representation of some animals, such as the horse, the later Greeks produced some wonderful examples, but in the depiction of animals other peoples have rivalled them, whereas in the depiction of men and women they stand alone.

I

Humanism. Three great discoveries lay open to the awakened spirit of man, when he began to realize and reflect upon his surroundings. The first was the discovery of God, which was mainly the work of the Prophets of Israel, though no doubt Greece added much on the intellectual side ; and the religions both of Judaea and Greece were carried to a higher point by Christianity. The second was the discovery of man himself, which was in all essentials the great work of Greek thinkers and writers. The third, begun in Greece, has been carried very much farther in modern times, the discovery of nature and her laws. I think that reflection will show that of the three discoveries the last is the least important, for though it has vastly changed the habits and the surroundings of mankind, and has offered him long vistas of material progress, yet it has not changed his nature much, nor added greatly to his happiness. We know how the delights of thought, of art, of poetry and music have overcome barbarism and given to multitudes a new pleasure in existence. But the results of scientific progress have not as yet done all that we might have hoped for mankind. Every great discovery in physical science has been turned, primarily, not to the welfare but to the destruction of mankind. The ocean-going ship is tracked by the submarine ; air-ships are used to drop bombs on defence-less cities, some of the most notable achievements of chemistry are poison-gases. We may of course hope that this is but a passing phase, and that brighter times are before us. But I venture to suggest that the true road to progress cannot be found unless we preserve the Jewish and the Greek points of view. We must not lose sight of the ethical and religious bearing of science, and not be content with merely regarding it as a means of exploiting the material world. Instead of harnessing the forces of nature to true human ends, to happi-ness, we have allowed them to be used for any purpose, moral or immoral, by any one who by cunning or pushing has gained control of them. We have dehumanized the world, and allowed it to ride rough shod over human life.

The discovery of man and his capacities, then, is the great gift of Greece to the world. There were epics before the *Iliad*, but no epic full of charm, of tragedy, of tears and laughter. There were philosophers before Socrates ; but they were busied in trying to find the physical constituents of the world. Socrates took up the motto of Delphi ' Know thyself ', and became the progenitor of all who study the nature of duty and of happiness. In the same way there was much art in the world before the rise of Greece, in Egypt, in Mesopotamia, in Crete. But it was not a humanist art. It represented the worship of the Gods, battles, and sieges, the life of the fields. But the human figures in these scenes were conventional : there was nothing in them to stir the finer feelings, to produce a love of beauty, to raise man above the ordinary daily level. The Greeks knew of earlier works of art ; but they declined to be seduced, as the Phoenicians and Etruscans were seduced, into a facile imitation of them. They realized, no doubt subconsciously rather than consciously, that they were called to set forth a new and human art, and had in them powers which could produce it. They began a process which developed with astonishing rapidity, and which cannot cease, unless, as seems now not impossible, barbarism reinvades a weary world.

' Man is the measure of all things ' is the doctrine ascribed to Protagoras of Abdera, which shocked the people of Athens and is attacked by Plato in his more constructive mood. It is a doctrine lending itself to abuse, and still more to caricature ; but it is really the teaching of Socrates no less than of Protagoras ; and it has held its own from his times to those of the Utilitarians and Pragmatists. Certainly it is at the basis of the Greek view of life, in which man with his feelings, his faculties, and his endeavours, stands in the foreground, and all else appears as a vague background.

It was quite natural that as the Greek thinkers interpreted all experience in relation to human powers and faculties, so the artists of Greece thought of all nature in terms of the human body. Thus while the stern monotheism of later Israel absolutely prohibited the representation in art of any living thing, and especially of man, Greek artists entirely devoted themselves to such representation.

The great result of the working of the spirit of humanism in Greek art was the representation of the Gods in human form.

There is still prevalent among us a survival of the Jewish hatred of the representation of the divine element in the world by the mimetic art of sculpture. We still repeat, day by day, the Jewish commandment, ' Thou shalt not make to thyself any graven image '. Now I am not going to find any fault with the intense feeling of iconoclasm, which was one of the main-springs of Jewish religion. I have no doubt that in the develop-ment of that religion, hatred and contempt for the idols of the surrounding nations was of inestimable value to the race. The struggle, ever renewed, against the invasion of idolatry was necessary to the development of that pure pro-phetic religion which it was the highest mission of the Jewish race to set forth and propagate in the world. I would not even speak against the echoes of it in the modern world. To the Moslems of our days, as to the ancient Jews, it appears to be a necessary corollary of any lofty and spiritual conception of the divine. And when we read of the destruction of religious images by our Puritan ancestors we cannot withhold from them an inner sympathy. The hatred of images was one side of the pure and passionate belief in spiritual religion which it was the mission of the great Reformers to revive and propagate in Europe.

But it is possible to appreciate this side of religion without being blind to other aspects of it. Our religion comes not only from Judaea, but also from Greece. The Jewish passion for the divine righteousness lies at its roots. But that passion is consistent with narrowness, bigotry, inhumanity. For the modifications of it which come from the working of the spirit of humanism we have to turn to the Hellenes, for the feeling of the likeness in nature between God and man, the love of the beauty of the created works of God, the joy in whatever is sweet, whatever is comely, whatever is charming. The beauty and majesty of God appealed to the Greek, as the unapproach-able transcendence of God inspired the Jew.

So it fell to the Greek artists to try to set forth in marble

Fig. 1. VASE REPRESENTING SUNRISE

Fig. 2. CARYATID
of Erechtheum

Fig. 3. CARYATID
by Rodin

and in bronze the gentler and more social side of the divine nature. There is a sweet reasonableness in the words of Maximus of Tyre: ' The Greek custom is to represent the Gods by the most beautiful things on earth—pure material, the human form, consummate art. The idea of those who make divine images in human shape is quite reasonable, since the spirit of man is nearest of all things to God and most godlike.'

The whole history of Greek sculpture, from its rise in the sixth century to its decline in the third, is inspired by this desire to represent the divine by the most beautiful things on earth. The sculpture of the great nations of the East, Egypt and Assyria, is full of figures of the Gods, and of scenes of worship. But these figures do not rise above the human. The gods appear as conventional figures, mere ordinary men and women. And to distinguish them from mortal beings, the artists of the East proceed in the manner of symbolism : they make additions to the human types which are to signify the divine attributes, but do not really embody them. They add wings to represent the swiftness of the deity, wings not meant for actual flight, but only symbols of rapid motion. They represent them as victoriously overthrowing wild beasts and monsters, which stand for the powers of evil, ever bent on thwarting their action. In some of their most archaic works, the Greeks fall into the imitation of this way. They represent Apollo flanked by two vanquished griffins, Artemis with wings, and holding in her hands captive lions. But their artistic sense soon revolted against such crude and clumsy ways of representation. They began to try to represent the divine character of their deities, not by arbitrary and external symbols, but by modifying the human types in the direction of the ideal. Sometimes, indeed, in later art we find survivals of early symbolism in the form of an attribute. Hermes is still winged, but the wings are transferred to his cap or his boots. Zeus may still carry the thunderbolt, the symbol of his rule over the storm. Apollo may be still radiate, combining human form with the rays which proceed from the visible sun.

But these are only survivals, and do not affect the process, carried on by artist after artist and school after school, by which the gods absorbed ever more fully the qualities of the most perfect manhood. Zeus, as father of gods and men, is an idealization of the human father, combining justice and dignity with benevolence and kindness; Athena becomes the embodiment of the divine reason and wisdom, perhaps the most fully idealized of all the forms of the gods, since this armed and victorious virgin with wisdom seated on her brow had little in common with the secluded and domestic women of her city of Athens. Apollo has not the muscles of the trained athlete, but in his nobleness of countenance and perfect symmetry of shape, he stands for all that a young man might grow towards by self-restraint and aspiration. At a somewhat lower level Herakles bears the form of the wrestler, admirably proportioned but more powerful than even the greatest of athletes; Hermes is the ideal runner, every muscle adapted to swift and lithe movements.

Thus in the types of the gods which were produced when Greek art was at its best we have a series of supermen and superwomen who represent the highest and best to which mortals can hope to attain, types embodying the highest perfection of body and mind. The influence of those types has gone on from century to century, never in the darkest ages wholly forgotten, and serving at all times to redeem human nature from foulness and degradation. All through the history of art they have been acting as a raising and purifying element.

It was not until the decay of the Olympic religion in the fourth century that these types fell to a lower level. The sense of beauty in the artist remained as keen as ever, the technique of art even improved, but the religion of humanism was debased by less noble tendencies, and the gods took on too much not the nature of man as he might become, but the form of man as he actually is in the world.

Not the forms only of the gods, but the history of their appearances on earth and their dealings with mankind found expression in painting and relief. Plato, as we know, condemned the myths of the gods as unworthy from the ethical point of view. But we shall misjudge myths if we suppose that they were actually believed in, or served to regulate conduct. What they did was greatly to further the picturesqueness and joy of life. And when they became less important in cultus they survived in poetry, and served greatly to temper the harsh prose of actual life. We must remember that some of the Jewish tales which have so much interested and charmed our forefathers are hardly to be defended on strict ethical principles, yet they have been a leavening and widening influence. Who would wish to expel from churches the stories of Adam and Eve, of Joseph and David, on grounds of ethical purism? The life of the many is not so highly decorated that we should wish to expel from it elements so pleasing.

As the Gods tend more and more to take forms beautiful but entirely human, so do the notable features of the landscape, rivers and mountains, sky and sea, take on themselves human shape. Sun and moon, wind and storm, are completely humanized. The society of Olympus, the powers manifested in nature, appear in sculpture as a human society, but of more than human beauty and dignity. And such rendering of the gods leads, as we shall presently see, to an ideal rendering of men. As the gods come down in the likeness of men, so men are raised to the level of the gods. Hence the intrinsic and inexhaustible idealism of Greek sculpture, to which I will presently return.

Few works of art more fully and more attractively show the anthropomorphic tendency of Greek art than the sunrise vase of the British Museum. It shows us the whole morning pageant of nature humanized. On the right appears the sun-god driving a chariot of winged horses, who rise out of the sea. Before him the stars, represented as youths, plunge into the water. To the left is the moon-goddess on horseback, setting behind the hills, on one of which is a mountain-god in an attitude of surprise. Before the sun hurries Eos, the winged dawn, who by a bold citation of mythology is represented as pursuing Cephalus the hunter, of whom she was enamoured. We have the features of the daybreak; but they are all represented not as facts of nature, but in their influence on Gods and men.

I do not figure this vase, as I have already done so in my *Principles of Greek Art*; but instead I give an almost equally beautiful representation from the lid of a toilet vase in the Sabouroff Collection at Berlin. We have here the same three figures of the sun-god, the moon-goddess, and the winged dawn, who, however, in this case is driving a chariot. The form of the whole group and the radiate symbol in the midst stands admirably for the vault of heaven (Fig. 1).

Another extreme example of anthropomorphism is the embodiment of the sustaining power of the pillar in the so-called Caryatids of the Erechtheum (Fig. 2). Really they are Corae, maidens dedicated to Athena, and willingly in her service bearing up the weight of the architrave of her temple. Possibly the notion is not wholly satisfactory; but if it be tolerated, could it have been more nobly carried out? The square and stalwart form of the women, the mass of hair which strengthens their necks, the easy pose, all make us feel that the task is not beyond their strength or oppressive.

Beside the Greek Caryatid I must be allowed to place a modern version, by Rodin. For the power and the technique of Rodin I have great admiration; but when his works are placed beside those of Greece, we feel at once their inferiority in dignity, in simplicity, in ideality (Fig. 3).

Fig. 4
CHARIOTEER of Delphi

Fig. 5
ARTEMIS of Gabii

Fig. 6. KNIGHT AND LADY
By Peter Vischer

II

The second lamp of Greek art is *Simplicity*. The artist sees quite clearly what he desires to produce, and sets about producing it without hesitation, without self-consciousness, with no beating about the bush. Of course the more primitive and less conventional a society is, the easier it is for artists to be simple. In a complicated society simplicity and directness are apt to be confused with what is commonplace or even with the foolish. The simplicity of Wordsworth and of Tennyson does sometimes cross the line. The Greeks had the great advantage of coming before other cultivated peoples, so that there was no commonplace to avoid. They could be simple, as the wild rose and the primrose are simple. What could be more simple than the *Iliad* ? The same simplicity marks Greek sculpture. It requires no great exercise of the intellect to understand it. It presents every figure in a clear and unsophisticated way.

As there is no more sure sign of a fine nature than the absence of self-consciousness, so there is no more sure sign of greatness in art than simplicity. The Greeks did not strive to be original, to make people stare, to do the unusual. One of the most usual subjects in Greek relief is a battle between male warriors and Amazons. Such battles adorn many temples. And in every case they are distinctive in style. One could not mistake a group from the temple at Phigaleia for a group from the Mausoleum. And there is no sameness : almost every group has some point or touch of its own, which makes it a variety on the usual theme. One Amazon is falling from her horse, one is asking for quarter, one is following up a retreating foe. But no group is insistent that the passer-by should look at it. The relief was the decoration of a temple ; and if its originality drew men's attention from the temple itself, or from the Deity seated enthroned within, it might justly be accused of impertinence, of exceeding due measure. The sculptor did his best ; but he was careful to do nothing which was out of harmony with its surroundings. He sank himself in his work. And even when he was engaged on a more serious substantive work, what he most avoided was the incongruous and unbecoming. He so worked that the attention of the spectator was concentrated not on the character of the workmanship, but on the person or the subject portrayed. The idea which he tried to incorporate in marble or bronze was not his own thought about the subject, but the character which really belonged to it in the mind of the people.

This singleness of purpose is well illustrated by a story about the painter Protogenes. He painted the figure of a Satyr, and beside it, as a trifle, he inserted a partridge. But when he found that admiration for the lifelikeness of the partridge tended to distract the attention of visitors from the main figure, he painted it out.

No doubt simplicity implies limitation. It is not easy in any age to strike the deepest note without some surrender of simplicity. The higher phases of the mental and spiritual life, mysticism, symbolism, and the like are not to be expressed with complete simplicity in any form of art. One cannot deny that the Greek view of life was limited ; that the Greeks did not attempt to represent in art the highest aspirations of the soul. It was an entirely perverted ingenuity which sought a generation ago to find mystic meaning in the representations on Greek vases. Attempts to portray the Deities of the Mysteries scarcely count as works of art. Such figures as Sabazius, Isis, Mithras, only come into ancient art in its decadence. I would not maintain that the modern world, with its infinitely varied emotions, or the higher aspirations of religions like the Christian or the Buddhist, could be satisfied with such simple schemes as those of Greek sculpture, which appeal to human instinct and human intelligence rather than to the more recondite emotions. Such emotions, however, in my opinion, do not find any appropriate embodiment in the arts of which I am treating—the graphic and plastic arts. In poetry they have at all times found a noble expression; and in modern days a perhaps still completer expression in music, which was in pre-Christian days in a very rudimentary condition. But painting is but ill suited to the rendering of these vague aspirations. And still more unsuited is sculpture, the most imitative and objective of all the arts. The attempts which have been made in recent years by some sculptors to give a mystic turn to their art seems to me doomed to failure by the essential nature of sculpture. A Western mind can have little sympathy with the art which has moved most on mystic lines, the art of India, which in such efforts has abandoned the search for beauty, and so given up the really artistic point of view. Mere prettiness no doubt is an unsatisfying ideal: but a loftier beauty, in harmony with the world around us and the soul within us, is another thing.

In order that simplicity may be in the highest degree admirable, it must be combined with two other qualities—intense love of beauty, and the utmost patience in execution. It must not lead on the one side to a mere unideal copy of nature, nor on the other to a hasty and slovenly kind of work.

The figure already mentioned, the Caryatid of the Erechtheum, is a model of perfect simplicity. For further illustration of the quality I have chosen the bronze charioteer from Delphi, and the Artemis from Gabii, now in the Louvre. The former (Fig. 4) is a youth of noble family, clad in the long dress necessary to protect from the wind a man driving a chariot. The latter (Fig. 5), a work of the school of Praxiteles, represents a young girl fastening her dress on her shoulder. Both are as free as they can be from any attempt at novelty or originality: yet no one with any taste could for a moment hesitate to pronounce them admirable. The object of the artist was to make works as perfect as possible. And to that end he goes straight, without any complication, and without the least care that others may have done similar works, against which he must assert originality.

Beside the two figures I have cited I place a more modern group (Fig. 6), also by a man of genius, Peter Vischer. It has the same simplicity and the same care in execution as the Greek works, but in beauty it will not compare with them ; and one feels regret that so great an artist should have spent his powers on so unsuitable a subject as the rivets and plates of a suit of armour. The lady, though not without charm, seems artificial and affected beside the exquisite freshness of the girl of Praxiteles.

III

The third lamp of Greek art is *Balance and Measure*, the recognition of limit and law. This is most obvious in architecture, and especially in its most characteristic production, the temple. The form of the temple, when once established, remained fixed, within certain limits of variation, for all time. A most accomplished writer, M. Boutmy, has admirably shown how all the constituent parts of the temple are related one to the other, how a plan, a consistent rhythm, runs throughout it. Each part has a definite function, which it accomplishes in the simplest and clearest way. The pillars are made simply to support, and their shape and slight decoration is in accordance with that purpose. Their form ensures a maximum of stability. The channeling or fluting carries the eye of the spectator upwards to the capital which swells outwards to support the heavy straight line of the cornice. Above the cornice, the grooves of the triglyphs carry on the lines of fluting from the columns towards the roof. The walls of the temple are not primarily intended to support, but to enclose the sacred cella, and are adorned only at their upper edge, as a curtain might be, with a decorative frieze. The whole building is thought out as a home for the statue of the deity which it encloses ; and no part is allowed to adorn itself except in subordination to this general purpose. Like the shells of molluscs or the hives of bees, it is the direct embodiment of an idea, a purpose, only a conscious and reflective, not a merely instinctive purpose.

The sculptural decoration, which is so striking a feature of the temple, is also carefully subordinated to purpose and idea. No part of the structure which bears a strain, if we except one or two early and unsatisfactory experiments, was decorated. The business of column and architrave was to bear weight ; and if they were ornate they would seem less well adapted to that purpose. Only in parts of the building which were from the point of view of construction otiose, such as pediment and metope, was the art of the sculptor allowed to play ; and even then it was bound to play appropriately to the nature of the deity within and the festivals of which the temple was to be the focus. There was no room for cross-purposes or disturbing thoughts.

This rigidity of form and subordination to reason is as characteristic of Attic tragedies as of temples. It would indeed be possible to work out a close parallel between the two forms of art. But we must return to our immediate subject, sculpture. Temple sculpture exhibits the qualities of balance and measure in the highest degree. In case of the pediment there is a central point, just under the apex, where the dominant figures of the scene portrayed are placed ; and on either side of this central figure or group, figure balances figure, until we come to the corners, which are occupied by reclining forms, dying warriors, or river-gods or spectators. In case of the metope, the square field is filled with two or three figures balanced about a central line, a scheme self-contained and harmonious, which may be compared to a geometrical diagram, and carries simplicity to the farthest point.

Rhythm, balance, symmetry are the translation into sculpture of the spirit of discipline and self-control, which the Greeks learned by hard necessity. The civilization of the Ionians in Asia is a brilliant sunrise, an overflowing of the delight in life, in beauty, in the exercise of all the faculties, which for a time dominated Greece itself. And their art was joyous and free. The artists of Ionia invaded Athens in the sixth century, visiting the luxurious court of Peisistratus, and inspiring Peloponnesus, even Sparta, as the excavations of the British School in Athens have abundantly shown. But the Ionians were trodden down under the heavy foot of Persia : excess of freedom and want of cohesion and discipline was their ruin. The Great King of Persia was determined to trample in a like manner on Greece Proper ; and he would have succeeded but for the discipline and devotion of the Dorians. It was the Spartans, aided by the brilliant military talent of Miltiades and Themistocles, who saved Greece from slavery. A military caste, like the Templars and Hospitallers of mediaeval Europe, they furnished the backbone of the Greek army and dispersed the hordes of Asia as easily as did the hardy Macedonians of Alexander the Great a century and a half later.

The Athenians, with their quick wits, understood whence came their salvation, and in the early part of the fifth century the tide of Ionian influence was turned back, and Dorian manners, Dorian dress, Dorian art, became dominant from Thessaly to Laconia. It is precisely the Dorian ideas of discipline, of measure, of self-control, which entering into the art of Greece made it a noble and continuous development, instead of a mere brilliant flash. Plato was well aware of the dangers which beset the Athenians from their extreme versatility and want of reverence, and he foresaw how these qualities would in the end destroy the civilization which they had adorned. He so clearly saw this that he was inclined to prefer the conventional and monotonous art of Egypt to the brilliant Greek art of his own time. This is, of course, to carry ethical prejudice to the length of fanaticism, and to transgress the very law of moderation which inspired him. But it was only in his old age that he went thus far.

This careful balance and proportion may be observed, as has often been pointed out, in the designs of Greek vases, where the painted subject not only is in itself a balanced scheme, but is also planned in relation to the shape of the vases themselves. A group suitable to an amphora would look out of place on a drinking cup. And in the cup itself the outside requires a different treatment from the inside. The whole is planned not merely to give free scope to the artist, but to be appropriate, fitting, harmonious. Our first figure well illustrates this thesis.

Even in the case of substantive sculpture, figures or groups made to stand by themselves in market-place or portico, the Greek love of harmony, or as they would have put it, of rhythm and symmetry prevails: ancient critics in those accounts of Greek sculpture, of which fragments have come down to us in the writings of Pliny and Quintilian, lay great stress on these features. They show us that whereas in early art a merely external and mechanical balance had prevailed, in the course of the fifth century this love of order and measure was taken into the very being of art. Pythagoras of Rhegium, whose works are unfortunately lost to us, made great progress in rhythm and symmetry. His contemporaries, Myron and Polycleitus, who carried the athletic art of Peloponnesus almost to its highest point, were celebrated, Myron for the rhythm in motion which he infused into his sculpture, Polycleitus for the careful balance of his athletes and the system of proportion which he embodied in their figures. Pheidias was more essentially ideal than either of these, as we shall presently see, but he also most diligently preserved in the Parthenon and other works a spirit of measure and reasonableness.

Measure and balance in art differ widely from mere convention. 'Order is Heaven's first law.' All fine character is formed, not by following random impulses as they arise, but by making them conform to reason and duty, disciplining them as wild horses are disciplined and taught to serve mankind. Horses indeed may be over-disciplined, and by cruelty all spirit may be taken out of them. And men may be over-disciplined, so that their impulses die away from inanition. The Spartans were over-disciplined; and through constant repression of natural tendencies they became mere machines, and before long died out. But reasonable restraint imposed on strong natural tendencies produces noble results in all spheres of activity.

The same thing is true in art. Measure and discipline do not of course make it easier to produce works of art; for in the nature of the case discipline is at first grievous and is felt as a barrier. But for the production of good and lasting works of art, discipline and law are necessary. Take as an example the art which is simplest, poetry. It is easier to write blank verse than to write sonnets. But it is far easier to write *good* sonnets than good blank verse, simply because the constant restraint of the form stimulates thought and invention, prevents too great haste, exercises the ingenuity. In the same way the somewhat rigid laws of composition of pediment metope and frieze compelled the Greek artist to think out schemes suitable to those forms.

It would not be possible to find a better example of order and balance in reliefs than is furnished by the magnificent sarcophagus from Sidon (Fig. 7), on one side of which is represented one of the victories of Alexander the Great. At first sight it may seem a confused mêlée. But when we look closer we see careful arrangement underlying the apparent

disorder. Alexander, charging from the left, is balanced by
Parmenio charging from the right : the horseman in the
middle between the leaders seems to come out of the background ; and on either side of him is a fighting group, to the
left a Macedonian foot soldier fighting a Persian on foot, to
the right a light-armed Greek resisting a Persian horseman.
Two Persian archers balance one another. There are in the
scene five Greeks to eight Persians, indicating the numerical
superiority of the latter. And if we knew more about the battle
we should probably find its principal phases hinted at in the
groups. The relief tells us far more about the battle than
would a naturalistic representation of one corner of the field.
The Greek artist could not work without using his reason and
his sense of order as well as his skilled hand.

IV

The fourth notable quality of Greek art is *Naturalism*.
Painting and sculpture, being representative or mimetic arts,
are dependent for their effects on the careful observation and
loving study of nature. Probably this is not the feature in
works of Greek sculpture which would be most conspicuous
to a modern eye. And it cannot be doubted that the habit
of exact observation produced by modern nature studies, our
familiarity with such helps to sight as telescopes and magnifying
glasses, our constant use of photography, have made most of
us better acquainted with the phenomena of the world about
us than were the Greeks. But compared with the works of
preceding ages, Greek sculpture must have seemed amazingly
naturalist. Even works of the archaic period, like the pediments
from Aegina, show a knowledge of the human form infinitely
more accurate than any to be found in Assyrian palaces or
Egyptian temples. There is probably always a good deal of
illusion in the minds of the schools which are constantly

springing up, which profess to break away from all conventions and to go back to nature herself. To reach nature except through human senses and human combinations is quite impossible. And any artist who determines to give us nature merely as the photographic plate or the mechanical cast gives it to us simply wastes his powers, and produces a result of no interest whatever to any one. According to Pliny Lysippus professed to take nature alone for his teacher; but in fact the works of Lysippus, so far as we can recover or trace them, are full of most definite style. An artist has to look at nature through his own eyes, and those eyes give to what he sees a character based in part on his own personality. Everything he sees is refracted in the waters of his subjectivity, from which he cannot escape.

Nevertheless, the whole historic course of Greek sculpture is steeped in the study of nature; and we see as it proceeds more and more clearly the results of careful observation. The artist had in fact opportunities for the study of what he considered the one important group of phenomena, human bodies, such as a modern artist cannot hope to compass. In the baths and gymnasia where all young men of free birth spent part of their mornings in running, leaping, wrestling, or swimming, he could daily watch the beautiful bodies of athletes in every variety of pose and action. He knew them as a trainer knows horses, or a fancier knows dogs. He would have little need of a special model; but would daily observe some fresh detail of muscles, some notable pose which he could add from memory to his conception of the human body.

But in the greatest periods of art naturalism is not predominant. Its constantly working tendency is kept in check by noble ideas and noble style. There is in the development of sculpture a constant approach to nature, but nothing of the nihilism which looks on all aspects of nature as equally fit subjects for art. The artists of the pediments of Aegina could

Fig. 7. SARCOPHAGUS FROM SIDON

not bring themselves to conceal the beautiful bodies of the fighting warriors by rigid armour like that copied in Vischer's group. Thus we find the paradox of armed men in battle, but without armour. The utmost pains are taken with the nude limbs. In the wonderful bronze charioteer found at Delphi (Fig. 4), which dates from about 470 B.C., the garment necessary to protect the man from the rush of air is very simply treated; but the arms and feet, which the garment does not conceal, are wrought with marvellous accuracy and truth to nature. It seems almost as if the artist were compensating himself for the extremely simple work on the drapery by an almost excessively close study of nature where it was possible. The head, on the other hand, is typical and not individual; for in fact individual portraits were scarcely possible at the time.

This would be the place to speak of Greek portraits, if space allowed it. I will only point out the erroneousness of the popular view, that Greek portraits were conventional and uninteresting; and that it was the Romans who introduced individuality into portraiture. It is strange that a view which is utterly false should have gained such currency. It is true that Greek portraits of the fifth and even the fourth century have in them much of the type, and individual traits are softened in accord with the strongly idealizing tendencies of the age. But from the third and second centuries we have a great number of portraits which are in the highest degree characteristic and individual, a wonderful gallery of philosophers and poets and statesmen which for lifelikeness cannot be surpassed. All the finest of the portraits of Romans were by Greek artists. I can give but one example of really fine Greek portraiture, a statue of Demosthenes of the third century B.C. (Fig. 8). It is a portrait indeed. The long lean arms and the pose are quite as individual and characteristic as the face with its melancholy expression and deep lines of anxiety. We have the man from head to foot; not as is so often the case in modern statues, a portrait head set on a conventional body.

For comparison with Demosthenes I set a statue of a great modern statesman, Abraham Lincoln, by Barnard (Fig. 9), not the best statue of him, but one which is approved by many. It aims at truth, but only attains caricature, by exaggerating Lincoln's awkwardness and angularity, the size of his hands and feet, and the anxiety in his face. This exaggeration has been proved by a comparison with many photographs of Lincoln, which show that he was careful in dress and by no means wanting in dignity. The statue of Demosthenes is marvellous for truth ; but it adds a touch of pathos ; the statue of Lincoln misses the truth, through exaggerating the least pleasing features of the subject.

When we want to ascertain how close Greek sculpture could come to actual fact, we turn from the great ideal age to the Hellenistic period. Lysistratus, the brother of Lysippus, began to take moulds in plaster from individual faces. At the great medical school of Alexandria the anatomy of the human frame, from which earlier ages in a spirit of piety had shrunk, became usual : some of the great physicians, such as Herophilus and Erasistratus, being noted for the completeness of their study of anatomy. In the art of the third century B.C. we see the inevitable result of such studies in a more precise and learned rendering of the muscles and the skin. And artists no longer hesitated to represent bodies wasted with toil and exposure to the weather, or emaciated with fasting. There are many such figures in our museums, showing a marvellously close study of the forms of peasants and old women and children. I figure one of these, preserved in the museum of the Conservatori of the Capitol at Rome, an aged shepherdess carrying a lamb (Fig. 10). But it will be observed that close as this form is to the facts of common life, there is yet in it nothing repulsive. It is in a sense a type rather than an

Fig. 8. DEMOSTHENES
By Polyeuctus

Fig. 9. ABRAHAM LINCOLN
By Barnard

individual, a poem of nature rather than a portrait. It is parallel to the pastorals of Theocritus. It strongly contrasts with such loathsome figures as some modern sculptors in their exaggerated love of fact, even if repulsive, have inflicted upon us, such as the Vieille Héaulmière of Rodin (Fig. 11), a figure of an aged and decayed prostitute. I know, of course, that some critics would defend the last-mentioned work on ethical grounds, as showing how hideous the decay of sensual beauty may become ; but I venture to doubt whether sculpture is an appropriate vehicle for a moral lesson of that kind, because it can only represent and cannot explain.

V

So we come to the fifth lamp of Greek art, *Ideality*. It is in the idealism of their rendering of the body of man that the Greeks have surpassed all other peoples and left an imperishable record. The history of Greek art is the history of a search for beauty, for poetry, for whatever can charm and delight.

In the earliest sculptural works of Greece, as Lange the Dane was the first to point out, we find not a direct imitation of the facts of the visible world, but impressions taken from that world, stored in the memory, and put together in accordance with subjective purpose rather than objective law. It is indeed thus that clever children work, when in the picture-writing of their sketch books they violate the laws of perspective by combining separate aspects and memories of an object into an inconsistent whole. They will not omit any peculiarity of a person which happens to have struck them, even when in the profile which they sketch it would be invisible. They think of a face as turned towards them, of legs as walking past them. Every face must have two eyes, every body two arms, whether they would be visible under the natural conditions or not. In early Greek reliefs it is common to find the body down to the waist full-face, the body below the waist in profile, with no transition between the two. The well-known metopes from Selinus in Sicily are good examples. It is a kind of procedure common to the early art of all peoples. But the Greeks differ from other nations in this ; that when they improved away these early crudities they retained the predominance of thought over things, of man over nature, in a word of the ideal element in art. They regarded the body of man not, as the materialists do, as man himself, but as a shell produced by the inner working of the spirit, to be seen by the eyes of thought and imagination, as well as by the bodily eyes. Hence they were always aspiring from that which exists in appearance to that which lies behind the mere phenomenon. They realized that nature, when she produces an individual, never wholly succeeds, she falls short of the idea. And the artist by a loving sympathy with the creative Spirit, may venture to improve what she has made, to carry out her intentions more fully, to incorporate more completely the idea. The Greek artist, appreciating and venerating the body, tries to raise it to a higher and more perfect level. A simple kind of idealism may be found in athletic art. In their practice of athletics the Greeks did not, like the moderns, think only of the number of feet an athlete could leap, or the space of time he would take to run a distance. They thought also of his *form*, of the rhythmic and harmonious character of his action. If an athlete showed ugly form, they would hiss him, as they would an incompetent actor. Most of their exercises were done to the accompaniment of the flute. In all the statues of athletes which have come down to us, not one shows an inharmonious development, powerful chest and weak legs, or muscular legs and poor arms. It is more than probable that as the features of Alexander the Great influenced the portraits of his officers and followers, so the specially beautiful forms of some of the athletes who were most admired, tended to create a type, something of which appears in all the athlete figures of the time.

No doubt any one who is well acquainted with Greek types and with the forms of modern athletes will observe that the Greek physical build is not identical with that of our days. The equable climate and the unstrained life of the young men produced something more rounded and fleshy than we see in the north. Our athletes are less harmoniously built, with more prominent sinews, more harsh and wiry in type. An American trainer who is also a sculptor, Dr. Tait McKenzie, working as some of the Greek sculptors worked, from the average measurements of a number of young men, has produced types of strength and beauty, by no means exactly like the statues of Greece, but in their way almost equally beautiful. I instance the beautiful fifth-century figures of Greek boxers, softened by idealism, but admirable for strength and symmetry ; and the Apoxyomenos, a man scraping himself with a strigil, as was the custom in the baths (Fig. 12). This is a work of the third century, after the artists had imported their knowledge of anatomy into their works, which had effects both good and bad. And beside the Apoxyomenos I place an athlete by Tait McKenzie, produced from the careful comparison and measurements of hundreds of young athletes of Harvard and Philadelphia (Fig. 13). This is a work of modern idealism produced by similar processes to those to which we owe the excellence of Greek athletic sculpture.

The types of female beauty come into Greek sculpture later than the types of male beauty. In Ionian and early Attic sculpture women appear closely wrapped up in drapery. Pheidias and his contemporaries did not venture to represent undraped women. They showed the beauties of the female form not apart from, but by the help of, drapery. It was reserved for the age of Praxiteles and Scopas to represent the Goddess of Love in the guise of a nude woman ; and Praxiteles made an apology for the innovation by introducing the motive of bathing as an explanation and a palliation. And even the

Aphrodite of Praxiteles is remarkably free from all attempt at sensuous attraction, or self-consciousness. Solid, noble, and stately in form, she is a type or model rather than an individual. Later sculptors, it is true, departed from this line of simple harmoniousness, and tried to make the figure more attractive to the average man. But it does not become weak, and it does not become vulgar. The noble Aphrodites of the fourth century have fixed the type of female beauty in school after school of artists down to our own time.

This ideal is perhaps for us best incorporated in the Aphrodite of Melos in the Louvre, a work of the Hellenistic age, combining with the great fourth-century tradition a perfection of detail and an informing life which belong to a later time. But while most people of taste profess a devotion to her, that devotion is usually untinged by knowledge or real appreciation; for there could hardly be a greater contrast than that between the bodily forms of the Goddess of Melos and those of the women who are most admired in our days. I was almost disposed to figure side by side the Goddess and the bodily forms which figure in our fashion plates. The fashion plates do not represent women as they are, but as they would like to be; they represent not the actual, but the modern ideal. And what an ideal!

Some readers may smile at the notion of taking seriously these ephemeral productions. But no one would take them lightly who was familiar with the facts of psychology. We well know that when certain types of women are set constantly before the rising generation as beautiful and to be imitated they will necessarily exercise a great influence on the future of the race. Young men will look out for such types to admire and to court : young women will try to resemble them. The hideous mistake in aesthetics will exercise a constant dragging power, pulling the young away from the light and the air of heaven towards the caves of evil spirits.

Fig. 10
AGED SHEPHERDESS
Alexandrian

Fig. 11
LA VIEILLE HÉAULMIÈRE
By Rodin

Few more charming representations of young womanhood in Greece exist than the Artemis from Gabii already cited (Fig. 5). One must confess that the divine element in it is but slight. But what could be fresher, simpler, more exquisitely natural ?

No doubt as in the case of men, so in the case of women, we must make allowance for race and climate. A full and rotund development of physique is far rarer in northern than in southern Europe. The English race is taller, less solidly built, slighter than the ancient Greek. Among us hard tendons usually take the place of solid muscles. And the practise of athletic games by women undoubtedly tends to make them in some respects conform more to the male type. In moderation physical exercises may improve health and strength without tending to deprive the vital organs of nourishment. But the overtrained woman is farther from the healthy life of nature than the overtrained man. And whether the over-exertion be of the body or of the intelligence, it tends to destroy true womanliness.

It is a pity that some sculptor does not do for the ideal of womanhood what Dr. Tait McKenzie has done for the ideal of athletic manhood. Of course the process would not be the same. No one wants an ideal type of the female athlete, unless we wish to restore the race of Amazons, but we do sorely need to have before our eyes types which embody the physical ideal of efficient womanhood. At present while nude womanhood in art conforms in a great measure to the Greek tradition, clothed womanhood follows the types of the street, modified by the baseless caprices of fashion. The two stand in unreconciled contrast. The Greeks when painting women on a vase often drew their figures in outline before they added clothes. But any one who tries to draw the outline of the female figure beneath the clothes on a fashion-plate will stand aghast at what he has produced.

Cicero repeats an instructive story in regard to the painter Zeuxis, who lived about 400 B.C. He was commissioned to make for the people of Croton a painting of Helen of Troy. He first inquired, what seems to have been a matter of common knowledge, who were the most beautifully made young men in that city, which was noted for its athletes. He next asked that he should be allowed to study the forms of the sisters of these men, judging that the sisters must partake of the beauty of the brothers. Out of these he selected five girls for more continued study, and by such aid produced his picture. We cannot suppose that he would be so clumsy as to select at random beautiful details from each of the five ; in that way he would produce only an eclectic monstrosity. But, working in the presence of beautiful examples, his sense of beauty would rise in tone to the highest of which he was capable.

In this story several points are noteworthy. It shows that the type of beauty in men was more advanced and more generally recognized than the type of beauty in women. And it shows the Greek artistic mind ever on the watch to catch some new note of beauty to add to the traditional stock. Professor Brücke, in his excellent work on the beauties of the human form, observes that in the ideal statues of Greece many features may be discovered which in the actual world of men and women are very rare, but the charm of which can scarcely be disputed. There went on from school to school, and from period to period, a sort of accumulation of beauty which was ever increasing. Every beautiful model which was studied added something to what Brücke calls the stock of beauty at the disposal of artists.

VI

The sixth lamp of Greek art is *Patience* in striving after perfection. In the finer work of Greek sculptors one finds an utterly ungrudging expenditure of time and care which

Fig. 12
ATHLETE WITH STRIGIL

Fig. 13
ATHLETE, by Tait McKenzie

reminds one of the working of Nature herself, Nature who is never in a hurry, who is never contented with a hasty sketch, but works regardless of time. We are told of Protogenes that he spent seven years on a single figure, and I think he would have spent seven more if he had thought that he could thereby have improved his painting. Nothing strikes one more strongly in such works as the charioteer of Delphi and the Hermes of Praxiteles than the pains taken with every detail. It is by careful work, continued through successive generations, that sculpture attained such mastery in the representation of the muscles of the body as we find in the Borghese fighting figure of the Louvre, and such delicacy in the rendering of drapery as we find in the Victories of the Balustrade at Athens, or the Victory of Samothrace.

But the delicacy and minuteness of Greek work is of course most obvious in the reliefs of coins and in gems. The coins were not primarily meant to please the eye, but to circulate in the fish-market ; yet a multitude of the dies are so exquisitely finished that they lose little when magnified to many diameters, and will bear the most critical examination. The intaglio gems were meant for the sealing of documents, the seal taking the place of the modern signature ; but the figures upon seals are in their way as finished as great works of sculpture. Seals even more usually than coins gain rather than lose if they are enlarged. Yet they were executed without the help of magnifying glasses. Their subjects are taken from the widest field, the figures of deities, tales from mythology, portraits, animal forms ; like the coins they introduced as an undercurrent to the prosaic life of every day an element of poetry and imagination.

VII

The seventh lamp, which goes as naturally with idealism as care and patience go with naturalism, is joy, *joie de vivre.*

Keats has expressed the Greek sense of art in an immortal line, ' A thing of beauty is a joy for ever '. It was the over-flowing gladness which lies at the root of creation and evolution which took eternal form in the painting and sculpture of the Greeks and inspired all their works. The same irrepressible joy which gives colour to the flowers, sweetness to the fruit, song to the birds, and sexual desire to mankind reached here one of its most perfect manifestations. The life of the Greeks was by no means one of unmixed happiness. Each city was not unfrequently at war with its neighbours ; and the penalty of complete defeat was sometimes the razing of its walls, the slaughter of its men, and the enslavement of its women. Disease, even plague, constantly ravaged the land ; and the resources of modern surgery and modern anaesthetics were not present to curb their ravages. The life of the majority in country huts, and still more in the slums of the cities, most of all in the mines, was rougher and more sordid than is the case in the modern world, in countries in their normal state. And the people had not even that hope of a blessed hereafter which sustained the people of the Middle Ages. Yet under all these clouds, their spirit was hopeful and aspiring. And their art reflects ever the brighter side of things. Surely they were wise and right. We seek out works of art not to foster pessimism but to inspire optimism, not to show us the world of nature on its repulsive side, but to reveal to us how much underlying beauty is to be found in it. ' 'Tis life not death for which we pant, More life and fuller that we want.'

At the same time, Greek art in some forms was extremely serious and keenly alive to the darker side of existence. The Greeks invented tragedy, the poetical reflection of the severity of fate. Would any modern audience be found, which would be prepared to sit for a whole summer day listening eagerly to the grand expression by such poets as Aeschylus and Sophocles of the power of Nemesis, the instability of all prosperity, the misfortunes which hunt those who have the ill luck to displease the gods? Surely not. And not in Greek tragedy only, but in elegiac poetry and in epigram, we find perfect reflections of our most gloomy moods. But for such expressions of sorrow and despair the Greeks felt that sculpture, and even painting, were not suitable vehicles. They belong to moods, and are not suitable for illustration in the market place and the temple. The roads which led to Greek cities were frequently bordered with monumental tombs. If in the reliefs and inscriptions of these tombs there had been any telling echo of the sorrow and regret of bereaved survivors, every one would have entered the cities in a black mood. As it is, as every one who has been in the museums of Athens knows, the sepulchral artists carefully avoided anything which might harrow the feelings. They represented the dead at their best, engaged in victorious warfare, or in athletic sports or in the happy family circle. A gentle air of melancholy could not be avoided; but there was nothing to shock, nothing to oppress the spirits. The deceased represented seemed still to share the occupations and pleasures of the living, not to be shut off from the world of happiness.

Milton has expressed, in his magnificent prose, the profound joy of the world of the Renaissance at the recovery of the Bible, and free liberty of reading it, after it had been shut away from the laity by the organized Church. Equally intense, and more exuberant, was the delight of scholars and artists, when the asceticism and pessimism of the Middle Ages, which had given birth to such bodies as the Carmelite monks and the mendicant friars, gave way before the revival of Greek litera-ture and art. The world seemed suddenly to have renewed its youth. No doubt the sudden expansion led to foul excesses; but it was yet a great landmark in human progress.

VIII

The eighth light of Greek art is *Fellowship*. Perhaps there is no quality in it which is more instructive for our days than this. The extreme individualism which is the most remarkable characteristic of modern times lays the utmost stress on the right or the duty of an artist to express *himself* in his work, to work out his own vein of originality, to give to the world a rendering of his own qualities and individuality. And no doubt no great artist can help doing this in a measure. When he works he must be himself; he can only see the world through the medium of his character and talents. And as every man is a microcosm, a reflection in miniature of the great world of human beings, what is really good and original in an artist must appeal to something in the human world; must have a meaning for people of a certain class or a certain training, or a certain country. But whether an artist is the better for a conscious attempt thus to externalize his personality; whether he is improved by being self-conscious and reflective in his art is a different question.

Scarcely any feature of Greek art is more impressive to a student than its continuous and uninterrupted course. When once it has started it does not turn back, but goes forward steadily, for a time rising superior to difficulty after difficulty, attaining a higher and higher level, then in the fifth century branching out in various directions into styles and groups, then going on with great technical skill, but with a loss of inspiration. It is a course of evolution as steady as that of any kind of plant or animal. This shows that it did not depend upon the rise of successive men of talent or genius, each of whom was intent on expressing himself; but upon the rise and influence of successive artistic schools, each of which did not merely follow the personality of a founder or teacher, but stood for a phase in the development of the common life of the Greek people. The schools were Ionian or Dorian, Attic or Argive, and harmonized with the whole civilization of such fractions of the race. Ionian art went with the gay and pleasure-loving ways of the Asiatic coast. Dorian art reflected the restraint, the balance, the self-control of the people of Peloponnesus. Attic art not only conformed to the refined taste of the people of Athens, but suited also the strong mental bias of the most intellectual city which ever existed. Of course these schools did not flourish in complete isolation one from the other; city influenced city and artist artist; but in a far less degree than would be the case now. A school of sculpture was a species; and all the individuals of the species were more like one another than they were like any of their contemporaries outside.

Thus when we examine any work of Greek sculpture, before the eclectic schools came into being, we find it easy to determine its period, often within narrow limits, and we are usually able to assign it with confidence to a particular school, imperfect as is our knowledge of the history of Greek art. But we can scarcely ever say that it is the work of an individual artist, unless it stands on a basis bearing the author's name, or unless ancient critics and historians have left us detailed descriptions of a work which survives. I am speaking of Greek originals; the copies of earlier works made by Greek artists of a late period for Roman galleries are often so confused in style and so careless in execution that they serve only to mislead, even if they have escaped the Italian restorer of recent date.

Great and connected series of statues and reliefs, such as constitute the sculptural adornment of such temples as that of Zeus at Olympia or the Parthenon or the Mausoleum, are the joint productions of a number of sculptors who worked together, no doubt under the general supervision of some architect or chief mason, but probably under very little control. Such works combine considerable variety in execution with a general similarity so great that a superficial observer does not see their differences. Public opinion in London seems to hold that Pheidias made the whole of the pediments and the frieze of the Parthenon ; though in some cases contiguous figures are so markedly various amid the general likeness as to prove separate hands. In the case of the Erechtheum at Athens there is extant a long list of payments to a number of artists for the several figures of the frieze. There was no general contractor, no artist who hired his masons by the day, but every man who produced one of the figures in relief was paid for it sixty drachmas, without regard to its difficulty or its simplicity.

It is comparatively easy to get a set of skilled stone-masons to carry out with exactness a plan of which all the details are worked out for them, and which requires only faithful copying. And it must have been easy for a set of Egyptian sculptors who made their figures according to a rigid conventional pattern to produce a uniform result. But for a number of skilled workers who were allowed great liberty in detail to produce an harmonious whole was infinitely harder. And that the Greek masons regularly accomplished this result shows how strong upon them was the influence of the school. Nor did they merely work from nature ; but their production was of an idealizing kind. It is clear that they must have had not merely similar tools and similar mechanical processes, but the same purposes and ideals. They must have had what we should call a collective personality. It is more than probable that among the workers on the Parthenon were Alcamenes and Agoracritus, two sculptors who rose to great fame. It is certain that among the workers on the Erechtheum was Praxias, a pupil of Calamis, and probably a relative of Praxiteles. The distinction between artist and mason, so marked in our day, scarcely existed in Greece. The mason who had talent became a noted sculptor ; and the sculptor, instead of making a model in wax or plaster, set to work, like Michelangelo, on the block of marble himself. Probably sometimes, like Benvenuto Cellini, he cast his own bronze statues.

Generally in all great periods of art there is such fellowship. And in sculpture in particular the design and the execution are so closely connected that it is an abuse to assign the two functions to different men, and even to different classes of men. Greece was pre-eminently the land of productive guilds, of families of artists, of groups of workers who were of one heart and one spirit, and who therefore worked in one style. One of the closest parallels to a Greek school of sculpture is to be found in the group of Pre-Raphaelite artists of the middle of the last century, Morris, Burne-Jones, Rossetti, Millais, Collins, and their companions. This group had a religious or ideal starting-point in the revived Anglo-Catholicism which arose in Oxford at the time, and they had principles of art in common which they embodied in their work. Their paintings, before they diverged one from another, form a distinct species, and have an interest for the historian of civilization greater than that of any other English school.

IX

In order that we may estimate the influence of Greek art on the civilization of Europe, it is necessary briefly to trace its reappearances through the ages. Its first conquest was Rome. The victorious Roman Generals, Marcellus, Scipio, Flamininus, Mummius, and others, brought to the imperial city, to adorn their triumphs, an immense quantity of Greek sculpture and paintings, of which they robbed the great storehouses of works of art in the temples and stoae of Hellas, Sicily, and Asia Minor. The earlier Emperors, especially Nero, followed their example, so that in the time of Pliny the naturalist all the public places of Rome were crowded with sculptures of bronze and marble and with the painted masterpieces of great artists. It became fashionable for wealthy Romans, such as Hortensius and Cicero, to stock their country-houses with such works. Even so, the demand was not satisfied; and Greek artists were imported into Rome, where they set up great workshops, and poured out an incessant stream of fresh works of art. Of such our modern museums are full. Generally speaking they are of little artistic merit, copies of various degrees of excellence of the great works of earlier generations. For the Roman plutocrats had little taste. Because certain figures or groups had a great reputation, and especially because they had been purchased at a high price by Greek cities and kings, the Roman collector liked to have copies of them in his villa; and the artists who produced these copies were mere workers for hire, without originality and without aspirations. Sometimes when employed on such works as the Arch of Titus, or the Column of Trajan, the novelty of the theme stimulated the artist to attempt something of a more original kind. And occasionally the fire within took course and produced a finer work than ordinary. Under the art-loving Emperor Hadrian there was a sort of St. Martin's summer of sculpture; but its productions were smooth, elegant and refined rather than original or interesting. The charm of art was not appreciated by the Roman people; only the few who professed cultivation really cared whether a figure was good or bad, and even the few were a little ashamed of their preferences.

Into the Roman Empire, in the first three centuries of our era, Christianity gradually ate its way. It originated among the Jews, to whom all representation of living things was hateful. And it developed under the influence of Greek oriental mysticism, which had no kinship with sculpture and painting; and so far as it had any expression in those arts worked in the direction of that symbolism against which Greek art was a protest. Thus we could not expect any fresh inspiration for art from early Christianity; on the contrary, Christianity would work upon it as a blighting influence. If we examine the remains of Christian art in those early centuries, in sarcophagus and mural painting, we find that it merely copied the contemporary pagan art, only changing the subjects portrayed, and introducing a further development in the symbolic interpretation of ordinary scenes.

Christianity offered almost no field for the exercise of Greek anthropomorphism. The latter was closely bound up with polytheism and hero-worship. The Christian Apostles and Saints, who took the place of the pagan Deities, were men who had lived on the earth and whose deeds belonged not to mythology but to history, although at the time the line between history and mythology was not clearly drawn, and history was largely diluted with myth. A few impersonations of nature, such as river-gods, lingered on in the paintings of the Roman catacombs. And winged genii were common there, whether cupids or cherubs it would be hard to say. But there was no realm into which artistic fancy could stray, filling it with super-men and super-women. Angels might be portrayed; but they all came from the Jewish angelology; and there was no artistic tradition as to their types: it was only later that the types of Michael, Raphael, Gabriel, and others were distinguished.

The second principle of Greek art, balance and symmetry, had almost disappeared in pagan art in the Antonine age. The reliefs of triumphal arches and of sarcophagi are crowded with figures inserted without order or method. Even the mural paintings of Pompeii have escaped from control; and show no purposeful arrangement. Law and order have given place to individual fancy, unless in cases where earlier schemes are adopted. And with artistic arrangement has disappeared all attempt to idealize, to produce forms nobler and more beautiful than those seen every day. The figure of Antinous is the latest in which we find any attempt to produce a type of ideal beauty. Even the Virgin Mary and her Son are depicted without any attempt to render them beautiful. Nor indeed does naturalism fare better than idealism. The representation of the human body is no longer studied. The figures are clothed : and the clothing is purely conventional, while the features of the landscape are far less carefully introduced than in Hellenistic Greek art.

In fact one feels that the artist had little interest in his art. Scenes from the Old and the New Testament are the usual subjects. But the depiction is little more than picture-writing, mere copies of traditional groups. The only thing regarded as of any interest is the meaning. The ethical and spiritual point of view overlies and smothers any interest in the representation.

And this predominance of the didactic element over the sense of proportion, the love of beauty, the appreciation of nature prevails more and more as Europe slowly moves towards the dark ages. The lamps of Greek art burn more and more dimly. They are never wholly extinguished ; for in all ages there are born artists to whom they are the light of life ; and in mediaeval carvings one finds here and there a touch of humanism, most often in grotesque or satyric figures. We must never forget that some of the later masterpieces of Greek work, such as the Column of Trajan and the Arch of Beneventum, were always to be seen. And little as they were appreciated by ordinary people, an artist here and there derived from them some appreciation of the beauty of humanity.

Then in the thirteenth century the dry bones began to come together. The breath of fresh life stirred Europe, or at least parts of Europe, such as North Italy, Southern Germany, Eastern France. The magnificent Gothic Cathedrals rising in the north called forth the talent of the painter and the sculptor for their adornment. A great Christian art arose, and in the thirteenth and fourteenth centuries flourished widely. Certain qualities of high art it certainly had. It was lighted by the lamp of fellowship. The sculpture was the work not of individuals, but of guilds, groups of workers of the same style, and inspired by the same motives. It attained to great beauty in decoration, in the adaptation to architectural purpose of the forms of plants and flowers. Where it was most defective was in the rendering of the human form, whether nude or draped, for in such matters the artists had no schooling to be compared with that of the Greeks.

When the full Renaissance came with the dispersion of the educated Greeks through Europe, there was a conscious reawakening of the artistic influence of Greece, contemporaneously with the revived interest in Greek literature and philosophy. A few great works of ancient sculpture, the Laocoon, the Dying Gaul of the Capitol, the Apollo Belvedere were discovered; and collections of ancient gems and coins were formed by many of the wealthy. We can judge from the life of Benvenuto Cellini how profound was the effect produced by such discoveries. The great Italians of the fifteenth and sixteenth centuries felt as if they had climbed out of darkness into light. To rival works of Greek art was looked upon as the highest ambition which an artist could cherish. Sculptors so great as Donatello and Michelangelo took the scanty remains of Greek masterpieces as their models, and measured their attainments by the degree of success which they reached in copying them. The lamps of Greek balance and symmetry, Greek idealism, and Greek naturalism were rekindled, and the crowd of artists vied one with another in walking by their light.

We may mark four stages in the rediscovery of Greek sculpture. The first is the Italian Renaissance already mentioned. The second originated in the visit of Winckelmann to Italy in 1755, and the application by Goethe and Lessing of his discoveries to the judgement of contemporary art. It tended greatly to the raising and purifying of the artistic taste of Europe. The splendid promise of the Renaissance had degenerated into the mannerism and extravagance of Bernini and his contemporaries. Winckelmann called it back to simplicity, to self-restraint, to ideality. But before long this teaching also was perverted; and such sculptors as Thorwaldsen and Canova were misled by the defects of the inferior examples of Greek sculpture, which were the only ones accessible to Winckelmann, into a slavish copy of the antique or works of an artificial grand style. Then came the third wave of revived Greek influence, when the sculptures of the Parthenon found a home in London, and critics were able to observe how infinitely superior the masterpieces of a really great age were to the copies of Roman times and the adaptations of the Hellenistic age. When Haydon the painter first saw the Parthenon marbles he was immensely impressed; but that which struck him most strongly was not the ideality, for which they have since become proverbial, but the wonderful naturalism of much of their detail in contrast to the grandiose conventions of his contemporaries. The fourth stage in our knowledge of Greek sculpture comes from the very fruitful excavations on Greek soil, especially at Athens, Olympia, and Delphi, which have shown us how widely varied is the range of the ancient sculptors, how many their styles, how admirable their technique. This extension of our knowledge has not, it is true, as yet much affected contemporary art, as art was affected by the teachings of Winckelmann and the publishing of the marbles of the Parthenon. Until last year there was no book in English setting forth the results of the excavations of Delphi; and there is even now no book in English performing the same service for the excavations at Olympia. Sculptors are so little educated in the history of their craft, that they do not easily learn from new sources of knowledge. But by degrees, beyond doubt, the new views of Greek art will filter down to them. A few recently discovered sculptures, such as the Charioteer of Delphi, the Hermes of Praxiteles, the bronze head from Beneventum in the Louvre, the Demeter of Cnidus, have by their overpowering charm affected artists and art. And most sculptors profess a great admiration for Greek works, notably Rodin, who, although the tendency of his works is not in a classical direction, yet uses the strongest language in praising the Greek masterpieces. But in general the tendency of art towards extreme individualism and the search after novelty have more than counteracted the somewhat shallow admiration of sculptors for what is antique.

X

At present religion and culture alike are struggling against the waves of barbarism reinvading. It is not my business to speak here of the forces which are trying to crush religion among us. But I may fitly conclude by sketching some of the tendencies against which culture based upon that of Greece is our best antidote. If I have rightly set forth the principles of Greek literature and art in past pages, the nature of their influence under present conditions will be clear.

I must venture on a parallel which seems to me very suggestive, though some readers may regard it as risky. There are two great standards set up in the past, to control the wayward fanaticisms of men, and to keep them within the bounds of reason and good sense. The standard in religion is set by the New Testament : the standard in art is set by Greece. As at the Renaissance the peoples of Europe went back for their inspiration and their models to the literature and the art of Hellas, so at the Reformation they, or at all events the Teutonic races, went back to the early records of Christianity, appealing to them against the venality and corruption of the dominant

Church. And ever since, at intervals, there has arisen, alike in the field of culture and in that of religion, an echo of the appeal to the classical past. It is to the New Testament that Apostles like John Wesley and George Fox made their appeal, setting up in opposition to the conventions and worldliness of the Church in their times the spirituality and simplicity of the apostolic age, just as Goethe and Lessing turned men's minds from what was contrary to reason and good taste in their surroundings to Greek beauty and simplicity. And however some of the followers of Wesley and Fox may have gone beyond due bounds towards fanaticism, yet in every branch of the Christian Society the influence of those modern prophets has been renovating and purifying, just as the schools of critics which followed Goethe tended greatly to increase among us sweetness and light.

In our schools and colleges, until quite lately, the religion of the New Testament and the tradition of the Greek and Roman Classics have gone together, the one preserving us from superstition and materialism in religion, the other making war upon the inherited barbarisms and brutalities which we have from our not very distant ancestors. The spirit of anarchy in religion would persuade us that there is no divine sanction for goodness and no eternal stamp on vice, that morality is a matter of convention which every society and every nation has a right to invert if it judges such inversion in the line of its interests. The spirit of anarchy in art proclaims that all the works of nature are equally beautiful or equally ugly, that nothing which exists is unfit to be represented in our galleries and public places, that so long as a picture or a statue arouses a sentiment it does not matter whether the sentiment be one of delight and aspiration or one of horror. If once the idea of beauty as the end to be aimed at be expelled from art, art sinks like a stone to the bottom of the sea. Some people are ready to tolerate any monstrosity in art, however remote from nature, however offensive to decency, however repugnant to humanity. The whole artistic inheritance of the race from the day when men began to climb out of barbarism is liable to be thrown away by an age which has unbounded confidence in its own wisdom.

I should, however, be sorry to stop at this point, for I might leave on readers the impression that I am in favour of the mere imitation of works of Greek art. That is by no means my view. In the last century several sculptors, overpowered by the charm of the antique, produced statues which closely followed ancient patterns, such as the Hope and the Hebe of Thorwaldsen, some of the statues of Rauch and Schadow, and the tinted Venus of Gibson. Such works were necessarily stillborn; they had not in them any breath of the life of a new age, any attempt to conform to changed conditions. Very different was the following of the antique by Michelangelo. He admired with enthusiasm such works of the Greek chisel as he knew; but he produced not dull and academic reflections of them, but works of the most splendid originality and the greatest charm. He imbibed not the letter but the spirit of Greek art; and even succeeded better than most artists in combining that spirit with a breath of Christianity.

The parallel which I have drawn may be carried farther. A reversion to the letter of the New Testament writers has been often attempted by considerable religious leaders of our time, especially Tolstoi and the Quakers. They have gone back to the injunctions of the Sermon on the Mount, and tried literally to abide by them. But it has become apparent to all but fanatics that such procedure would be fatal to civil government and civilized life. It is the spirit not the letter of the teaching of Jesus which is life-giving. In just the same way an acceptance of the mere externals of Greek art would not help us at all; but a revival of its spirit would be a great inspiration to modern artists. The lamps of Greek art will give light in any age. Greek idealism, Greek balance and measure, Greek love of what is natural and healthful, Greek simplicity and moderation are of the very essence of good art in all ages. We can no more revive the exact conditions under which art arose than we can import into England the clear air, the bright sun, the clear-cut shadows of the Greek landscape. But we can still look up to the philosophy, the poetry, and the art of Greece as classical, as a revelation of what is most pleasing and most enduring in human nature. And if we neglect them and reject them from the education of our children, we shall destroy what has been ever since the Renaissance the source of pure joy and refined feeling in the majority of cultured men ; we shall make a great gap which material prosperity, a deeper knowledge of the secrets of nature, the invention of fresh modes of amusement, can never fill. And if we trust merely to the reflections of the Greek spirit in modern literature and art, we shall be acting as the Roman Church in its darker ages has acted, in shutting away from the people recourse to the primary documents of religion, and obliging them to be content with such interpretations of those documents as the ruling hierarchy judged to be useful. We must retain the right of appeal to our classical examples, whether in religion, in literature, or in art. Arnold was right. The Bible, Homer, Shakespeare, Greek art remain the stars by which we may direct our course over stormy seas.

P. GARDNER.

ARCHITECTURE

NOBODY has ever disputed the beauty of Greek Architecture. We recognize the justice of a description of the Parthenon as 'le suprême effort du génie à la poursuite du beau'; but the layman must sometimes ask himself what does it mean? Where did it come from, where did it go to, why is it thought so beautiful, how was it that this people relatively insignificant in power, in territory, and in numbers, was able to attain to this astonishing supremacy in art? These are questions not easily answered. The evidence is fragmentary and not always conclusive, the ruins of a few temples and buildings, a technical treatise by a garrulous third-rate writer in the first century A.D.,[1] the anecdotes of an indefatigable collector[2] a little later, the notes of a traveller in the second century,[3] and the materials collected by the patient research of scholars and archaeologists, pieced together on more or less ingenious hypotheses. Indeed, a great part of what is written on Greek Architecture is simply hypothesis. There is not much to go on, yet Greek Architecture (and by this I mean the architecture of the sixth and fifth centuries B.C.) remains one of the great outstanding facts in the history of the Architecture of the Western world, and the Art of the age of Pericles is the fountain-head to which artists still return.

Where that art sprang from, and how it grew, is largely a matter of speculation. There have been legends of civilizations wiped out in tremendous cataclysms that left no trace behind them. Vague suggestions are made that the cradle

[1] Vitruvius, *De Architectura*.
[2] Pliny the Elder, *Historia Naturalis*, xxxvi.
[3] Pausanias, Ἑλλάδος Περιήγησις.

of the race was in Asia. All we know for certain is that the earliest civilizations of which actual historical evidence remains are those of Chaldea and Egypt, and that the art of these countries reached a high degree of attainment long before we come upon the earliest traces of art of any sort in Greece. That both these countries contributed in varying degrees to the art of Greece is certain, but that is not the whole of the story. As we shall see, another element comes into play, which made of that art almost a new creation, differing in outlook and ideal from any art that preceded it, stamped by the genius of a vigorous northern race with a character all its own. The art of the East and the art of the West never really fused. There is a difference in kind between the joyous vitality of pure Greek art, and the gloomy vision of Asia, with its craving for the vast and terrible, its sombre imagination, its lack of humanity and indifference to the individual.

It is not, however, till far down in the progress of history that this differentiation asserts itself. Greek art is relatively a late development. The Great Pyramid at Ghizeh was built some 2,000 years before a stone was laid of the masonry of Mycenae. The Hall of Columns of Karnak, with its columns sixty feet high, was probably coeval with the Treasury of Atreus : in other words, when the art of Greece and of the islands was scarcely out of the barbaric stage, a wonderful art had been in existence across the Mediterranean from time immemorial. Both Egypt and Chaldea attained a high degree of civilization long before the Dorians were ever heard of. At some remote period the Egyptian influence penetrated to Crete and Cyprus, the islands of the Aegean, and the mainland of Greece ; and the intermediaries were the Phoenicians, that enterprising race of merchant adventurers, whose home was in Syria, and whose fleets traversed the Mediterranean from East to West. The Phoenicians were traders and not artists. In Egypt they came into contact with a highly developed art, beyond their comprehension in its essential features, yet including details which could easily be apprehended by their quick commercial intelligence. Wherever they touched on their voyages, Cyprus, Crete, the southern islands of the Aegean, the mainland of Greece, the south of Italy, Sicily, Carthage, the Balearic islands, Spain in the far west, they probably carried with them, for trading purposes, minor articles of Egyptian workmanship which may have supplied hints to the indigenous peoples. Where they established settlements, they reproduced what they could recollect of the methods of Egyptian architecture, possessing at second-hand a knowledge of technical methods in advance of anything within the knowledge of the people among whom they settled. Rudimentary anticipations of the Ionic volute are found in Phoenician capitals, vague reminiscences of what the traders had seen in Egypt and elsewhere. Moreover, the Phoenicians, who possessed the skill of sailors in the use of tackle, would have had little difficulty in handling large stones set dry in more or less regular courses, which was a characteristic feature of Cretan and Mycenaean building. It is too soon to describe the work as architecture. It is doubtful if the Phoenicians possessed any aptitude for the arts. Their rôle was that of intermediaries only.

Obscure as was the part played by the Phoenicians in the early origins of art in Greece and the islands, there was another channel through which Eastern influences came to bear on its development, which is even more uncertain. To the west of Chaldea and north of Syria, dwelt a race of which little is known, the Hittites. Carchemish, their capital, was on the upper Euphrates, north-east of Antioch, and their power appears to have extended westward through Asia Minor to the shores of the Aegean. Dr. Sayce says that in the thirteenth century B.C. it extended from 'the banks of the Euphrates to the shores of the Aegean, including both the cultured Semites of Syria and the rude barbarians of the Greek Seas', he even says that the Hittites ' brought the civilization of the East to the barbarous tribes of the distant West'. What actually remains of Hittite art hardly bears out this statement. When the Hittite power was at its height, Minoan ' art ' had long been practised in Crete, and according to the most popular chronology, had already passed its prime and given way to the art of Mycenae and Tiryns. The scanty evidence of Hittite art consists of bas-reliefs of figures and animals cut on the face of rocks along the natural caravan routes through Asia Minor from East to West. This and the evidence of seals and engraved gems show that Hittite art was derived first from Chaldea, later from Egypt. It undoubtedly exercised some influence on the art of the early Greek settlers on the eastern side of the Aegean, and gave it an Asiatic cast, which it never lost throughout all its later developments. For the Greeks of Asia Minor never really understood the austere ideal of Doric art. Ionian art crossed westward to Greece, but the Dorian never went east. It was the art of a strong northern race, that found no place for itself among the softer peoples of Asia Minor.

At this point we can take up the first rudimentary beginnings of Greek art. The discoveries of the last forty years have proved the existence in Crete and Cyprus, Southern Greece, and the islands of the Aegean, of an archaic art of obscure origin, of very great interest, and of remarkable attainment in certain directions, long before the earliest beginnings of what we mean when we speak of Greek architecture. So far as architecture is concerned, this archaic art is of relatively minor importance. It plays a small part, if any, in subsequent developments, and though enthusiastic explorers claim to find in it anticipations of the details of modern domestic architecture, the evidence produced is unconvincing. Great movements in the arts always owe some debt to the periods that

Fig. 1. LION GATE, MYCENAE

have preceded them, but Minoan and Mycenaean art, at any rate in regard to architecture, was rather the last word of a decaying civilization than the first herald of the glorious art of Greece in the sixth and fifth centuries B.C. We are still far back in remote ages, remote that is so far as Greek art is concerned, anywhere between 2000 and 1000 B.C. or even earlier,[1] back in the Minoan age of Crete with its rudimentary architecture, and its relatively high excellence in the crafts, and in the age of Mycenae and Tiryns, the age that produced the Lion Gate at Mycenae, and that strange half-barbaric work, if I may be pardoned the term, the Treasury of Atreus. It is worth pausing to consider these archaic buildings, not so much to show a relationship to later work (which scarcely existed), as to call attention to the fact that the Minoan and Mycenaean builders were moving unconsciously in a direction that would never have led to the column and lintel architecture of the seventh and sixth centuries B.C. It might have led to some form of dome construction, it could never have led to the Doric of the Sicilian temples. No stronger evidence of the genius of the Dorian invaders could be produced than that, with this unpromising art in possession, they were yet able in the course of three or four centuries to create Greek architecture. The design of the Lion Gate is a strange jumble of ill-adjusted motives. It is set in a wall of great stones roughly squared and laid dry. Two monolith jambs support a huge lintel, cambered in the middle like the tie-beams of our sixteenth-century roofs. Above the lintel the courses are gathered over, leaving between their lower faces and the top

---

[1] Sir Arthur Evans has drawn up an ingenious chronology of Early Minoan (2800–2200 B.C.), Middle Minoan (2200–1700 B.C.), and Late Minoan (1700–1200 B.C.). The evidence is almost entirely that of pottery discovered on the site. The whole question of the relations of Minoan to Mycenaean art, and of this archaic art to the earlier civilizations of Egypt and Chaldaea, is very obscure and uncertain.

of the lintel a triangular space of a steep pitch (about 60°), in which was inserted a frontispiece carved on a single stone representing two lions standing up on either side of an archaic column supporting a fragment of a rudimentary architrave.[1] The heraldic pose of the lions and the technique of their sculpture, so suggestive of Assyrian reliefs with their splendid sense of muscular form and energy, are far ahead of an architecture that is still barbaric, scarcely architecture at all. There is here nothing to suggest the Doric of Paestum and Selinus, much to recall the megalithic buildings of Syria, and the sculpture of the farther East.

The Treasury of Atreus is still more remarkable, not only because it shows more skill in building, but because its design is based on a structural motive which seems to have been wholly abandoned by the successors of the Mycenaean builders. The Treasury of Atreus (or Tomb of Agamemnon) was excavated in a hill, and consists of a long passage about 120 ft. by 21 ft. wide, with retaining walls of megalithic masonry on either side, terminating in a great entrance doorway. This doorway is flanked on either side by columns tapering downwards, and decorated with chevrons in a manner very similar to Norman work of the eleventh century, and apparently intended solely for ornament.[2] The entrance opened into a circular domed chamber about 48 ft. 6 in. in diameter, 45 ft. 4 in. high, out of which opened another smaller chamber. The dome, in section, is built on the curve of a parabola, formed with courses projecting over one another, and not set out radial to the curve of the dome—in other words it is not a true dome or arch, but a succession of corbels. The internal face of the dome is dressed down, and was covered with ornament of some sort, whether metal rosettes,

---

[1] The heraldic treatment of the lions is of Eastern origin. The Greeks had a tradition that the chieftains of Mycenae came from Lydia.

[2] Portions of these columns are now in the British Museum.

or enamelled terra-cotta, or wholly in metal, possibly the famous gold of Mycenae, is not known. The whole of this chamber was covered in with a mound of earth, in accordance with the primitive custom of concealing the chieftain's grave. It is impossible to find, in this extremely interesting monument or in the domed chamber of Orchomenos in Boeotia, any trace of future developments in Greek architecture. Both in intention and in its psychological background it seems almost as remote from the Doric Temple as the Great Pyramid itself. In point of fact architecture was still in a rudimentary stage. It has been proved abundantly that Architecture comes late in the sequence of the Arts. People could draw well, long before they could design. Among the cavemen, for example, there were admirable draughtsmen, but they had to make their drawings on the sides of caves. That there existed in the Minoan and Mycenaean ages skilful potters and metal-workers, is shown by the vases of Knossos and the gold cups found at Vaphio near Sparta; that they built habitable buildings and decorated them to the best of their ability is also proved, as, for example, the palace of Tiryns, but it has not yet been shown that their builders reached the degree of skilled design, at which building becomes architecture. Architecture had not yet found itself in Greece.

Then somewhere about 1000 B.C. came the Dorian invasions, and the art of Crete and Mycenae vanished into space—possibly the legend was right which said that the conquered people of the mainland carried it away with them to Asia. Anyhow, the three or four centuries following the Dorian invasions are a blank which future research may fill out for us, and so far as art is concerned, there appears to have been a *détente*, during which the new race was settling down to its conquest, finding itself, and assimilating something at any rate of the older civilization. The survival of such buildings as the Treasury of Atreus show that the Dorians were not simple barbarians, destroying all that came in their way. Even Sparta in its earlier days was not a mere military machine. Discoveries made in 1906-9 suggest that from the ninth to the seventh centuries B.C. Sparta had some sort of an art of its own showing traces of Asiatic influence in its pottery— a little later Sparta concluded an alliance with Croesus, King of Lydia, and Bathycles, an artist of Magnesia in Ionia, was treated with honour in Sparta. The Dorians were something more than fighters, they seem to have possessed some sort of civilization, and to have been endowed with a natural capacity for the arts, which after two or three centuries of experiment will find its own splendid expression within very definite and original lines. The legend of the return of the Heracleidae was to be justified by their later history. No merely imitative race could have evolved the perfect manner of the great Doric temples from the scraps of Egypt and the East, and the rudimentary buildings of Crete and Mycenae.

Greek architecture for the purpose of this study is Dorian architecture, and its elements are simple. It was evolved in the design of their temples, and with the exception of their theatres it was summed up in these temples. From the period during which Greek architecture was being built up to its maturity, say from the seventh century B.C. to the completion of the Parthenon in the fifth century B.C., the whole life of the Greek was coloured and dominated by his religion and its observances; and his religion was not the sinister mystery of Egypt, but on the whole a cheerful open-air Pantheism that gloried in the life and beauty of the visible world in which he lived. He himself was content to live in a poor house, so long as he had his market-place, his ceremonial theatre, and the glorious temples of his Gods. Moreover, to whatever depths the Athenians may have sunk in the time of St. Paul, in the heroic days of Pericles they were remarkable for constancy of purpose and the steadfastness of their ideals. They stood on the ancient ways, and it never occurred to them to abandon the tradition of their fathers, their business was to carry it forward to perfection. The result was that the architecture of their temples proceeded on lines that long use had made sacrosanct ; and its technique is summed up in the history of two orders, the Doric and the Ionic.[1]

Now, the order, its character, dimensions and disposition, with the wall of the Cella (or enclosed shrine) within the colonnade, summed up the elements, the vocabulary, if one may so put it, of Greek architecture ; and we come here at the outset on a curious quality of the Greek genius, and one that differentiates it from the Roman. The properties of wood and stone as materials are clearly different, things can be done with the one which are impossible with the other ; but the Greeks either did not realize this or did not trouble their heads about it. They found that the post and lintel was a simple means of building, and they adopted it as their permanent method of construction. If the span became too wide, they thickened the posts (the columns of Paestum are 7 ft. in diameter) and increased the strength of the beam (the architrave). Hence the vast solidity of the Doric order of the temples of Sicily and Magna Graecia. The Greek was incurious about construction *qua* construction. He found, in the column and the lintel, means perfectly adequate to realize his ideal of high unalterable beauty, and he was content. The Romans, who for a time were satisfied with these simple methods, became impatient of the constructive limitation of the post and lintel. They wanted to cover in great spaces,

[1] The order, I may say for the uninitiated, means the complete ordonnance of the column, the architrave resting immediately on its capital, the frieze and the cornice. It is the final expression of the simple device of the post and lintel, of the beam resting on the heads of two or more posts ; and there is little doubt that in its ultimate origin, the Order is the translation into stone of the details of a rudimentary wooden construction.

and to leave the floor unencumbered ; and concentrating on this they arrived at the arch, the vault, and the dome, and so became the greatest builders of the world. To them, the orders were a mere appanage of decoration, which they never properly appreciated, of which they mistook the intention, adopted the worst elements, and often enough made a gross misuse. The Greeks took another line. They adopted the column and lintel once for all as the only possible method of construction, and devoted all their labours to the incessant refinement of this type, eliminating the unessential, arriving by constant selection at the most perfect expression of their purpose, and their purpose was not that of the Roman and the modern architect, mainly utilitarian, it was directed entirely to the aesthetic appeal, the appeal to the emotions through beauty of line, of form, and in a less degree of colour. ' The whole fabric of Greek art goes to pieces when it is brought into contact with a purely utilitarian nation like Rome.' [1]

Of the two orders, the Doric and the Ionic, the Doric seems to me the purest embodiment of the true Greek spirit, in its faultless form, and its austere restraint and rejection of the unessential. It was, moreover, the order *par excellence* of the Greek temple of the mainland. The Erechtheum was the only Ionic temple of first-rate importance in Greece, and the employment of the Ionic order in Greece was confined to interiors and minor buildings. As for the Corinthian order, the favourite order of the Romans, it was scarcely recognized by the Greeks. In all their great temples, in Greece, in Sicily, and Magna Graecia, they used the Doric order.

How this order was arrived at we do not really know. Ingenious conjectures have been made as to its origin in

---

[1] *Hellenistic Sculpture*, by Guy Dickins, p. 85. The author, who wrote with something of the insight of the artist as well as the accurate knowledge of the scholar, died of wounds, on the Somme, in 1916.

Fig. 2. TEMPLE OF NEPTUNE AT PAESTUM

wooden construction, and though some of these conjectures are more probable than others they leave us pretty well where we were in regard to the stages by which it reached its final form. It has been suggested that the Doric column originated in the wooden post of the earliest temples, such as are supposed to have existed in the Heraion at Olympia. The square post would have its angles taken off, and become an octagon, and the further elimination of the angles would gradually produce a form nearly circular in plan, in which the arrises of the chamfered angles would remain, and this might easily suggest to artists so sensitive as the Greeks, their further refinement and definition by a slight hollow between the arrises which would constitute the flutings of the Doric column. Its derivations from the Minoan and Mycenaean columns seems most improbable. There are two essential parts in the Doric column, the shaft and the capital (the Greeks did not use any base for this order). The Minoan columns taper downwards instead of upwards, an utterly unconstructional form, and though in the palace of Knossos and at Tiryns columns of this shape appear to have been used to carry lintels, the stone columns on either side of the entrance to the Treasury of Atreus at Mycenae were used for decorative and not for structural purposes. On the other hand columns of great massiveness tapering upwards had been used long before in Egypt; and though there is evidence against it, it still seems probable that the suggestion of the shaft of the Doric column may have come from Egypt. We first find it in Greece in the seventh century B.C. at the period when Psammetichus I (671–617 B.C.) opened Egypt to Greek trade and settlement. The Greek colony of Naukratis on the west side of the Nile delta was founded by Milesians about 650 B.C. and by the middle of the sixth century B.C. definite trade relations were established between Naukratis and the mainland of Greece. The Greek settlement at Daphnae on the eastern arm of the

Nile appears to have been founded at about the same time as Naukratis, in both cases with the sanction and encouragement of the Egyptian king. The earliest Doric temples in Greece, Sicily, and Magna Graecia date from the end of the seventh century and early part of the sixth century. The nearness of date makes it probable that the shaft of the Doric order had its origin in the Egyptian column seen by some quick-witted Greek when trading in Egypt. When we come to the capital of the column, the rôles seem to be reversed, for we find nothing in Egyptian architecture to suggest the echinus moulding under the square abacus of the Doric column; whereas the Mycenaean column had a rudimentary capital which may have suggested the idea of the Doric capital. But the notable thing about it is that when we first come across the Doric capital in Sicily and Greece, it is already far in advance of anything that had gone before it in Greece, and it is quite different from the columns of Egypt. In the Doric temple of Corinth (650–600 B.C.) the columns have already reached the type form, the tapered shaft with its entasis or slight convex curvature in outline, its massive solidity (the ratio is one of diameter to four and a quarter of height), and the bold parabolic curve of the echinus moulding under the abacus of its cap. In this form, the Doric column was an absolutely fresh note in architecture. Archaic though they were, these columns at Corinth show that the Greeks were already on the track of those refinements of form, those optical corrections and compensations, which differentiate Greek architecture from that of any other race. The exaggeration in the entasis of the archaic column disappears, its tapering was diminished, its height increased, and the overhang of the capitals reduced, till in the Theseion (465 B.C.) and the Parthenon (450–438 B.C.) we reach the final inimitable type. The column, which at Paestum was not much over four times the height of its correct diameter, is now over five times, the great over-

Architecture   409

hanging capitals are reduced to reasonable dimensions, the
depth of the entablature is diminished, the axis of the column
is slightly inclined inwards to give the impression of stability,
the shafts have the slight curve or ' entasis ' just sufficiently
marked to prevent the outline of the column looking incurved ;
the lines of the stylobate, or continuous base, on which the
columns stand, and the entablature which they carry, have
a slight rise toward the centre in order to correct the impression
of the lines sinking in the middle ; the columns at the angles
are thickened, because standing free with the light all round
them they would otherwise appear smaller than the columns
standing against the background of the building.   Nothing
was left to chance ; every aspect of the building, the relation
of every part to the whole, and of the whole to its part, was
studied profoundly, so that there should be no failure in its
perfect harmony.   Except in Egyptian architecture, and there
to a much smaller extent, nothing like this had been done
before.   What the Greeks did, was to formulate a rhythmical
architecture, in which each part stood in a definite and considered relation to the whole, so that even in their ruined
state these Doric temples give an irresistible impression of
a great idea, a great architectural epic, in which each detail,
however beautiful, was subordinated to the unity of the conception as a whole.   It is this abstract quality which lifts
Greek Doric so far above the ambitious art of later ages, and
indeed above all but the very finest work of any period of
architecture.

Many attempts have been made to discover the secret of
this wonderful perfection of proportion.   That the Greeks
had a system of their own, that they worked to definite ratios
of dimension and number, and employed graphic methods of
determining their proportions, such as the use of triangles and
the like to determine the limits of their designs, seems certain.
But no contemporary account of any such system remains ;
and all the explanations that are given are *ex post facto*, made

by theorists analysing existing buildings, not by architects designing new ones. Some four or five hundred years later Vitruvius compiled a treatise on architecture, in which, following the doctrines of the school of Alexandria, he expounded a Greek theory of proportion on the basis of the human figure. Vitruvius is obscure, and does not seem to have been certain himself whether the proportion of the parts of a design were to bear a relation to the whole, analogous to that of members of a human body to the body as a whole, or whether the proportions of the order were to be taken from the actual proportions of the human body; and he complicates the position by reference to the ' perfect numbers ' of the Greeks. But here again he was uncertain whether the ' perfect number ' was ten or six. After which, and having, in his reference to the human figure as the canon of proportion, unwittingly set a trap for the scholars and artists of the Renaissance, he drops the subject and digresses into a general classification of temples, with formal rules for the placing and dimensions of columns, which have formed the staple of treatises on classical architecture ever since. One should speak with gratitude of the labours of Vitruvius, because, after all, his is the only technical treatise left us on the subject; but he applied to the pure Greek temples a system evolved centuries later by critics and theorists; he was thinking chiefly of Roman versions of Greek architecture, and he was more interested in technical rules and precepts for the use of architects than in that abstract beauty which was all the Greek cared for. No classification, however laborious, will reach the mystery of Greek architecture. Its beauty is too subtle to be reduced to any formula.

The Doric order reigned supreme throughout the great period from the sixth till the end of the fifth century B.C. It failed with the failure of the high ideals of Athens. Other forces came into play to which it no longer responded, and later Greek critics even found fault with the Doric order

Fig. 3. DORIC TEMPLE, CORINTH

for certain ' mendosae et inconvenientes symmetriae ' ;[1] but that order, the true symbol of the sons of Heracles, was one of the most momentous contributions ever made to the art of architecture. It was the keynote of Greek architecture throughout its finest period. Later it was superseded by the Ionic order, and when Rome became paramount in the western world, that, in its turn, yielded its place of pride to the Corinthian order, opulent, luxurious, a little vulgar, a true register of the lowering of the sense and standard of beauty that followed the downfall of Athens.

Meanwhile, on the other side of the Aegean, the Ionic order was reaching its perfect form through a similar process of systematic thought on a type definitely adopted. The Greek colonies in Asia Minor were of very early origin. Legend attributed their foundation to the earlier inhabitants of Greece, driven out by the Dorians. By the sixth century B.C. the Greek colonies were well established on the west and south-west coasts of Asia Minor, and had evolved their own characteristic architectural idiom in the Ionic order and its column, more slender than the Doric, with its moulded base and its strange characteristic capital, unsuitable from the constructional point of view in stone or marble, yet ultimately attaining the exquisite beauty of line and modelling of the capitals of the Erechtheion at Athens. Two things seem fairly certain as to the origin of this capital ; first, that it was derived from the wooden horizontal head-pieces fixed on posts to reduce the bearing of the primitive wooden lintels ; and, secondly, that the first suggestion of the volute reached

---

[1] *Vitruvius*, iii. 1. The difficulty was, that if the triglyph was placed on the angle of the building (the practice of the Greeks) and the next triglyph was placed over the axis of the column, the metope (or panel) between these two triglyphs would be larger than the metopes between the triglyphs axial over the other columns. The Greeks solved it by reducing the width of the end intercolumniation, but later critics disliked this, and solved it by removing the end triglyph from the angle and placing it axial over the end column.

the Ionian Greeks from the East. A crude anticipation of the volute is found in Phoenician work, and it also appears on a Hittite relief at Boghaz Keui in the middle of Asia Minor. Its origin in either case was oriental, and we have here the other motive in Greek architecture, Eastern, at any rate exotic, and, as compared with Doric, almost alien to the true Greek genius. Yet this astonishing people gave it a form as far removed from its barbarous originals, as the Doric capitals of the Parthenon from the capitals of the columns of Mycenae, and when the Greeks of both sides of the Aegean drew together after the defeat of the Persians, the Ionic order crossed the sea, and assumed a place of honour in the temples of Greece, still, however, with rare exceptions, in subordination to the Doric order. In the colonies in Asia Minor, the supremacy of the Ionic order had long been recognized. The Ionic temple of Hera at Samos, 368 ft. long by 178 ft. wide, is supposed to have been built at the end of the sixth or early in the fifth century B.C., and this was the forerunner of the great fourth-century temples of Ionia, built when Architecture had changed its direction and Hellenistic Art was beginning its adventurous career.

With these two orders as the terms and idioms of expression the Greeks built up the architecture of their temples. Their plans were the simplest possible. The rudimentary type was a simple chamber or cella, with a loggia open to the air except for two columns standing between the two extremities of the side walls, which terminated in pilasters known as ' antae '.[1] The next stage was to bring the colonnade forward,[2] stage number three repeated the column at the other end of the building,[3] stage number four continued the colonnade along the sides,[4] stage number five doubled the colonnade on all

---

[1] Vitruvius gives this as the ' aedes in antis '.

[2] Pro-style (colonnade in front).

[3] Amphipro-style (colonnade at both ends).

[4] Peripteral (single colonnade all round).

four sides,[1] and stage number six retained the outer rows of columns but omitted the inner row along the sides, leaving a wide passage-way all round the main building.[2] Vitruvius gives a further classification by the spacing of columns which will be found in all the handbooks of classic architecture. With minor variations in detail, these types remained constant for the temples of Greece and Rome. The principal altera- tions occurred in the extension of the temple proper, at the expense of the surrounding colonnade. In the Archaic temples, such as the older temples of Selinus in Sicily (sixth century B. c.), the portico and colonnade occupy three-quarters of the site. In the temple of Hephaestus (Theseion) at Athens (fifth century B.c.) the cella occupies only a little more than half the total area, and in the Parthenon, built some twenty years later, the size of the cella is still further increased. Most of these temples were covered in. Hypaethral temples, in which the cella was open to the sky, are mentioned by Vitruvius, and it is probable that some of the larger ones at any rate were partly open to the sky. But how the openings were arranged is almost entirely a matter of conjecture. The roof used was of a very flat pitch, one of height to four of base, later it was even flatter, and this dictated the slope of the pediments. This roof covered the whole of the building, that is, both the cella and the colonnades on either side of it, and as the Greeks were ignorant of the principle of the triangulated truss built up of beams in compression and tension, they were at a loss to know how to carry their roof without pushing out their walls. Hence the great solidity of their buildings, and the rather clumsy expedient of the colonnades in the interiors of temples which appear to have been the only means they could think of to carry the roof. One has to bear it in mind in thinking of Greek architecture, that the Greeks were not constructors in the sense that the Romans were; they built well, and the

[1] Dipteral (double colonnade all round).

[2] Pseudo-dipteral (inner row of columns omitted).

best of their masonry was extraordinarily skilful—only by unusual skill in the cutting and setting of stone could they have carried out the delicate curves in the columns and other parts of their buildings—but construction, in the sense of the invention of new methods to meet difficult conditions, did not interest the Greek, and one cannot help thinking that the Greeks may have been more successful with the outside of their buildings than with the inside. It seems clear that they devoted most of their attention to the external elevations. It is not really known for certain how they lit their temples, though of course all sorts of suggestions of top-lighting have been made. It is possible that in some cases they were lit only from the principal entrance, and it is certain that the Greek did not want for the interior of his temple any such floods of light as are necessary under our northern skies. In the first place, he enjoyed a most brilliant and penetrating light, so that within his colonnades reflected light was amply sufficient to show the friezes and other ornaments, and he did not hesitate to use strong primary colours to heighten and explain their effect, wherever he found it necessary. In the second place, within the shrine itself, other considerations came into play. A certain luminous atmosphere, rather than positive light was what was aimed at, and the deep shadows of these internal colonnades might have helped this effect, adding to the mystery of the figure of the God.

This, too, may be the explanation of what must strike an architect as an anomaly of design, the Greek habit of placing enormous figures in the interior of their temples. The Greek, in his own way, was a very religious man. In his temple, he was doing his utmost to set forth the majesty of his God, and if it was necessary for this purpose he was even prepared to sacrifice his principles as an artist, to ignore the scale of his interior and the rhythmic harmony of his design, by the introduction of gigantic figures. The eye judges by what it

knows, and the readiest way of arriving at some idea of the size
of a building or a monument is by relating it to the normal
size of the human figure. Vitruvius, in his confused way,
suggested that the human figure was the canon and standard
of architectural design, but how is it possible to determine
the scale of a building which contained a figure at least six
times the size of a man, reaching from the floor to the roof ?
The chryselephantine figure of Zeus at Olympia, made by
Pheidias, is supposed to have been some thirty-five feet high,
and to have reached nearly to the roof, passing the double
tier of columns and the gallery above the aisles of the cella.
Moreover, this god was represented as seated on his throne,
so that by no possibility could it have been in scale with the
building so far as the architecture was concerned. Even the
gigantic temple of Zeus at Agrigentum with its external
columns 61 ft. 9 in. in height, and large enough for a man to
stand within one of the flutings of the columns, could hardly
have stood up to figures on such a scale as this. Such a violent
contrast in scale broke the principle of συμμετρία, that
strict relation of the part to the whole which the Greek artists
maintained elsewhere with scrupulous care. Artists with
such a consummate sense of proportion as the Greeks possessed would hardly have made a mistake here, and the
conclusion one comes to is that where their religion was in
question, everything had to give way. Indeed, one can
imagine the tremendous effect of this colossal figure seen
dimly in the half-light of the cella, filling the whole temple
with its presence. The same anomaly in scale occurred in the
Akropolis at Athens, where the vast figure of Athene Promachos
must have reduced the beautiful Caryatides of the Erechtheum
to insignificance. M. Choisy makes a gallant effort to show
that this want of relationship in scale, and also in the siting
of the temples, was deliberate and considered. As a fact,
the general rule that seems to have been observed in the time
of Pericles was that new temples should always be built on

the site of the older ones,[1] but axis lines were neglected, and even the masses of the Propylaea, beautiful building as it must have been, did not balance. The Akropolis was just a collection of unrelated buildings, and in the great Temenos of Delphi the various monuments were all anyhow.[2] The Sacred Way meandered about like an **S**, and the only method it observed was to clear the various treasuries and shrines which appear to have been scattered about within the enclosure, with a disregard of each other little less than brutal—a rather suggestive symbol of the internecine rivalry of the small Greek states. At Delphi, also, there was a huge figure of Apollo Sitalkas said to have been seventeen metres high, which must have been hopelessly out of scale. The fact was that Greek architects of the fifth century had not yet arrived at the conception of the city as a whole. They had an admirable eye for a site, for example, the position of the Parthenon itself, and the temple of Hera Lacinia at Agrigentum placed high above the sea, but it is unhistorical to invest even the architects of the Parthenon and the Propylaea with a knowledge and outlook which was not thought of till a hundred years later. Even the Greek architects and sculptors of the fifth century B.C. were not omniscient, yet within their limits, in their mastery of what they set themselves to do, the artists of the age of Pericles remain unapproachable, and theirs was the Golden Age of Architecture. They had fixed for all time essential elements of the art, and had set up a standard of attainment in pure form which no subsequent architecture has ever been able to reach.

The fall of Athens closed this splendid chapter, but Greek

[1] The Erechtheum was an exception.

[2] See *Delphi*, by Dr. Frederick Poulsen, p. 52. It is suggested that the Sacred Way was in existence before the shrines were built, and that its wanderings were necessitated by the gradients of the hillside. No sort of attempt, however, seems to have been made to correct this, or to treat it as an element of design.

Fig. 4. TEMPLE OF THESEUS, ATHENS

architecture was by no means done with. The Silver Age, the Hellenistic art that followed, is of intense interest. With the rise of the Macedonian monarchy the stage of history shifted from the mainland to the Ionian colonies on the coast of Asia Minor. Cities such as Ephesus and Miletus became immensely prosperous, Mausolus of Halicarnassus, the Attalids of Pergamon, possessed wealth that would have been unimaginable to the Greeks of Marathon. The City State, fighting desperately for its existence, inspired by high ideals of patriotism and religion, was a thing of the past. These Greeks of Ionia were well content to enjoy the comfort and prosperity of a settled civilization without having to fight for it ; and the whole atmosphere of their existence must have been different from the strenuous life of Greece in the fifth century. Moreover, the Ionian Greek, influenced, even if subconsciously, by the spirit of Asia, was by temperament unable to maintain the intellectual level of the Doric architecture of the mainland ; and a difference appears in the whole orientation of art, in sculpture perhaps even more than in architecture. The history of Hellenistic art has yet to be written. It has been described as decadent, and it was undoubtedly responsible for some very poor stuff, but it also produced the 'Victory' of Samothrace, one of the finest things ever done in sculpture, and some very remarkable developments in architecture. It is not to be judged by the standards of the art that preceded it. The Ionian Greek of the fourth and third centuries B.C. broke away from the tradition of the mainland, a tradition always rather alien to his instincts. His interest lay less in a somewhat impersonal religion than in the assertion of his own individuality. He did not understand the lofty patriotism, and the high ideal of abstract beauty that had inspired Pericles and his artists in the Akropolis ; indeed, there is a curiously modern feeling about much of his work, which became more marked as he came under the dominance of Rome. The individualism, the realism, the revivalism, and the commercialism of modern art, were all anticipated by the Hellenistic artists of Ionia, of Rhodes, of Alexandria, and of Athens itself in the Roman period. Civilization was becoming more complex, and one finds this reflected in Hellenistic art, at once more florid than the Doric of the fourth century, yet also more skilful in its handling of complicated problems of planning and design. No one wanted archaic simplicity when the wealth of Asia was flowing into the treasuries of the Ionian states, and the expression of this opulent ease is found in their magnificent temples, such as the third temple of Artemis at Ephesus, of which the outer colonnade measured 342 ft. 6 in. by 163 ft. 9 in., or the vast temple of Apollo Didymaeus at Miletus, 165 ft. wide by 360 ft. long out to out of the colonnades ; or the amazing monument of Mausolus of Caria at Halicarnassus, or the great altar of Pergamon. Fragments of the columns of the Temple of Artemis, now in the British Museum, tell of its size and richness, they also give the first hint of the downfall of art and civilization which was to follow centuries later. The Greeks of the great period had kept the structural parts of their building free of ornament. It would never have occurred to them to interfere with the lines of the column in any way that would contradict its purpose ; but the Greek architects of Ephesus not only placed their columns on pedestals (making them so far less stable in appearance), but they adorned the lower part of their Ionic columns with figures, of admirable execution, but perfectly inappropriate in the position they occupy. One cannot imagine Pheidias making a mistake such as this. Splendid in execution as Hellenistic sculpture often was, it won its place at the expense of architecture ; one looks in vain for that selection and restraint which give its undying distinction to the earlier work.

The Greeks of the fifth century realized that architecture is an art with a definite purpose other than that of a mere vehicle for sculpture, and that it makes its aesthetic appeal by its own inherent qualities of rhythm, and proportion, spacing, mass, and outline. Though they used sculpture and colour to heighten and intensify the effect of their architecture, they saw very clearly the function of the arts in relation to each other, and kept their sculpture and their colour in strict relation to the aesthetic purpose of their architecture. It is a point on which later architects went lamentably astray. A great deal of early Renaissance work is mere ornamentation of buildings, indeed in buildings such as the Certosa of Pavia the architecture has almost ceased to exist ; and most of the bad architecture of the last fifty years is due to the deplorable fallacy that ornament is architecture. The columns of Ephesus, the sculpture of the altar of Pergamon, brilliant as they were in technical accomplishment, were the first hint of that decline which was in time to undermine the whole fabric of the Arts. Architecture was deposed from its high intellectual dominance. It tended more and more to become a conventional affair, and it was an easy transition from the exuberance of Hellenistic art to the point-blank vulgarity of Roman ornamental architecture.

It was, however, inevitable that the fine simplicity of Periclean art should vanish with its ideals, and one finds a certain compensation in the extension of the range and outlook of architecture, which we owe to the Hellenistic architects of the fourth and succeeding centuries B.C. So far as perfection of form was concerned, it was impossible to carry the art beyond the stage to which Ictinus and Callicrates had brought it ; but there still remained something, and something very important, to be done. Axial planning, the consideration of the relation of building to building, seem to have been outside the consciousness of Greeks of the fifth century, and each building was treated as an unrelated unit. But the inconvenience of this, its loss of opportunity, and the necessity of order and method, must have become apparent, as civilization became more complex and more exacting. By the end of the fourth century B.C. the tradition of architectural technique was firmly established, and architects were able to turn their attention to problems of large planning, and these they seem to have handled with extraordinary skill. So far, what had been done in this direction had been due to religious inspiration, as in the processional ways leading to the Egyptian temples or the avenue of figures at Branchidae. What the Hellenistic architects did was to think out consecutive schemes of city planning, in which the dominant motive of arrangement was artistic. They had learnt to treat the temples, the public buildings, the open spaces and approaches, as the elements of one harmonious composition, in which the utmost use was made of the natural opportunities of the site. At Ephesus, for example, there is supposed to have existed a consecutive scheme, larger than anything of the kind carried out even in France in the eighteenth century, though the evidence, it should be noted, is largely conjectural. As presented by sanguine and enthusiastic restorers the scheme was magnificent. Next the port, and facing it on one side, was the Arsenal, a regular building opening on to a court surrounded by a colonnade, which again opened on to the great 'Place', a square enclosure some 850 ft. wide north and south, by 650 ft. east and west,[1] surrounded by a colonnade on all four sides, with exhedrae, or semicircular recesses. In the centre of this Place was an oblong water-piece, about 300 ft. by 200 ft., and on the farther side, opposite the Arsenal buildings, were the Senate House and other public buildings; and behind these and to the right and left of them the Theatre and the Stadium, partly excavated in Mount Coressus. The Arsenal, the great Place with its water-piece, and the public buildings, were laid out on an axis line, and on a regular rectangulated plan.

A scheme such as this (if it is possible to accept a conjectural

[1] The Place Vendôme measures 450 ft. × 420 ft.; Grosvenor Square about 650 × 530; and Lincoln's Inn Fields about 800 × 630, measured from wall to wall of buildings.

restoration), thought out in all its bearings, meant a real advance in the range of architecture. It is useless to look for the faultless beauty of the fifth century, but the resourcefulness and skill of the Hellenistic architects gave a new meaning to the art ; and indeed they might almost be said to have established the first stage in the development of its modern practice. It was from these able Hellenistic architects that the Romans learnt the monumental planning of their cities, and for centuries the architects most frequently employed were Greeks of Asia Minor. At this point, Hellenistic architecture merges into Roman, and loses its distinctive character. Through Roman it passes on to modern architecture, and so in a sense the chain is complete ; but between this later art and pure Greek architecture there is a great gulf fixed, differences not only of technique but of outlook, of ideal, and of temperament. The mighty Doric of Paestum, Selinus, and Segesta, the Theseion and the Parthenon, remains for all time the perfect expression of the soul of ancient Greece.

It is one of the ironies of history that when in the fifteenth and sixteenth centuries scholars and artists awoke to the fact that there had been a great architecture in the past they should have known of no other version of it but the Roman. What splendid developments might have followed if the finer spirits of the Renaissance, Alberti, Bramante, or Peruzzi, had founded their theories of architecture on the temples of Sicily and Magna Graecia, instead of on the debased examples of Imperial Rome! They, at least, would have caught a glimpse of the beauty of abstract form and perfect harmony, the secret of which seems to have been revealed to the Greeks alone among the peoples of the world—and to them for only a transient period of their history. Unfortunately, when Greek architecture was discovered in the second half of the eighteenth century, it became the shibboleth of the ' virtuosi '. The national traditions, both of France and England, were lost, Greek architecture became the fashion, and the misguided enthusiasm of pedants and amateurs insisted on literal reproductions which completed the extinction of architecture as a vernacular art, and replaced it by the series of revivalisms from which it has suffered for the last one hundred and fifty years. Conscious and deliberate tinkering with the art of architecture ended by destroying it.

We can never hope to revive Greek architecture, nor should we attempt to do so. There was once a well-known Scotch architect who held that the column and the lintel was the only permissible form of construction, and with this limitation and ill-selected Greek details he produced some fantastically ugly buildings. Following a similar line of thought a famous critic of the last century condemned methods of construction not sanctioned by the Old Testament. Both were wide of the mark; because, above and beyond all technical details of architecture is the spirit in which it is approached, the intellectual outlook of the artist on his art, and this may express itself in widely differing forms. In Greek architecture of the Golden period, that outlook was definite and distinctive, and it was one that has a very urgent lesson for us to-day. The aim and ideal of the Greek was beauty of form, and this beauty, which he sought in the first instance as the expression of his religion, ultimately became almost a religion in itself. To the realization of this ideal he devoted all his powers, sparing himself no pains in chastening his work till it had attained the utmost perfection possible. He merged himself in this work, without thought of the expression of himself in his vision of a divine and immutable beauty. It hardly occurred to him that his individual emotions were worth preserving. (In the sculpture of the great period the expression of the face is usually one of unruffled calm.) Although religious emotion was the source and inspiration of his work, his work was impersonal. He was aloof from that feverish anxiety for self-revelation which has made much modern art so interesting pathologically, and so detestable otherwise. Nor again had he anything of

the virtuoso about him. To him technique was not an end
in itself. In Hellenistic art it became so, but not in the Golden
Age. Indeed, he was sometimes almost careless of exact
modelling, and in architecture he did not use the order as
a mere exhibition of scholarship. In his search for beautiful
form, he stood upon the ancient ways, patient and serene,
moving steadily to his appointed end. ' Ainsi procède le génie
grec, moins soucieux du nouveau que du mieux, il reporte
vers l'épuration des formes l'activité que d'autres dépensent
en innovations souvent stériles, jusqu'à ce qu'enfin il atteigne
l'exquise mesure dans les efforts, et dans les expressions l'absolue
justesse.' [1] There have been rare periods since, when Architecture has moved with the same calm unhesitating purpose,
Gothic architecture, for example, in the twelfth and thirteenth
centuries, and certain phases of eighteenth-century architecture in France and England, when tradition was still active
and vital, and artists were content to let well alone.

Modern conditions seem to be wholly against the Greek
standpoint in art. The Arts are in the melting-pot, the old
standards of attainment are trampled under foot, and the
prophets prophesy falsely. Quite lately we were asked to
find our inspiration in the fetishes of the Gold Coast, and if
the aim of the artist is to outstrip his brethren in brutality,
the advice is sound. A recent critic justified the antics of
certain artists by the necessity they were under of advertising
themselves. That, no doubt, is the readiest way to immediate
success. But the question for the critic is, not the personal
advancement of the artist but the value of his work ; and one
would ask if any good work at any period in the history of art
has been inspired by this ambition to shout louder than one's
neighbours. Certainly, the standpoint of the Greek was the
exact opposite. He did not seek advertisement and notoriety.
He was happy with his inner vision of beauty, and intent only
on its realization. He had not the smallest desire to shock or

---

[1] Choisy, *History of Architecture*, vol. i, p. 298.

startle any one. There are occasions when shock tactics are necessary, but they are not necessary every day in the week, nor is it necessary to make a clean sweep of the past before one sets to work in one's own little corner of art.

What is wanted in modern art is some consciousness of this old Greek spirit, some recognition of its value. The Greeks of the age of Pericles wanted neither revivalism nor revolution; they moved forward, without haste or anxiety, on traditional lines, and they were able to do so because their art was so interwoven with their life that, in the plastic arts, they could no more have changed their methods of expression than they could have changed their manner of speech. That high outlook on life is lost and hardly to be recovered under modern conditions of social life and political government. It was perhaps only possible under the true democracy of the small Greek city state, when every citizen took his share in the ordered life of the community. Yet the Greek ideal remains. In our fitful fever of honest intention and wrong judgement, high endeavour and point-blank commercialism, Greek art, the art of Pheidias and Ictinus, is still the wise mother to whom we must return. The lesson of the Parthenon is the lesson of a stedfast vision of beauty, held high above individual effort and failure, realizing itself not in complex detail or calculated eccentricity, but in a serene and exquisite simplicity of form. It teaches us that in the arts there are no short cuts, and that anarchy, the destruction of what has been won for us in the past, is not advance but the straight road to the bottomless pit of barbarism. Instead of repudiating the work of his fathers, the Greek carried it on to its perfection, and built his palace of art on a sure foundation because he turned neither to the right hand nor to the left, but steadily set his face towards the light.

REGINALD BLOMFIELD.